A FAMILY OF WOMEN

JANE H. PEASE AND WILLIAM H. PEASE

A Family of Women

The Carolina Petigrus in Peace and War

The University of North Carolina Press | Chapel Hill and London

Designed by April Leidig-Higgins
Set in Centaur type by Keystone Typesetting, Inc.

The paper in this book meets the guidelines for permanence and
durability of the Committee on Production Guidelines for Book
Longevity of the Council on Library Resources.

Publication of this work was aided by a generous grant from
the Z. Smith Reynolds Foundation.

Library of Congress Cataloging-in-Publication Data
Pease, Jane H. A family of women : the Carolina Petigrus in peace
and war / Jane H. Pease and William H. Pease.
p. cm. Includes bibliographical references (p.   ) and index.
ISBN 0-8078-2505-0 (cloth: alk. paper)
1. Pettigrew family. 2. Women—South Carolina—History—
19th century. 3. Women and war—South Carolina—History—
19th century. 4. South Carolina—History—Civil War, 1861–1865
—Women. 5. South Carolina—History—Civil War, 1861–1865
—Social aspects. I. Pease, William Henry, 1924–   . II. Title.
HQ1438.S6P43 1999   305.4'09757—dc21   99-12599 CIP

03 02 01 00 99 5 4 3 2 1

In memory of Emma and Ned Pyle,

who, in our youth, introduced us to cousinage,

and in appreciation for Jack Noble and Bill Grundy,

who continue to teach us about the meaning

of extended family

CONTENTS

Maps

ACKNOWLEDGMENTS

For thirty years, we have pursued the South Carolina history of which the Petigru women are a part. In this endeavor, many librarians, friends, and acquaintances led us to a wide variety of sources and confronted us with numerous questions, insights, and qualifications that made us dig still deeper. To all of them we owe a debt of gratitude. But here we have room to thank only those who have shaped this study directly. Without the rich resources and helpful staffs of the South Carolina Historical Society, the Southern Historical Collection at the University of North Carolina, and the South Caroliniana Library at the University of South Carolina, we could not have written this book. Also, Donald Yacavone's knowledge of the Edward Everett Papers at the Massachusetts Historical Society allowed us at last to conclude that Everett's correspondence with Caroline Carson had, in fact, been destroyed.

The timely award of an Archie K. Davis Fellowship from the North Caroliniana Society as well as the hospitality of friends David Moltke-Hansen, Connie and Carl Schulz, and Lee and Cheryle Drago made extended periods of research away from home both more efficient and more comfortable. Martha W. Daniels was most kind in allowing us to use the extraordinary Mulberry Plantation collection over which she presides. Ashton and Lavonne Phillips were similarly generous in giving us access to their extensive collection of Caroline Carson's paintings. Elise Pinckney, who also provided a variety of research leads, introduced us to Petigru descendants Adele Wilson, Sally Simons, and Margaret Allston, who shared their family portraits, artifacts, anecdotes, and genealogical knowledge with us. Chris Marlowe arranged a wonderful tour of Allston territory, during which the present owner of Chicora Wood, Jamie Constance, explained its architectural history and W. C. Grant showed us the remaining half of the Allston summerhouse on Pawleys Island. In North Carolina, Alex King introduced us to Mitchell King's summerhouse in Flat Rock. Members of the Division of Parks and Recreation, North Carolina Department of Environment, Health, and Natural Resources, helped us locate the site in the present-day

Pettigrew State Park where Bonarva once stood. Angela Mack of the Gibbes Museum in Charleston, South Carolina, and Nancy Benjamin and Catherine Wahl of the Morris Museum in Augusta, Georgia, arranged for us to see Carson's works in their institutions.

Finally, we are indebted to Bertram Wyatt-Brown for his helpful reading of the revised manuscript and to Alice Wilkinson for her partial reading and an anonymous referee for his or her full reading of its predecessor. So too we are grateful to Lewis Bateman of the University of North Carolina Press for edging us into and through the extensive revision of the manuscript and to Paula Wald for her sensitive copyediting.

The following institutions have kindly given us permission to quote material and/or use images from their collections: the South Carolina Historical Society, the Southern Historical Collection at the University of North Carolina, the South Caroliniana Library at the University of South Carolina, the University of South Carolina Law School, the Division of Archives and History of the North Carolina Department of Cultural Resources, the Gibbes Museum, and the Hargrett Rare Book and Manuscript Library at the University of Georgia.

The following presses have given us permission to quote material from books they published: the Seajay Society, the University of South Carolina Press, Yale University Press, and the University of Chicago Press.

The following persons have graciously allowed us to reproduce images in their possession: Mrs. Donald McK. Allston, Jr., Mrs. John H. Daniels of Mulberry Plantation, and Mrs. Irénée duPont May.

Because the bulk of the narrative in this book comes from thousands of letters in a few collections, we have noted only the sources of direct quotations. Our practice has been to rationalize ambiguous punctuation marks when periods, commas, and dashes are indistinguishable in the original but to place in brackets any inserted punctuation not indicated by some mark in the original. Inserted letters or words are also enclosed in brackets. When misspellings occur in the original, we have left them as they were without the benediction of "[sic]." We have capitalized or lowercased the first letter of the initial word in a quotation to accord with the capitalization our text requires but have left irregular capitalization as it was in the original. And in the interest of smoother reading, we have sometimes changed first- or second-person pronouns to the third person but have indicated that shift by putting the third-person pronoun in brackets. Words printed in italics represent underlined words in the manuscripts from which they are quoted.

Regarding names, we have used the collective "Petigru women" to refer to all women in the Petigru connection whatever their surnames. Since all of his siblings adopted James Louis Petigru's distinctive spelling of his last name, that spelling defines the South Carolina branch of the Pettigrew family. For each person, we have employed the most common first name or nickname the family used both to differentiate among those who shared the same first names and to avoid yet greater confusion had we tried to refer to them by their surnames, which are even more repetitious. In only two cases, Jane Amelia Petigru and Mary Blount Pettigrew, have we departed from the most common family practice by adding their middle names to differentiate them from others bearing the same first name. The following are names we have used to refer to Petigru family members throughout.

Addy   Adele Allston (King) Middleton Kershaw
Adèle   Adèle Theresa (Petigru) Allston
Ann   Mary Ann (LaBruce) Petigru
Annie   Ann Blount Shepard (Pettigrew) McKay

Arnoldus	Arnoldus Vanderhorst
Ben	Benjamin Allston
Bessie	Elizabeth Waties (Allston) Pringle
Carey	Jane Caroline (North) Pettigrew
Caro	Caroline Pettigrew
Caroline	Jane Caroline (Petigru) Carson
Carson	William Augustus Carson
Charles	Charles Lockhart Pettigrew
Charles	Charles Petigru Allston
Charley	Charles Louis Pettigrew
Charley	Charles Porcher
Chris	Christopher Columbus Bowen
Dan	Daniel Elliott Huger Petigru
Della	Adele Petigru (Allston) Vanderhorst
Ebenezer	Ebenezer Pettigrew
Ellen	Ellen Stanley (Robinson) Allston
Hal	Henry Russell Lesesne
Harriette	Harriette (Petigru) Lesesne
Henry	Henry Campbell King
Henry	Henry Deas Lesesne
Jack	John Petigru
James	James Petigru Lesesne
James, Brother, Uncle	James Louis Petigru
Jane	Jane Gibert (Petigru) North
Jane Amelia, Sister	Jane Amelia (Postell) Petigru
Janey	Jane Louise Porcher
Janey, Jane	Jane North (Pettigrew) Williams
Janie	Jane Louise Allston
Jem	James Petigru Carson
Jinty	Jane Louise (Allston) Hill
Joe	Joseph Blyth Allston
John	John Gough North
Johnston	James Johnston Pettigrew
Leila	Harriette Leila (Lesesne) Smith
Little Min	Marion Johnston (Porcher) Ford
Lou	Louise Gibert (North) Allston
Louis	James Louis Petigru II
Louise	Louise Guy (Gibert) Pettigrew
Louise	Louise (Petigru) Porcher
Loulie	Louise Valery (Pettigrew) Woodson

Editorial Note

Louly	Louise Porcher
Lucy	Louise Porcher (Allston) Meade
Mary	Mary Petigru
Mary Anna	Mary Anna Porcher
Mary Blount	Mary Blount (Pettigrew) Browne
Mattie	Martha Pawley Petigru
Minnie	Mary Charlotte (North) Allston
Phil	Philip Johnston Porcher, Jr.
Philip	Philip Johnston Porcher
Robert	Robert Francis Withers Allston
Sue	Susan Dupont (Petigru) King Bowen
Tom	Thomas Petigru
William	William Shepard Pettigrew
Willie	William Carson

A FAMILY OF WOMEN

In romantic tales of the antebellum South, brave and honorable men pro-vided bountifully for gracious and beautiful wives on plantations where the labor of contented slaves produced rice and cotton crops that supported unequaled leisure and luxury. In Carolina's low country, the aura of that world lives on. Stately manor houses enveloped in wide piazzas lure visitors who first see them at the end of long avenues shaded by great live oaks festooned with Spanish moss. No less awed, tourists climb gently curving steps to enter Charleston town houses where once upon a time privileged Carolinians from across the state mingled, gossiped, and partied in the social frenzy of the winter high season.

To visit such houses is to enter a cherished past. A soft-spoken docent greets us at the door. She tells of a culture that flourished until, after four devastating years of war, outnumbered Southern troops surrendered and came home to poverty. As she recounts the tales of former owners, she notes the structural damage that invading armies and emancipated slaves inflicted on the property of those who had opted for secession and war to secure the peculiar institution. She chronicles the changes in the lives of mistresses, who pressed both husbands and sons to fight for Southern independence, sewed battle flags and uniforms, and, for the first time in their lives, oversaw the field work that produced crops desperately needed to feed both soldiers and civilians. As we proceed through the house, our docent sympathizes with the women who mourned kinsmen killed in battle and loved ones killed by the contagious diseases that spread rapidly among ill-nourished troops in crowded camps. Perhaps, like so many others, the mistress of this house was driven by the threat or reality of enemy invasion to flee her home and when she returned found a house badly vandalized or nearly destroyed. The docent also alludes to African Americans who had endured the same war and whose refusal to return to the old labor system contributed, along with hurricanes, insect plagues, and plummeting farm prices, to the end of plantation prosperity.

Seldom, however, can tour guides explore what underlies their narrative.

It is true enough that the low country's fabled riches disappeared in the 1860s. Many enterprising men, unable to restore the tattered vestiges of their old lives, sought their fortunes elsewhere. Some went west to farm new land. Others pursued businesses or professions in bustling competitive cities like New York and Atlanta, so unlike old familiar Charleston. Some women who were or had long expected to become plantation mistresses did reclaim their prewar dependence on husbands or fathers. Others sought new ways to support themselves, their children, and often a husband who returned from the war too damaged to resume his former role.

Like most myths that posit a golden age in the past, that of the Old South is partly rooted in reality. But in framing their narrative to solace a region that endured economic depression for seventy-five years after the Civil War ended, storytellers forget the preceding half-century when South Carolina had also known hard times. In the early 1820s, the mid-1830s, and most of the 1850s, skyrocketing commodity prices produced boom times, but soil exhaustion, the doldrums of the late 1820s, and the severe decade-long depression that began in 1837 impelled so many South Carolinians to migrate that by 1860 more than half of those who had been born in the state resided elsewhere. Furthermore, in those years, major trunk lines of the emerging railroad network that was revolutionizing marketing bypassed Charleston. And because of the westward shift of cotton production, shipping from the state's only port city lagged far behind that from Mobile and New Orleans. So by mid-century, if not well before then, neither plantation ownership nor the urban occupations dependent on the staples trade guaranteed financial security and the luxuries it made possible.

Therefore, no matter how much they enjoyed the amenities associated with rice and cotton cultivation, South Carolina's most privileged women were insecure in that enjoyment. Few ladies knew when their husbands' economic problems were about to subvert their own well-being, and still fewer took a significant part in managing family finances and business affairs. Because husbands seldom informed their wives about burdensome debts and other monetary obligations, women seldom even recognized the many financial uncertainties that might end their comfortable existence with little advance warning.

All, however, were painfully aware of other dangers. The subtropical climate and the swampy marshes so propitious for bumper crops of rice and long-staple cotton also fostered disease. In winter, cold damps along the riverine coast enhanced the risk of tuberculosis. In summer, malaria raged endemic, while ships entering Charleston harbor spurred fear of cholera, dengue fever, and yellow fever epidemics. Always parents dreaded the deadly scarlet fever that threatened children in all seasons. Between mid-May and the first fall frost, plantations and city alike were deemed so hazardous that come summer the wives and children of planters took refuge either in beach houses made safe by ocean breezes or in villages like Plantersville and Pineopolis where the towering longleaf pines marked well-drained sandy soil. Similarly, Charleston families went to Sullivans Island or traveled north or to Europe. Whatever their precautions, however, disease was a constant hazard, and death struck often.

Being privileged neither sheltered ladies from the perils of South Carolina's climate nor exempted them from experiences common to almost all nineteenth-century women. For women of their class, marriage and motherhood, the roles that cultural values imposed on women generally, were made yet more compelling because parents urged alliances with other families of similar—or better—standing. So the personal compatibility of future spouses, to which nearly all gave lip service, was often overshadowed even in the minds of much-courted belles by the pressure to marry well and soon. And in a state with absolutely no provision for divorce, the bonds once tied were indissoluble.

Yet the possibility of being trapped in a bad marriage seldom blocked the rush to the altar. Indeed, white women in Charleston—the only part of South Carolina for which mid-nineteenth-century statistics exist—were half again as likely as their Northern counterparts to be married by the time they were twenty-five. Once women married, childbearing began and continued, as long as the husband lived and the spouses were not geographically separated, until the wife reached menopause sometime in her early to mid-forties. Throughout those years, women generally gave birth at eighteen-month to three-year intervals. For some, perhaps many, additional pregnancies ended in miscarriages that threatened their health as much as deliveries attended by lay people, midwives, or even trained physicians who, ignorant of germs and careless about cleanliness, not infrequently carried puerperal fever to the birthing room. Consequently, however much they wanted children, most women associated pregnancy and childbirth with deadly dangers and feared each pregnancy accordingly. In a time and place where one in every four white children died in infancy and where one-third to one-half of all recorded deaths were those of children under five, mothers commonly saw at least one child die. Moreover, because the men they married were generally five to ten or more years older than they were, even women in their early thirties were 20 percent more likely to be widowed than were their Yankee counterparts.

The age difference between spouses had implications for women beyond the increased likelihood that they would outlive the men who had pledged to support them. Particularly in the first years of marriage, men cultivated their wives' complete dependence by treating them like children to whom they condescended as they instructed them in their matrimonial duties. This stance both justified and was justified by patriarchal assumptions as well as every gentleman's honorable duty to protect the weak and helpless. For women, however, such treatment implied a personal inadequacy so great that they were obliged to rely on a husband's superior strength. It was poor preparation for those who, possibly in their thirties but more likely in their forties and fifties, would become guardians of their children and managers of their families' assets.

Many women, in fact, had been obliged to become heads of their households long before war compelled most able-bodied white men to leave their homes. Nonetheless, the losses and trials of war tested all Southern women as never before. Exasperated by constant military defeats, furious at the ineptitude of both civilian and military leadership, and constantly on guard against enemy invasion and slave rebellion, they grappled with the death of kin, the upheavals of refugeeing, and shortages of even the most basic necessities. Nor did peace, when it finally came, restore old ways. Men who had lived through years of war came home defeated, depressed, and unprepared for the continuing social revolution that excluded them from the power they had once enjoyed. In the country, they returned to plantations stripped of stock, supplies, and equipment and deserted by newly freed laborers. When they attempted to resume their former occupations in town, they found few who could afford their services. Not infrequently, they could provide neither the food nor the clothing for which their families were desperate. Therefore, women who had once lived in luxury but who now faced both the impotence of their husbands and the absence of servants saw no alternative but to work at whatever tasks would assure their families' survival. At the same time, they struggled to reconcile their new lives with the expectation that they should resume their former subservient stance. Confused by the contradictions in their personal lives and bitter at the social revolution that had stripped away their privileges, many vented their rage not on the politicians who had launched the war or the husbands who had elected them but on the few servants they could hire but whose compliance they could not command.

Never in the postwar years were women exempt from the conflict between seeking a return to something like the ladylike dependence of yore and continuing along the more independent paths the war had forced them to take. In part, their responses were generational. In part, they were determined by individual personality. And in part, they hinged on how well husbands or sons could restore the privileges ladies had once enjoyed. Women whose midlife coincided with the war often retained the autonomy they had achieved. Older women were decidedly more likely to opt for, even insist on, prewar patterns of dependence and support. Those who came of age after the war were the most likely to depart from antebellum values and make their own way. There was, however, no sweeping move from patriarchal compliance to feminist self-assertion.

For nearly a century after the Civil War, historians who gave any attention to these Southern ladies enshrined them in the still familiar stereotypes of comely belles, hospitable plantation mistresses, noble supporters of the Confederacy, and brave survivors eager to surrender their wartime burdens to returning fathers, husbands, or sons. But since the 1970 publication of Anne Firor Scott's *The Southern Lady*, historians have explored those myths and exploded many of the stereotypes.[1] Some dispute Scott's contention that at no time in the nineteenth century did privileged Southern women fit this model. Others assert that such women had seldom challenged patriarchy until the war swept their men into military service and shifted male responsibilities onto female shoulders. Controversy swirls just as fiercely around what these ladies expected from their men when they returned home to a ruined economy, an emancipated African American work force, and temporary exclusion from political power. Had these women been so changed by their wartime experiences that they contested old forms of patriarchy, or did they revert at least to an outer shell of ladylike reticence in their eagerness to bolster white men's self-esteem after humiliating military and political defeats?

The story of the Petigru women, spanning the years in which this process was played out, underlines the diversity among both prewar and postwar Southern ladies. Although their history is not that of all Southern women, it does portray an outer world and bares an inner turmoil common to the privileged ladies who graced the antebellum South, endured the deprivations and despair of civil war, and experienced a social revolution. Their diaries and letters reveal the many contradictions that coexisted in the minds and lives of Southern ladies far better than any house tour could possibly do. They demonstrate that women were well aware of the restrictions that hobbled them and of the choices they had to make. Because neither looking at one woman's writing over a long period of time nor reading the diaries and letters that many wrote in response to a particular event can chart the shifts and shoals of a century, the rich record that the South Carolina Petigrus compiled provides a rare opportunity to understand how three generations of related but distinctive women conducted their individual lives, shared one another's triumphs and defeats, and sustained their collective courage as they weighed the dangers and possibilities that confronted them.

This is their story. It begins on a modest farm in the South Carolina upcountry from which education offered a path to low country wealth and social standing for both daughters and sons. It winds its way through Charleston's urban excitements and the luxuries of life on rice and cotton plantations. It heaves with the dislocations of war and mourning the dead. And it ends only after a long struggle with loss and defeat. The Petigrus' is a story worth telling about women worth knowing.

PART ONE

The Rise of the Petigrus

CHAPTER ONE

Establishing the Petigru Connection

When Louise Petigru Porcher learned that Adèle Petigru had become engaged to Robert Francis Withers Allston, she rushed to her sister's side. It was "simply madness" for Adèle to "bury" herself on Allston's remote rice plantation when a contending suitor would provide her a fine Charleston home and make her "the centre of a brilliant social circle." No matter how handsome or rich Robert was, life as his wife would be a "dreadful thing." Adèle half smiled and half scowled. "Louise, you want to know why I am going to marry Robert Allston? I will tell you:—because he is as obstinate as the devil. In our family we lack will-power; that is our weakness."[1]

This is not just an anecdote of Louise's or Adèle's preferences. It is part of the story of an entire Southern family, of three generations of Petigru women who were the daughters, daughters-in-law, granddaughters, granddaughters-in-law, and great-granddaughters of Louise Guy Gibert, a South Carolina Huguenot who in 1788 married William Pettigrew, a boisterous upcountry Scotch-Irishman. But defined by their time and place, they were the wife, sisters and sisters-in-law, daughters and nieces, granddaughters and grandnieces of James Louis Petigru, Louise's son, who, in changing the spelling of his family name, set his kinswomen apart from all other Pettigrews.

The first-generation Petigrus began their lives in rather humble circumstances. Their father, who had been born in 1758, grew up in the Abbeville

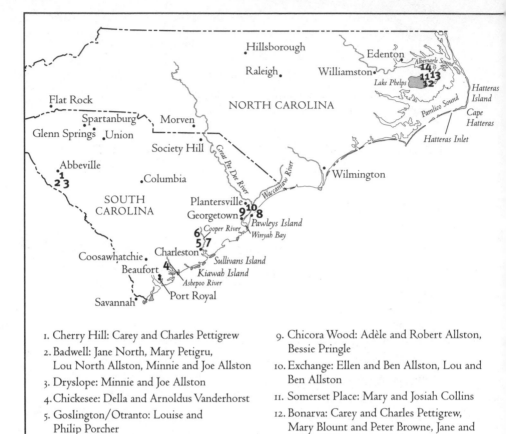

1. Cherry Hill: Carey and Charles Pettigrew
2. Badwell: Jane North, Mary Petigru, Lou North Allston, Minnie and Joe Allston
3. Dryslope: Minnie and Joe Allston
4. Chickesee: Della and Arnoldus Vanderhorst
5. Goslington/Otranto: Louise and Philip Porcher
6. Keithfield: Louise and Philip Porcher
7. Dean Hall: Caroline and William A. Carson
8. Waverly: Minnie and Joe Allston
9. Chicora Wood: Adèle and Robert Allston, Bessie Pringle
10. Exchange: Ellen and Ben Allston, Lou and Ben Allston
11. Somerset Place: Mary and Josiah Collins
12. Bonarva: Carey and Charles Pettigrew, Mary Blount and Peter Browne, Jane and Miller Williams
13. Magnolia: William Pettigrew
14. Belgrade: William Pettigrew, Carey and Charles Pettigrew

MAP 1. The Carolinas

district on the southwestern South Carolina frontier. Few of his neighbors boasted substantial wealth, and the Pettigrews surely did not. But they had prospered enough for William's widowed mother to leave him seventy-five acres of farmland, two slaves, two horses, and two cows—half of all of the property that his Irish-born immigrant father had accumulated in the forty-four years during which he had migrated south along the Appalachians. His youngest son, however, soon lost even that modest patrimony. An undistinguished Revolutionary War veteran with little education and less ambition, he read, drank, and gambled more than he cleared, planted, and harvested.

In 1788, when he courted and married, William had just inherited his

THE RISE OF THE PETIGRUS

property and, despite its limited amount, stood among the richest 20 percent of local folk. His bride, Louise Gibert, dark-haired, fair-skinned, and barely twenty, had grown up in more prosperous circumstances. Her father, Jean Louis Gibert, was a Huguenot cleric who in 1764 had led his persecuted parishioners from France to upcountry South Carolina, where they founded the town New Bordeaux. There his wife bore three children. There, in the nine years before he died, he accumulated extensive real estate, a store, ten slaves, nine horses, and fifty to eighty head of cattle, all of which he bequeathed to his wife. But French-born Jeanne, widowed and unhappy on that isolated frontier, promptly took her children to Charleston, where she met and married retail merchant Pierre Engevine, a fellow immigrant. Louise, who was only six when she arrived, spent most of her childhood and early adolescence in Charleston. It was a good place for her to grow up. Although Pierre was neither part of the city's sophisticated culture nor at the center of its revolutionary politics, he was able to introduce his stepchildren to many of the amenities and advantages of urban life.

When Jeanne Gibert Engevine died in 1783, Pierre gave up his business to take his stepchildren back to their birthplace. There he built a new house and began to cultivate the land the children had inherited from their mother. On that farm, appropriately named Badwell, William Pettigrew courted Louise Gibert, drawn by her citified ways as much as by her physical charms. Undoubtedly repelled by the loneliness of life on a remote farm and surely intrigued by her suitor's dashing frontier zest, Louise was equally attracted to him. They married in May 1788.

At once she moved to William's farm in even more remote Flat Woods. For twelve years, the couple occupied what was probably little more than the two ground-floor rooms and loft of a double cabin. Their only near neighbors were William's close friend Thomas Finley and his wife Jeanne, Louise's younger sister. It was with Jeanne's inexperienced support, therefore, that on May 10, 1789, Louise bore the first of her nine children, whom she named James Louis for her father. In succession, two more sons came, John in 1791 and Thomas two years later. Also, in 1795, after Jeanne died, Louise virtually adopted infant Louis Finley.

As the Pettigrew family grew, its prosperity declined. Easygoing, fonder of fishing, hunting, and horse racing than of farming, William soon stumbled into debt. The hard times of postrevolutionary social disorder and economic upheaval gripped the upcountry, while the plantation low country continued to monopolize the state's economic resources as well as its government. Stripped of his farm by his creditors, William moved his pregnant wife and their four boys to the Gibert family farm in 1800. There, property-less and humiliated, he merged his household with that of Louise's bachelor brother, Joseph, who occupied Badwell after both his sisters married.

The family had barely settled in when Louise gave birth on August 17 to her first daughter, whom she named Jane Gibert after her mother and her sister. Thereafter, at regular two-to-three year intervals, she bore the rest of her children: Mary in 1803, Charles in 1806, Louise in 1809, Adeline Theresa in 1811; and Harriette in 1813. At Badwell, Louise watched her sons grow sturdy as they worked in the fields side by side with the few slaves left from Jean Gibert's estate. Despite her restricted means, she found a way to send James to Moses Waddel's nearby academy and then, with borrowed money, to pay his tuition at South Carolina College. Established quite explicitly to draw talented upcountry boys into the state's low country ruling class, the recently chartered college did just that for James. In 1812, three years after he graduated, he was admitted to the bar. Shortly thereafter he changed the spelling of his name from Pettigrew to Petigru, and in so doing he allied himself with his mother's Huguenot heritage rather than with the Scotch-Irish heritage of his father. Subsequently, all of his brothers and sisters followed his example.

More than a simple change in spelling, becoming a Petigru signaled the transformation of James's and his siblings' expectations and aspirations. It also confirmed the reality of the upward mobility the young lawyer was already achieving. The social style he had polished by association with his low country classmates so enhanced his native endowments that he soon attracted a powerful mentor, Daniel Elliott Huger, with whose aid he rose rapidly, becoming state attorney general in 1822, the same year he took over James Hamilton's Charleston practice after Hamilton went to Congress. By his early thirties, therefore, James Petigru's steady rise in social and profes-sional prestige had given him the critical financial and psychological re-sources not just to assume major responsibility for his parents' support but also to forward his brothers' careers and enhance his sisters' social status.

In 1816, the same year he was appointed state solicitor for the Beaufort district, James married Jane Amelia Postell, the daughter of a local planter, who two years earlier had spurned him. The marriage confirmed his new social acceptability. A low country belle with dark eyes, clear complexion, and auburn hair, Jane Amelia was a Southern beauty whose flashing smile and graceful bearing attracted many admirers. Well educated at Mademoi-selle Julia Datty's Charleston finishing school, she displayed a polished sociability and exuberant style that pleased everyone but her serious and pious mother-in-law. All the rest of James's family were pleased by his good

James Louis Petigru. Caroline Carson portrait painted from memory
and photographs, ca. 1880. Courtesy of the University of
South Carolina Law School.

luck in marrying a woman whose father was able to give her ten slaves as a
wedding present. And even Louise was somewhat mollified by Jane Amelia's
mother's Huguenot ancestry. The whole family, in fact, clearly benefited
from the rise in social standing brought by their new connection with the
bride's grandfather, Colonel James Postell, a Revolutionary War hero, at
whose plantation near Abbeville Jane Amelia and James were married.

Before they established their own home, the newlyweds lived for over a
year with Jane Amelia's cousin, Jane Caroline Porcher North, and her husband, Edward, on his plantation near the Beaufort district seat of Coosaw-

1. Home of Sue and Christopher Bowen, corner of Bull and Smith Streets

2. Home of Ann and Thomas Petigru, Bull Street

3. Home of Harriette and Henry Lesesne, Green Street, 1837-53

4. Home of Jane Amelia and James Petigru, Broad Street

5. Home of Mrs. James Carson (William's mother) to 1849; Harriette and Henry Lesesne, 1850s, Tradd Street

6. Home of Sue and Henry King, Tradd Street

7. Home of J. Johnston Pettigrew, Tradd Street, 1860-63

8. Home of Adèle and Robert Allston, Lower Meeting Street

9. Home of Ann Petigru, Lower King Street, 1858-69

10. Home of Louise and Philip Porcher, South Bay

11. Home of Jane and Albert Hill, South Battery

12. White Point Garden

13. Home of J. Johnston Pettigrew, St. Michael's Alley, 1856-60

14. James Petigru's law office, St. Michael's Alley

15. St. Michael's Church

16. Home of Della and Arnoldus Vanderhorst, Chapel Street

MAP 2. Charleston

hatchie. There their first son, Albert Porcher, was born in 1818. After their move to Charleston in 1819, their first daughter, Jane Caroline, also named for her mother's kin, was born in 1820. The next two children, Daniel Elliott Huger in 1822 and Susan Dupont in 1824, were given the names of family friends.

All the while, James's legal career thrived. His government salary, added to the ever-growing income from his private practice, gave him a comfortable security his parents had never known. But prosperity was no buffer against personal tragedy. On September 11, 1826, eight-year-old Albert, who loved to coast down the railing from the third to the ground floor although forbidden to do so, took advantage of his parents' brief absence and the inattention of a servant to mount the banister on the top floor of the house. He lost his balance and fell thirty feet to the first floor hall. Badly injured, he died thirty-seven hours later. That same day, James's fifty-nine-year-old mother died at Badwell. James was devastated, racked with guilt over his son's death, which he might have prevented, and his mother's suffering, which his presence might have eased.

Characteristically, he muffled his emotions by assuming new duties. His mother had appointed him trustee of her property, to be used to benefit her unmarried children as well as her spouse, and in so doing had implicitly charged him with still other responsibilities. After their mother's death, James's three youngest sisters lacked the guidance they needed if they were to overcome the backcountry isolation of Badwell and their alcoholic father's lax standards. James, therefore, brought them to Charleston to live with his family. In 1827 he purchased a summer cottage on nearby Sullivans Island so that the entire family could enjoy the healthful vacations that so many affluent Charlestonians sought there. The next year, to accommodate his expanded household, he bought a big house on a fashionable downtown block of Broad Street.

For Jane Amelia, introducing three adolescent girls into her grief-stricken home exacted a heavy toll. Emotionally high-strung and physically stressed by the birth of four children in six years, she had been shattered by Albert's death and was ill-prepared to supervise six youngsters ranging in age from four to eighteen. Her emotional equanimity was destroyed by the death of her firstborn and by the almost simultaneous addition to her household of three nubile sisters-in-law with whom she had to compete for her husband's affections. Moreover, she was ill at ease with her husband's oldest sister, Jane, even though Jane, like the next oldest sister, Mary, had chosen to remain at Badwell with their father. Ignoring that discomfort, James soon invited Jane for a long visit, partly out of brotherly affection and partly to introduce her to the Charleston society from which a suitable husband might emerge. One did. John Gough North was not, however, a casual acquaintance encountered at a party. He was James's former law student as well as Jane Amelia's cousin.

After their courtship and marriage at Badwell in August 1827, Jane and John set off at once for Georgetown, where John had just opened a law office. James was as pleased with his sister's marriage as he was with his former student's career plans and hoped both would flourish. "I have no idea that a woman should marry at all, unless she is willing to devote herself heart and soul to promote the good of her husband. . . . If she has the sense of virtue and honor . . . [she will] show it, like Solomon's good wife, in rising betimes and setting her maidens to work."[2] Thus did the thirty-eight-year-old brother affectionately instruct his twenty-seven-year-old sister—she the first sister to marry a man to whom her brother had introduced her, he an emerging fratriarch.

From then on, the marriages of his sisters and one brother and their generation of children created an ever broader fratriarchy, enhanced by James's legal and political prestige. All of them acknowledged his standing as the Petigru family's head. One after another, his sisters married prosperous men whom their brother's professional and social status had first attracted. After each sibling married, Brother, as they called him, expanded his nurturing encouragement to encompass the spouse and children. He was equally well pleased with John North's success as a planter and lawyer and with the comforts Jane now enjoyed. By 1830, John owned the couple's house in Georgetown as well as a nearby rice plantation employing sixty-seven slaves. Soon the couple boasted three daughters, all named for kin: Jane Caroline, born in 1828, for her North grandmother; Mary Charlotte, born in 1832, for her Aunt Mary Petigru; and Louise Gibert, born in 1833, for her Pettigrew grandmother. But given their society's patriarchal values, they vested their hopes for the family's perpetuity in their second child, Albert Porcher. Consequently they were devastated when the boy died in 1833, before his fourth birthday. For Jane, who nursed him with the painful cuppings doctors then prescribed for scarlet fever, the child's suffering was nearly unbearable. Yet, although she never ceased to mourn his loss, she pulled back from the debilitating grief into which Jane Amelia had sunk under similar circumstances. That iron self-discipline was her salvation, for on February 13, 1836, John died, apparently of congestive heart failure. Only then did Jane discover that during his gradual physical decline his property had become heavily encumbered. Unable to save anything, even with Brother's legal intervention, and drained of emotional strength, she returned to Badwell with her three daughters to live with her sister Mary and their ailing father.

Mary, a homebody, plain, and by then thirty-three, seemed fated to remain a spinster. For the eleven years between her mother's death in 1826 and her father's in 1837, she oversaw Badwell's domestic management. Indeed, she would live at Badwell for the rest of her life, for although she made occasional visits to Charleston, where the opportunities to meet eligible men were extensive, she attracted no suitors and never married. So it was Louise, the third oldest sister, who was the second to marry.

Louise celebrated her eighteenth birthday soon after James brought her to live with him. Although no beauty and never a popular belle, in the next two years, while she was part of Brother's household and social circle, she attracted several suitors. Like Jane, however, she too chose a cousin of Jane Amelia's, Philip Johnston Porcher. Trained as a physician, Philip had recently given up his medical practice to manage the 1,200-acre Keithfield plantation, which he had purchased along with its sixty-seven slaves in 1828. As soon as they were married on October 13, 1829, the couple left for the plantation in St. John's Berkeley parish. They lived at Keithfield for the next six years, although they spent the summer months in the nearby pineland village of Cordesville to escape country fever, as malaria was then called. At Keithfield, Louise bore three children, two of whom died in infancy. Not surprisingly, in her distress, she yearned for the companionship of family and friends in Charleston. But because Philip no longer maintained a residence there and they hesitated to wear out their welcome with his kin, they visited town only rarely. In 1836, however, either in response to Louise's misery at her isolation or his own dissatisfaction with planting, Philip bought a house on Charleston's South Bay Street. He moved his family there almost at once, even though he did not sell the plantation until nearly three years later.

James Petigru's marriage to a Postell, Jane's to a North, and Louise's to a Porcher each represented gratifying upward mobility. Brother Tom's marriage, however, catapulted him in one bound into great planter wealth. To all appearances, he was not much of a catch. Tom had joined the U.S. Navy in 1812 and remained a midshipman for the next ten years. When, in 1829, he finally became a lieutenant, it was only after James had pressed his political contacts to make sure that Tom's long service was not overlooked. Tom's distinctly marginal career did not deter Mary Ann LaBruce, the daughter of a Georgetown rice planter, whom Tom had probably met when he was visiting Jane and John North. For her, engagement to a reasonably attractive naval officer her own age betokened an unexpected escape from life as an old maid dedicated to her brother's children. For Tom, her family's wealth was apparently a greater attraction than the personal charms of a thirty-six-year-old spinster. Still, although it may not have been a marriage made in heaven, their union in November 1829 was an earthly compromise by which Ann (so called in the Petigru family to distinguish her from sister Mary) brought Tom two rice plantations, a town house in Georgetown, and 111 slaves and Tom gave Ann a home and children of her own: Martha, named for Ann's mother, born in 1830, and James Louis Petigru II, born in 1832.

Of all the sisters, Adeline, who in her adolescence had renamed herself Adelle and after her marriage spelled her name Adèle, was undoubtedly the most attractive. A ravishing Charleston belle, she almost swept Brother himself off his feet with her radiant beauty. Her long brown curls were a perfect frame for her oval face with its high cheekbones and slender, straight nose. Her mind sparkled engagingly, cultivated by extensive reading under James's guidance. Even twenty years after he had overseen her introduction to society, James confessed that he had "never loved any one more, never received from anyone more proofs of affection." Ten years later, he still believed there was "none or hardly one" whom he had "loved with such an enduring affection."[3] Such an intense attachment could hardly have pleased Jane Amelia, but it was not a selfish one. James wanted Adèle to marry and to marry even better than had her sisters. He encouraged her and was not disappointed when she accepted not another cousin of his wife's but his wealthy and prestigious client Robert Allston.

Robert was the younger son of a major Georgetown rice planter who had died when both of his sons were small children. As an adult, Robert turned to lawyer Petigru for help in rescuing his share of the family estate from the challenges and disputes that had reduced its value during the years in which his mother had managed it. Robert, however, did not wait idly for the resolution of such problems. For five years after his graduation from West Point in 1821, he put the engineering skills he had learned there to profitable use as the official surveyor of South Carolina. And by the end of the decade, he had brought his inherited Matanzas plantation, which he later renamed Chicora Wood,[4] back to high productivity with the labor of the eighty slaves he had added to the forty-six he had inherited from his mother in 1824. Moreover, in 1828, when he first plunged into politics, he was elected at only twenty-seven to represent Georgetown in the state House of Representatives. By 1831, therefore, when he courted Adèle, he was obviously a man accustomed to getting what he wanted. So intense was his pursuit of the twenty-year-old belle that her brother whisked her off to Savannah for the Christmas season to give her a cooling-off period in which to consider her future. But although she also attracted a bevy of beaux in the Georgia city, when Robert proposed in January, she accepted.

THE RISE OF THE PETIGRUS

Robert's aunt and "most indulgent friend" Elizabeth Blyth was delighted. But Robert himself was somewhat buffaloed, for, although Adèle had promised to marry him, she refused to set a date. Very much in character, he pressed her. If, he wrote, she "could fix upon the 28th Feby. or 1st of March, at the same time that it would consummate my bliss, this arrangement would add very much to my convenience." Robert's convenience was not, however, Adèle's. Like many of her contemporaries, she basked in the excitement of courtship and staved off as long as possible its frightening culmination in the realities of marriage. She well knew that at her wedding she would surrender her power as the center of attention for obligations that would almost inevitably include the dangers of childbirth and the anxieties of motherhood. Robert, sensing her fears, promised not to abridge the freedom of which she was "so jealous" until 1833 if only Adèle would set an early date.[5]

It was then that Louise Porcher, in town for a brief respite from Keithfield's isolation, warned her sister against marriage to Allston and the lonely exile at Chicora Wood it would bring. Adèle ignored her advice. But she also set limits on Robert's demands. She rejected both February 28 and March 1 as wedding dates. An April wedding was her choice, and she stuck with it. So it was on April 21 that, surrounded by family members and given in marriage by Brother, she pledged her future to the man their daughter would later characterize as "severe," "stern," and generally unwilling or unable to express emotion. Still, in the eyes of the world, it was an excellent match for Adèle. Brother, although he considered it a personal "sacrifice," blessed it, but Jane Amelia responded to the event with a "derangement of stomach," including "throwing up bile," that kept her from playing any role in the wedding festivities.[6]

In his first letter to her at Chicora Wood, James advised his sister to accommodate herself to the "employments and pleasures" of country living. That charge well-nigh overwhelmed her. As Mrs. R. F. W. Allston, she was the mistress of a large plantation as different from the Badwell of her childhood as it was from the urban sociability of Charleston. Although she and Robert were not Chicora's only white residents—an overseer and his family lived there as well—Adèle felt totally isolated in a sea of black workers. Furthermore, Robert insisted that the well-being of these workers was largely her responsibility. Fortunately, his Aunt Blyth came to the rescue. Long a widow and the efficient manager of her own plantations, she guided her nephew's new bride through the uncertainties that terrified her. Under Aunt Blyth's tutelage, Adèle began the transition from "a pleasure-loving, indolent woman" to an earnest one, whose "power of organization, grasp of

Harriette Petigru at age twenty-two. Charles Fraser miniature reproduced in
Alice R. Huger Smith and D. E. Huger Smith, *Charles Fraser*
(Charleston: Garnier, 1924).

detail, perception of character, power of speech . . . [and] endless self-
control" developed over time to make her in fact the mistress of Chicora
Wood. But as a young person who believed it was "absolutely necessary to
express . . . all she felt," she had to struggle to follow Brother's encomium
that wifely duty demanded a constant "endeavour to make others happy."[7]
Many tensions surfaced between the voluble and inexperienced wife and her
older and taciturn husband.

Undeterred by the mixed blessings that marriage brought her older sisters, Harriette, the youngest and shyest, proved also the most eager to assume the duties of matrimony. Never the belle or beauty that Adèle had been, her straight hair pulled back tight on her head, her nose puggish, her chin somewhat protruding, she too had been introduced to the exciting circle of Charleston's elite young. But she had not shone. She was not much of a conversationalist, being neither very lively nor well informed. She preferred the domestic arts to books, lacked any talent for music, and was too bashful for quick repartee. Her preferences and talents, however, attracted Henry Deas Lesesne, an accountant who had entered James Petigru's office to study law as his clerk. He had progressed so swiftly that he was admitted to the bar when he was barely twenty-one. Before he was thirty, Petigru made him a partner in his extensive and extremely remunerative practice. But that came only in 1840, after the young lawyer had already made the most of his easy access to the Petigru family circle to woo Harriette. They were married in May 1836, when Henry was twenty-five and Harriette, twenty-three. For several months, they lived in Brother's commodious Broad Street house until they could move into the more modest one on the edge of town that Henry soon purchased. Having earlier been "very busy and very giddy too" in preparing her trousseau, Harriette now delighted in putting her linens and household equipment to use. As her teenaged niece Caroline put it, the newlyweds "jog[ged] on in a most sober, quiet and pleasant way." Henry might have lacked a sound constitution, but his frequent illnesses did not lessen Harriette's pride in her professionally "industrious" spouse, who was "never idle."[8] Even though they had no children in their first six years of marriage, they seemed to all a very well matched pair.

Harriette's marriage was the last among Louise Gibert's daughters. Her youngest son, Charles, an army officer, died in 1835, having courted one woman after another without success. Jack, the black sheep of the family, whom, after their mother's death, James sent west until he should end his dissipations, later married Tempe, whose surname is unknown but whose origins were apparently very humble.

Jack alone broke the pattern that his six married siblings established by marrying well. And Mary Ann LaBruce alone broke the pattern of women marrying in their twenties. All but Harriette bore a child in the first year or two of marriage and demonstrated thereby the fertility expected of good wives. Of the men the sisters married, all were professionals or planters or both, men of notably higher status than their father, although, with the exception of Robert Allston, not of higher status than their brother James, within whose circle they were all wooed. And the Petigru sisters-in-law, with the probable exception of Tempe, contributed, at least initially, to their husbands' increasing prestige.

Between Brother's marriage in 1816 and Harriette's in 1836, the children of Louise Gibert and William Pettigrew had begun to create an extended family. James was its hub; each sibling, a spoke linking spouse and children to that hub. Together they formed a rim strongly bonded to the hub by resilient spokes. Together they formed the Petigru connection.

CHAPTER TWO

Begetting Offspring

Whatever hopes Petigru brides held for married life, whatever fears they harbored as they promised to love, honor, and obey until death—and only death—broke that vow, they knowingly faced a future in which childbearing and child rearing were central. No matter what their forebodings during pregnancy, when their time came, they, like most women, lavished love and attention on their newborn infants. Almost always, the first of their children produced an intense sense of maternal fulfillment. But such satisfaction came only after months of physical discomfort that culminated in the childbirth they feared might kill them. Their responses to pregnancy, therefore, embraced conflicting emotions—joyous anticipation and stark terror held in balance by their determination to accept the inevitable.

In an era when babies were born at home with women friends and family members in attendance whether or not a doctor or midwife was present, the Petigru girls learned much about their future tribulations in their childhood home. At Badwell, as many as eight siblings had lived with their parents and their uncle in no more than five rooms. Necessarily they overheard the nocturnal noises of parental intimacy. Both Jane and Mary probably attended their mother when she gave birth to their youngest siblings. Later on, the younger sisters assisted the older ones in similar ways. All of them, without exception, had as girls helped care for young infants and recuperating mothers. But familiar as they were with the realities of childbearing, they also followed the mores of their time by discussing such matters only obliquely. In their letters at least, sexuality and the commonplaces of child-

Adèle Petigru Allston at age twenty-three. Thomas Sully portrait reproduced in
James Petigru Carson, *Life, Letters, and Speeches of James Louis Petigru:
The Union Man of South Carolina* (Washington, D.C.: W. H. Lowdermilk, 1920).

birth were cloaked in a language of reticent ambiguity. They announced
their pregnancies with coded references, urging family members to be on
hand at dates when they anticipated being "sick." By doing so, of course,
they supplied the probable dates of the intercourse that led to conception.

As the Petigru girls matured, married, and became pregnant, their own
observations and the confidences of others were their best sources of infor-

mation. Despite ladylike restraints that limited their written communication, they managed to inform each other of miscarriages as well as live births. Jane Amelia Petigru, Adèle Allston, and Harriette Lesesne all miscarried at least once. Adèle, Harriette, and Louise Porcher all experienced nearly fatal deliveries. And every mother in that first generation endured the death of at least one child. Collectively, these six married women, while they were still relatively young, lost sixteen children, eight of them under ten.

Adèle's experience typifies the perils and triumphs they all faced. Married in April 1832, she was already pregnant by early June. Racked by nausea and severely depressed, she sought moral support from Jane North, then living nearby in Georgetown. Even though her own three children were all under five, Jane hurried up to Canaan beach house, the Allston's summer place, to stay with her younger sister while Robert was away on business. When he returned and Jane left, he asked the rest of her family to help buoy her spirits. James wrote at least one cheering letter, and Charles wrote several. That December, Louise entertained her younger sister at Keithfield while Robert attended the annual legislative session. Toward the end of her pregnancy, James and Jane Amelia housed her in Charleston to ensure that she would have the best medical help available for her confinement. Then, after underweight and rather puny Benjamin was born, Harriette nursed Adèle through an illness so severe that her doctors ordered all her hair cut off. When she recovered sufficiently to return home, sister Mary came down from Badwell to accompany her to Chicora Wood and stay with her there. Once she was home, the neighborly rituals began. Almost exactly four weeks after Ben's birth, a Pee Dee plantation mistress made the first mandatory social call on the new mother.

During the next twenty years after her initiation into the trials and rites of matronhood, Adèle bore eight more children. Before Ben was fifteen months old, his mother was back in maternity clothes. Her sister-in-law Jane Amelia prescribed the latest style, a dress hanging loose from a wide yoke, the skirt held in only by a belt that could be discarded when appropriate. With characteristic officiousness, she also virtually ordered Adèle to return to Charleston for her second lying-in despite Robert's opposition. His notion that it was her confinement in Charleston that had made delivering Ben so difficult was sheer nonsense. "A first child," Brother's wife proclaimed, "always gives more trouble than those that come after."[1] Robert clearly knew nothing about such things and should leave them to women. Nonetheless, either because Robert believed that a second child would come easier or because he remained convinced that Charleston was inherently unhealthful, baby Robert was born at Chicora Wood on December 31, 1834.

His father entrusted Jane Amelia only with the limited responsibility of choosing the Charleston nurse-midwife who attended Adèle. Happily Mrs. Murphy arrived in time, for Adèle, very frightened anyway, was doubly terrified by Aunt Blyth's observation that her size suggested twins. To her infinite relief, however, she bore a single child, large and healthy, as big at birth as his older brother had been after a year.

Three years later, Adèle feared a harder time, in part because she had suffered a miscarriage in late 1836. Her premonitions were well founded, for on November 23, 1837, the birth of her first daughter nearly killed her. The attending physician attributed the long period of fever, "great distress of body," and "excitement of mind" that followed the delivery to the morphine and quinine he had administered to ease her pain. When she finally recovered, she thought that assuredly she had been "raised from the brink of the grave." Yet even during her long weeks of pain and delirium, Robert had remained in Columbia, attending the regular winter session of the South Carolina Senate. Reflecting a year later on her "great deliverance from the bed of death," he addressed the baby's moral future more than his wife's suffering. On Charlotte Frances's first birthday (they had named her after his mother), Robert exhorted Adèle to devote herself to "that precious life, so spared," and to rear her "innocent, tender charge . . . 'in the nurture & admonition of the Lord.'"[2]

Robert's concern for the souls of his children was heartfelt, but Adèle, although she shared his religious commitment, worried more intensely about her own and her children's physical survival. That she had nursed each of her sons for a full year only disheartened her further when her illness so disrupted lactation that Fanny—only Robert called the child Charlotte—had to be fed by a wet nurse. Then in March 1839, four-year-old Robert died from scarlet fever. And less than three months later, at the Canaan beach house, Adèle again miscarried while she was far from medical help. The double tragedy of that spring, added to memories of the early months of her awful first pregnancy, convinced her never to return to that doomed spot. Accordingly, by the summer of 1840, Robert had built her a bungalow in the isolated pineland about eight miles north of Chicora Wood, a spot believed to be as safe from summer fevers as the beach. There Adèle, pregnant again, became sick once more. Her fear and misery were compounded by the fact that the local physician was an inexperienced young country doctor, but she was saved from his unskilled ministrations by the fortuitous arrival of an able monthly nurse from Charleston. Mary Holland had been in Georgetown on another case and was about to return home when she was summoned to aid Adèle. Grateful that his wife had once again narrowly escaped death, Robert insisted that this daughter be named Adele in her honor. But once again the mother had been traumatized by childbirth.

Nonetheless, the cycle continued. In her twenty years of childbearing, Adèle experienced at least eleven pregnancies, from which seven children survived infancy. Louise Gibert was born without complications in 1842, as was Elizabeth Waties (named for her Great-aunt Blyth) in 1845. Perhaps because these deliveries had been so easy, only Maum Mary, a slave midwife from a neighboring plantation, attended Adèle in 1848 when Charles Petigru was born. Then, two years later, Adèle spent most of her last successful pregnancy at the family's new summer cottage on Pawleys Island. Here, because Robert was traveling in the North, she was accompanied by her twenty-two-year-old niece Carey North as well as her children and servants. By the time she bore her fifth daughter, however, she had returned to Chicora Wood, where Mary Holland, who had arrived a full month in advance, was on hand to attend her. Also with her were her sisters Jane North (for whom and sister Louise Porcher the baby was named) and Harriette Lesesne. Because Adèle was now thirty-nine years old, her sisters were especially concerned. Once again, however, all went well. Five days after Jane Louise's birth, Robert, now president of the South Carolina Senate and more than ever tied to Columbia for the December legislative session, wrote ecstatically to his wife. "Honor to your sex for its beautiful symmetry, its wonderful & admirable perfection in fulfilling the responsibilities imposed by nature!" Then he paused before he went on to send "love to your own dear self, as being one of the truest and the best of that same!"[3] One final time, in 1852 Adèle again faced the dangers of pregnancy. That summer, while the family was in New York on vacation, she became so ill that she was rushed back to Pawleys Island, where she gave premature birth to one last son, who died immediately. Adèle, now forty-one, had had her last child.

None of her sisters quite matched Adèle's fertility, although in the thirty years that elapsed between the birth of Jane North's first child in 1828 and the birth of Harriette Lesesne's last in 1858, there was rarely more than a year during which one of the sisters was not pregnant, and on at least six occasions, two or three bore children in the same year. Jane, whose childbearing was cut short by her husband's death, had already borne four infants between the time she was twenty-eight and the time she was thirty-three. Between her twenty-third and fortieth birthdays, Louise Porcher delivered eight children, and Harriette, from the time she was twenty-nine until she reached forty-five, added six to the family circle. On the other hand, Ann Petigru, who had not married until she was thirty-six, had only two children before she reached forty, and Jane Amelia Petigru, although she may have had a miscarriage when she was thirty-seven, had completed her family of four by the time she was thirty. With the exception of Jane Amelia, therefore, those of the first generation of Petigru women who married spent the most fertile years of their marriages bearing and nursing infants just as Louise Gibert Pettigrew had done. And except for Jane Amelia, they were still rearing their progeny in their late fifties.

Not surprisingly, much of the support the Petigru sisters gave each other addressed the trials and needs of motherhood. Sometimes it was as limited as Louise's proffer to Adèle of a set of very large corsets she had worn during her last pregnancy and had found "quite easy," unlike the stiff-boned corsets that were troubling her sister. Sometimes it was as prolonged and intense as the aid Jane gave Harriette, pregnant and severely depressed over her six-year-old daughter's recent death. When Harriette and her two sons arrived at Badwell in December 1852, she found in Jane's household a large assemblage of women that created a cheerfully reassuring haven. Then in April Jane went down to Charleston to attend Harriette in what turned out to be a difficult delivery. Their youngest sister, Jane reported to Adèle, "had an hour of desperate pain," but because "no physician was by to make her ashamed," she "screamed at the top of her lungs, and that . . . did her good."[4]

In the flow of advice back and forth, the sisters occasionally tripped over differences of opinion. Nevertheless, they shared an underlying and reassuring consensus on child care, which they doubtless had derived from their mother. With the exception of Jane Amelia, who scoffed at the practice as making oneself "a slave to ones children," all of the sisters nursed their babies for at least a year unless postpartum illness or the depressions that both Harriette and Adèle suffered precluded this practice.[5] Similarly, they agreed that the naming of their children should reinforce family bonds by entrenching Petigru names in the next generation. The Porchers called their first son James Petigru, but also honored the paternal line when they christened the third one Philip after his father. The Lesesnes reversed the process, naming their first son after his father and the second after his Uncle James. Adèle's and Harriette's third sons and Louise's fourth all bore the name Charles to honor the memory of their youngest brother, who had died before any of those children were born.

In naming sons, the traditions of both parents' families were generally evenly balanced. Of the sixteen sons born to Petigru mothers, seven were named for maternal kin, whereas six derived their names from their fathers' families—three from the fathers themselves. Only one was named for an outsider. The central role that James Petigru played in his family was made clear in the process. His brother Tom's son as well as two sons of his sisters bore his name. Christening daughters was even more intensely familial. Twelve of the seventeen baby girls acquired names already in use by their mother's kin. Although paternal preference may explain the three who were called by their mothers' names, it was clearly the mother's choice that led every one of Louise Pettigrew's daughters to name one of her own Louise. Not a single son, however, was named for William Pettigrew.

Yet mere naming did not guarantee the perpetuity of family lines. No one could assume that a child born would become a child grown. Only seventeen of the thirty-three children born to first-generation mothers outlived their mothers, and of them, none transmitted the family's name in its distinctive spelling. Of the five adult males who died before their mothers did, all were single. And five of the eight children who died in infancy or early childhood were boys. It is not surprising, therefore, that fears for a child's survival sometimes overshadowed the joy of a child's birth. Few trusted the power of nineteenth-century medicine to cure common childhood diseases. Each of Louise Pettigrew's daughters had to watch virtually helpless while a loved child suffered and died. Such solace as they had came from the sympathy of family members and the strength of their religious faith. Little Robert Allston's death when he was barely four years old taught Adèle a "terrible lesson of the vanity of earthly hope." Her sister Jane, recalling her own mourning after her little Albert had also succumbed to scarlet fever, had no worldly advice to offer. Nonetheless, Louise, who was an evangelical Christian, tried to reassure her sister that the death of a child too young to know sin was a sure guarantee of the child's eternal life in heaven. And when her daughter Louise died in 1850, Harriette, drawing on a similar faith, was certain that "God saw that I needed something . . . to bring me out of myself, come nearer to Heaven, & he has taken our only Daughter, the sprightly one of our household," to that end.[6]

It was not her sisters but rather her brother James who staked out an alternative path of secular stoicism when Adèle mourned the deaths of five-year-old Fanny and her infant sister within months of each other in 1843. Recalling his own despair at the death of his eight-year-old son, Albert, he concluded: "If we had no better consolation, necessity would compel us to be reconciled to a doom, which we cannot avert, and time that robs us of so many joys, softens if it does not altogether remove the sense of grief." Perhaps this, more than her sisters' pious consolations, brought Adèle the strength she needed to deal with the guilt imposed by her belief that her children's deaths were punishments for her own sinfulness. Seven years later, a similar but more transitory sense of personal failure tinged twenty-two-year-old Carey North's response to Louise Lesesne's demise. Burdened with guilt for her own indiscreet recent behavior, she almost envied her little cousin. The child was "taken in her early innocence before the world [was] strong in her heart . . . [and] before she cost her parents one pang or gave them cause for one sigh!"[7]

However they responded to the deaths of young innocents, all of these women desperately sought ways to save their children from disease and the suffering it brought. Thus Jane North celebrated the new medical treatment that allowed her to nurse her eleven-year-old nephew through a siege of scarlet fever in 1859. "Instead of [the] blistering & poultices" that she had inflicted on her son years ago, she tended Charles Allston by "frequent sponging with cold vinegar & water," the effect of which was "so soothing & comforting, that if there is no other recommendation that is a great one. I can scarce keep back my tears," she added, "when I remember the terrible suffering of my poor child, how he burnt, burnt, for so many days."[8]

Motherhood was never easy. Whether their pregnancies ended in miscarriage or in childbirth, the Petigru women faced and feared the possibility of death. Nonetheless, when they bore children, each of them committed themselves to their care and nurture. Each prayed for a propitious future. Each mourned the suffering and death of at least one child. Their triumph lay with those who survived and thrived.

CHAPTER THREE

Managing Complex Households

When J. Johnston Pettigrew, a young cousin from North Carolina, first visited Badwell in 1849, he could scarcely believe his eyes. There, in "a wild part of the Country," he found forty-nine-year-old Jane North living with her three daughters, aged sixteen, seventeen, and twenty-one, and her forty-six-year-old sister Mary with not "a solitary person as a protector." Never before had he encountered a woman of such "great strength and force of mind: accompanied by independence of feeling and fearlessness somewhat of the masculine order."[1]

After John North's death in February and her return to Badwell in May 1836, Jane had little choice but to reassess her future. The family farm was in no shape either to support the Norths in their previous Georgetown style or to sustain even Jane's most minimal aspirations for her daughters. Nevertheless, when her seventy-nine-year-old father died the following January, Jane stoically accepted her fate. By April, she had, with Brother's help, begun a substantial addition to the house, which gave Mary, the three children, and Jane a total of five bedrooms for themselves and guests, a comfortably large sitting room, a new piazza for summer living, and a separate kitchen house. At the same time, Brother began to buy up surrounding land, which, he hoped, would make the plantation productive enough to support the Norths respectably. Regrettably, the new well he ordered to replace the old one was no better and forecast much of Jane's future.

Still, she did not abandon Badwell. With no viable alternatives, Jane stayed on, although she resented being trapped. "God knows if I will ever be able to leave."[2] For the first year, she retained the white farmer who had worked the acreage for Mary, but he did not produce the crops she wanted. And Badwell's role as the Petigru family homestead drained her limited resources. The additions to the house were still unfinished when Harriette Lesesne, sick and needing much attention, arrived in June for a long summer visit. Then came brother Tom with Ann and their two children. Although she welcomed them all warmly, they strained Badwell's facilities and fed her nostalgia for the summers she and John had spent at the beach near Georgetown.

The bleaching drought that threatened all of Jane's crops by mid-July was nearly the last straw. She contemplated alternatives to farming and considered opening a school in nearby Abbeville. Brother encouraged her. He thought that teaching might well provide her "an honorable independency." But her prospects faded when the school's potential sponsors backed out because they feared she "would teach the children fine manners" instead of "what the people wanted."[3] So she stayed where she was and worked hard to make Badwell more productive.

If the ownership of at least twenty slaves was the measure of a planter, Jane more than qualified by 1840. But only ten of her thirty-two hands were, in fact, physically fit for the field work necessary to support her own family as well as two elderly slave couples and sixteen black children under ten. So it was more than inadequate water, poor soil, and erratic weather that kept Badwell from providing fabled plantation luxury. Occasionally, Jane prospered enough to afford visits to her sisters in Charleston and the Allstons on their Pee Dee plantation. Usually, however, she yearned for the amenities of urban life while she was obliged to stay at home, coping with one agricultural disaster after another: parched crops, gardens blackened by late frosts, chickens that laid no eggs. Weighing promise against probability, she once wrote that "the only flourishing things" on the place were her goslings, and "they incur the malediction of Aunt May because next to pigs they are the most detestable of creatures."[4] She expected that even they would soon die.

By the time Johnston paid his 1849 visit, Jane was long inured to the struggles and frustrations Badwell imposed. But she was never resigned. She deplored the constraints her sex imposed on her career as a planter. She dreamed of the difference "ten more workers" would make if she could only buy them. "Were I a man," she wrote, "I would go to Virginia and get them" and thus "make a drive for a fortune." But she was not a man, and despite Johnston's assessment, she could only chafe at being "always cramped and stinted" by the demands of womanly propriety.[5]

Nevertheless, by 1850 Jane was farming 225 acres of improved land with the thirty-five slaves she then owned. Still, not more than ten of her eighteen male slaves were likely field workers, and of them, one was sixty-eight and two others were barely over ten. Doubtless some of her ten female slaves between the ages of ten and sixty-five also worked in the fields, although how many is unclear. Sister Mary contributed the labor of her two slave boys, aged thirteen and fifteen, as well. But her two adult women and any of their seven children under ten who could be useful were Mary's personal house servants. Since a premechanized farm such as Badwell usually required one worker for every ten acres under cultivation, Jane's work force was, in fact, minimal.

Circumstances over which she had no control always limited Badwell's modest returns. In 1849, one of her most successful years, Jane produced 14 bales of ginned cotton, 2,000 bushels of corn, 500 bushels of oats, and 100 bushels of sweet potatoes; made 700 pounds of butter; and pastured 41 pigs, 60 sheep, and 90 head of cattle. That crop generated a reasonable cash income and produced the basic staples needed to feed Badwell's black and white residents and the fodder its animals required. But that was not the norm. The previous year, the cotton crop barely paid the taxes and outstanding farm bills. And 1850 was a real disaster. A severe drought in midsummer was followed by torrential rains and high winds in August that destroyed much of what the drought had spared. Jane empathized with the "dismal stories of suffering and want" of others as she confronted the "trammels imposed" by her own "narrow fortune."[6]

Despite her meager income, Jane was determined to rear her daughters in a style that comported with her high social aspirations for them. Only occasionally did she contemplate whether it might be more prudent to prepare them for a "rustic farming life," with its "pleasant equilibrium." Once, in a particularly dreary moment, she wished for the security a convent might have provided at least one daughter. But Jane entertained more fantasies of what she would do if she were a man than visions of "find[ing] an asylum" in Old World religious institutions. The 1849 gold rush attracted her to California, a place that seemed "more like fairy land than common earth."[7] Closer to home, she dreamed of the wealth that cheap and swift transportation might bring. When a railroad from Charleston through nearby Abbeville to the West was proposed in 1853, she decided that she would invest $500 in its stock—if only she had $500.

Mostly, however, Jane faced the realities confronting a woman trying to make a go of a small, minimally fertile plantation. She never found a satisfactory overseer. From 1850 until 1854, she employed a Mr. McGrath, who presided over one disaster after another. His first year produced "the most entire failure" she had yet known. The next year, he eked out a harvest plentiful enough to feed humans and animals, but the cotton crop was mediocre and the oats intended for the new plow horse died in a summer drought. In 1852 a flash flood on the Little River wiped out the cotton crop and only a swiftly arriving dry spell saved the corn. In 1853, although the cotton crop survived yet another drought, it fell far short of making up for the previous year's losses and the debts they had generated. Furthermore, the food crops were so poor that Jane predicted that they would "assuredly starve" the following winter.[8] Perhaps unfairly, four years of McGrath had exhausted her patience, and in 1854 Jane hired a young and inexperienced Mr. Tolbert. He promptly ruined the corn crop when all of the farms around Badwell produced abundantly.

Thoroughly discouraged by 1855, Jane became her own overseer. The first year, she did well enough to wish she had "taken this stand before."[9] But her success was not without its price. Although she did not plow, plant, or pick herself, she was constantly in the saddle during the sowing and harvesting seasons. Exposed to burning sun and sudden downpours, her health began to deteriorate. She could keep up the killing pace only so long. Consequently, in 1860, when she turned sixty, physical exhaustion drove her back to using a hired overseer.

Whether or not she was in the fields, Jane also undertook the domestic chores women like her were expected to perform. She oversaw, if she did not actually prepare, meals for her family and her guests. She coordinated daily household routines and supervised the dairy and the garden. She attended to the manufacture of clothing for her family and her laborers. And perhaps more frequently than most, she entertained the guests who visited the family homestead over which she presided.

Nearly every year, Brother vacationed there during August and often stayed into September. Less regularly, his sisters made separate or overlapping visits. Louise Porcher might arrive alone or with several children. Adèle Allston and Harriette Lesesne sometimes brought some of their youngsters to visit. Whether or not their parents accompanied them, Jane encouraged all of her nieces and nephews to spend long periods at Badwell to strengthen their connection with the old homestead. Despite her additions to the house, it was often too small to accommodate its multitude of guests comfortably. The spatial pressures in 1859 were not atypical. Three Lesesne children were squeezed into one room. Their mother shared Mary Petigru's room and bed. Brother, of course, was privileged with his regular corner room. Jane shared her room with a North Carolina cousin. And sixteen-year-old Lou North was edged out of the room of her own that she had acquired after her sisters had married by three male cousins who were in school nearby and spent the weekends at Badwell.

To feed them all, Jane cultivated a huge vegetable garden, which, along with fruit from her orchard and products from her dairy, provided a major part of early summer meals. By July, however, chickens hatched in the spring and lambs and calves birthed only months earlier added variety and substance to the menu. Fall fruits not eaten when they were picked went into preserves and desserts or were dried for winter use. Altogether, Jane regularly set a good table. Her youngest daughter had learned to churn excellent butter. Visiting nieces collected berries from which Jane and women visitors made jelly. All three North girls were instructed in the mysteries of the kitchen, learning to make yeast from homegrown hops and to concoct the desserts of which both Jane and Mary were masters.

Despite the joy with which Jane received her many guests, they sometimes strained her patience. Although she never confronted James openly, his role as Badwell's trustee and the family fratriarch occasionally sparked her resentment. Although she devoted massive efforts to making Badwell a paying proposition, her brother sought to turn it into an impressive country estate flaunting a grand avenue of oaks. The incompatibility of their purposes regularly peaked when Brother's demands for workers to carry out his decorative projects competed with Jane's urgent need for field laborers. It is true that James sent fifteen of his own slaves up to Badwell. But mostly they were the children of his Charleston domestics, too young to work productively in either field or house but requiring food, shelter, and much looking after. Likewise, James, who had excused the last of his grandfather Gibert's African-born slaves from all labor, did little to provide the special care Old Tom needed by the mid-1850s after he rejected manumission. Jane grumbled when James sent two craftsmen up from Charleston to teach two of her young male slaves carpentry just when she needed them to prepare the fields for next year's crops. She came close to exploding when, after she had fired her overseer and was preparing to supervise all field work herself, her brother directed her "above all things" to mind his "nursery of oaks. . . . Let everything give way to them." No matter if the crops were lost; securing the "fruits of the acorn" must come first. The more Brother indulged his hobby and taxed Badwell's resources for it, the more Jane's patience was tried. Finally her resentment boiled over in a letter to her sister Adèle, but aghast at her own outburst, she retreated before the ink had dried. "Blot all this out & forget you ever saw it."[10]

Even among themselves, the women seldom criticized their menfolk openly. Jane did so this time in part because she, unlike any of the others, was charged with not only the domestic responsibilities but also the full economic responsibility for her household. More often than not, it was she who managed to smooth family ruffles, but some frictions, particularly those between sister and sister-in-law, could only be papered over. The differences between Jane Amelia's style and temperament and the more serious natures of James's sisters produced ongoing tensions. As Sister (the name James preferred his sisters call his wife) drifted into invalidism, her personality became an ever-less-predictable mixture of charm and cantankerousness, sweetness and spitefulness, generosity and selfishness. While the Porchers still lived at Keithfield, she refused to allow them to stay in her Charleston home after, on one visit, their very young slave boy had stolen a silver fork and dessert spoon and sold them on the street. Thereafter, others hesitated to make prolonged visits at Brother's ample Broad Street house lest similar explosions occur. When they visited Charleston a little later, the Allstons chose to stay in the Lesesnes' small house, where they were, despite its size, sure of a more consistently cordial welcome. Months later, in the summer of 1838, they even avoided staying in the same New York boarding-house with Jane Amelia. Such evasions convinced the ailing woman that she had become a packhorse for family animosity. But for the most part, her sisters-in-law tolerated her with as much grace as they could summon, despite a consensus that she faked many of her ailments and behaved inexcusably even when they were genuine. "I suppose," Mary wrote from rural Badwell just before Adèle and Jane Amelia were to cross paths in New York, "she will be the gayest of the gay, & return looking as smart as fine clothes and trinkets can make her. Poor soul[,] she lives for the world, & perhaps the world may reward her with a little brief attention." But the attention she gained came only from public behavior that, in Mary's eyes, lowered her "in the esteem of the respectable class."[11]

Tom Petigru's wife, Ann, although she was less flagrantly offensive, was also a not fully agreeable addition to the family. Her personality was bland and unattractive, and her bearing toward her sisters-in-law put them off. When Ann first came to Cedar Hill, the isolated plantation near Badwell that Tom bought after his marriage, Jane North did what she could to make his wife feel at home. She particularly praised Ann's "gentleness" and acquiescence to a life in "these back woods," for which she had "anything but a predilection." Ann's airs, however, made Louise Porcher notably less forgiving. She resented Ann's expectation to be *"adored"* and vowed to "treat her with civility" but only because she was, after all, Tom's wife. Ann, she concluded, "ought to be amply satisfied with that."[12]

When affection flagged, however, sheer domestic practicality fostered mutual accommodation. Managing a household could be eased by an inter-change of goods and services between country and city dwellers. Because regular steamboat service between Charleston and Georgetown was particularly convenient, the exchange between Adèle and her sisters and sisters-in-law was the most obvious and abundant. From Chicora Wood came butter, chickens, turkeys, guinea fowl, mutton, hams, potatoes, and game. Once Ann even borrowed a milk cow. In return, her kinswomen sent Adèle imported citrus fruit and coconuts as well as bakers' goods and garden seeds that Charleston shops offered in greater variety than any store in Georgetown. Similarly, they shipped yard goods, ribbons, shoes, and spelling books, much needed in the country but more available in the port city. People also went back and forth. When required, the city folk took charge of servants sent to town to learn skilled trades. Charlotte came to Charleston from Chicora to learn dressmaking from a Miss Barrett, who made a business of teaching various household skills to plantation slaves. Somewhat later, Hibby came down to learn dressmaking from a Miss Nell, and still later Caroline pursued the needle arts with a Miss Bonner. Each of them stayed in either the Porcher or the Lesesne yard.

Throughout the antebellum period, the Petigru women never let the sense of family and family obligation weaken. Constantly in contact with one another, they shared not only the closeness that letter writing and frequent visiting provided but also the mutual support that the exchange of goods and services and the sharing of joys and sorrows brought them. Thus, they cemented their family ties and kept the old homestead intact as a focus for their collective life.

CHAPTER FOUR

Educating the Young

Despite the antagonisms that sometimes set tempers flaring, the Petigrus remained a cohesive family as they added to their number. Binding the first generation together as they brought up their offspring were memories of their own childhood and youth at Badwell that provided basic guidelines. But the opinions of spouses and the intervention of in-laws modified familiar practices. Thus, although all of the mothers shared the expectation that their children should be a credit to themselves and their family, they nonetheless watched each other's disciplinary practices, discussed each other's educational strategies, and commented on each other's successes and failures.

Their discourse on discipline often began as gossip about how youngsters, generally not their own, were being spoiled. In 1839, when Phil and Janey Porcher were still toddlers, James and Jane Amelia agreed that Louise's children were often quite out of control. Explaining their behavior to Adèle Allston, James tried to shift the blame for it to the children's doting Porcher aunts. Nonetheless, he was sure that unless Louise managed better, the children would never have "the bad propensities weeded out . . . and the good qualities made to grow up and be strong." Ten years later, Jane North said the same thing about the Lesesne children. Allowing that her youngest sister was "a very sweet little woman," she lamented that Harriette was so "surprisingly childish in the management of her children," lavishing too much individual attention on them and failing to correct their naughtiness. Harriette countered that poor health left her unable to do more. Jane had little patience with such excuses. When Harriette came up to Badwell in

June 1848 with her brood of three, Jane was indignant at how sickly and "feeble minded" six-year-old Hal, who was the oldest, had become. So she and unmarried Mary set out at once to shape him up and to correct Harriette's overprotectiveness.[1]

Perhaps in self-defense, Harriette criticized her sisters with equal vigor. She condemned the Allstons' white nurse, Mary O'Shea, for endangering year-old Jinty's health by dressing her in excessive clothing and urged Adèle to read Dr. Moore's manual on the preservation of good health. Adèle may or may not have heeded Harriette or Dr. Moore, but she surely paid attention to her husband's advice, even though she might not follow it. Robert's ideas about child rearing were as firm as his ideas about plantation management and politics. As a grown woman, Bessie remembered how hard she had striven to win her father's approval—although it was rarely more than a smile. She recalled all too well the "severe switching" he had once given her for telling a lie and the numerous spankings that were meant to cure her temper tantrums.[2]

For all his rigor, however, Robert's letters to Adèle when he was away from home carried a rather mixed message about discipline. He warned her that excessive severity might damage the children as much as coddling undoubtedly would. That advice only intensified Adèle's quandary. She was already torn between her own strict standards and her wish to be gentle and found it almost impossible to reconcile the discipline she believed essential with sympathetic understanding. Generally her determination to exact proper behavior took precedence. She justified switching five-year-old Bessie, admittedly a self-willed and difficult child, on the grounds that all children "require training" and that Robert expected her to instill principles of "self-control and denial" in her "precious charge." Still, she was not sure that such punishment was appropriate for a child so young. Yet how should she respond to Robert's advice to treat one-year-old Fanny with patience when she was "out of temper" but also fulfill his order to "fail not from any motive of indulgence or indolence or any other, to make [the child] submit to what is right & to deny her in any habit that is wrong"? Such, he insisted, was a mother's "sacred duty," which Adèle could not "delegate . . . and . . . ought not to postpone; for 'tis easier done, the earlier 'tis begun."[3] Small wonder Adèle was torn.

Without a husband's urging, Jane North was just as firm but distinctly more evenhanded and consistent with her children. After she sent her eldest daughter, Carey, to school in Charleston in 1840, she deluged her with letters designed to reinforce behavior learned at home. Jane commissioned the twelve-year-old to buy various sewing materials for Badwell but at the same time admonished her that after several months in the city she should "have learnt to look at all the pretty things" in King Street shops "without wanting so much as a sugar plum." Again and again, she pressed the need for self-control. Three years later, pinched as always for money, Jane chastised Carey for her carelessness about her clothing. Being so "hard on shoes and gloves" unnecessarily taxed the family budget. Moreover, at fifteen, it was high time the girl learned to take care of her clothes so that they would "not only last longer but look so much better." In all things, her mother urged her to extract the maximum benefit from expenditures made on her behalf. Accordingly, Jane reprimanded her daughter for failing to practice the piano and thus wasting the money spent on piano lessons. It was not that she begrudged the lessons, for when it came to education, Jane seldom stinted. It was rather that she was determined that her most talented daughter improve every opportunity to become the polished young lady her mother envisioned. She must shun "dull laziness" and "base mediocrity" by pursuing the "great blessing" of an accomplished mind. She must excel not only for her own future benefit but also to provide her younger sisters the best possible model.[4]

Just what were the accomplishments that Jane pressed so vigorously? For the very young, they were the skills that aunts, sisters, and cousins as well as mothers taught at home: the first lessons in reading, writing, and arithmetic, then the introduction to history and geography, French, and music. Sporadic and informal as it often was in the Porcher and Lesesne households, home education at Badwell was a rigorous, stimulating central experience. In 1841 Jane built a small schoolhouse in which her own children and whichever cousins were then visiting studied together. One perceptive visitor observed that Badwell was, in fact, an academy "in which the pupils are exempt from the spirit of rivalry that usually exists where intellectual pursuits are a part of the employment." Accordingly, however much Jane directed the young people's reading, insisted on language and music practice, and otherwise spurred their intellectual development, she pledged herself never to "lose sight of the necessity to cultivate the *heart* even more than the understanding."[5]

She also recognized the limitations that her managerial responsibilities as well as Badwell's isolation imposed on the scope of her pupils' education. Consequently, in 1841 she welcomed Ann Petigru's proposal that during the summer her two children should join Jane's younger daughters to be taught in the Badwell schoolhouse by Mary Ayme, the English governess Ann had just hired. Thus Miss Ayme boarded at Badwell rather than at Cedar Hill and was endured there as an overbearing bore whose intrusions at the family table and into the evening circle were equally offensive.

Subsequently, in 1851, despite her grating personality, Ayme was hired to teach the Allston children. But she was not their first governess. In 1850, when Della, the oldest daughter, reached ten, her mother engaged Miss Wells, a forty-five-year-old woman who clearly knew her business and performed it enthusiastically. She beefed up the curriculum to include French, music, drawing, grammar, geography, and writing. Della responded positively to the rigorous new regime: from 9:00 to 10:00 A.M., she practiced the piano; then she spent two hours in the schoolroom before dinner and another hour after; then she had a change of pace with drawing lessons before a final stint at her desk until the school day ended at 5:30 P.M. To her mother's delight, she progressed remarkably. Long "the cause of great anxiety," Della blossomed into a "clever child," who, under Wells's tutelage, promised to become an "accomplished and pious woman."[6]

Then suddenly and for unclear reasons, Wells left. Within three months, the search for another governess began, only to be interrupted when Carey North, by then twenty-two, came to spend the summer and early fall with her aunt and cousins on Pawleys Island. There she taught Della the music and French her own mother had insisted she master. And when winter approached, she took Della home with her to Badwell, where, under Jane's watchful eye, Carey undertook still more systematic tutoring. At first her regimen was too demanding. Sent to bed exhausted at eight o'clock each night, Della was rousted out early the next morning for another full day of school. Even her letters to her brother Ben became exercises in composition and penmanship, copied over and over until "as neat and nicely done as could be desired." Very soon, Della taught Carey a lesson. She rebelled and surrendered only when Carey allowed her an hour and a half of playtime in the regular schedule. Even that concession, however, became a form of discipline, for if Della pouted about her piano practice or recited poorly, she forfeited that time. In the end, Della understood that self-discipline brought its own rewards, and Carey learned that sensible moderation was "better and far more improving than two or more hours against the will of the pupil."[7]

While Carey forwarded Della's education, Robert Allston continued his search for a new governess. Finally, he invited Ayme to return from a prolonged visit in England. When she arrived in Charleston in January 1851, Adèle at first refused to hire her, ostensibly because the English woman had brought an uncouth young cousin with her. But she probably also recalled the friction Ayme had generated at Badwell. For a while, the unemployed governess and her cousin Caty stayed with the Porchers in Charleston while Adèle dithered. Harriette Lesesne visited Ayme there and was sufficiently impressed to deplore her sister's reluctance. Likewise, Jane North, who believed the governess's intellectual accomplishments outweighed her social flaws, thought that the Allstons "must engage Miss Ayme" because "they cannot get a better—how far superior to Miss Wells." Nor could they "be so unjust as to bring her across the Atlantic and send her adrift."[8] Finally, Adèle agreed to engage Ayme as long as the governess agreed not to bring slow-witted and ungainly Caty with her.

Carey was sure the arrangement would not work. "They wont agree long," she guessed. "Miss Ayme's ways are *aggravating.*" But despite the initial flurry of conflicting opinions, Ayme stayed on at Chicora for two years. She received $500 a year as well as room and board in return for teaching the older Allston daughters "all the branches of an english education, music[,] drawing[,] french[,] italian[,] and the rudiments of latin." Their mother even surprised herself, conceding that Ayme could in fact teach everything she had said she could, that if she was not a fast teacher she was a thorough one, and that she was personally "a simple-minded honest-hearted woman." Furthermore, she knew enough about children's health to make sure that they got physical exercise every day. She introduced them to formal calisthenics, made them exercise with poles and dumbbells, and managed to correct Della's slight stoop by making her lie on an inclined plane for an hour each day while the governess read to her. Nevertheless, the adult Allstons sighed with relief when Ayme left. Robert was positively delighted because, as daughter Bessie recalled years later, "Miss Ayme also believed in telling children many of the truths of nature, which at that time was considered very indiscreet if not immoral."[9] Moreover, her insistence on a place at the family table and in the drawing room created unpleasantness similar to that which she had generated at Badwell.

Almost balancing the irritations to which governesses gave rise was the satisfaction Adèle derived from educating her daughters at home. There family nurture was assured equal footing with academic training. By keeping them under her own roof, Adèle could be sure that the Calvinist moral training she so valued was transmitted to her children. But like her sisters, who shared similar sentiments, she also wished to endow her girls with a broader knowledge of the world than her own education had provided and give them the graces to function smoothly in appropriate social circles. So when Della was thirteen, her mother decided that the time had come to send her eldest daughter off to school. She had long believed, as did all of her Charleston kin, who had pursued similar courses, that "the discipline, order and regulations of a good school are . . . of inestimable importance to children in bringing their faculties into exercise."[10] Now she was ready to try it.

Caroline Petigru, the oldest of Della's cousins, had already set the pattern for her generation. In the early 1830s, she attended Miss Susan Robertson's school in Charleston, which excelled in teaching English and history. But when she reached fourteen, her father insisted that she be sent north to finish her education, especially to perfect her French. Luckily James Petigru had political and professional colleagues who were well informed about educational possibilities in both Philadelphia and New York. Ultimately he chose Madame Binsse's school in New York, which was patronized by a number of prestigious South Carolinians, including his former law partner James Hamilton.

From the start, Caroline was dissatisfied and unhappy at the school. Madame was, the new pupil wrote, "a little fat lady"—"very *very* fat" and "very ugly." More relevant, she liked "very much to scold" without reason. Neither Monsieur Binsse, who was "an excellent gentleman [who] never scolds or if he does he forgets his anger in five minutes," nor Mr. Mills, her first-rate English teacher, redeemed Madame's ogreish character. Then Northern weather intensified her homesickness. New York was "a most horrible place . . . so cold and . . . so dismal." Caroline wallowed in exaggeration as she described her situation. She was often "inclined to hang" herself she was so thoroughly "tired and dissatisfied with this place."[11]

But despite the snow, slush, and scoldings that made her sure the place would kill her before it "finished" her, she applied herself conscientiously to her studies. She must "not be a *dishonor*" to her family. Her education must not "be as Papa has often predicted, a *failure*." In fact, her Papa was delighted with his daughter's progress. Her improvement, especially in French, was well worth the $170 a quarter he paid Madame Binsse. But Jane Amelia took a different tack. She wanted Caroline to return home to take over household duties that she, in her semi-invalidism, could not manage. So tenaciously did she press her husband that, after only a year, James, who hated arguments, gave in and ended Caroline's formal schooling. He knew well enough that fifteen was "not an age to finish one's education" and confessed to his sister Jane that in taking his daughter from school at that age he did "wrong" and did it "knowingly."[12] Not even his subsequent oversight of Caroline's continuing education at home relieved him of that guilt.

Like her older sister, Sue Petigru was also sent to the best available schools. In Charleston, she attended Madame Talvande's, where French was the language not only of instruction but also of conversation. The latter particularly riled Sue. During an extended period in 1837 in which her parents traveled in the North with Caroline, Sue boarded at the school, where she felt trapped in a life of nothing but "lessons, lessons, 'tout le tem[p]s.'" "*Parlez Francais Mademoiselle vous parlez toujours Anglais*" was "bawled in [her] ears from morning till night."[13]

The following year, at age fourteen, Sue was sent to Madame Guillon's boarding school in Philadelphia. She liked it no better than Caroline had liked Madame Binsse's. Although her denunciations of the school differed from her sister's, they were just as harsh. She had left home excited by the social prospects a big city offered, but her father decreed that "she should dine out but once a month," and her mother insisted that she "wear fewer petticoats and hold herself up." Sue was thoroughly frustrated. After only a month, she wrote her sister, she was "in quite a *reduced* frame of mind." Her father simply could not understand it. Why was Sue making so little academic progress? Her French had improved but only somewhat; James lamented that her letters were "French only in the words." Furthermore, in his eyes, the home of the one family he permitted her to visit in Philadelphia introduced her to far "better society" than she would meet in Charleston. Indeed, her father thought, she "could not have a better model nor visit a house by which she will improve so much." But that was just what put Sue in "great wrath." She wanted an exciting life, not an improving one. And she had only scorn for the education Madame Guillon's academy offered. In a novel published seventeen years later, she questioned whether a finishing-school education was of any utility at all for girls doomed to a life in the domestic sphere. "Look at all the women we know at home. They are taught French, music, drawing, 'geography and the use of the globe,' and as soon as they marry, they shut the piano, never open a French book, give their paints away, and might a great deal better have had all the money spent on these accomplishments put in the Savings' Bank instead. It is a great waste of time and dollars to study."[14]

Sue's aunts, as well as her father, disagreed. The schooling at Madame Talvande's that had been such a bore to Sue not only enriched Carey North's lifelong enjoyment of music but later enabled her to provide her daughters a superior education. Within the school's handsome buildings, some twenty to thirty boarders and at least as many day students—whose parents cheerfully paid up to $500 a year for their tuition—studied not just French but also chemistry, astronomy, and botany; literature, rhetoric, and German; art, dancing, and music. And despite spending their school days behind high brick walls topped with broken glass, they enjoyed the amenities of Charleston's social life, acquiring the skills and grace that would allow them as belles to attract the beaux who would ultimately make them wives and mothers. Well chaperoned and dressed uniformly in narrow skirts short enough to show their ankles and bodices whose puffed sleeves drew attention to their slender arms, they promenaded on the fashionable Battery, took part in weekly dances at Lege's long room, attended the theater, heard concerts, and received guests at Madame Talvande's soirees.

Jane North wanted all of that for her daughters. But it was primarily for her intellectual development that she scrimped and borrowed to send twelve-year-old Carey to Madame Talvande's as a boarder. Urged to devote "every hour of [her] precious time" to her studies, Carey mastered much of the usual academic fare and honed the musical talent that her mother hoped would "soothe . . . solitary evenings" at Badwell.[15] Even so, Jane, financially pinched, had to withdraw Carey from school after her first year. When, two years later in 1843, her Uncle Tom and Aunt Ann Petigru invited Carey to live with them and attend Madame Prudhomme's school with her cousin Mattie, she did so even though the school was less distinguished than Talvande's. Yet it, like the schools her younger sisters subsequently attended, added to the girls' fluency in French and introduced them to subjects their mothers could not teach them. Minnie was only eleven when she lived first with Aunt Harriette and Uncle Henry Lesesne and later with a North aunt and uncle while she studied at Miss Cattenet's school. And Lou, who did not begin her studies in Charleston until she was fifteen, lived with the Lesesnes and then with the Porchers, whose daughters Janey and Mary Anna attended Mrs. Dupre's school with her.

Adèle Allston watched all of this carefully and learned much from her nieces' experience before Della enrolled in Mrs. Dupre's school in 1851. Although she originally had intended to send her as a boarder, she reconsidered after Louise Porcher warned her of the potential for corruption that living with some sixty otherwise unknown youngsters might visit upon a naive child from the country. Agreeing with her sister that parents should "not voluntarily relinquish the supervision" of their children's principles and conduct, Adèle decided that Della should live with the Porchers.[16] But the home influence there and then at the Lesesnes', to which Della later moved to be nearer the school, could not make Dupre's a satisfactory institution. Even Louise, whose daughters had studied there for several years, was so dissatisfied with the language instruction that she hired a French tutor for them. So after only four months, Della returned home to study botany, music, and French with Miss Ayme, who was still at Chicora as Bessie's governess.

Faced with institutions they believed added little to their daughters' "slight store of knowledge," the Petigru mothers welcomed Acelie Togno, who came to Charleston from Philadelphia in 1853 to open a first-class

Madame Acelie Togno's school for young ladies on lower Meeting Street, Charleston. William H. Pease photograph, 1996.

school. Relying at first solely on Togno's credentials, Louise enrolled her daughters immediately and rejoiced that she had. She assured Adèle that Madame "thoroughly understands her business, & is a sensible & [a] very good woman without flourish or pretence."[17] Moreover, like Ann Talvande before her, she conducted her school exclusively in French, except for the equally well taught classes in English language and literature. Her emphasis on moral and religious education reassured mothers that their girls would be safe under her tutelage. Also like Talvande, she was skilled in polishing her pupils' social deportment. Clearly all of this was well worth hefty tuition fees, with extra charges for instruction in Italian, German, Spanish, drawing, and music, as well as for board and room.

Such fees constituted no obstacle for the Allstons, and Adèle quickly followed Louise's example, sending Della to the new school in January 1854. This time, there was no question that, at fourteen, she was old enough to be a boarder. And Adèle was so satisfied with the quality of care and instruction that the next year she sent Della's ten-year-old sister there as well. To Adèle's immense pleasure, both girls improved in deportment as well as scholarship. Della learned to rein in her quick temper and to overcome the lassitude and procrastination that had impeded her instruction at home. Bessie gradually gained enough self-control to change her "volatile & restless" ways, although they still tempted her to skim over lessons to get on with the amusements she found more appealing.[18] She never did quite conform. She saw little point in struggling to speak French when she could express herself perfectly well in English. And learning to sit still long enough to practice the piano effectively was a long time coming.

For Della it was the cultivation of the social graces on which Madame Togno insisted that was so burdensome. She despised the parties that the schoolmistress obliged her pupils to attend so they might learn the conversational arts and the personal bearing appropriate to the adult world. Moreover, the conversations so necessary to Togno's purposes often bored the young girls with whom the adults shared few interests. Sometimes the girls tried to hide in corners, but sharp-eyed Madame soon spotted the rebels and rousted them from their chairs in ones and twos to talk with the grownups. It could, as Della once complained, make for "a very long evening indeed."[19]

But whether their daughters learned their lessons eagerly, passively, or resentfully, whether they were taught at home or at school, Petigru mothers, except, perhaps, for Jane Amelia, expected them to cultivate their minds. Likewise, they guided them toward piety and high moral standards while they insisted that they behave politely and exert self-control. Thus, shy or bold, the girls were included early in adult social activities to improve both minds and manners. Theirs was a broad education, deemed essential to their futures first as belles who could attract appropriate spouses and later as wives and mothers.

CHAPTER FIVE

Marrying for Money

When the Petigru girls were well into their teens, their parents formally introduced them to society and headed them toward marriage. The first of their generation to be launched as belles were the daughters of James and Jane Amelia Petigru. Already well schooled in the intricacies of Charleston's social life and eager for the partying and flirting it encouraged, they thoroughly enjoyed the wooing. About the marriages expected to follow they rhapsodized less.

When, in the winter of 1836–37, Caroline made her debut, she anticipated several glittering years as the center of attention. Her Papa, despite his humble beginnings, was not just a prosperous lawyer. In 1835 the 137 slaves on his recently acquired Savannah River rice plantation had produced as much income as his lucrative law practice. And should his vast Mississippi land speculations and a corporate venture in Alabama cotton planting bear their promised fruit, his purse would indeed bulge. Moreover, his post as solicitor for Charleston's largest bank and his recent election to both the city council and the state legislature betokened his public successes, while his positions as vestryman of the prestigious St. Michael's Episcopal Church and an officer of Charleston's exclusive St. Cecilia Society further enhanced his daughter's social standing.

Jane Amelia, perhaps recalling her own days as a belle and surely excited by her daughter's still brighter prospects, totally redecorated the ground floor of her Broad Street house for Caroline's coming out. She transformed one large room, previously a bed chamber, into a dining room adorned with a Turkish carpet that Captain Tom Petigru had brought back from the Mediterranean. Then she defied Charleston custom by moving the drawing-room furniture downstairs to another ground-floor room that boasted an elegantly molded plaster ceiling. In every way she could she prepared for the festivities that would mark Caroline's first season.

But no sooner were her preparations completed than the panic of 1837 touched off an economic upheaval that turned James's promising investments into financial obligations he could not meet. By 1839, he had been forced to sell his Savannah River plantation at a loss; ultimately, he would assign virtually all of his property to his creditors. Necessarily, he cut household expenses ruthlessly. With each cut, Jane Amelia's spirits plummeted and her health suffered. She spent five days out of every seven in bed, complaining of severe edema in her legs and shortness of breath. With his wife "still very poor in health" and himself "poor in every thing else," James introduced economies that disrupted domestic harmony. Forced to sell his horse and a recently purchased carriage, he could only suggest that Jane Amelia borrow a horse to draw their old carriage. She summarily refused to make do in so humiliating a fashion. So after Caroline's first year as a belle, her home became "at the very time when other people brush up and look as smart as they can to bring out a daughter" more dark and gloomy than it had ever been.[1]

Even so, Caroline's social life was not wholly disrupted. Festivities at home were, to be sure, smaller and fewer than they had been in brighter days. But from time to time, family members and close friends still gathered there for waltzing parties. More commonly, however, Caroline spent her evenings in the drawing rooms of friends or at privately sponsored balls where Jane Amelia occasionally pulled herself together to act as a chaperone. Her husband thought she enjoyed "seeing Caroline surrounded by beaux" and took as much pleasure in so doing "as she once did in flirting with them herself." But Caroline, whom her father and mother thought an excessively sober child, seemed "indifferent to that sort of attention." Always eager for her father's approval, she won his praise for coping graciously with her mother's semi-invalidism and the financial restraints imposed by James's near bankruptcy. "She never grumbles," her father boasted, and "takes everything quietly and gains more upon my esteem by her habitual good humor and cheerfulness, as she has more occasions and opportunities of showing her willingness to submit to circumstances." Nonetheless, her maiden Aunt Mary criticized Caroline's gaiety in bad times. Accustomed to the slow pace of rural life, she heartily disapproved of her niece's busy social schedule and complained that the child was quite "given up to the world."[2]

Caroline Petigru at age eighteen. Thomas Sully portrait reproduced in James Petigru Carson, *Life, Letters, and Speeches of James Louis Petigru: The Union Man of South Carolina* (Washington, D.C.: W. H. Lowdermilk, 1920).

Behind her apparent frivolity lay troubling questions about her future. Jane Amelia's fury at her husband's business ineptitude and reduced circumstances placed new strains on their marriage. Her insistence that, as a consequence, her daughter marry for money heightened old tensions between mother and daughter. Furthermore, her jealousy of the attention James paid Caroline increased her determination that the girl not only marry well but marry soon. So in October 1841, when she was just twenty-one and not at all in love, Caroline suddenly accepted William Carson's

THE RISE OF THE PETIGRUS

proposal. Whether she simply gave in to her mother's pressing counsel or chose marriage as a way to escape it, she did first ask her father's advice. Either too perplexed by her choice or too immersed in his own financial predicament, he told her only to "consult her own feelings."[3] His refusal to say more left Caroline high and dry, for he was the parent to whom she was closer and he well knew it. Nonetheless, he did not share with her the doubts he expressed to his sister Adèle that Carson at age forty-one had long seemed too much the confirmed bachelor ever to marry and that Caroline was lured by his wealth more than his person.

Why else would this popular and beautiful young woman choose to marry a man twice her age? From Jane Amelia's vantage point, William Augustus Carson was certainly a prize catch. The son of a wealthy Charleston merchant, he had attended Harvard College, where he had been a member of the Porcellian Society, which Carolinians considered the college's most acceptable club. After graduating in 1821 (the year after Caroline's birth), he bought Dean Hall, a rice plantation on the east branch of the Cooper River. On its spacious grounds, he built an imposing square brick house, whose large rooms and wide piazzas proclaimed riches passed from father to son. He frequently traveled to Charleston to oversee the major wharf he had purchased in the boom years of the 1830s and to discharge his duties as a bank director and a trustee of the New Theater. While in town, he shared his mother's imposing house on Tradd Street, only a block from the Petigrus' home. He, too, escaped summer sickly seasons at a beach cottage on Sullivans Island, whose municipal government he had once served, first as a councilman and later as mayor (intendant), much as he had earlier represented his plantation's parish in the state legislature. Although he had thus dabbled in politics, William Carson was preeminently a club man, being a prominent member of the Jockey Club, whose races and race week ball marked the culmination of the city's high season, and a convivial participant at Strawberry Club dinners, where Cooper River planters celebrated their good fortune.

Who could better meet Jane Amelia's specifications? Carson was a planter, he was rich, and he had good social credentials. For his part, James could find no positive reason to reject him as a son-in-law. Yet he was somewhat uneasy that his fellow theater enthusiast and Sullivans Island neighbor had used the intimacy of their summertime proximity to join the throng of suitors surrounding Caroline. And he was thrown off balance when Caroline, usually so independent and self-assured, had come to him for advice about marrying. Left to his own inclinations, he "would not have said a word to promote the match." If his explanation to Adèle that Caro-

Dean Hall. The Carsons' plantation house was moved in the 1930s from the Cooper River to a site near Gardens Corner in southwestern Colleton County. William H. Pease photograph, 1993.

line's choice followed the "old rule" that a great mansion that speaks and a woman who listens cannot be kept apart implicitly endorsed marriage as a socioeconomic institution, it was an endorsement edged with doubt. Comparing his daughter's impending marriage with Adèle's to Robert Allston, he recalled his regret at seeing his favorite younger sister leave his home. But he was "prepared to resign" Caroline if only the outcome might "be as auspicious to her happiness." So without any explicit objection, Caroline Petigru married William Carson on December 16, 1841.[4]

At first early doubts seemed quite misplaced. The Carsons settled easily into their new roles. Caroline was delighted with playing lady of the manor, entertaining her family and friends at Dean Hall. This was the idyll she had envisioned. But just four months after her wedding, when she discovered that she was pregnant, her happiness crumbled. Caroline simply did not want a child—at any rate, not so soon. When William was born, almost a year after her wedding day, Caroline displayed no joy in motherhood. Nor did her husband offer the new mother much support. He expected her to take complete charge of the baby, denied that she needed an experienced woman to help her, and only grudgingly assigned a "little girl" to serve as nursemaid. None of this sat well with Caroline, who was "*quite sick*" after her delivery. More lastingly, as her Aunt Louise Porcher observed, she was "*not *pleased* with her prospects[.] You know she rather dislikes children & says the idea of *a baby* is odious."[5] Furthermore, her husband's behavior deteriorated. He took no pleasure in his son and became increasingly uncivil toward his wife. Soon family members began to comment on his ever more obvious nasty disposition, a display of temperament that was exacerbated by the financial woes that soon beset him.

Like a number of other public-spirited Charlestonians, Carson was a trustee of the New Theater, rebuilt after the fire of 1838 destroyed the heavily mortgaged original. When the theater fell victim to the long depression that followed its reconstruction, Carson, like his fellow board members, was liable for both its old and its new mortgages. At the same time, vagaries of nature were destroying Dean Hall's profitability as prolonged droughts reduced the Cooper River's flow, allowing brackish sea water to contaminate plantation fields. In response, Carson simply defied nature. Dedicated to planting rice, he refused to shift to cultivating cotton, which needed no irrigation. As a result, he reaped nothing but financial losses in 1844 and 1845. With little money coming in and with debts heedlessly incurred in better times coming due, he was forced to sell his Charleston wharf in 1846 for $20,000 less than he had paid for it—largely with borrowed money— little more than a decade earlier.

Just as her husband faced this financial crisis, Caroline bore her second and last child, named for her father and destined to become her favorite. But James Petigru Carson's birth in April 1845 brought his mother only misery. She suffered from a repetition of the skin eruptions that had followed Willie's birth and also developed a panoply of eye infections, pains, fevers, spasms, and weaknesses so debilitating that she could not even nurse Jem as she had his older brother. As he had when Willie was born, her husband had little sympathy for her plight. When doctors recommended that she take the curative waters of the Virginia springs, William declined to accompany her. Thus it was her father who took Caroline on the rounds from Warm Springs to Sweet Springs to White Sulfur Springs, whose medicinal waters she both drank and bathed in. While there, she also tried other remedies: warm poultices, chicken water, asafetida, mercury-laden "blue pills," and laudanum. When by summer's end nothing had cured her, her father took her to Philadelphia, where she consulted the city's most prestigious physicians. After his legal business obliged him to return home, Sue came north to keep her sister company.

Sue's thoughtfulness somewhat surprised her father, for there had long been considerable rivalry between his daughters. Caroline, with her blond beauty and commendable behavior, had generally outshone her sturdily built and rambunctious younger sister. And Sue had resented the preference given Caroline. Shortly after she returned home from boarding school, she had joked that her presence would probably drive away the swains whom Caroline's magnetism had drawn to the Petigru home. Although it did not, Sue never made the splash as a belle that Caroline did. She lacked the winsome expression, the long curls, and the delicate coloring that contemporary ideas of beauty dictated. Severely nearsighted, she stumbled and bumbled when she most wanted to be graceful. Worst of all, her thoughtless pursuit of adventure and her quick temper provoked gossip and repelled sympathy. At her very best, she was, as Uncle Allston described her when she turned sixteen, "all life & a[n]im[a]tion."[6] But because she was both rebellious and indiscreet, she constantly fell into awkward scrapes and occasionally provoked outright scandal.

She later fictionalized one such escapade in a short story entitled "Gossip." The young heroine's reputation was ruined when, her dress badly torn, she had to be carried to and from the carriage that brought her home after a theater party. In fact, she was innocent of the indiscretions invented by the "ribald tongue" of a nosy old lady to explain her condition. After the performance, she had gone to her uncle's house with some friends. There, while she was looking for a Shakespeare citation relevant to their discussion of the play, she had fallen from a library ladder, injuring herself so badly that she could not walk. So the mean gossip of two withered busybodies whose warped minds imagined the worst cast totally "undeserved shame" on a pure young woman. Family discussions of Sue's behavior suggest that the story was, at least in part, autobiographical. After at least one such real scrape, her Aunt Louise Porcher lamented that scandal was so "busy with her name" and "her situation" was so deplorable that she had to be rusticated to Badwell until gossip about her simmered down.[7]

As Louise explained the situation to Adèle Allston, Sue's intractable disposition was intensified by the constant warfare she waged with her mother. She refused to tolerate Jane Amelia's idiosyncrasies silently. In return, Jane Amelia refused to shelter or defend her daughter's reputation. Indeed, she spoke of her in ways that invited the malevolence of others. So instead of nudging Sue toward more prudent conduct, her mother chose to marry her off before the gossip she provoked rendered her altogether unmarriageable. Another of Sue's published stories casts only a thin veil over her own experience. "A Marriage of Persuasion" describes a mother who pressed the heroine so hard to marry an unattractive rich old man that she finally agreed to a match that tied her to an "owner of houses and lands—gold and silver" at the cost of "a perjured conscience and a bleeding heart."[8] In fact,

Henry Campbell King was neither old nor very rich when Jane Amelia chose him as Sue's best chance for a husband. Clearly he was not the catch she had believed William Carson to be. But given Sue's indiscretions, she could hope for nothing better. The son of Mitchell King, a wealthy lawyer and close friend of James Petigru, he had promising prospects, for as one of ten children he would ultimately share an estate that, in 1990s terms, was worth between $3 million and $4 million. In addition, although he was not a Harvard graduate, Henry had studied law in Germany and was thus prepared for a respectable position at the Charleston bar.

Sue, however, assessed Henry's eligibility from a different perspective. For her, his lineage and his prospects could not compensate for his unattractive physique. Despite the fact that he had a character her nephew later described as one of "manliness, kindness of heart and geniality," Sue saw only a man who was "very *short* very *broad* & very round shouldered, & withall a little lame." Even Aunt Louise, who respected Henry's "intelligence & industry," had to admit that a girl contemplating marriage might very well think his appearance "a substantial objection." But could Sue afford to object? She would "probably get no better offer" because her much-discussed behavior was "a most unfortunate thing for herself." Nonetheless—and on balance—Louise concluded that it would be "safer & wiser to refuse than accept under the circumstances" and added that she could not "bear that so young a girl should be urged on that subject, as it is a step one cannot retrieve when once taken, & all the trials it may entail must be borne alone & in silence, as it is one of the few trial[s] that the sympathy of friends cannot alleviate but rather enhances."[9]

Despite her aunt's forebodings and long before she had any desire to marry at all, Sue suddenly accepted Henry. A month later, on March 30, 1843, they were married. Her father was "well pleased" with the "nine days' wonder" and expressed no reservations that his daughter, then only nineteen, should marry so young. In fact, she was the only Petigru woman in three generations to marry before she was twenty. Jane Amelia was pleased that, for once, her daughter had given in to her advice. Sue, however, viewed her hasty surrender as an escape from her mother's eternal nagging. Her aunts, although they still feared for her future, hoped that her marriage would separate the mother and daughter who were "in constant opposition to each other" and succeed better than their own efforts to "pour oil upon the waves & still the frequent raging of the tempest." For Sue's father, the wedding promised to ease the domestic disruptions that made it difficult to "keep the even tenor of [his] way without becoming a party to either." At least it should curtail Jane Amelia's using those occasions on which she actually joined her family at table to recite her complaints about Sue during "those spare intervals between changing plates and waiting to be helped, which are usually thrown away."[10]

Sue's marriage, however, produced neither peace for her parents nor freedom for herself. Although it may have calmed mother-daughter hostilities for a while, nothing else changed. In his sister Harriette Lesesne's eyes, James was still plagued by an "unnatural" wife who "lies in bed from morning till night with every luxury about her & complains of poverty" and "makes her husband's time at home wretched." James himself doubted a lasting resolution of "the truth so generally known that near and dear friends are very apt to spend all their time in wrangling. Of the generality of this observation," he added, "every one may judge for himself. Of the application to Mother & Daughter in this case, I have been a witness too well qualified to speak."[11]

As for Sue, after she and Henry returned from their scarcely propitious honeymooning at Dean Hall, they lived with Henry's parents and unmarried siblings in Mitchell King's spacious Charleston mansion. That in itself was not so unusual. After all, Sue's parents had begun marriage the same way. But it was a bitter pill for the independent-minded bride, who signaled her displeasure with outrageous banter. When the young couple arrived at Badwell just four months after their wedding, Aunt Jane North was much upset by Sue's flippancy, which so resembled her mother's. Henry "will say Sue is too lazy sleeping all day. Well Henry says she, why did you not find that out before? It would have saved a great deal of trouble both sides." It seemed to be "said in good humour and taken in good part," Jane admitted, but such repartee was "nevertheless playing with edged tools, especially in one so indiscreet" as Sue.[12]

Henry, although he was five years older than Sue, was no more ready for marriage than she was. He exasperated his feisty wife by refusing for two-and-a-half years to leave his parents' home for one of his own. It galled her that she bore her only child, Adele Allston King, there and spent her first fifteen months as a mother under the watchful eyes of her in-laws. Finally, Henry gave in to Sue's prodding to go "to house keeping." In 1845 his parents and his five sisters all joined Sue's pleas that he strike out on his own. Even then, he did nothing until his stepmother arranged for him to buy a house she had inherited and convinced his father to lend him the money to do so. So the actual move late that year to their own home on Tradd Street hardly marked a major declaration of independence for Henry. It did, however, for Sue. And Henry believed it presaged a new and better married life. "Sue is very much pleased with the house," he assured his father, "& I have very great hopes will make a good & economical housekeeper."[13]

But Sue, who had just turned twenty-one that October, found neither economical housekeeping nor mothering a satisfactory substitute for the fun and adventure she craved. When she looked back wistfully on her last Christmas as a single girl, when "the hours did dance away right joyously," Henry appeared "very reproachful." And when she yearned for their return, Henry called her " 'a great goose for talking so' with a side glance at little Addy to point his remark."[14]

For a while, however, establishing her own home and planning the parties she would give there offered excitement enough. And little Addy brought joy to both parents. So the Kings' future looked far brighter in 1845 than did the Carsons', albeit at the time of their weddings Caroline's marriage had seemed more propitious. Both sisters had married socially correct men with money—or the prospect of inheriting it. But each had accepted a suitor to whom, for whatever reasons, she could not or would not make a strong emotional commitment. What each had done in haste she would repent at leisure, for in South Carolina only death could end a marriage. There was no provision for divorce. The conditions for separation generally implied disgrace. There was simply no way out of marriage bonds once they were contracted—ever.

CHAPTER SIX

Reigning as Belles

As their younger cousins speculated about their own future lives, they studied the paths that Caroline and Sue Petigru had charted. When Carey North prepared to enter the social whirl in which South Carolina's privileged youth mingled and mated, she was especially wary of its pitfalls. Unlike her older cousins, who had grown up in Charleston and tasted sophisticated Northern society while they were in boarding school, Carey had spent most of her youth in rural Abbeville district and had never left her native South. Nonetheless, by the time she reached adolescence, she too had been inducted into the social rituals of elite urban society.

During her school days in Charleston and on her occasional visits to the Allstons at Chicora Wood, Carey never escaped her mother's admonitions to behave properly, pay calls on her mother's friends, write thank-you notes to those who entertained her, and observe all of the social amenities that family and family friends expected. Jane North insisted that her daughter look on all social intercourse as an occasion for practicing the proprieties of adult life—from writing her letters legibly to utilizing every opportunity to cultivate the favor of planter society. Moreover, as her mother encouraged thirteen-year-old Carey when she was about to visit a North uncle in Norfolk, she should make the most of the experience, for it "ought to do every one good to see a little of the world."[1]

But the social world for which Carey was being prepared was largely Charleston. There family and friends, young and old alike, provided a sheltered atmosphere in which girls and boys were steered through the parties where they first practiced the social graces they had been taught at home. Those whose parents lived in town had an obvious advantage. In May 1858 Bessie gave her own "little party" at the Allstons' Charleston house to celebrate becoming a teenager. By then, she was already an experienced party goer, maneuvering readily among people her own age. At her first such Charleston party the year before, she had been asked to supper by a "small boy." Fearful of being a wallflower, she had quickly accepted. Almost at once, however, she rued her haste. When older and more desirable boys issued similar invitations, she was stuck, for she could not, in honor, accept them. But as she confessed to her diary, she made the best of it and was somewhat consoled by the copious amounts of ice cream and cake with which the boy plied her. Actually, she concluded, the party had been quite a personal success. Although it did nothing to contradict her belief that she was ugly, numbers of boys had obviously liked to talk and dance with her, and that, after all, was the "main thing."[2]

It had not been so easy for her older sister. "I dare say I am very foolish," seventeen-year-old Della reflected after one miserable party in 1857, "but it does mortify me when I go out to sit in the corner all the evening receiving no sort of attention while girls who are very affected [are] very much attended to and admired." "Little Jimmie Simons's" attentions at another party did nothing to improve the situation. "When I once get a gentleman in tow there is no getting rid of him," she wailed, and "unfortunately there are few gentlemen who can stand one or two hours without becoming horribly tiresome at least to me."[3]

It was much easier to handle the ritual exchange of visits that made up a large part of Charleston social life. In the morning, ladies, often with young daughters in tow, called on other ladies. In the evening, when men as well as women exchanged calls, drawing rooms presented a less intimidating stage for young people's sociability than did formal parties and balls. And a city custom governing evening visits gave girls a distinct advantage, for the same curfew—nine in winter and ten in summer—that summoned slaves from city streets announced that beaux should leave the drawing room, unless they had been explicitly invited to remain longer.

Small afternoon or early evening parties at home were also less threatening than large parties or even smaller ones at other people's houses. But it was hard to keep parties small, and some so-called small parties had as many as fifty guests. That, in turn, led to the facetiously named "hard time parties." Louise Porcher suggested just how "hard time" they were when, in January 1851, she "limited" the refreshments to "two kinds of ice cream, oysters, punch and wine—nothing else allowed."[4] Sometimes, too, parents or friends gave dinner parties expressly for young people. In April 1852 a Mr. Hopley gave one for Louise's daughters. He asked ten-year-old Louly to invite the ladies, and he selected the gentlemen. Reflecting the customary practice for such events, she asked her mother, her nineteen-year-old cousin Minnie North, and her married cousin Sue King before she went outside the family.

As girls became courtable young ladies, the transition was formally marked by a coming-out party generally held at home. When nineteen-year-old Janey Porcher was introduced to society in 1857, her parents' house, which looked out on Charleston harbor, was totally given over to the brilliant affair. "The two Piazzas were enclosed and carpetted and decorated with festoons of flowers and wreaths." The two first-floor rooms were stripped of carpets and given over to dancing. Upstairs "the guests were received of course in the Drawing-room, and the supper was laid in Aunt Lou's room, so the house was literally thrown open." Not only was the party a success, but Janey became a tremendously popular belle. Sprightly and charming, she was "engaged five and six deep" for each dance at every ball all that winter.[5]

For sheer display and high-pitched exuberance, balls were the most complex festivities. At the height of the season, private balls were more numerous than public ones. In late February 1851, the Petigru women spun from one to another. On the first night of race week, they attended a grand affair at the Pringle mansion. The next night, they hurried to Dr. John Bellinger's ball, and, not yet exhausted, the following night, some of them graced the huge party that Dr. and Mrs. John Geddings threw. Finally, the most spectacular of all that winter's fetes was the "grand 'rout'" over which the very rich and ambitious hostess Mrs. William Aiken presided only a few days later.[6]

Less concentrated, quasi-public affairs abounded throughout the winter. Self-chosen groups of men staged balls organized to celebrate a particular occasion. Select societies sponsored other festivities. Each season, the St. Cecilia Society held three balls for its rigorously circumscribed membership and their guests. Less exclusive but nonetheless respectable and very popular was the annual Jockey Club ball that concluded race week festivities in late February. And December commencement balls were held at the College of Charleston for graduates, their families, and their friends.

Like almost everything else in this heady social life, balls were highly choreographed. Ritual and restriction governed the dancing at all times. No socially aspiring young woman could afford not to dance. The wise ones learned to dance well. A scantily filled dance program marked a pariah. A card endlessly repeating the same name spurred gossip that deterred other potential partners. To be a success, a belle had to attract beaux more numerous than her available sets, and the number of those sets was at the mercy of tight-laced mothers who limited the steps they permitted their daughters. Square dances, especially the restrained quadrille, won universal approval. Round dances, in which the gentleman might hold the lady too closely about her waist, drew a mixed reception. Nice girls might perhaps dance the schottische; more daring ones were permitted to waltz; but only the most liberal of chaperones smiled on the polka. Adèle Allston and Louise Porcher agreed with their oldest sister, who urged both her daughters and her nieces to dance and dance well, in part because refined dancing taught them to "walk well" and move gracefully. But Jane North drew the line at the waltz, let alone the polka. She had no sympathy for her daughter's protests that the ban forced her to sit out too many sets. If Carey did "not like to sit down desolate," her mother advised her, she should "find some agreeable person to stand up and talk to." Because Carey found her mother's objections simply "absurd," she took advantage of maternal absence not only to waltz but also to polka. Yet as an adult when she herself was a chaperone, she disapproved of Janey Porcher's dancing the steps the fast set preferred. Arguing that it was not the dance itself but rather the association with those who "polked" that made doing so objectionable, she advised her young cousin to hold back until "more reliable people than Mrs. Joe Heyward & Sue [King]" took the lead.[7]

Whatever the occasion, young ladies must not spend time alone with men who were not part of their family circle. To attend an evening concert or lecture, they needed the protection of a suitable male escort. To venture to a ball without a female chaperone was unthinkable. Even at home, they seldom spent extended periods alone with men not their kin. Nor did marriage free them from the beady eyes of Mrs. Grundy. Louise Porcher was positively shocked when young Mrs. Blacklock, who was nearly eight months pregnant, "ponderous [of] figure & disdain[ing] all concealment," swept onto the dance floor and pranced about as if she were a "jeune fille." Such dismay at the lack of concealment, like anxieties about round dancing, reflected prevailing mores. It was not Blacklock's presence at a party when she was so obviously enceinte that raised eyebrows so much as her failure to clothe and carry herself more discreetly. Indeed, prudence admonished all ladies to dress and behave with decorum, whatever their age or condition. Jane Amelia was considered comically overage for a ball dress with "low neck & short sleeves" that she wore when she was sixty-three.[8]

When Minnie North, at age fourteen, had to decline an invitation to

Caroline North Pettigrew at age twenty-five. Photograph of a lost portrait attributed to Thomas Sully. Courtesy of Mrs. John H. Daniels for Mulberry Plantation.

spend a week in Abbeville because she lacked the requisite clothing and her older sister confronted the dilemma of garbing herself for a wedding while she was in mourning, they illustrated how demanding dressing appropriately could be. For years, Jane North strained her meager budget to provide just one of her three daughters at a time the outfits she needed to take part in the Charleston social season. No wonder that these girls also borrowed one another's clothing, those at home lending their finery to the one who was in town. Happily, the small inheritance each girl had received from her North grandfather supplemented Jane's sparse resources for dressing them well.

Jane's budget seldom allowed her to accompany her daughters when they were in Charleston for the high season. Determined nonetheless to exert her maternal influence when her eldest and most talented daughter was introduced to society, Jane tried to make up for her absence by sending a steady stream of letters. Her advice, Sue King observed, often only confused Carey. At first Jane tried hard "to make little Carey interested in the coming balls." But having infused "a wish for gayety, into the young débutante," she became alarmed that her daughter was becoming "too fond of the world" and "rather forward for so little a girl."[9] She fretted that Carey, who from the first enjoyed the attention of many beaux but showed little interest in marrying any of them, would return home to accept a persistent but unacceptable suitor from Abbeville. As her mother and aunts puzzled over her failure to seize any of her many opportunities, the young debutante reveled in being courted by many but avoided accepting any of them.

For two long and arduous seasons, Carey dodged making any commitment. Then, early in 1849, without consulting either her mother or her Aunt Ann Petigru, with whom she was staying, she tentatively accepted Joe Pyatt's proposal. She was more attracted to him than to any other of the eligible young men who danced attendance on her. Edward Pringle and Charles Prioleau, young men from old and prestigious families, had wooed her ardently. So had future congressman William Porcher Miles, who, although less moneyed than the others, was more gifted of mind. And Kirkwood King, Henry's brother, who had recently returned from legal study in Germany, had also joined the circle of eager devotees. None of them, however, could, if a good match was measured by riches, compete with Joseph Benjamin Pyatt, a Georgetown planter whose Rosemont plantation employed 291 slaves and that year produced 570,000 pounds of rice. Like Joshua Ward, Jr., whose father owned six plantations and over 1,000 slaves and who had wooed Carey quietly ever since he had first met her at Chicora before her debut, Joe Pyatt clearly had her Aunt and Uncle Allston's approval—perhaps even their encouragement.

Moreover, her mother was growing ever more anxious as she observed Carey's crowded social life from afar. She certainly wished Carey to have a happy marriage, but she saw no reason why it should not also be a prosperous and financially easy one. So she coached her daughter in worldly wisdom and prudence. Since the young woman was a "little votary of love in a cottage," her mother countered such romantic fantasies with pragmatic advice. She must not ignore a friend's warning "never to marry a poor man." Jane North, however, was not Jane Amelia Petigru. She balanced her advice to marry well with homage to a marriage grounded in a solid emotional attachment. "I prefer you should not marry at all than to be induced to that step without your heart and affections going with it." But with Carey in Charleston or visiting relatives elsewhere, how could she be more precise? "God help us in our girls," she exploded to Adèle. They were such "a source of pleasing anxious pain."[10]

After she had tentatively accepted Joe, Carey also was torn by an ambivalence more painful than pleasing. As soon as he gave her a ring, she pulled up short. As she thought it over, she concluded that she did not love him. Belatedly realizing that despite his wealth, Joe fell short of her prescription for an ideal husband, she beat back her initial reluctance to speak out and told him that he had not won her heart. But even so, she managed only an indefinite withdrawal from her amorphous commitment. When reports of this stumbling ineptitude reached Badwell, her mother was appalled and angry. Looking for a villain, she suspected that Sue King had persuaded Carey to cast off the secure, luxurious life the Pyatt fortune promised. Sue denied that she had had "a shadow of influence with Carey," but reflecting on her own marriage, she admitted that if she did profess "such influence, it would most assuredly be exercised in urging [her cousin] never to marry where she did not love."[11]

The denouement did not come until the next spring when Joe's engagement to his wealthy cousin Joanna Ward was announced. Thoroughly mortified, Carey then asked her Aunt Louise to return the ring Joe had given her the previous winter. At first he refused to take it back. But he had to admit that he had changed his mind and shifted his affection elsewhere after Carey had said she did not love him. Louise replied that "it was fortunate that such had been the case, that C[arey] accepted him precipitately, & was then frightened & embarrassed by her own act, that to marry without giving her heart was a thing she could not do & that she felt immediately &c &c." The painful part of their conversation ended there. Louise congratulated the young man on his engagement, "thankful to have it over & C[arey] happy to get rid of the ring." But privately she mused that Joe was "very much without a *real manly heart*."[12]

Her Aunt Adèle Allston, however, whose ambitions for Carey had been as great as her mother's, was "greatly distressed." The news of Joe's engagement to Joanna Ward caused her "a sleepless night," ending as it did her "fond vision" of her niece's marital success. Still, she too blamed Joe more than Carey. He had not "been strictly honorable in this matter." Worst of all, the hubbub surrounding the affair now made it likely that Carey would "never marry." When the news reached Badwell, conveyed by Jane Amelia, who scented in it a good scandal, Jane was distraught at her daughter's conduct. Adèle sympathized with her sister's chagrin at Carey's behavior. " 'How sharper than a serpents tooth it is to have a thankless child,' " she lamented, adding that "an undutiful child is a thankless one." Indeed, the whole family was indignant at Carey's conduct, although whether the indignation was at accepting Joe in the first place or rejecting him later differed from kins-woman to kinswoman. In any case, there was naught else to do but take comfort in Louise Porcher's judgment. Although her aunt grieved that Carey had "lost her opportunities" by her own folly, she accepted the fact that "the past can not be recalled." The family should therefore "take refuge in the hope that 'whatever is, is right' " and get on with life. Carey herself, despite much inner turmoil, did carry on. With a stiff upper lip, she wrote a distant cousin that the engagement of "Mr Pyatt to his cousin Miss Ward" gave her "great satisfaction. . . . It is very suitable in every respect & they have my best wishes for their happiness."[13]

Hoping to rescue Carey's marital chances, Aunt Harriette and Uncle Henry Lesesne invited her to accompany them and their two young sons on an expedition to the Virginia springs and on north. She assented, and in August 1851 the party began its quest for health and relaxation, first at Warm Springs and then at Hot Springs, White Sulphur Springs, Salt Sulphur Springs, and Red Sweet Springs. At their first stop, nine-year-old Hal Lesesne let out the real reason for Carey's presence. Pleased with the atten-tion that John Gadsden, one of the two acceptable beaux at Warm Springs, had paid him—perhaps as a device to enjoy Carey's company—Hal, in an unsettling faux pas, eagerly told him the saga of Carey and Joe Pyatt. Carey hoped that his subsequent "walk in the woods" with his father, who there "administered an effectual admonition," would tie his tongue in future. She took what comfort she could in the fact that it had happened "at this early stage" and fervently hoped it would not happen again.[14]

It did not. And Carey, with the verve that had attracted so many to her in Charleston, was soon making friends with the men and women, both old and young, who flocked to the South's prime resorts. One of the older women who took her up was Mrs. William Seaton, whose connection to Washington's political circles as the wife of the publisher of the *Na-tional Intelligencer* reverberated with the younger woman's loyalty to her Uncle James's Whig politics. Attracted more by Carey's musical abilities, Ann Vanderhorst, wife of a wealthy planter and Charleston businessman, took Carey under her wing and promoted a romance with her son. Among the younger set, Carey joined Stricker Coles, his sister, and his cousin Mary in a merry foursome until Stricker, like John Vanderhorst, grew serious and proposed—to her dismay. And even worse, a young West Point graduate with no known social credentials made himself a consummate pest until Carey, who thought she had done everything to avoid yet another proposal, turned Lieutenant Riall down flat.

No doubt about it, Aunt Louise had guessed wrong when she mourned the passing of Carey's life as a belle. Despite so many gallants showering attention on her, her enthusiasm for life at the springs reached its peak only when, toward the end of her stay, Gales Seaton arrived to become at once her most steady beau. A "manly well bred looking person," although not handsome, his exotic aura of sophistication, acquired during five years in Europe, was especially appealing. Except for his proclivity to take "a glass too much of wine," he was, Carey bubbled, "the most agreeable man we have met in Virginia."[15]

Gales did not confine himself to Virginia. When Carey and the Lesesnes went on to Washington, he was already there and at once offered himself as their guide. Although it was not he who took them to President Millard Fillmore's White House reception, he took them everywhere else. At the Capitol, he escorted Carey through the House and Senate chambers, while Aunt Harriette and Uncle Henry were left "rather groping their way" alone.[16] Later he ushered them all through the Patent Office, the Naval Observatory, the White House, and the Smithsonian Institution. Most exciting of all, when they toured Mt. Vernon, he induced Augustine Washington to invite the whole party into the family parlor, where Washington himself served them wine, cake, and biscuits. After that, Carey's first visit to New York was a distinct letdown.

When she returned to Charleston, rumors were already flying that she was engaged to one of her new "Summer acquaintances." She denied the charges vigorously, but when Gales Seaton arrived in town in February, her denials seemed so much subterfuge. Aunt Adèle believed without doubt that he had come to "make his addresses" to Carey. Carey shook her head. She "liked him well enough," but she "was not the least in love." In the end, everyone was relieved when his courtship, too, fell through. Adèle credited "the report of his character which Brother received" for having kept Carey from accepting Gales. Her Uncle Robert, noting the couple's different levels of sophistication, assessed matters somewhat more astutely. "If he makes up his mind to do so, he will win our little niece, and bear her away to the Metropolis, the centre of fashion & gayety, as it is of political influence & intrigue." Although he concluded that the ambitious heir to the *Intelligencer* would do no such thing, he was sure that the women in the family would surrender to a careful campaign of ingratiation if Seaton decided to launch one, whereas the men, especially James Petigru and Philip Porcher as well as himself, would like "to have a friend always at Court!"[17]

Carey, however, fooled them all. The rumors she had heard about Seaton made her uneasy. She knew that Mrs. Seaton had pushed them together at the springs, and she sympathized with the older woman. But she concluded that if "all 'they say' be true," she could only be sorry for Gales's mother.[18] Thus another courtship died—another for which Carey did not mourn.

The next summer, after she had just turned twenty-four, Carey traveled north again. Offered a grand tour that would take her over familiar ground to Washington and then on to Niagara Falls, Montreal, Boston, and New York, she at first hesitated, held back by unexplained "shadows" clouding her future. Nonetheless, when the time came, she set off with Aunt Ann and Uncle Tom and their daughter Mattie. Even without Seaton as a guide, Carey enjoyed her return visit to the capital, where the professional connections of Captain Thomas Petigru U.S.N. opened social and political doors. They were invited to a White House concert and to an evening tea at the home of Congressman William Aiken of South Carolina. Best of all, however, was hearing Senate debates from the gallery and being recognized on the Capitol steps by Senator Andrew Butler.

After spending only a few days in Washington, Uncle Tom led the ladies on a fast-paced round of conventional sightseeing in Philadelphia, New York, West Point, and Saratoga. Until they reached Niagara Falls, the trip had been, except for Washington, a pretty dull affair, and Carey's diary mechanically reported little more than minimally interesting scenery, poor accommodations, and major tourist sites. Niagara Falls, however, marked a precipitate change. She waxed ecstatic when she viewed them in all their grandeur from the suspension bridge that led to Canada. She watched the water flowing "in a slow steady current" until it broke "in a thousand waves of whitest foam over the sunken rocks." As she looked back from the western shore, the water assumed the color of "a stream of melted Emeralds" spraying and spouting over huge rocks until it reached the falls, where it plunged and leapt "like a mad thing of life," creating a "great sheet of foam" from which a "white mist rises, & circles & eddies, constantly beaten back by the rushing waters into the depths below from which it seems struggling to escape." Nothing she had ever seen before had so impressed her "with a sense of the Deity—with the power of the Creator 'who holds the waters in the hollow of his hand.'"[19]

From then on, the trip exceeded Carey's expectations. The voyage down the St. Lawrence River to Montreal was extremely pleasant. At Montreal, amusing social activity added to sightseeing delights when their North Carolina cousins, Charles Pettigrew, Johnston's brother, whom Carey had met three years earlier in Charleston, and their sister Mary Blount, whom she had met the year before in Washington, joined them. Although Charles had been the one to make "pretty speeches" about traveling with Tom Petigru's party, Carey was, at first, more pleased about becoming "good friends" with Mary Blount. About Mary Blount's thirty-six-year-old brother, she had less to say until Charles proved to be a far more lively escort than Uncle Tom. When they all went on together to Quebec City, sightseeing became even more exciting, especially after George Webb, commissary general of the British troops stationed there, offered to guide them around the Citadel and Montmorenci Falls.

To reach the falls proper, they had to clamber over a precipitous rocky slope and then descend hand over hand on a rope ladder. Mattie, Mary Blount, and Carey, exhilarated by both the scenery and the company, did so fearlessly despite brisk autumn winds that billowed out the skirts of their impractical silk dresses. That tricky descent to a rock below the falls proved to be well worth the discombobulation it caused, for the young women thrilled at the view of the flume from so unusual a perspective. But at least part of the fun was making sport of their two escorts, who hung back from the edge of the rock on which the women gleefully perched. Carey especially mocked Charles for urging them to stand back and only "peep out from behind the trees." She later boasted that neither the heights nor, she assured her mother, Charles's presence had made her giddy. "Any fears of a flirtation &c, dear Mamma pray dismiss from your mind."[20]

So pleasing was their collaboration that the Petigrus and Pettigrews continued to travel together. After a brief return to Montreal, they journeyed south, cruising by boat down Lake Champlain and going on to Boston by train. Soon after they settled in at the Winthrop House, they received an unanticipated call from a Mr. Smith. They greeted him with some perplexity, for no one knew the stranger with the "fierce yellow mustache, whisker[s] and short cut hair." Although he was well dressed and seemed civil, the conversation lagged until Charles almost shouted his delight as he suddenly realized that the stranger was his younger brother Johnston. Right away, the rest of them saw through Johnston's new trappings. Mary Blount of course recognized her brother, but so did the others, who had known him in Charleston while he was studying law with James Petigru. But the changes in his appearance that two years of European travel had produced absolutely astounded Carey. He was "so altered" as to be unrecognizable.[21]

Her astonishment was even greater because she had gotten to know James Johnston Pettigrew exceedingly well during his sojourn in Charleston. Called Johnston to distinguish him from an older but long-dead brother named James, he had arrived there as a callow youth, unfashionable in appearance and ill at ease in the social milieu of his South Carolina kin. Although he was believed to be something of an intellectual and mathematical genius and had mastered the law so swiftly that his mentor predicted a great legal career for him, he had been thoroughly uncomfortable when he first arrived in the city. It was "a strange place, without one person" with whom he could sympathize, for James Petigru was "too old" and the young men he met were "too stupid" and conceited. Moreover, most of his female relatives had found him brusque and offish.[22]

Carey was the exception. As soon as they met, Johnston and Carey, who were exactly the same age, became the closest of friends. Her flair for making friends and her well-cultivated intellect attracted Johnston powerfully. Within a month of their first meeting, he asked for either a painted miniature or a daguerreotype of her. Before long, he sought permission to escort her when she went home to Badwell. Carey, wondering about propriety, referred his request to her mother, noting that "Uncle does not disapprove at all, . . . [but] *you* keep silent." Whatever that silence betokened, Jane North soon assented to the arrangement so wholeheartedly that she invited Johnston to spend the summer at Badwell. Johnston's enthusiasm for those plans made his older sister, Mary Blount, smile. "Are you not head and toes in love with our fair cousin Carie?," she asked but then cautioned, "Mind out! before you know it you will be irretrievably lost."[23]

Johnston fully affirmed his sister's belief that "Carie must be a love of a girl," but he defined that love rather surprisingly when he sent her a gift of Thomas Moore's *Poetical Works*, which he inscribed "To my charming *sister* C. North." Carey was quick to see his meaning. "I have been annoyed at some of the wise ones in the family saying he 'was smitten.' This is altogether a mistake[;] in the first place he *highly objects* to *cousins*, in the next he regards me as a sister[,] calls me so very often, besides being quite too wise a person to let any foolish notion take possession of his head." Seemingly the two saw eye to eye, for Johnston was curious whether any of the family had said anything to Carey "about a *flirtation*" with him and laughed at the idea as much as she did.[24] At least on the surface, they were not as others saw them, although their extreme closeness would have been unusual even for siblings.

At first Jane North viewed Johnston favorably as a matrimonial prospect for her daughter. His father, Ebenezer Pettigrew, had owned three plantations on Lake Phelps in eastern North Carolina employing some 100 slaves to produce primarily corn but also wheat, rice, vegetables, wine, lumber, and lumber products. Moreover, he had served a term in Congress and had remained a political presence in his state until his death in 1848. The prospects even of his youngest son, therefore, promised financial and social acceptability. It was Johnston's intentions that were at issue. His attitude and bearing, from the time of his first visit to Badwell, made Carey's mother skeptical. "Ambition is his mistress and if he ever marries," she predicted, "it will be some high match to advance his views." Carey's spinster Aunt Mary, however, simply could not understand why her niece did not press forward toward marriage to Johnston. The girl was, in her opinion, too "satisfied with the present & does not look to the future."[25]

Johnston's two years in Europe made any future with him less likely. On his return, Carey found him "sterner than formerly, & (truth might as well be told) scarcely so amiable." When he reappeared so abruptly in Boston, she and his sister at first joked casually about those changes, only to have Mary Blount blurt out, "I do wish you would marry Johnston, just seize upon & take him up to the priest." But if that had ever been a possibility, it was long past. Louise Porcher sized it up well. Paris not only had altered Johnston's dress and manners but also had made him less interested in Carey and strengthened the ambition that would "dictate his choice if he should ever marry." And even that was unpropitious, for, as Louise added, "his heart occupies so diminished a portion of his individuality that I do not think his wife will be an enviable woman."[26]

Carey herself retained much of their old footing. Her letters, now written in Italian, called him "carissimo fratello" and ended simply "sua Sorella."[27] In that, they were predictive.

CHAPTER SEVEN

Surviving Miserable Marriages

However convoluted her reluctance to marry, however conventional her elders' eagerness that she do so, Carey North found little encouragement in the marriages she observed most closely. Her mother's had ended with her father's death when Carey was only seven. The marriages of her aunts, although they all fulfilled the legal obligation that a husband support his wife and children, were, to varying degrees, emotionally strained. The marriages of her older cousins, whose courtships she had watched in anticipation of her own, were positively disastrous. And just as she was balancing the importunities of one suitor against another, the family miseries of James and Jane Amelia Petigru turned precipitately worse.

In the mid-1840s, after their daughters had married and mesmerism had apparently restored Jane Amelia's health, James expected the happiness of the early days of their marriage to return. His wife was now "far more reasonable than she ha[d] been for years," so much so that he dared invite Jane North to stay in their Charleston home for an extended visit. Her recovery, however, was brief. By 1849, Jane Amelia's "reasonableness" and her good health had quite faded. Moreover, as both daughters spent longer and longer periods with their parents to escape their own unhappy homes, old family frictions resurfaced and sharpened. The situation had become so tense by that summer that her mother absolutely refused to allow Sue King to stay in the family's house on Sullivans Island. Lou North reported that her aunt was in such "a terrible rage with Sue for something or other" that

Jane Amelia Petigru at age sixty. George Flagg portrait. Courtesy of the
Gibbes Museum of Art / Carolina Art Association, Charleston.

when Sue's "things were brought down she would not have them arranged in
her room and forbade any dinner to be cooked."[1]

Enraged by her daughters' harsh criticism of everything she did and made
wretched by the pains and other discomforts of her revived ill health, Jane
Amelia reverted to the behavior that made her so difficult to live with. Later
that summer, she balked at her husband's spending his customary month's
vacation at Badwell, where she adamantly refused to go. Louise Porcher

thought it was just another "specimen" of her sister-in-law's "heartless selfishness" and her insistent demand for his "flattery & adulation." Although James still paid her the "attention which contents other women," he had finally "ceased to act the lover, or to suffer anguish under the cloud of her ill humour."[2]

Despite his courtroom prowess, he tried to evade domestic conflict whenever he could. Yet he continued to spend most summer vacations at Badwell. In 1852, however, he gave way; making a "great sacrifice . . . of inclination and feeling," he took his wife to the Virginia springs instead. Still, he lamented, happiness remained "a thing rare" in his household. The couple's miseries were increased by Jane Amelia's own evasions. She ordered Henry Lesesne, who handled her trust funds, to reinvest all of her income and not to "tell Mr Petigru one word even if he should ask you. He likes secrets and mysteries," she went on, and although she did not, because it was now "his way," she had determined to make it hers. Her little game undoubtedly reflected as well her enduring bitterness that James's financial failure had so strapped the family a decade earlier. Over time, this resentment became ever more overt. Writing to her cousin William Porcher Miles in 1860, she insisted that her husband "certainly had no business to get married, as no mule is more [obstinate] than he is, and he has no right to involve so many in misery, because he chooses to go his own way." James's quip that all Jane Amelia needed "to complete her career" was "to come out as a widow" was not far off the mark.[3]

Although James doted on his daughters, as he did not on his wife, both Caroline and Sue caused him almost as much anguish as did Jane Amelia. As a successful lawyer, he spent at least a third of each year on the road, and even when he was in Charleston, he spent little time at home. As a result, the girls had been reared primarily under what their Aunt Louise labeled the "demoralizing influence" of their mother. Jane Amelia admitted that she had abdicated parental duties on the grounds that her invalidism had made her "able to do nothing, but pray to God" for her children.[4] At this, her sisters-in-law could only shake their heads. Significantly, none of them blamed Brother either for his only son's drift into personal and professional failure or for beautiful and charming Caroline's choice of spouse and clever but quick-tempered Sue's defiance of convention and unstinted quest for excitement.

Once his daughters had married—Caroline, "an opulent planter," and Sue, the son of his "friend and contemporary at [the] Bar"—their father apparently assumed that they would live happily ever after. But six years later, Adèle Allston found them both "so little prosperous or happy" that merely seeing them distressed her. Clearly, their father must have anticipated some of their troubles. Less than two months after Sue's wedding, he had

Caroline Petigru Carson at age twenty-five holding Jem. Zeno Schindler portrait.
Courtesy of Mrs. Irénée duPont May.

warned her against the damage her unleashed temper could wreak. Aware
that she was driven by the same temperamental volatility he had struggled to
overcome in himself, he urged her to exert self-control. It was as inappropri-
ate for her to rant and rave at her dressmaker for a botched job as it was for
her to disdain her mother openly. He could account for neither of these two
recent explosions when he recalled "what a sweet child" she had been, "so
docile, so gentle and so lively, as to get the imputation of being Pa's pet." Her

"love of distinction" and desire to shine should, he thought, cancel out such demeaning displays of ill humor. At the same time, he tried to reassure her. He praised the literary quality of her letters and her ability to portray people and events so wittily. He fed her curiosity with confidences about his legal triumphs and political defeats. But this careful coaching came, as his sister Louise observed, rather too late to do much good. Even he lamented that as far as being a father was concerned, his "life had been in vain."[5]

At the heart of his daughters' present troubles were their ill-considered marriages, which simply could not be undone. As William Carson's financial troubles engulfed him and his domestic behavior revealed his overwhelming contempt for Caroline, she openly expressed her misgivings about the contract into which she had entered so thoughtlessly. At first she largely confined them to her commonplace book, in which she copied passages from her reading that she found of particular relevance to her life. A few lines from Thomas Babington Macaulay's *James II* addressed her early forebodings: "No man was ever a greater slave to his passion than ——. Few had ever less judgment to poise his passions; none ever listened less to that little. He was rash in his undertakings, violent in his proceedings, awkward in his carriage, brutal in his expressions, and cruel in his disposition; impatient of the least contradiction, as slow to pardon as he was quick to resent." Fearful of his physical abuse, Caroline chose a passage from the *Rambler* to express her vulnerability: "Thus am I condemned to solitude: the day moves slowly along, and I see the dawn with uneasiness, because I consider that night is at a great distance."[6]

From the disillusionment these entries reflected there was no escape. South Carolina law, as her father himself had summed it up in court, made "marriage . . . the only indissoluble contract." Doubtless each spouse's disaffection fed the other's. Caroline made her very real ill health an excuse for frequent and prolonged absences from Dean Hall. More and more, William stayed alone there, even during the long, hot, and humid summers that in earlier years would have driven him to Sullivans Island. While he drank juleps in the company of house servants, Caroline went to the island to stay in her parents' cottage. When visitors found both Carsons in residence at Dean Hall, they reported that at best William treated Caroline with the "coolest civility" and at worst displayed shocking brutality.[7]

For a brief period in early 1849, William's grief over his mother's death and Caroline's support through his fits of violent weeping "softened" his temper. But before long, familiar financial pressures and new agricultural disasters drove him back to the bottle. By fall, their marriage was again a center of family gossip. Aunt Louise was sure that "things have gone too far ever to be accomodated between her & her husband" and hoped only that "decencies will still be preserved." Caroline herself was unsure even about preserving the decencies. According to Louise, "she does not know when she is right or when she is wrong & therefore is never firm in the right place except by some lucky accident." Finally, the situation grew so tense that her father "sought an interview formally with Carson. . . . It was a very stormy debate but ended happily . . . as he made every conssession."[8]

William's concessions, however, were short-lived. He did buy Caroline a showy new carriage, but he did not curtail his drinking. And he retained Matilda Blanche and her (and probably Carson's) daughter Meta as very special house servants. In short, he made little change in his "brutal habits & low propensities." Nevertheless, Louise, who considered him a "very bad man," reflected both conventional propriety and legal wisdom when she insisted that "in becoming his wife" Caroline had committed herself permanently to marital duties that were "plain, tho most unwelcome & arduous."[9]

Caroline, however, was determined to avoid those duties as much as possible. The following spring, she went with her father to Philadelphia for medical treatment of a uterine tumor. But because James had to return to the law practice that paid for such ventures, Sue King again came north to stay with her sister. When the treatments in Philadelphia proved unavailing, the sisters traveled to New York for a brief stay and then went to the health resort at Sharon Springs, some fifty miles west of Albany. By early July, Caroline and Sue had been away from home long enough to provoke comment. "Their situation is dreadful," Aunt Louise fretted, "calculated to excite the suspicion of all discreet people." There they were, "two young women without their husbands, & far from all those upon whom they have any claim" or who, like their children, had a claim on them. Soon thereafter, Sue returned, but Caroline stayed on, settling in to spend the winter in New York. To Robert Allston, it looked like desertion pure and simple. She had chosen to live on her own "in a manner which seems to suit her."[10] Even Sue was a bit scandalized by her sister's extravagances, which included redecorating her hotel parlor with furniture upholstered in blue satin damask. Like Uncle Robert, Sue was convinced that Caroline had little intention of returning to her husband's hearth.

Caroline did return to South Carolina but only after a nine-month absence. And when she did, it was not to Dean Hall but to her parents' Charleston home. There her sons, who had meanwhile been shunted among the relatives, joined her. But following her father's counsel, she took them periodically to Dean Hall for prolonged visits. If the plantation was to be their patrimony, the boys should be familiar with it and develop strong ties to it. Occasionally, Caroline even entertained friends and family there. The large Christmas house party in 1853 actually made Dean Hall jolly for a while. But that was the last time she took any pleasure in the Cooper River plantation. Before long, she refused to return at all or to allow Willie and Jem to visit their father unless they were accompanied and supervised by one of her own kinsmen.

By the summer of 1856, her husband's alcoholism was clearly killing him. But Caroline had become so alienated that she remained in Charleston while he lay dying on Sullivans Island. Moreover, after August 18, when his remains were buried in St. Michael's churchyard, Caroline did nothing to hide her relief. It was, however, relief bought at a price, for the man she had married for his wealth had "died insolvent, or next to it so that his poor widow and children," as her Aunt Adèle described it, were "very poor." When his estate was settled, Carson's debts of $87,500 devoured three-fifths of his property. Only Dean Hall remained to his heirs. Two years later, they sold it to Elias Nonus Ball, who paid down a third in cash and gave the Carsons a mortgage note for the rest, on which, in fact, he failed even to pay interest after the first two years. Caroline, whose share was confined to the legally mandatory widow's third, thus received only a minimal income from capital little more than the annual income her father derived from his law practice. Her kin, who had long criticized her "very expensive" habits, sympathized far less with her than with her sixty-seven-year-old father, on whom "she and her children must depend . . . entirely."[11]

In comparison with the miseries of her parents' marriage and the shambles of Caroline's, Sue King's seemed not so bad. At least she and Henry kept up appearances better and longer. She did return from her occasionally prolonged absences to the home they shared. Still, her "public demonstration of the want of cordiality or even of hospitable civility" and her utter lack of self-control threatening further "quicksands and shallows" drove her father to despair. Sue, however, considered her sharp-edged confrontations with others an essential defense of her persona. Social restraint would constitute a self-imposed hindrance to her quest for the personal independence and fun she demanded of life. The "delicate little suppers and recherché dinners" she threw, like the "altogether successful" evening parties that she patterned on Parisian soirees, did not comport with Henry's ideas of pleasure. Nor did her enthusiasm for dancing, which Aunt Mary deemed the immature "tastes of 16 fresh."[12]

In 1849, after the Kings had been married for six years, Aunt Louise decided that they were "by no means more comfortable or happy in each other" than were the Carsons. That year, Sue made her first prolonged trip north alone without her husband's approval but with his, as well as her father's, financial support. Henry did, however, refuse to allow his wife to take four-year-old Addy with her. But that did little to dampen her eagerness. "I feel so much pleasure in the anticipation," she wrote a week before she left, "that my old presentiments are quite strong, & I am constantly fancying that it is quite impossible that I am really & truly going to New York. I have so longed to take a peep out of our confined limits, to spread my wings ever so little, & the wish has appeared so utterly *unrealizable*." She brushed off Henry's disdain for the venture since he was "quite willing to go back" to his parents' home in her absence.[13]

When Sue returned three months later, Jane North thought Henry seemed again to be "distractedly in love with his wife." Even Sue, somewhat "paler & thinner," was in rare good spirits and appeared positively glad to be back. Aunt Louise went so far as to predict that the trip might have given Sue "some idea of the propriety of *reserve* which is a new idea for her," for "her relations with Henry" were now "apparently harmonious."[14]

Harmony, however, was short-lived. The next year, after Sue spent four months in the North with Caroline, she returned unwillingly and to an angry husband. Part of his ill humor was undoubtedly brought on by disappointment that Sue chose to absent herself just when his professional life seemed to be turning around. Before then, Henry's independent legal practice had been so negligible that it produced little income. Then in the summer of 1850, James Petigru made Henry his law partner, and he began to apply himself diligently. When Sue returned, she was blind to any change. She saw only the same unprepossessing, short, fat, dull husband, happier to drink and gamble with cronies than to cavort with her. Henry, in turn, found fault with Sue's excesses. Even with a now-quite-reasonable income, he could not keep up with her demands for money. Since he could rein in neither her spending nor his own prodigality, he continued to borrow heavily from his father and his siblings, plunging ever deeper into debt. Accordingly, it was imperative that both he and Sue cultivate smooth relations with all of the Kings, who at least expected them to attend weekly family dinners at the elder Kings' home.

Henry found subservience to his parents considerably easier to bear than did Sue. Her father-in-law, who had never fully approved of her, watched her carefully. But he was not altogether rigidly conventional in his expectations. He beamed with pleasure when Sue's first book, a novella and four short stories titled *Busy Moments of an Idle Woman*, appeared late in 1853. It was, he thought, "very clever," a "production of much talent." Indeed, her fiction won noticeably more of his approbation than her everyday conduct. Only months before he praised *Busy Moments* so highly, he had asked its author what she would do "if any one else acted as you are doing," for she was then in the midst of another one of her blowups. Even Sue was so unsettled by the incident that she became "very much indisposed." Harriette Lesesne observed Sue's symptoms with some care. "She can't eat, suffers from nausia &c, & looks poorly, is of course out of spirits." Indeed, "if it was anyone else," her aunt would "think she was in a 'delicate situation' but she says that is *impossible* & I suppose she must know best."[15]

Six months later, when her *Busy Moments* was winning critical praise, Sue and Caroline went with their father to spend six weeks in Washington, where his many friends entertained them extensively. Sue basked in her new popularity. When they returned home early in March 1854, she bragged that "no *women* before had ever had such a successful career in Washington." Clearly Aunt Harriette thought their stay in the capital had gone to their heads and sniffed that they both seemed "triumphant & *saucy*, & ready for almost anything." Only two days after their return, they joined a family dinner party at the Lesesnes dressed so "very richly" that their appearance offended their kin even more than their boasting. Indeed, Caroline's pink silk dress, which was cut "very low in front making truly a meagre display," positively shocked her aunt.[16]

Stimulated by her daring assault on Washington society, Sue became ever less restrained at home. Later that year, her battles with her mother were so intense that Louise Porcher concluded the two "ought never to be together except formally, & never attempt to occupy the same establishment." More publicly disgraceful was Sue's uninhibited coquetting and flirting with young men. Even her conversation reeked of indiscretion. If family lore is correct, when her father congratulated her as the author of *Busy Moments* with the toast, "Quick in conception and easy in delivery," Sue promptly raised her glass to toast, "A man of large parts and deep penetration."[17]

Sue's risqué repartee and suggestive coquetry, however enticing, failed to secure the loyal devotion she expected from her young bachelor following. In December 1854, when Arthur Hayne abandoned her drawing room to wed the actress Julia Dean after what Louise Porcher called a "nine days wonder," Sue expressed her resentment openly. That a son of the late South Carolina senator and governor Robert Y. Hayne should marry an actress defied even her sense of propriety. That he should tolerate his wife's continued career on the stage was downright indecent. The vehemence of Sue's response to Hayne's desertion seemed to confirm that she had been engaged in something more than a casual flirtation with him. As Aunt Louise again lamented, "our poor Niece has lost all discretion & exposed herself dreadfully."[18]

Still, Sue charged ahead undaunted. At a dinner party her father gave in 1855 for William Makepeace Thackeray, in town on a lecture tour, Sue equated herself with the well-known English novelist. Displaying the hubris of a first-time author, she observed that as far as the criticism of their books went, he and she were *"in the same boat."* "A dead silence fell," one guest reported, "a thunder-cloud descended upon the face of Mr. Thackeray, and the pleasure of the entertainment was at an end."[19]

Soon after Thackeray left town, another teapot tempest came to the boil. On March 4, 1856, Sue appeared at a "Bal costume" dressed as a "Marquise of Louis 14th time & of course," so her Aunt Louise reported, "was something we are not likely to see again." Her hair, "turned with two curls hanging down," was powdered, piled high, and set off by "a little pink silk hat or cap with pink streamers." The bodice of her dress was "open and drawn attached with beautiful opals or pearls set with diamonds. [And] round the neck and arms was the most beautiful lace." It was, in fact, less the lacily veiled décolletage that sparked gossip than the "great many diamonds and jewels and things of that sort," which had been lent her by Sara Felix, an actress and, still more distressing, the sister of a well-known Charleston madam whose brothel was reputedly equally magnificent.[20]

Not satisfied with the frisson she had created at the ball itself, Sue wrote a full report of the occasion and the costumes for the *Charleston Courier*. When the men who had sponsored the ball, among them her cousin Johnston Pettigrew, heard of the anonymous article's impending publication, they demanded its suppression. The ball had been a private affair, and publicizing it would infringe on the standards of the time even if the ladies who attended were not named. Ignoring that protest, the *Courier* published the article, although the editors subsequently apologized for doing so. The many who, by that time, knew that Sue King had written it were disinclined to believe her disclaimer that it was a personal letter published without her consent. And the fact that three of those whose costumes it described were Henry's unmarried sisters did little to help her relations with her in-laws.

That summer, Sue and Henry's marriage became so severely strained that it invited direct family intervention. In his diary, Mitchell King recorded frank talks with his son. Henry's "reference to Sue [was] very very unhappy." A few days later, as they again discussed his marriage, Henry gave his father "very briefly & unsatisfactorily . . . a very lame account of their relations." That lameness may have been only a matter of embarrassed reticence or it may have stemmed from a rumored relationship with a black woman. Whatever it was, his marriage was going from bad to worse. By this time, her father-in-law was clearly running out of patience with Sue's temperamental outbursts and her defiance of convention. But because he also realized that Henry's actions as well as Sue's were subverting their marriage, he scarcely knew how to proceed. About her most recent scrapes, he noted that Sue was "apparent[ly] insouciant" but feeling it all "deeply," whereas Henry was "moody & unwell" and growing careless about his professional obligations. As for himself, he concluded, "My headache increases."[21]

Her cousin Carey came to share Mitchell King's uneasiness about Henry and was "truly sorry" for Sue. "She is nearly mad, unfortunate woman, but others are not blameless." Sue, who saw no way to resolve her marital crisis, attempted instead to evade it. She spent more and more time in New York or visiting the plantations of various South Carolina friends. Those friends, however, grew ever fewer in number as, one after another, she blew up at them. And instead of making any effort to relieve her husband's growing moodiness, she continued to flirt quite openly with young bachelor acquaintances. To her father, she seemed "the prey of discontent and nervous irritation to an alarming degree," so much so that he feared that even her affection for him might be "perverted into downright hatred."[22]

Despite her predicament, Sue's talents as a writer were still, her father assured her, "an object of . . . just pride." By now, writing was almost the only way she could handle the dissatisfactions that wracked her life. In fiction, she could satirize the customs of Charleston and the mores of her class. Although the "witty and sparkling" dialogue and "circumstantial and striking" descriptions in *Busy Moments*, rooted as they were in her observations of the society she knew so well, delighted her father, they irritated many of her kin. Johnston Pettigrew saw in both *Busy Moments* and her first full-length novel, *Lily*, published in 1855, "the mere embodifications of what she has seen," which he considered a severe limitation because "her circle of immediate experience is of course small." Aunt Jane agreed with that premise, but her chief objection was that Sue had situated the opening scenes of *Lily* at Chicora Wood. Lou North cringed at the clearly autobiographical nature of the stories her older cousin published as *Sylvia's World: Crimes Which the Law Does Not Reach*. She found them "extremely mortifying" because "every body recognizes them." That Sue could so mock the institution of marriage and feminine propriety convinced Lou that "judgment . . . so warped" indicated a mind "seriously affected."[23]

Lou's older sister Carey was similarly upset "to recognize so many of the anecdotes," though she praised Sue's ability to "express such excellent sentiments" and to write "remarkably well, & very easily." Nevertheless, she was discomfited by the disparities between the "excellent sentiments" of *Lily*'s heroine and the author's own conduct. Other kin were disconcerted by Sue's authorial interventions. Her explicit recollection of the misery she had endured as a wallflower at her first ball revived memories of Sue's rivalry with her popular sister. Her condemnation of a mother who left "her young daughters to enter upon the state of grown-up life without the watchful guard of a parent's eye" resounded with the real-life hostility between Sue and Jane Amelia. Most unsettling of all was Sue's open criticism of marriage and the restrictions it placed on the lives of women. Although that criticism was a deliberate challenge to Charleston customs, it just as clearly was a public reflection on her own marriage. In "Every-Day Life," one of her earliest stories, Mrs. Mordaunt, a woman wedded to a man she despised, advised a younger woman to marry only for love. In another, Sue broadened her scope to deplore the institution of marriage as a whole. Even the most happily mated of the several young matrons its heroine asked for advice warned against it. "A life of strict seclusion, a life of mourning and of sorrow," was infinitely better than "a miserable double existence, dragged on in continued wretchedness, bringing children into the world to follow, possibly, in their parents' footsteps; or, worse still, have some horrible, disgraceful wind-up of an ill-assorted union." In Sue's stories, the major force promoting such ill-assorted unions was usually either parental pressure to marry wealth or parental failure to guide a daughter and shelter her from designing men who were after her money. Lily's guardians had consented to her engagement to a fortune-seeking cad "without an inquiry made into the habits, the principles, the morals, the antecedents of the man to whom she becomes the veritable legal slave."[24]

Likening marriage to slavery was a direct challenge to the male domination that fabled Southern patriarchy demanded. So too was Sue's challenge to women who colluded "in making their husbands despots or Jerry Sneaks." The caustic Mrs. Mordaunt charted a better course. In the first days of her wretched marriage, she was "conscious" of her spouse's "injustice" but passively "received his insults and submitted to his anger." She came to enjoy married life only when she began to exert her will to subdue him, when she asserted her "rights" and "forced him" to treat her "with more respect."[25]

Although her own marriage produced not even that perversely happy outcome, Sue's writing gave her the opportunity to critique the social demands and domestic restraints that her class, her time, and her place imposed on women. It even permitted her to construct an alternative persona as the racy litterateur who defied convention. Both at home and on her trips to Northern cities, she projected herself as a liberated woman whose standing as a published author put her on level ground with the prominent writers with whom she associated. In that guise, she identified herself with

Thackeray, wanting to be both as shocking and as respected as he was. So she gloried in her second encounter with the English novelist, when he was the guest of honor at a little supper in her home. She basked in the daring repartee the occasion sparked. He confessed to being "agreeably disappointed" to find that she was not, as he had heard, quite the "fastest woman in America." She was "agreeably surprised" by Thackeray for she had heard that he was "no gentleman."[26]

Despite such literary suppers, Sue remained on the outer fringes of her city's intellectual life, which was dominated by "The Club," who met at Russell's bookstore for wide-ranging discussions. Its members included Charleston's leading lawyers, doctors, editors, and ministers—occasionally even a poet. Without exception, however, all were men, whose attitudes Mitchell King caught in summarizing their discussion of "Woman's Rights." The gentler sex were "Higher morally—Inferior—Intellectually—Physically—more sensitive & yet more enduring—Less robust. Formed to rear a family—Design of Heaven conformity to nature."[27] Sue's higher morality was at best questionable. Clearly she was robust—even tough—both physically and intellectually. Her nonconformity was most certain of all. But then so was her sister's and her mother's.

Conforming more closely to Mitchell King's prescription for femininity, Louise Porcher and Ann Petigru never addressed the misery of their marriages so openly. Louise's problems stemmed largely from Philip's drinking, but it was only after their daughter Janey died of yellow fever in June 1858 that her father's problems were openly admitted and candidly discussed. And then it was because the death of his debutante daughter shook him so severely that for the first time ever he took communion at Louise's evangelical St. Peter's Episcopal Church and vowed to overcome his drinking and wenching proclivities. Louise celebrated his conversion in a letter to their oldest son reporting that his father had become "very active & industrious" and had "been called to a new & better life than he has ever lived before."[28] But the respite was brief as Louise's constant ill health and Philip's dwindling business success propelled him back to his old ways.

Janey's death was not the first death of a young adult to expose marital strains and feed general family anxieties about a strained marriage. In September 1853, when Tom Petigru and his son were at their Cedar Hill plantation near Abbeville, Louis Petigru had set off with a single servant to visit neighbors who lived on the far side of the Little River. When their boat capsized, both men were drowned. Two days later, Tom discovered their bodies. The next day, he saw to Louis's burial in the family cemetery at nearby Badwell and, with Jane North for support, took the train to Charles ton to tell the dread news to his wife and daughter. As soon as they saw him get off the train without Louis, Ann and Mattie broke down. Very quickly, the gloomy news spread to other family members. For them all, the loss was doubly mourned, for Louis was one of the two surviving males of his generation who bore the Petigru surname. The other was James's son Dan, universally believed to be a black sheep beyond redemption.

But it was her husband's subsequent behavior that made Ann's sorrow almost unendurable. Their marriage had long been strained. Even in its early years, Adèle had found "little happiness between them," and Mary had fumed at her brother's "terrible improprieties," which gave his wife "so much just reason to complain." Neither sister saw any likelihood of resolving the frictions between the two except in Tom's long absences at sea. His excessive drinking both at home and away had caused problems even before implications of lewdness, violence to subordinates, and repeated drunkenness on duty had surfaced during an 1850 court-martial on charges that he had used government property for his own profit while on a naval mission to Mazatlán on Mexico's Pacific coast. Whether or not being cleared of charges of misuse of his ship altered his consumption of alcohol, it decidedly did not curtail his womanizing. Ann was forced to display her "first passion of grief for her lost son" in the presence of Tom's slave mistress in her own home, where Linda was an ever-present "ready lighted firebrand between them." This "particularly dreadful circumstance" almost overwhelmed Ann, for Linda "intruded her hateful presence upon her with her child."[29]

Tom's subsequent appointment as superintendent of the Washington Naval Yard, although it removed one cause of Ann's distress, did not end her mourning. Little more than two years after the death of her only son, her only daughter died suddenly at age twenty-five. Mattie's death came only a month after retrenchments in the navy had forced Tom's retirement. A year and a half later, in March 1857, Tom himself died at age sixty-six. His vigorous campaign, with his family's full support, to reverse the navy's action was intended to redeem Petigru honor. Instead it sparked another public airing of his behavioral improprieties. Once again, the public airing of his excessive drinking shamed his sisters. "How dreadful," Jane shuddered, "that an enemy should have the power to make charges so odious & proffer the proof."[30] Nonetheless, Tom's death shocked the family and thrust it once again into mourning.

The death of her husband fell less heavily on Ann than the loss of her children. Even as a childless widow, however, she remained a Petigru in more than name. James immediately assumed the same duties he had undertaken for Jane North when, twenty years earlier, she had been widowed. The difference was that Ann, who at Tom's death regained the property she had brought him by marriage, was left with wealth rather than poverty. Accordingly, James helped her sell off her Georgetown and Charleston mansions and buy a small house near his. He arranged for Robert Allston to buy the land and slaves on her Pipedown rice plantation near Chicora. Jane North, who had earlier defended her sister-in-law from her sisters' criticisms, again came to her aid with the solace of shared experience and joined James in praising Ann for papering over the discords of a troubled marriage by maintaining her husband's memory "with an affectionate sense of all his good qualities, and cover[ing] his defects with the mantle of charity."[31]

Ann responded to this sympathy by developing new ties to her in-laws. From 1858 until her death in 1869, Lou North was her almost constant companion. Ann nursed her Charleston kin when they became ill. She funded a trip upcountry to Glenn Springs to improve Louise Porcher's feeble health. She paid her godson Charley Porcher's tuition at boarding school. All told, it seemed that Tom's death strengthened rather than weakened family bonds, a proposition that Carey Pettigrew later confirmed by naming a daughter Ann and a son Thomas.

Despite the shame that Tom brought on the family, it was Jack who was the black sheep of the first generation. But after thirty years of exile in the West marked by drinking, womanizing, and gambling, he sought his family's aid in 1854 when he begged Jane North to allow him and his wife to come live at Badwell. His only slave, who had supported them by farming and acted as their domestic servant, had recently died. Jack had no place else to turn. The prospect of coping with him at Badwell made his unmarried sister Mary "sad & anxious," but she saw no alternative. It was "the only thing that could be done. He is so desirous to come & finish his course where he began." It was, however, Jane on whom responsibility for the "forlorn couple" fell when they arrived that December.[32]

The best that could be said for Tempe was that, although she was a woman of appalling commonness, she was humble and seemed "grateful." Jack, only minimally better off than his wife, displayed the physical and mental deterioration of an alcoholic. Nonetheless, Jane and Mary fed and sheltered them both at Badwell until James built them a small house nearby when Tom, who had at first welcomed their coming, denied them the use of his deserted Cedar Hill house. Driven perhaps as much by shame as by family loyalty, Jane and Mary continued to provide Tempe with clothing, hoping to give her, if possible, a more "genteel appearance."[33] In any case, they were relieved that the couple seldom came to Badwell once they had their own house and a slave whom Brother gave them to produce and prepare their food. Still, for the next fifteen years, Jane and then Mary saw to their physical needs as they drifted into helpless senility.

Jack and his wife provided one more test for the Petigru women, who, no matter how trying the circumstances, always closed ranks to maintain family honor and cohesion. This demanded much of them even when their kinsmen and women had kept up the external proprieties their class expected. It demanded even more when those to be shielded had defied such proprieties.

CHAPTER EIGHT

Governing at Home

Of all the Petigru women, none so understood yet so flouted Southern conventions as did Sue King. None so firmly rejected her native region yet so held to the aristocratic prescriptions for a Southern lady as did Caroline Carson. None quite so completely abandoned the responsibilities of the traditional Southern matron as did Jane Amelia Petigru. And none, however well or ill she reflected the stereotypical plantation mistress, grappled more determinedly with the stern necessity of fulfilling the socially prescribed roles of both planter and mistress than did Jane North.

Yet in fact no woman in the Petigru family matched the complex stereotype of the Southern woman exactly, although some came closer to conventional wisdom about the uniform nature of Southern ladies than did others. Each in her own distinctive way faced the particular demands of domesticity and the pressures of family that fell to her lot. And each lived within a framework imposed by kinship as well as by the society and the class to which they all belonged. It was a framework that expected men to be economic managers and providers and women to be domestic managers and emotional guardians. The Petigru women seldom debated financial questions arising from plantation management or professional performance. Yet some of them were aware of the debts their husbands found difficult to pay and the credit they had unwisely extended. When they were, they recognized that the resolution of such difficulties, like the planter's deployment of field laborers and the attorney's conduct at the bar, lay with their menfolk. Inside the household, however, they usually decided the matters of domestic economy that affected the management of their homes. They kept track of the cost of clothing, the market price of foodstuffs, and the expenditures required for other items that, as mistresses of their domiciles, they needed. In addition, the very nature of the slaveholding world required them to manage the unpaid labor that worked daily in their kitchens, washhouses, dairies, and gardens. Whether or not they themselves shunned doing household chores, these women supervised the servants who performed those tasks in their stead. Their domestic economy depended on slave labor as much as the cash-crop plantation economy did. So it was natural that they often discussed labor management as well as the allocation of other critical resources both with their spouses and among themselves. How should they manage workers to whom they paid no wages? How could they motivate slaves who were already quite aware that it was as much in their mistresses' interest as in their own to provide them with adequate food, housing, and clothing? What were the effective techniques for defusing tensions and adjudicating differences between slave and mistress?

From the day of her marriage to Robert Allston, Adèle assumed responsibility for a larger and more complex domestic labor force than any that her sisters oversaw. But her preparation for such a role was shaky. While she was part of Brother's Charleston household, she had observed the management of the thirteen or so slaves present in his Broad Street yard. But she had not been in charge of them, nor, as a youngster at Badwell, had she ever seen so many domestic servants. Consequently, she had no idea how to manage the large staff she found at Chicora Wood. The house itself presented no problem. No larger and perhaps even smaller than the Broad Street house, it had eight rooms. Four were part of the original structure. The two on the first floor were each about twenty feet square. From the wide center hall, stairs led up to the low-ceilinged second floor, which was similarly divided. An addition to this older part contained two somewhat more spacious rooms on each floor, which were divided by an even wider hall. For this ample but not vast house and its two white residents, the young bride supervised a staff of over ten. Mary, the cook, aided by George, the scullion, prepared the Allstons' meals in the separate kitchen house, and Peter, the butler, and Andrew, the waiter, carried the dishes to the main house. Milly, the laundress, worked in a separate washhouse, where, in all probability, space was also set aside for Cindy, the seamstress. Aleck, the coachman, presided over the stables, and Moses, the gardener, kept up the grounds. In the house, Lavinia, Brother's wedding gift to Adèle, was her personal maid, and Caroline and Beck made the beds, dusted, and swept.

Finding constructive work to occupy the servants' time was a challenge.

So was establishing authority over them. Even Aunt Elizabeth Blyth's advice, however much it helped, did not make domestic affairs run smoothly. Only gradually did Adèle learn to take charge. At first she relied heavily on advice from her older sisters and her aunt. The gravest early test was how to handle evasion of her orders. Here, sister Louise Porcher was especially helpful, for when she had "commenced keeping house" at Keithfield plantation, she had coped with similar difficulties. Finding her new servants badly trained, she suspected that some were also unreliable or intractable. "I had not one that I could place the least dependence on, or that was capable of doing any thing. I had to assist in ironing myself besides being a great deal in the kitchen." But she reported that she had conquered the situation by taking a firm stand until her "trials" were "much diminished." Adèle was determined to attain like results, but she was puzzled about how to achieve them. When she caught Beck trying on her clothes, Louise warned her against being "too lenient," for if she was, she would "only have to be more severe in the end." What Beck needed was immediate and "strict discipline." At the same time, Adèle should give Beck "every chance of amendment" before she went "to extremities."[1] Such advice apparently worked, although persuading Mary to change her style of cooking took a year and a half. But at last the improvement was sufficiently marked for Robert to congratulate the cook.

In contrast to Adèle's persistent efforts, Jane Amelia, after her severe illness in 1832, avoided responsibility for managing the Petigrus' Broad Street home. At first she hired a "white woman to keep house." A few months later, she charged nineteen-year-old Harriette with attending to the housekeeping. But Sister expected far more from Harriette than merely keeping track of supplies and servants. Soon she criticized her youngest sister-in-law for preferring to "write and read" rather than to make clothes and quilts. Nonetheless, Harriette gained sufficient experience to feel confident about keeping house when, almost five years later, she and Henry Lesesne moved into their first home. She concluded after only a few days that she would like it "more & more" as she grew "more accustomed" to it.[2] Indeed, she took special pride in making her own curtains and stretching her limited food budget to its maximum.

No matter how involved the other Petigru sisters were in performing such domestic tasks, they all had to manage the work of others. Even after Louise was reduced to a single servant as a result of the 1837 panic and Philip's financial problems , she fretted about that one. All of the second generation, despite being brought up in better-staffed homes than their seniors, needed instruction in supervising servants when they acquired their own. When Sue and Henry King finally moved into theirs, she faced a test of wills as determined as any that had perplexed her aunts. Her cook, a woman of twenty-four, claimed that Christian piety required her to attend Sunday church services "morning, afternoon, and evening." Yet that piety did not preclude her dancing every Tuesday evening. Clearly such "kitchen fancies" must be "nipped in the bud." But when Sue did nip, the cook staged "a regular 'strike' . . . for higher breakfast luxuries." Quite brazenly she informed her mistress that "in all decent yards butter or meat was given to each individual" and that "hominy, skim milk, and sugar with nothing but coffee grounds to wash them down . . . was a style of living not suited to the times." At twenty-two, Sue was not yet the self-assured woman she would become. But she understood how her pocketbook would be affected if she were to distribute daily "a slice of ham to each, or a spoonful of butter," and she also recognized the potential for her own discomfort if she did not. So she turned to Aunt Jane North for advice and in "cabinet counsel" learned how to hold the line and keep the upper hand.[3]

Not all crises were resolved that simply. Ten years later, in 1856, William, the Kings' butler for the preceding eight years, disappeared. After Henry notified the police, who promptly apprehended William, the Kings decided to sell him out of the city and away from his family. Similarly, Ann Petigru's Virgil, Peter, and Joe, after they stole an expensive velvet cloak and several boys' caps from the home of a neighbor, were caught with the goods almost as soon as the police were notified. Their punishment, mandated by their owner, was equally severe. Virgil, the "little wretch," was consigned to "solitary confinement" on the ground floor of Ann's house and then sold. Joe and Peter, both young adults, were whipped. Within two years, there was no male slave under thirty-six on Ann's staff of eight. But it was, of course, Ann with whom her extended family sympathized. The "great deal of annoyance and distress of mind" that the incident caused made her look "very badly."[4]

Even biddable servants troubled their owners. The three young women (aged nineteen, twenty-one, and twenty-seven) whom the 1850 census also listed as the Kings' servants manifested less rebelliousness than William. But since slavery was largely defined by race, they raised the touchy issue of color. One was black, two were conspicuously of mixed blood, and Rosaline, a mere child capable only of running errands, according to Sue was "fearfully white."[5] Even in noting that, Sue failed to address just why a white slave should induce fear, for she enjoyed the leisure that having five servants allowed her and wished for still more. By 1860, she and Henry and their only daughter were waited on by a staff of ten.

When James Petigru had faced bankruptcy, he had cut his household staff. But as times improved, he, like the Kings, doubled the number of servants from the eight who lived in his yard in 1850 to seventeen by 1860. In buying a family of six to provide his wife the personal maid she wanted, he acknowledged that "an increase of servants [was] only an increase of expense."[6] But he excused himself on the grounds that spending the $1,000 for Nannie and her children probably did Jane Amelia more good than the same sum spent on medicine would have done.

Unless hard times forced them to sell or hire out some of their slaves, all of the Petigrus increased rather than diminished the number of their slaves over time. What differentiated one household from another was thus not the presence of enslaved domestics but their number, their nature, and their relations with their owners. Harriette Lesesne preferred to employ whites to nurse her young children and to supervise her black servants, whom Mary Petigru characterized as "very inefficient & sickly."[7] Nonetheless, in 1860 the Lesesnes had thirteen slaves living in their yard. Nor did the Allstons reduce the number of their black domestics when, after the birth of her last daughter, Adèle hired Irish Mary O'Shea to care for the younger children.

The circumstances that led to employing white women for positions of special responsibility were not simply a matter of racial prescriptions. Both before and after the Allstons employed O'Shea, black Caroline gave excellent care to the younger children, who, in turn, were encouraged to form attachments not just to her but also to other house and field slaves. When Jinty was ten years old, her mother encouraged her to go, as her older sister Bessie had formerly done, "where the people are" in order to nurture an identification between white family and black servants. That identification of interests was consciously furthered in letters between white folk that became conduits for communication among black friends and family. When Jane North left Georgetown for Badwell in 1836, she took Sukey with her. Two years later, Sukey's sister, who belonged to a Mrs. Wilson in Georgetown, asked her owner's neighbor, Elizabeth Blyth, to help her get news of Sukey. Aunt Blyth passed on the request to Adèle, whose next letter to Jane included the message: "Please beg Mrs North to tell maum Sukey her Sister belonging to Mrs Wilson sends howdye for her & Do say how Sukey is, for her Sister has not heard of her for 2 years she says." Back came word that Sukey had married carpenter Jim. Similarly, two years after Lavinia, Brother's wedding present to Adèle, had gone with her new mistress to Chicora Wood, her mother begged Harriette Lesesne to ask Adèle "to mention in your letter to me, how she gets on, if she behaves well, & how her health is, & if she is married." And after 1845, when Adèle presented her godchild Addy King with little Phoebe for a maid, Old Phoebe repeatedly asked that letters from Chicora seek news of "little Fib."[8]

It was even easier to relay news when key domestic servants at Chicora accompanied Adèle during her long stays in Charleston in the 1850s. But it also exposed a hazard. Once, in the mistress's absence from Chicora, Sally, who had been left in charge of the poultry house, turned her responsibility over to Charlotte so that she and Molly could visit old Clarinda. Also, when Phoebe ran out of fabric for the sleeves she was making up, she stopped sewing altogether, as did Lavinia when she had finished all of her specifically assigned sewing. Even when the mistress was at home, idleness—real or potential—was a matter of concern. In the Allston household, there were always more servants than routine domestic chores demanded. Robert, who expected his plantations to operate efficiently and profitably, implored Adèle "to adopt a system of better accountability" for her domestics, requiring that work be done "at the appointed time," establishing "a system of monthly rewards," and punishing "delinquencies by diminishing or withholding" those rewards.[9] But neither rewards nor punishments proved universally effective.

A surplus of servants, however, was never the issue at Badwell. There, the difficulty lay largely with Mary Petigru's inconsistent treatment of her slaves. As Jane North gently put it, her sister had "some little attendant discomforts . . . as relates to servants." Her faultfinding made them frantic. She slapped them when she was angry. She pressed favors on them unpredictably. Her emotional life largely centered around them. In 1853 she was busy with "two little maids . . . who are to be educated . . . for Liberia," although Jane doubted whether Mary would "persevere in the educational part." When one of her "little boys" hurt his neck so badly the wound had to be cauterized, she nearly went wild. And when Rose, whom she loved "better than any human being," died of complications from typhoid fever, she went into mourning.[10]

Her capricious responses to her servants so irritated family members that one niece wished openly that "Aunt M's negroes would be disposed of for the wear & tear of temper & comfort to all concerned is tremendous." By 1859, Mary apparently agreed, for that year she arranged to sell her slaves. She had determined that they must be sold as a group to a nearby Gibert relative so that no families would be broken up. Nonetheless, when she announced her decision to her slaves after she had made all of the arrangements, they "just refused to go." Harriette Lesesne huffed disapprovingly that her sister would in future have to "consult her negroes & have their decision before she acted."[11]

Jane North, hardheaded as she was, also raised family doubts about labor management at Badwell, where, in the 1850s, her twenty-one slaves and

Brother's fifteen interacted with Mary's nine. On her first visit to her old home after she had married and moved away, Carey worried about the servants' "free & easy air" and her mother's tolerance of it. Seen from her new vantage point, it revealed "very little authority." The slaves might "look very contented, work well too," but at day's end and on Sundays, they asserted their right to go "pleasuring." Comparing Badwell discipline with that on her brothers' North Carolina plantations, Mary Blount Pettigrew was shocked at how "much more freedom . . . the negroes" enjoyed at Badwell.[12]

However it looked to others, Jane realized that Badwell's productivity and thus the quality of her life depended on having a capable and willing work force. So she weighed discipline against responsibility. In February 1858, having left the place in Mary's charge, she dashed back from Charleston as soon as she heard that an "awful Fever" had struck the slave quarters and threatened widespread death. Here there was no conflict between self-interest and benevolence. But when conflicting cultural values were at stake, decision making became more complex. Granting or denying permission to marry was a particularly thorny issue. Like most owners, Jane preferred that her laborers intermarry on the place. She had consented in 1837 to carpenter Jim's request that he be allowed to marry Sukey, a woman considerably older than he was. Jim had earlier courted a younger woman on a farm several miles away, and Jane had denied him permission to marry her on the grounds that this otherwise acceptable woman would be unavailable to wash and iron for him. But living with him at Badwell, Sukey could readily perform those services. So Jane approved this match, despite her adherence to the patriarchal assumption that a husband should never be younger than his wife. She rationalized this exception by conceding that "we must not judge for them by the criterion of our own feelings and opinions." Still, some twenty-three years later, a slave's age at marriage again troubled her. This time it was the extreme youth of the proposed bride that bothered her. When Susan, age sixteen, and Ned, who was somewhat older, sought her permission to marry, Jane gave her consent only after "the parents on both sides counsel[ed] better let them marry than do worse." But she remembered that several months earlier she had refused to allow Ned to marry a woman owned by a neighbor for the same reason that she had denied Jim's similar request. Ned had then spoken "so touchingly" about his disappointment that Jane "resolved never to interfere again between two loving hearts, even tho they be the children of Ham."[13]

In the cases of both Jim and Ned, denying permission to marry off the place was clearly a function of self-interest, for those whose spouses belonged to others would inevitably spend time and energy visiting their mates. Moreover, the husband's progeny would belong to the wife's owner. So in rooting her laborers' family attachments at Badwell, Jane quite consciously acted to develop a more settled work force. But although she never questioned her right to regulate the personal lives of her workers, she did temper the economics of self-interest with humane considerations. Others, however, saw in that tempering a reprehensible laxity made the more offensive by Jane's governance not just of domestic servants but also of field laborers, customarily the preserve of men. Nevertheless, all of the Petigrus depended on slave labor and needed to direct it to their own purposes. That was as true for women as it was for men.

CHAPTER NINE

Marrying for Love

Like her disastrous equivocation with Joe Pyatt two years earlier, Carey North's engagement to Charles Lockhart Pettigrew in 1853 startled her family. By then, she was twenty-four. Already her mother had begun warning her against the aridity of a spinster's life. Recalling a distant cousin who had never married, Jane drove home the point that "an old maid helpless looking" was inevitably "rather a sight." She quoted Dr. Johnson that "an ill assorted marriage is better—tho' that is to be deprecated too."[1] But reflection on the ill-assorted marriages of her cousins Caroline Carson and Sue King had taught Carey to ward off the beaux who offered wealth and luxury but little emotional fulfillment. In doing so, she had dismayed her aunts. Now, in accepting Charles, she baffled them. He was, in their eyes, little more than a somewhat overage and minimally distinguished cousin from far-off coastal North Carolina.

Nevertheless, there was a promising context for Carey's choice. Back in 1844, Charles had interrupted a business trip with a brief stopover in Charleston to meet James Petigru and several other descendants of his grandfather's brother. The next year, on another brief visit, he had met Jane North and two of her daughters, who were staying in Charleston with relatives. Over the next several years, he had corresponded with Jane, who was almost sixteen years his senior. By 1850, however, his attention focused on her oldest daughter, now twenty-one and twelve years his junior. He was so attracted to Carey that he prolonged his stay in the city that year. Although he seemed to Jane much "graver and older," he still displayed the "vigourous understanding and strong principles" she so admired.[2] Further-more, he was a graduate of the University of North Carolina, the grandson of an Episcopal bishop, the son of a former congressman, and, since 1848, the master of Bonarva, oldest of the Pettigrew plantations in North Carolina's Washington and Tyrrell Counties.

The casual interchange between the learned young belle and her approving older cousin allowed Carey and Charles unusual freedom from the common imperatives of a belle-beau relationship. During Charles's three weeks in Charleston in 1850, each discovered the other's fondness for music, which became first a playground for whimsy and later a vehicle for more serious ploys. After Charles went home, Carey teasingly urged him to return to hear the famous soprano Theresa Parodi, and Charles protested that Parodi would be a "small . . . motive for my visit when there is so weighty a one in the back ground." Then, only half in jest, he added that he hoped Carey would take an agricultural "interest in corn"—Bonarva's chief crop—as well as the cotton and rice her South Carolina kin grew.[3]

Thus they jousted and bantered back and forth, each chastising the other for neglecting to write more frequently. By 1852, Charles realized that letters would not carry him much further, so he planned the trip on which he and his sister Mary Blount joined Tom Petigru and his family and Carey in Montreal and traveled with them for the next three weeks. Even then, Carey assured her sister Minnie that Charles was a good friend but not "a favorite" and that to keep it that way she was "strictly *uncoquettish*, behaving extremely well." A short month later, she praised Charles to her mother as the "most amiable man, & most devoted brother" she had ever known, "rather prosy" but with "good qualities" that made up for his defects.[4]

That Christmas, Charles arrived at Badwell to spend the holidays. When he left shortly after New Year's, he regretted that in the excitement of his stay he had said less than he meant to say. But he had at least proposed, and Carey, although she had not accepted, had not refused him. Then, a month later, on February 1, she capitulated. "I have no objection," she wrote him, "to your telling your brother William the circumstances relating to yourself which at Badwell I was opposed to your doing, you have my entire permission."[5] Thus did Carey North and Charles Pettigrew become engaged.

Their wedding, on April 19, 1853, united not just Charles and Carey but also the North Carolina Pettigrews and the South Carolina Petigrus. With Charles's sisters Mary Blount and Annie and his brother Johnston members of the wedding party, their brother William rejoiced that, "excepting a few (two or three), the entire family connection was present, making a display of numbers that quite surprised" him. After the ceremony at St. Michael's

Church, they all traipsed uptown to Tom and Ann Petigru's house for a "collation" and then at 2:30 hurried down to the wharf to see the bridal pair set off for North Carolina with Minnie and Mary Blount, who would travel with them on their wedding trip.[6]

After these four had left, the bride's mother walked with her sisters Louise Porcher, Adèle Allston, and Harriette Lesesne across town to Harriette's house, where they drank several cups of tea, and then they went on to Louise's to spend a quiet but "not a dull" evening together. Her sisters praised the "womanly dignity" Jane had shown that day. And why should she not? For nearly five years, she had planned for that event in vain. Now Jane thanked God, who had "so blessed" her orphan daughter with a spouse who made Carey "really happy." She pronounced herself content, but the mother of the bride was not fully happy. As Robert Allston sized it up, Carey's marriage was like a "tooth drawer," its pain not fully relieved by the satisfaction that one of her daughters bore the Pettigrew name.[7]

The journey to Carey's new home at Bonarva was a letdown. The boat trip to Wilmington and the railroad connection to Goldsboro were comfortable enough, but the continuation was almost disastrous. Their hired carriage broke down just outside of Goldsboro, and the only substitute Charles could find was "a sort of bread cart concern," in which the bride, groom, and two bridesmaids jolted through the night until they reached Raleigh at dawn.[8] But once they were there, Charles's aunt, uncle, cousins, and grandmother welcomed Carey as warmly as the Petigrus had welcomed the Pettigrews.

Carey and Charles remained in Raleigh for five days before they went on to Bonarva, where at last the couple finally found themselves alone and free to explore the intimacy of marriage. But brother William was perplexed by the newly married couple's preference for lonely isolation over the company of kin. He was "unable to perceive the necessity of this," although he grudgingly yielded "to what does not meet my approbation, as all cannot view things in a similar light."[9]

Only three weeks after their arrival at Bonarva, Carey and Charles left on their European wedding trip, of which William also disapproved. To modern eyes, inviting Mary Blount and Minnie to travel with them on their honeymoon is perplexing. But in the nineteenth century, it was common for a few friends or relatives to accompany the bride. So it was as a party of four that they boarded the steamer *Pacific* in New York on May 18.

The crossing to England outdid the "bread cart" adventure. Only Minnie escaped the thorough "cleansing of the stomach" William had predicted. But as soon as they landed and headed south through country made familiar by the novels and histories they had all read since childhood, they became enthusiastic tourists. In London, they marveled at the crown jewels and enjoyed the box at the opera, from which they saw Queen Victoria, a "little ugly, common looking woman with a red face," and were charmed by her "handsome" prince consort. Then, after only a week, they set off for Paris. They thrilled to its exotic atmosphere, shopped enthusiastically for clothes, praised French cooking, which killed any taste for "bacon and Hominy," and, except for Charles, felt quite comfortable—if not quite Parisian—in their command of French. At Versailles, although the treasures on display "beggar[ed] all description," Carey was American enough to damn the palace and its grounds for their absurd pretentiousness, especially the Grandes Eaux, which she found "very ridiculous to a plain republican."[10]

Before long, however, the fast pace of travel, the expenses incurred beyond Charles's estimates, their growing nostalgia for home, and Carey's bad back contributed to tourist surfeit. Nonetheless, after a stay at Baden-Baden that cured Carey, the party made a swift tour of northern Italy from Genoa to Venice. In August they returned to Paris for a final two months of shopping and sightseeing. It was a sad denouement to an overly long honeymoon. Only Minnie and Mary Blount could take advantage of the American consul's offer to show them the Paris he knew well, while Carey, in the early stages of pregnancy, was cooped up in her hotel room and Charles, fretting that they had already spent too much money, busied himself with arrangements for packing and shipping their too many acquisitions. Getting home was little better. Seasickness confined Carey to her cabin for all but the last two days. Getting through customs in New York was an interminable hassle. On the train to Baltimore, their luggage was looted of all the wonderful silver and jewelry Carey had bought. And the new house ordered to be ready on their return to Bonarva was not even begun. Although she tried to put the best face on it all, Carey spilled out the full extent of her desperation to her mother: "Now[,] beloved Mamma, pray come to me *as soon as* you possibly can[.] I am crazy to see you, & I *want you* Oh! so much!"[11]

Nonetheless, it was now incumbent on Carey to carve out her new life among "new friends and new scenes" and to make Bonarva a pleasant refuge for all Petigrus and Pettigrews. Mary Blount and Annie came for extended visits. William made frequent calls from his Magnolia plantation. And then there was Johnston. His close intimacy with Carey had ended even before they became sister- and brother-in-law. After her marriage, her tone toward him changed markedly. Gradually she became more distant, advising him as an older woman guiding a younger man rather than as an intimate of the same age.

Simultaneously, any distance the twelve-year age difference between Charles and Carey had first imposed diminished as their emotional bonding strengthened. Their initial compatibility flourished with the willingness of each to adapt to the other. Their letters became more openly affectionate. During their first separation, in the summer of 1854, Carey missed Charles dreadfully. But after writing seriously that if he could "think of anything dearer or nearer than a wife[,] let me be that to thee," she almost laughed at herself for having written "a real *love letter*." Charles, although less given to humor, showed no less warmth, addressing his letters to his "dearest darling" and closing them as her "most attached and devoted husband."[12]

Most of the time, however, they were together at Bonarva. It was there, aided by her mother and her two sisters, that she bore her first child, Charles Louis Pettigrew, on April 5, 1854. His grandmother and aunts stayed on for a month as the new mother spent two weeks recovering in her chamber and another two confined to the house. Even after Lou and her mother returned to Badwell, Minnie stayed on to help Carey care for "Toodles." It was not until early June that Charles took the exhausted mother and the sickly baby to stay with the South Carolina relatives.

Not having seen her since her wedding more than a year ago, her Charleston kin scrutinized both mother and child. Louise Porcher bubbled happily that this niece, in marked contrast to Caroline Carson and Sue King, was "all that one could desire in a young wife," fully prepared "to do her duty in that state of life it has pleased God to place her." She had, as Charles also maintained, calmed down and "become a great deal more quiet" since her marriage. Still, Carey's physical capacity to care for her baby raised auntly doubts. Judging "from present appearances," Louise questioned whether "nursing will agree with her & if the quality of the nourishment is of the best."[13]

Although she was "thin, & pale, & worn looking," Carey proved to be a strong mother. With a single exception, she nursed all of her children, six of whom were born during her first nine years of marriage. At the same time, she proved to be a cheerfully competent plantation mistress at Bonarva. The challenges there were great. Except for the Collinses at nearby Somerset Place, the Pettigrews had few planter neighbors. Surrounded by swampland, Bonarva fronted on Lake Phelps, from which a canal connected it to Albemarle Sound. But even by water, access to the outside world was difficult. Luckily Carey, long familiar with rural isolation at Badwell, was content that "those who live together should sometimes *be alone* with themselves."[14]

She graciously entertained the many visitors who came for stays of varying lengths. But unlike Carey's sisters and sisters-in-law, who were always welcome, the virtual strangers who invited themselves and arrived on very short notice did try her patience. Nonetheless, traditional hospitality demanded that she accommodate the Edenton clergyman and his two daughters who asked to spend the 1855 Christmas holidays at Bonarva with no thought to the fact that their hostess was nursing a six-week-old baby, that her house was already filled with family, and that her winter supplies had not yet arrived from Norfolk. But Carey managed to joke about housing these additional guests, regretting only the lack of a "condensing machine" to press everybody into the available space. Furthermore, Carey was almost constantly either pregnant or nursing in these years, and Minnie could "only wonder" at her sister's "cheerful hospitality" when she was obviously "so far from *fitted* for it."[15]

Neighborly visits, anticipated or not, were easier to handle and usually gave pleasure. William always felt free to drop in. Even more frequently, Carey or Mary Collins would walk the short lakeside path between their houses to spend a few hours with the other. When either of them had houseguests, they commonly invited each other and more distant neighbors to their formal gatherings. At the first dinner party Carey attended at the Collinses' home, she took note of the local customs and preferences to prepare herself for similar occasions. In December 1854 she gave her first dinner party. Mullins, the butler, assisted by Grace, served the four-course dinner that Carey had planned and Caroline, the cook, had prepared. After the first course of soup and boiled beef came boiled chicken and a ham surrounded by vegetables and rice. That was followed by a boned turkey, wild duck, and sweet potatoes. After the dessert of pudding and stewed prunes, coffee was served.

To produce such a feast required considerable effort and ingenuity on the part of both servants and mistress. Staples like salt and sugar had to be ordered from Norfolk. Specialties, like the sausage and cheese Minnie once sent up from Charleston, might spoil en route. But Bonarva's own resources generally furnished a varied and satisfying menu. Game and fish were abundant locally. Poultry, beef, and pork fattened in the plantation's barnyard, and its fields produced the corn and sweet potatoes that were staples in the diet of master and slave alike. Carey, following her mother's example, planted an extensive kitchen garden that provided fresh vegetables throughout much of the year. By June, she could count on having Irish potatoes, beets, peas, beans, carrots, and artichokes. Some kind of fruit was available throughout the summer as peaches and pears followed the early strawberries. In the fall, Carey's supplies were so ample that she once sent her Collins neighbors a large mess of cranberries and nine bunches of celery, an act of generosity reciprocated with specialties grown at Somerset Place.

Like the experience of her aunts and older cousins, Carey's inevitable "servant problems" provided greater challenges to her ingenuity than did supplying her household with food. Ellen, the personal maid her mother had given her when she married, presented the first test. When, in the summer of 1854, she accompanied Carey to Badwell, she immediately confided to her mother, who in turn told her mistress, who then passed the news to her daughter, that Ellen was "in a 'situation.' " Carey already suspected that Ellen might be pregnant.[16] But ostrichlike, she had tried to ignore it. Now she was indignant that Ellen and Edmond, the Bonarva field hand with whom Ellen was in love, had not asked permission to marry before she left Bonarva.

Not quite sure what she should do, Carey sought clarification from Ellen's mother, who assured her that Charles had consented to Edmond's marrying Ellen and that she was therefore "as good as his wife."[17] In the end, Carey had to accept the facts as they were, although she still disapproved. She told Ellen that since she was apparently married, she must henceforth act like a proper wife. But in the back of her mind, she still thought that Ellen had deliberately deceived her and that she had been too lenient.

Although Carey's conscious dismay stemmed from her disapproval of sexual mores not her own, beneath it lay the personal inconvenience Ellen's pregnancy caused her. When her mistress returned to Bonarva in the fall, Ellen was too close to term to travel, so the baby was born in late October at Badwell. Minnie tried to console Carey, predicting that the newborn boy would eventually "make a famous valet" for little Charley Pettigrew, who was just six months older than the slave child.[18]

Ellen did not return to Bonarva until the following February. She was sent down to Charleston in January, where she waited for some reliable man who was headed for North Carolina and would see that she got home. For several weeks, she lived in the Lesesnes' yard. It was, therefore, from Ellen, when she finally arrived home, that Carey learned that Aunt Harriette was in "an 'interesting' & promising 'situation.' " The grapevine that carried this information was part of the black network that linked the North and South Carolina Petigru households. Through it, Badwell carpenter Jim learned in July 1854 that Jane North planned to send him to Bonarva with Carey when she left in the fall, causing Carey to ask, "How do things get out?" But she already knew the answer: "Servants I suppose." She recalled that her mother had recently "heard Rose giving an account in the kitchen of the contents of a letter received" from Bonarva, to which the servant added "her own comments, (rather displeasing ones too)." It was, she concluded, a lesson she had "laid up to remember & *act* upon."[19]

Similarly, Bonarva's slaves' response to her well-intentioned effort to organize a Sunday school perplexed her. They sang the hymns with gusto, but Carey suspected that their enthusiasm reflected secular pleasure far more than religious uplift. And however much she wanted to believe that her servants were trustworthy, her faith was unsettled when $50 disappeared from a locked desk. "How miserable" it was "to be forced to suspect those around one" of "picking & stealing"! Ignoring the inherent conflict between her expectations and servants' resentful responses, she heartily approved when three-year-old Charley rebuked his nursemaid for replying to his question in a "drawling indifferent" manner and ordered her to say instead "yes Master."[20]

During the first year of her marriage, Carey never questioned the financial stability and security of her new life. A month before their wedding, she had asked Charles's permission to turn over to her mother the modest capital that she, like her two sisters, had inherited from their grandfather North. He had consented at once to a proposal she deemed a "high compliment" to her future husband, conveying her absolute trust in him and her unspoken faith in his ability to support her and their children. But what, in fact, underlay his ability to do so? Before the marriage, Charles had probably said little about his debts, of which he kept poor records. Carey may have known that the $40,000 mortgage he had undertaken in 1846 to buy the land and slaves of a plantation adjacent to Bonarva was still outstanding. But because the capital was not due until 1861, his debt did not curb his proclivity to spend. Indeed, when he spent far more than he intended on the European honeymoon, he shifted the blame "to the capacity of inexperienced women for spending money."[21]

Carey, however, was no spendthrift. As soon as she began to realize the limitations of Charles's purse, she dug in her heels against unnecessary expenditures. A year after their marriage, when Charles announced that he intended to buy a group of slaves because they were a bargain, she spoke openly against his accumulating more debts. That same year, the destruction of crops in a violent June storm led her to call an abrupt halt to their plans for building a new house. If they were ever to replace the old house that Charles's grandfather had built before 1800, she realized she must become "a desperate stingy woman" for even "'screwing' does'nt express faintly the extremity I must practice!" So tightly did she pull in the reins that she urged her sisters to ask their Uncle Henry Lesesne, who was their trustee, to divide a sum of $1,200 that had been left to the sisters jointly. Less than two years into a marriage that she had believed would make having her own money unnecessary, Carey perceived that having even $400 of her own was "not to be sneezed at in tight times, or indeed at any time."[22] Uncle Henry, however, did not send the money, and Carey was forced to look to her husband. When the crops flourished the next summer, she naively rejoiced that they would soon be free of debt. By March 1856, however, Charles's financial plight was desperate. Not just his own mortgage but huge debts incurred in a disastrous speculation, undertaken with a partner whose avarice knew no bounds and who kept no written records, weighed upon him. Charles's own records showed that he had bound himself to S. S. Simons for about $40,000—fully as much as his mortgage. Even that much he thought he could cover. But when the full extent of his partner's wild scheme to engross all of the available land in the North Carolina low country came to light, he and several others who had cosigned notes found they had committed to obligations of at least $400,000 above and beyond all of Simons's liquid assets.

Before the national financial crisis of 1857 worsened Charles's situation, William offered to pledge all of his property as collateral for a loan if doing so would rescue his brother. But Charles, overconfident, declined the offer. Later, even if his brother had not changed his mind, the amount William could raise by mortgaging all of his assets would have availed little, for each of Simons's cosigners was in fact pledged to cover his entire debt. And Johnston, whose legal training allowed him to grasp the realities of Charles's situation early on, offered no help at all. Even so, Charles avoided complete disaster by finding buyers for some of Simons's many farms and plantations.

Throughout the 1850s, as their financial resources shrank, the Pettigrew family grew. Little Charley, who began life underweight and sickly, became strong and healthy during his first summer at Badwell, while Carey gained new confidence in her mothering skills. Still, as Charley's siblings arrived with great regularity, his mother would have had a much harder time without Mary Armstrong, an experienced and able nursery governess, who stayed with her for most of the next fifteen years. Engaged at first to look after Charley, Armstrong saw her charge expand in November 1855 with the birth of Jane North, a large, healthy infant christened for her grandmother North. Once again, Carey's mother and sisters were at Bonarva for the delivery. Soon Annie and Mary Blount Pettigrew arrived for prolonged visits. In addition, William came over from Magnolia twice weekly to check on mother and child.

Janey was not welcomed as warmly as Charley had been. Her Uncle

Nursery governess Mary Armstrong. Photograph.
Courtesy of Mrs. John H. Daniels for Mulberry Plantation.

Johnston Pettigrew openly acknowledged the child's deficiency when he congratulated his brother on being a father "for the second time" but could not "refrain from regretting" that the baby was a girl. Boys were "the thing for this world." Carey resented that "quite unnatural" preference, which even her mother and sisters shared. Sixteen months later, when the third child arrived and was christened for her great-aunt Ann Petigru, the family clung to the same "boy-ward" values and took little interest in the child.[23] Neither Jane nor Minnie North went up to Bonarva that time. And Lou, who did go, was not the mature married woman deemed appropriate to the occasion. So her cousin Caroline Carson, now a widow, came up to Bonarva with her. It was good she did so, for Carey, who was depressed by the Simons mess and unsettled by Charles's frequent absences on business, had a difficult delivery. Although she pulled through, the frightening experience was still with her when, in October 1858, only sixteen months after Annie's birth, she bore her second son, named for his recently deceased great-uncle Thomas Petigru. This time no female kin were on hand.

Her kinswomen now assumed that Carey was experienced enough to face such ordeals confidently. They were wrong. Although she remained in excellent health and had the competent Armstrong in constant attendance, she approached her fifth lying-in more fearful of the "perils of childbirth" than ever before. Fortunately, the delivery in February 1860 was far easier than Tom's. And for the first time, her usually dour brother-in-law William delighted that the child was a girl and that she was to be named Caroline for her "respected & beloved mother."[24]

When Caro was born, Charley was almost seven, Janey was five, Annie was nearly three, and Tom was barely sixteen months old. By this time, child rearing had become as challenging as childbearing. But with black nursery maids to assist Armstrong, Carey devoted much of her time to educating her older children. Praised by Ann Petigru for being "a Mother who really care[d] for her children," Carey had to ward off excessive attention from the aunts and uncles who would otherwise spoil them. Great-aunts and uncles were even more subversive of discipline. When the Pettigrews were at Badwell, Aunt Mary insisted that "any check to such a good child" as Charley was "dreadful & wld soon make him outrageous." Potentially as disruptive was great-uncle James's unstinted adoration of four-year-old Janey, in whom he already saw a future "belle and . . . beauty," as "comely and clever" as her mother.[25]

Generally, Carey's firm restraining hand won family approval, even though Henry Lesesne for a while actually believed Johnston's jest that it was Carey's "custom to walk into the nursery every morning & whip all the children good or bad." In fact, she very much followed her mother's gentle practices. But although remembering her own rearing made bringing up her girls comparatively easy, she was uncertain about rearing her boys. Enough of the Petigru men were poor models of manly behavior to make her rely more on prevailing moral and religious teachings than on her own observations. After Bishop Thomas Atkinson preached a sermon at the Episcopal church near

Bonarva "on the training of children especially boys, drawing his moral from late accounts of depraved vicious conduct," she prayed that she and Charles might, "with the Blessing of God, . . . bring up our boys, so that as men they will never play out fast & loose with sin." Convinced that "early training, *nursery* training," was essential to forestall their sowing "wild oats" later on, she struggled to rein in the boys, while she worked hard to draw out her daughters.[26]

As important as their education was maintaining the children's health. Family members' apprehensions about the swampy low country around them were shaped by the early deaths of Charles's four older brothers. By contrast, upcountry South Carolina seemed a health resort. Charles, therefore, ignored his financial difficulties and bought, in December 1856, a summer place near Badwell. Whatever its anticipated health benefits, his decision to pay $15,000 for Cherry Hill seemed imprudent. The house itself was nearly in shambles. Its eight spacious rooms and the eleven-foot-wide central hall desperately needed repair. Vandalism and neglect had brought the plaster down, destroyed the interior ornamental work, and left the surrounding grounds thoroughly overgrown. Nonetheless, Charles was so swept away by the remnants of past grandeur that, romantically quixotic as usual, he bought Cherry Hill as a present for Carey without telling her anything until his plans were complete.

From the start, the burdens it imposed pressed hard. In the very first year, Charles had to ask Johnston's help to make his mortgage payment. Luckily, this time Johnston responded positively, first by making him a small loan and then by buying a one-third interest in Cherry Hill for the entire $12,000 Charles still owed on the mortgage. He expected that his "investment must commence paying," but because Charles refused to spare hands from Bonarva to cultivate Cherry Hill, it never produced significant income.[27] Indeed he strove only to make the place self-sustaining. Probably his brother had known all along that it would be so. Probably, too, he knew that the $20,000 he lent Charles was an equally hazardous investment. As William Pettigrew calculated it, Charles's debt to non—family members then came to $108,000 (over $1 million in 1990s dollars). Johnston's subsidy for Cherry Hill and his loan only reduced that debt to a size that, at best, William believed Charles might someday be able to repay. But neither brother was at all sure that Charles had the managerial skills or the self-restraint to do so.

Even before Johnston came to his rescue, a new menace appeared. In the spring of 1857, an ominous sore developed on Charles's face. Apparently very healthy until then, he had been bothered only minimally by frequent sores in his mouth. But the large blotch that now appeared under his right eye was so

THE RISE OF THE PETIGRUS

painful that he hurried off to consult a Baltimore physician. The prolonged and rigorous treatment the doctor prescribed made Carey "very, very anxious."[28] But a strict diet and strong medicine seemed to improve the situation once Charles returned home. The improvement, however, was short-lived.

Six months later, the sore flared up again. This time Charles sought treatment from Philadelphia's prestigious doctors. But neither Pennsylvania physicians nor a course of treatment at Virginia's alum springs in the summer of 1858 stemmed the cancer's growth or alleviated the pain. Desperate for relief, the next spring Charles began consulting physicians in New York, where he lived for months at a time during the next two years trying one treatment after another.

His extended absences from Bonarva contributed to marked changes in the Pettigrews' marriage. Their initial relationship, cemented by romantic love and enshrined within prevailing patterns of patriarchy and male dominance, matured into loving friendship between nearly equal partners. A transition common in good marriages, this shift also reflected the transfer of plantation management that Charles's absences required. For three consecutive years, he was away during spring planting. Each time, of course, he gave extensive instructions to his white overseer. But he also encouraged Carey to take an active role in plantation oversight. At first he urged her only to "seem to take notice and at least approve if any thing is particularly well done." Soon "the people" were "reporting" to her, attaching "a certain grave importance to [her] being informed." Charles responded to her reports of specific problems with relevant observations and suggestions as he grew increasingly satisfied with her "ability to take charge." By April 1859, he had such confidence in her management that he predicted he would feel free to remain in New York, where he could attend "to the finances" while Carey carried on the "agricultural part of the business." His pride in his wife's managerial accomplishments made him sure that he could do no better than to leave Bonarva in her hands.[29]

By 1858, moreover, she had learned almost as much about his debts as he knew, for he assured her that in case of his death she would discover "no concealments" to astonish her. But it was not easy to endure the constant stinting that Charles's apparent inability to order his finances demanded. Sometimes Carey thought of what might have been. Once, much to Charles's chagrin, she even contrasted her wardrobe with those of the wives of her erstwhile suitors. Charles could say only that "what has been done cannot now be helped." Her only option was "to make the best of a hard bargain," and mostly Carey did.[30]

But she never quite gave up dreaming of the luxury she had anticipated as a plantation mistress. Despite their debts, in 1859 she spent a $300 windfall court settlement to buy a communion service for the Pettigrew chapel of ease, commission a portrait of her mother, and purchase some silver serving pieces for Bonarva. Surely that was understandable. Perhaps doing so helped her endure Charles's long stays in New York. Of course she missed him. Sometimes she openly resented being at Bonarva without him. Occasionally she intimated that he might be staying away longer than necessary. And Charles, who sensed that Carey's loneliness and her complaints about deprivations were connected, reminded her that his medical treatments were "a duty I owe to you, to my children[,] to my creditors, and to the character of my family."[31]

Charles was less quick to perceive Carey's growing jealousy. Alone in New York with little to occupy his time other than his treatments, Charles began to see a good deal of Caroline Carson. Only thirty-six in 1856 when William Carson died, she was beautiful, charming, and four years younger than Charles. Although allegedly she too was in New York for medical treatments, she lived the life of a very merry widow among the city's most glittering social circles. Like most of her kin, Carey bitterly condemned her cousin's life of unlimited pleasure at others' expense. She also suspected that Caroline was setting a snare to entrap Charles and his purse in her web of social folly. Charles's unabashed praise for Caroline's beautifully furnished Washington Square apartment, which he visited regularly, fed those suspicions. So did his reports of Caroline's repeated invitations to escort her on social outings and her campaign to spruce up his dowdy appearance. When she pressed him for a substantial loan, even though he refused firmly, she raised Carey's apprehensions to a peak. All of this Charles naively related in letters home. Carey fumed that her cousin's plan to make Charles "escort her where ever & whenever she wishes" was "simply ridiculous." To expect him to tag about "as a make weight to her respectability" was unreasonable. Her association with New Yorkers who were totally lacking "virtue or principle" was disgraceful. Rather than keeping such company, Charles should remember that he had left his "wife & little children" not for pleasure but to find a cure for the cancer that threatened his right eye. "I know my dear Charles you understand me, I have perfect faith in yr not doing anything against yr principles, but those people are corrupt & in with them you must allow many things wh if no great worry, wld scarcely have yr cool approval, & lead the way to others." Her assurance that she was "not in a panic" hardly rang true. Nor was it enhanced by Charles's next letter, which rehearsed a recent conversation with Caroline. "Really," he had said to her, "there is no other

THE RISE OF THE PETIGRUS

place worth living at in America but New York," to which she had replied, "I *entirely agree* with you Charles, but it takes a quantity of money."[32]

Shortly after she received that letter, Carey bundled up little Tom and headed for New York. There she stayed with Charles. There she conceived her fifth child. While she was there, Charles's cancer seemed to go into remission, and in August they returned home together, full of hope that he was cured. By November, however, lesions again threatened his eye. At first he returned to New York only briefly, but by January 1860, he had begun another prolonged course of treatment, leaving Carey eight months pregnant at Bonarva. Once again she was frightened. What did Charles's cancer portend for her future? What did his extended absences portend for their marriage? Already her Charleston aunts suspected "unhappiness" between them resembling the tensions that had wrecked the King and Carson marriages.[33] Charles too worried about their marriage, but from a very different perspective. Would his growing disfigurement destroy Carey's affection for him? He seems not, however, to have considered the effect of his continued association with Caroline Carson. All of this spurred Carey to take her two-month-old baby and go once again to New York.

She never made that trip. On Easter Sunday 1860, the old house at Bonarva burned to the ground. Carey then had little choice but to accept William's invitation to bring her five children and her domestic servants to his spacious house at Magnolia. There they lived for the next year while the house she had long dreamed of was finally built. In the interval, family ties were further cemented as William's hospitality almost overwhelmed her. They became "the best of friends." He deferred to her "about the house almost too much," telling his servants to consider her "their mistress."[34]

As Carey captivated the last of the Pettigrew brothers, friction between him and Charles over financial affairs largely vanished. Nevertheless, Charles's precarious finances, like his entrenched cancer, left Carey teetering on the brink of disaster.

CHAPTER TEN

Reflecting Power and Wealth

No Petigru sister had looked forward to a more glowing future on her wedding day than had Adèle. Robert Allston was a driver, rigidly self-controlled, and governed by a Puritanical work ethic. Through inheritance, trusteeship, exchange, and purchase, he steadily expanded his estates from the 922-acre Chicora Wood he had inherited as a child. By 1860, he was cultivating five separate rice plantations and directing a labor force of 600 slaves, four times the number he had owned thirty years earlier. In that peak year, his agricultural empire generated an income of over $45,000—nearly half a million in 1990s dollars.

Allston's accumulation of great wealth paralleled his accession to high political office. In 1850 he became president of the South Carolina senate, in which he had served since 1833. Six years later, the legislature elected him governor of the state. Thereupon he spent $38,000 for a Charleston mansion, thought by many to be the finest house in the city. In keeping with their new position, his wife and daughters rode in one of two handsome carriages drawn by a matched pair of imposing grays. And both family and guests were edified by his growing "gallery of paintings," most of which portrayed religious themes.

Such splendor cost Allston dearly. In the boom times of the 1850s, borrowing $250,000 to finance those purchases of land, slaves, and the Meeting Street house seemed reasonable. But by 1859, awareness that his mounting debts had caught up to his ability to carry them began to dampen his euphoria. At the same time as he contracted a debt of $58,000 to buy

Chicora Wood, the Allston plantation. William H. Pease photograph, 1996.

Pipedown from his sister-in-law Ann Petigru, he warned Adèle with good reason to be careful about money. "Pray dont either yourself, or suffer the children to acquire habits [of] cockney luxury. They are in danger of it."[1] Even James Petigru, whose own income never quite covered his family's extravagances, saw danger ahead for his brother-in-law.

As mounting financial woes subverted the Allstons' apparent prosperity, tensions between them gnawed at the solidity of their marriage. In the early days, Adèle had largely stifled the irritation produced by Robert's never-ending barrage of instructions about what she was to do, when she was to do it, and how she was to do it. When he was in Columbia for legislative sessions or participating in one of the Episcopal church conventions to which he was frequently a lay delegate, his letters poured forth a series of minute directions. Adèle followed them without protest. She ordered the annual hog slaughter at exactly the time he set, rewarded rice threshers with extra rations at his specific behest, instructed the servants about the special measures he advised to keep the turkeys away from the cows.

In the beginning, she expressed her displeasure only by writing less frequently and less fully than he expected her to do. But as her familiarity with plantation affairs increased, she gradually gained the self-confidence to act on her own in Robert's absence. By the late 1840s, Robert himself acknowledged her growing proficiency. The instructions about household

Robert F. W. Allston at age fifty. George Flagg portrait reproduced in
Elizabeth Waties Allston Pringle, *Chronicles of Chicora Wood*
(New York: Charles Scribner's Sons, 1922).

and plantation management became mutual. He trusted her to give directions to Jesse Belflowers, his longtime overseer. And she sent lists of supplies
for him to buy in Charleston.

As Robert came to recognize Adèle's competence in plantation matters,
he increasingly took her into his confidence about political issues. His
letters from Columbia became as full of legislative tactics as of the capital's
social life. They often spelled out the alternatives he faced, first as a senator
and then as the senate president, and invited her comments. Doubtless

aglow with his own liberality, he once "advanced the opinion," in a parlor discussion with his political colleagues, "that the influence of woman was greater in a Republic than elsewhere."[2] Thus far had the great rice planter and politician tempered his understanding of patriarchy.

Their new pattern of mutual responsibility allowed Adèle to participate increasingly in making business decisions. Robert consulted her when he contemplated selling Nightingale Hall plantation. He left the purchase of the Charleston house largely in her hands. When he was away during the critical planting season, he depended on her to receive and respond to Belflowers's reports. But he never surrendered his ultimate authority over his estates or his family. Nor could he ever bring himself to refrain altogether from giving those hateful detailed instructions that so riled Adèle. Once he concluded a letter to her by noting that he had not made a single mention of "Plantation affairs" only to add a reminder to make sure the overseer did not mix new rice with old when he sent it to be milled. Underlying Adèle's surging anger was Robert's persistent condescension. Even when she was forty, he addressed her as "my dear child."[3]

After Robert became governor, the social responsibilities of an active politician's wife made substantial claims on Adèle's energies for the first time. During the 1856 legislative session, which elected him governor, she spent a week and a half in Columbia. For the next two years, she was frequently called on to join his official party at balls, galas, and receptions in both Charleston and Columbia. Jane North praised the governor for "the generosity he continually bestows upon his wife." She understood that he was proud of Adèle and wanted her "to be made part of a spectacle" and to "enjoy it."[4]

Because of her increased social activities and Robert's ever more frequent and extended absences during the years he served in Columbia, Adèle also gained a new measure of financial autonomy. When they were first married, her husband had doled out the exact sums he believed his wife would need to supply the household and then instructed her, in detail, just how each portion should be used. For almost nineteen years, Adèle chafed under such minute supervision. Only in 1851, after she exploded in exasperation because she had lacked enough spare cash to make a decent Thanksgiving contribution to a church charity, did he finally realize how awkward his system was. In sending her a draft for $50, he pledged that she should never again "be out of money. . . . It is good and it is right to have some money by you." But he added the implied admonition that she had "arrived at a mature age which may be counted on for not spending money for the mere sake of spending."[5]

None of this, however, erased Adèle's underlying resentment of Robert's

Adèle Petigru Allston at age forty. George Flagg portrait reproduced in
Elizabeth Waties Allston Pringle, *Chronicles of Chicora Wood*
(New York: Charles Scribner's Sons, 1922).

paternalistic bearing. She appreciated that her marriage to a wealthy man ten years her senior whose lineage far outshone hers gave her substantial advantages. As she had approached their ninth anniversary, she had admitted that she had much "to be devoutly grateful for." But in the privacy of her diary, she confessed that her heart remained "ungrateful and unimproved." Robert displayed no such ambivalence. As he reflected on their tenth anniversary, he wrote his wife, "The longer I live, the more necessary do I feel that you are to me." She was second only to God in his affections and the person with whom he could "commune most freely, with most satisfaction & purity, with the least selfishness." Occasionally Adèle responded with equal warmth, as she did after receiving one long-awaited letter: "I am sure dearest I ought to be a better woman after receiving such a letter. . . . I know that I am a happier one."[6]

But, in fact, she was never happy for long. After sixteen-year-old Ben left for West Point but while her other children were still at home, she confessed that her life lacked purpose. She could tell a longtime acquaintance "little of our daily life" because "one day passes so like another and our occupations are so small and trivial[,] consist so entirely of the little routine which makes up home life." And although she missed Robert when he was away, she often found life rather dull when he was at home. During the long summers the family spent on Pawleys Island, her husband made daily trips to one or another of his mainland plantations. Every Friday he went to his club, where, with other gentlemen, he enjoyed "the very best eatables and drinkables" available. When he entertained fellow planters at home, the dinner parties most often included only men. Adèle, meanwhile, was left to drift into "a very profound quiet," as she suffered "from weariness, and an indescribable longing for something," which she could not define even to herself.[7]

As a counterweight, Adèle invited her sisters and nieces to make long visits to both Chicora Wood and Pawleys Island. But entertaining visitors could not long allay the unease that became more and more evident as she approached forty. "I have all my life been intending to do a great deal, to read, to cultivate my mind, to be a wise woman. . . . I know not how it is," she sighed, "that always intending to do so much I have done so little." Such depression was worsened by Robert's moodiness. As she awaited his return home from a business trip in 1850, Adèle scarcely dared hope that her husband would arrive in good spirits, for "he always returns in a fretful peevish State." To that diary entry she added two more sentences: "Many persons are happier from home," and "All persons ought to strive to be most agreeable at home." Adèle too could be disagreeable. Two weeks later, she agonized over having "offended Mr Allston very seriously by uttering the impression that past things and circumstances made on my mind." She knew at the time that she was foolish to do so and lashed out at her own folly: "I will never learn wisdom. It could do no good. I ought to control my thoughts and let by gones be by gones."[8] In the reconciliation that followed, Adèle became pregnant.

In contrast to Robert, who was openly a jealous and passionate lover, Adèle remained mute about her husband's sexuality. It is likely that her many pregnancies reinforced an ambivalence common among nineteenth-century women. In any case, as she matured, a self-assertiveness that Robert resented grew. He prayed that they both might achieve "a subdued will." But when she openly defied his wishes by extending a spring visit to Charleston in 1854, his anger swept away his self-restraint. Sulking about her "occasional reserved, self-dependent manner" and her "hard words," he reviewed their marriage. Acknowledging that "in the sight of [his] creator" he had "come short of fulfilling the thousandth part of [his] duty," he nonetheless bitterly defended the devotion of all of his energies to the "wor[l]dly welfare" of his family. In response, "the very source and head of that family aver[red] that she regard[ed him] as unjust, 'insincere & illiberal' as imposing hard terms, and exacting unreasonably!"[9]

Neither spouse made a public show of the marital friction to which they both contributed. As his niece Carey North complained well before her own marriage, Robert believed that "woman's legitimate sphere," her "proper and most useful duty," was "nursing babies." Adèle, at the end of her childbearing years, chafed at the limitations such values imposed. She conceded that Robert could be kind, but only "according to [his] notion of things" and when she submitted to "the imposition of [his] Will." Her husband utterly rejected that charge: "When you suppose . . . that I am about subjecting you to my arbitrary Will, you prepare at once to resist the imagined tyranny— 'Wont be Scared' & wont listen or heed any reason I can offer." He had, of course, exercised his own "judgement & firmness in the management of affairs." But "in respect to our domestic affairs and those things pertaining to your department particularly I have for years past exercised no 'Will.' " He ended by promising henceforth not to exercise any will at all in "every matter of domestic arrangements & of household servants."[10]

Nonetheless, four months later, Robert again exerted his will over the domestic arrangements he had pledged to leave alone. From Philadelphia, he wrote Adèle prescribing what she should drink at dinner, instructing her to make sure that his valet Stephen always accompanied their eight-year-old son when he rode his horse, and describing exactly how she should have her piano shipped from Pawleys Island to Chicora Wood. The letter reduced Adèle to despair. She had once hoped, she wrote her sister Louise Porcher, that as her children grew up their influence would "sooth and molify" her spouse's "naturally defective temper." But now she had "no hope of ever seeing Mr A come out of the narrow bounds he has placed for himself. He has not suavity or evenness of temperament enough to allow it." Still, her only recourse was to do her "duty in the station in life in which it [had] pleased God to place" her.[11]

Unable to change her husband's ways significantly, Adèle exhorted her children to master the "virtue and piety" that would make them "cheerful and content."[12] But during Ben's years at West Point from 1849 to 1853, her tutelage made him no more content than Robert's made her. The eldest son and the only one from the time he was six until Charley was born nine years later, Ben had been looked up to by his sisters and flattered by his many female cousins. Especially after little Robert died, Adèle had coddled Ben, even allowing him to sleep in her bed until, when he was ten, his father banned the practice.

As a result, Ben was ill-prepared for the inflexible military discipline he encountered at West Point. He undoubtedly would have preferred to study the classical curriculum that his mother and Uncle James had recommended and attend a liberal arts college. But his father was determined to send Ben to the academy, where he had received the scientific training that had served him well. Ben, with little interest in engineering and no desire to be a cadet, was so minimally motivated to study at West Point that he sank rapidly toward the bottom of his class as he also accumulated demerits for everything from minor infractions of dormitory rules to rank insubordination to officers.

Letters to Ben from his father were consistently cold. The tone of his mother's ranged from empathetic warmth to hot reprimands for his lack of "self command and self-denial." From his first to his last year, she urged him to meet standards that were far above his talents. When she challenged him to launch himself "on the stream of manhood . . . to battle and buffet with the waves of the great sea of life," Ben replied that he had no desire to ride "on the top of the billow." He would rather "float on the smooth surface of the ever calm, and tranquil wave, never agitated with the varying and ever shifting winds that blow over the Sea."[13]

In truth, Adèle really did not want her son to crest dangerous waves. She was devastated by Ben's choice of a three-year term of active duty in the West rather than a shorter term of less demanding service that also filled academy requirements for its graduates. Brother's warnings against "weak imaginations of impending evil" did little to lessen her suffering through three years of imaginary Indian attacks and desert thirsts.[14] Only when he came home did it cease.

Despite memories of her humble origins and austere childhood at Bad-well, which left her insecure about her own worth, Adèle found that prepar-ing her oldest daughter for the adult world was easier and more satisfying than sending Ben out into the world. Even so, nothing ever obliterated her sense of social inferiority. When the Allstons had visited Montreal in 1838 and were obliged to decline an invitation to the Countess of Durham's soiree, Adèle was sure she had missed "an opportunity we will never have again, of seeing how English people of consequence conduct themselves." But attending might have been even worse. "O that I had been educated, and could feel myself capable of maintaining a respectable station among edu-cated people."[15]

Similar anxieties plagued her at home. Occasionally even a family mem-ber would remind her that she had been born Adeline Pettigrew, had be-come Adelle Petigru when she entered Brother's Charleston circle, and had Frenchified her first name after her last had become Allston. Never did she forget that her standing in society derived not from birth but from marriage. When she was almost forty and attended the fabulous fete with which the richest planter on the Waccamaw celebrated his daughter's wedding, she contrasted it with the bareness of her own eighteen years earlier: "No fortune, ... few friends ... many faults." By 1850, however, she had learned to hide her own sense of inferiority from others. Even in the casual atmosphere of island living, Adèle avoided contact with long-established Georgetown planter families. By doing so, she intensified the loneliness and depression that, in turn, made her deplore her "insipid pliability," her "readiness" to yield to "circumstances," and her lack of "all grand and striking traits by which one asserts their superiority, and maintains a controlling influence."[16]

Determined to launch her daughter into a splendid marriage, she gave her all of the advantages she herself had lacked. In 1851, after she had resisted sending Della to school in Charleston, she suddenly gave in, mortified that she might have deprived her child of both educational and social advantages. How could she, who had "known a life long disappointment," inflict similar disappointments "knowingly upon another"? After the first school proved mediocre, she eagerly entered Della in Madame Acelie Togno's demanding new school, from which her daughter emerged with a certificate that James believed was fully the equivalent of a college diploma. Contrasting her graduation with his own from South Carolina College, he remembered that, as a poor upcountry youth, he had "straggled" out with nothing more than his diploma to commend him, whereas Della had "crossed the street" from Madame Togno's to enter the "palace" her parents owned on lower Meeting Street. Adèle had chosen that house, built in 1808 for Yankee merchant Nathaniel Russell, as a suitable mansion for the governor's family. But she valued it more highly as a grand base from which to launch Della into society. When Della quite willingly did "just what [her] mamma wanted her to do" to reign "supreme in belleship," her mother was "deeply gratified."[17]

Among Della's first and most persistent beaux was Pinckney Alston, scion of the one "l" Alstons, who Adèle believed looked down on the two "l" Allstons. But Pink was only one of the eager young men who sent Della bouquets, jostled each other to fill her dance programs, rode out with her in the afternoon, and called on her in the evening. When his courting grew serious, she refused him, albeit reluctantly, for he really was a favorite. She "regretted extremely to hurt him," but, like her cousin Carey, she would not accept a suitor she did not love. Pink, however, told Della that "he had known he would be unsuccessful" because he had been told that the Allstons "were opposed to him" from the first.[18] Other family entanglements made turning down Jimmy Simons even more uncomfortable. He proposed to her for the third and last time just a week after her brother had become engaged to his sister. Henrietta Simons, indignant at Della's refusal, which she perceived as an insult to her family, soon broke off her engagement to Ben Allston.

That breakup was yet another blow to his parents' plans for Ben's future. Although he had courted several young women, he was still unmarried at twenty-seven. His cousin Joseph Blyth Allston, who was exactly Ben's age, had, on the contrary, married at twenty-five. Yet Robert had been gravely displeased when Joe married Adèle's niece Minnie North. Minnie, even in her mother's eyes, was "shy and awkward," burdened with both "North indolence" and "Petigru idleness." Robert's opposition was not, however, a matter of frustrated aspirations for his nephew. He certainly "could have look'd upon" Minnie "as a dear daughter." Joe was the problem. As a boy, he had been a constant discipline problem both at home and at school. He smoked and drank. He read trashy novels and frequented "low company." As his Aunt Adèle put it, he might yearn to be "distinguished," but he was "unwilling to submit to the ordeal which alone could bring him worthy distinction."[19]

Unquestionably, Adèle's demands for proper deportment and intellectual rigor weighed on this orphaned nephew as heavily as they did on Ben. But during Carey North's stay with the Allstons in the summer of 1850, Joe surprised even his aunt. Carey, who was only five years his senior, managed

Adele Allston at age sixteen. Portrait, perhaps by John B. Irving, reproduced in
Elizabeth Waties Allston Pringle, *Chronicles of Chicora Wood*
(New York: Charles Scribner's Sons, 1922).

to get him to read significant literature and even convinced him to give up
smoking before he returned to South Carolina College in the fall. It was an
abrupt change of behavior, and Joe seemed to blossom in his final year at
college. After graduation, he went on to read law successfully with James
Petigru. All of this Joe attributed to Carey's influence, which led to his
feeling toward her as "a brother would feel towards a sister."[20]

Joe's attraction to Carey's sister Minnie was very different. Their Aunt Adèle, who early on sensed a romance, had discouraged it. Uncle Robert, who feared that his nephew might inherit his father's mental illness and who, in any case, opposed marriage between cousins, tried to block it outright. After Joe proposed to Minnie by letter in 1856, Robert insisted that he make the reasons for his uncle's opposition known to Minnie at once. He also demanded that Joe free Minnie from any commitment she might have made to him. Her Uncle James, however, had already told her something of Joe's misfortune, and Minnie had accepted his advice that it was her filial duty to break off the as yet unannounced engagement.

Nonetheless, within a year and despite persistent opposition, Joe again proposed and Minnie again accepted. That she did so without consulting her mother put Jane in a difficult position. At first she temporized, fearing that opposition would only strengthen the young people's determination. She conceded reluctantly that Joe's family connection was "a very good one." She acknowledged that the young people had known each other long enough and were old enough to "know their own minds." But the more she thought about it, the more anxious she became until everyone knew that she was "opposed to the engagement & much troubled on the subject."[21]

When Joe and Minnie remained resolute, most of their kin decided to make the best of a troubling situation. Some of them helped make the wedding, in December 1857, a success. Aunt Ann Petigru opened her Charleston house for a reception that Carey arranged, and Charles Pettigrew vowed to "break through ice" if necessary to get down to Charleston for the festivities.[22] Minnie's younger sister, Lou, struggled to overcome the stiff uneasiness she felt in the presence of Joe's prolonged silences. Their mutual cousin Ben, who was the best man, attended to the details necessary to make everything run smoothly. Only Robert's and Adèle's absence signaled the family's pervasive apprehension. They sent gracious but unconvincing excuses.

After the wedding, the disorder that would mark the newlyweds' lives together began. They almost missed the packet boat to New York because Minnie, ever dilatory, was still packing when the drayman pulled up to the door for her trunk. When the couple reached New York to embark for their honeymoon in Cuba, Joe could find no ship that would bring them back in time to reach Charleston for the January court session. So they simply stayed in New York shopping and sightseeing. Things improved when they returned to settle into their newly rented house and Minnie experienced the first signs of pregnancy. Almost exactly ten months after the wedding, Jane Louise Allston was born. She was named for Minnie's cousin Jancy Porcher, who had died in the same yellow fever epidemic that had almost killed Joe just before he became a father.

In January 1859 Minnie and Joe moved their baby and their belongings to Waverly, the plantation he had inherited from his father and that his Uncle Robert had managed up to that time. Robert had done so well that in 1857, with the labor of eighty-four slaves, Waverly had produced a rice crop of 300,000 pounds. The extraordinarily good price for which the crop sold convinced Joe to give up the law and become a full-time planter. Despite his total lack of agricultural experience, he naively thought he could manage as well as his uncle simply by asking his advice—although he did not necessarily follow it. He was so sure of himself that, ignoring Robert's warnings, he plunged recklessly into debt to buy more slaves and land.

His mother-in-law scorned Joe's "giving up law & taking to dig." Now more than ever she wished she could endow each of her daughters with capital sufficient to guarantee them comfortable futures. But lacking such funds, she looked to her sons-in-law to make her granddaughters "rather more than independent." Charles, she still hoped, might. But she had little faith that Joe would do so, even though in 1860 he harvested 450,000 pounds of rice. To buy the new hands that made that possible, he had just spent all of Minnie's modest inheritance from her grandfather North. When Jane arrived at Waverly for a spring visit that year, she was alarmed to find Joe looking "*wretchedly* sunburnt & sallow," although he seemed "strong as an overseer." The latter was grudging praise at best, for she feared it meant that he bid "fair to satisfy himself with that standard" and would likely be a poor overseer. By now, even Joe had to confess his inadequacies as a planter. He admitted that he knew nothing of "planting [and] carpentering" and almost as little about "the characters of the negroes." Even his bumper crop became an albatross, for the rice market collapsed as soon as Abraham Lincoln became president. And with a second daughter, Mary, born the previous November, Joe had "his hands full, heavy debts & nothing selling."[23]

For Minnie, the move to Waverly proved equally wretched. She had anticipated a pleasurable life as a plantation mistress. But like her Aunt Adèle almost thirty years before, she found herself lonely and isolated. When Janie was born in her Charleston home in 1858, relatives had surrounded her, eager to help and offer companionship. But for Mary's birth, Minnie had to leave home and return to Charleston to have the same support. When she came back to Waverly with her namesake, she brought a "white nurse" with her. As Ben observed, Minnie had less need of the nurse's skills and experience than of the comfort that "having a white face in the house with her" provided.[24]

Unhappily, the nurse's presence dispelled neither Minnie's unease at living amid so large a slave population nor the "ennui of 'protracted dullness'" that pervaded Waverly.[25] Even the mail came irregularly. And Joe's difficulties as a planter induced prolonged periods of silence that intensified her loneliness. Minnie had most certainly married a low country rice planter of large property and prestigious lineage, but she had gained thereby neither material comfort nor social pleasure. Like others of her kinswomen, she had embarked on a marriage that promised more than it delivered.

CHAPTER ELEVEN

Dealing with Public Issues

Whether the Petigru women lived in Charleston or in the country, they were never really isolated. Their reading made them aware of the world beyond. Local and national newspapers regularly brought news of foreign wars and national politics into their homes. English as well as American monthlies and quarterlies adorned their reading tables, supplementing the many books they read to relieve the boredom of plantation life and the ennui of the city. As children, they had all read narratives of ancient and modern Europe. As adults, most of them continued to read widely in British and western European literature and history, which made them more familiar with those cultures than with that of the American North. And they kept up to date. Those who bought the latest publications at Charleston bookshops regularly lent or recommended them to their country cousins.

Generally well informed, most of the Petigru women were prepared to follow public events and to draw their own conclusions. And they displayed no more unanimity than did their male kin. The nullification crisis, which dominated public life in South Carolina from the summer of 1830 until the spring of 1833, created partisan loyalties that sometimes pitted family members against one another. At issue were agricultural South Carolina's efforts to void federal tariffs designed to protect emerging Northern industry. James Petigru, a leader of the Unionist Party, denied that any state had the right to nullify a federal law. On the other side, Robert Allston energetically upheld a state's right to nullify burdensome federal tariffs. During the crisis, both James and his Unionist brother-in-law Philip Porcher served briefly in the state legislature. Robert, however, continued to serve in the legislature almost without interruption for twenty-eight years. Although armed warfare between state and nation was averted in March 1833 when Congress passed a lower tariff and South Carolina repealed its nullification ordinance, the crisis changed state politics permanently. Except for his election in 1836 to a second term in the state legislature and a seat on the city council, James Petigru never again won a popular election. Robert Allston never again lost one.

Despite the political gulf that continued to separate them, both men cultivated the cordial personal relations that predated their differences. Adèle, who was married in the midst of this political turmoil, mostly kept her own counsel, torn between her old allegiance to her brother and her new obligation to her husband. Even so, Louise Porcher could not keep from writing Adèle that nullification was "madness and wickedness," although she went on to warn her sister not to "show Mr Allston" that letter. But of all of the sisters, it was Jane North who, in the 1830s, followed state politics most closely. Even before her husband's death, Brother had kept her well informed about internecine Unionist squabbles. After it, his letters fairly bristled with public affairs. During the 1836 and 1837 legislative sessions, he vented his frustrations over a wide variety of state issues. After he left office, his letters to his sister ranged still more broadly, from patronage matters to fiscal policy. Jane, who shared her brother's Whiggish leanings, developed her own partisan assessments. She particularly damned the Democratic Party's pandering to popular opinion as "a wrong principle nay a bad one . . . the canker at the root of the whole matter." The "matter" addressed at that time was also a family affair—Robert Allston's stalled claims to the governorship.[1]

Jane's persistent attention to public affairs was unusual. During the years between the nullification crisis and the Mexican War, her sisters rarely commented on public issues. Indeed, it was not until 1848, when Mexico ceded 1 million square miles of its land to the United States in the Treaty of Guadalupe Hidalgo, that they again gave extensive attention to politics. From 1846 onward, heated debate over whether or not slavery should be banned from that territory nourished regional solidarity at the expense of party loyalty and had arcane repercussions within the Petigru connection. In 1848 only Robert Allston supported the Democratic nominee, Lewis Cass of Michigan. All of the rest opted for the Whig candidate, General Zachary Taylor, a Louisiana planter and the wartime hero of Buena Vista, although few really shared James's and Jane's Whiggish commitments. Sue King even ventured to advise her father-in-law: "My feelings, of course, go for Taylor, & would do so, were he a rank Democrat & avowedly so. It seems like sheer madness for Southern men to vote for Cass whose principles are openly against us, rather than for Taylor, of whom they can only say 'they don't know.' " Even if the old soldier "were to turn out an Abolitionist & make his slaves free the day he was inaugurated, he would only then be just equal to Cass."[2] As it turned out, he was perhaps even worse, for New York's anti-slavery senator, William Seward, quickly persuaded the politically inexperienced Taylor to support California's immediate admission to the Union as a free state.

Even before Taylor's plans were made public, Jane North dreaded his doing "all possible to excite the people on the subject of Slavery, a miserable subject," it seemed to her.[3] But heated debate had already done just that. On January 29, 1850, the dispute became still more rancorous when Senator Henry Clay of Kentucky proposed a compromise that would, among other things, admit California as a free state but leave the rest of the Mexican Cession open to slavery, protect slavery but eliminate the domestic slave trade in the District of Columbia, and strengthen the Fugitive Slave Law.

Like many Americans in both the North and the South, the Petigru women followed the extended Senate debate, whose major speeches they read in verbatim newspaper reports. For the first time, Carey North, then a young woman of twenty-two, was swept up in politics. She sympathized with her upcountry neighbor Senator John C. Calhoun, but she regretted the unconvincing and inferior quality of his speech, which was "not worthy of himself."[4] Sharing her mother's admiration of Henry Clay, she was disappointed at Calhoun's outright rejection of the compromise and disturbed by his prediction that the American Union would not survive its adoption. So she, like her mother and Uncle James, welcomed Yankee Daniel Webster's unambiguous support of the compromise.

In June, while the debate dragged on in Washington, opponents of the compromise from nine Southern states met in Nashville. Robert Allston was among the official delegates. No fire-eater, he opposed the immediate secession of the slave states that his fellow South Carolinian R. Barnwell Rhett urged on the convention. As a member of the more moderate majority, he supported a resolution to block the admission of California as a free state by extending to the Pacific the terms of the 1820 Missouri Compromise, which banned slavery north of the 36°30' parallel but left the territory south of it open to the peculiar institution. After they passed that resolution, the moderates declined to consider the other provisions of Clay's compromise until Congress had acted on them. At the time, Allston believed that, although the whole compromise package might possibly pass the Senate, the Northern majority in the House would do no more than vote to admit California as a free state and then reject all of the other measures. If that should happen, he predicted that "the House will be broken up in a general row, with perhaps bloodshed." Back home, Adèle had a somewhat different view of the matter. The Clay compromise, she wrote her husband shortly before he arrived in Nashville, could pass in neither house of Congress, so the convention should block Clay's treason to his section by forcing the extension of the 36°30' line to the Pacific. Thus, even before the delegates endorsed that very measure, she warned Robert that any tampering with "the Missourie compromise" would break Congress's "former pledge" to the South.[5]

Not quite a month after the Nashville Convention disbanded, President Taylor died. He was succeeded by Vice President Millard Fillmore. Southerners dreaded the possibility that this New Yorker might favor Northern interests even more than had Taylor. Louise Porcher predicted that Taylor's death would "hasten on that evil day of separation which looms portentous in the future." Although it was possible that God would "direct the good ship through the breakers," she prayed for no more than "sufficient public virtue & wisdom to construct an other [union] out of the wreck fit to be an arc of safety to us & our southern country." Even so, she foresaw a new war in Texas that would turn into a revolution whose leaders lacked the noble standards needed to re-create the "perfect government" that was now threatened by squabbling over territory shamefully seized from Mexico. "That iniquitous War for conquest," which had already destroyed "the spirit of the constitution," was "a crime for which we are going to reap the punishment."[6]

In the fall of 1850, that punishment was evaded. Although Clay's compromise package could not pass as a whole, it did pass bit by bit as Democratic Senator Stephen Douglas used his political skills to guide its separate parts through Congress. In the long run, however, the compromise only embittered South Carolinians, who increasingly divided between advocates of immediate secession and proponents of caution until broad Southern support for disunion was assured. Although surrounded by such deadly serious political discussion, Sue King reacted with her customary flip humor. On returning to Charleston from a visit to New York in December 1850, she found "'Crisis,' 'secession' & 'what will Georgia do' . . . the great staples of conversation," just as they had been when she left. She could only "laugh at the whole business—have not the slightest respect for the whole body of legislators." As she wrote her Aunt Adèle, her mother-in-law now envisaged a civil war with her son Gadsden "marching to battle, at the head of a troop of Columbia students." If only Sue could be made "Governor for a day or two!," she chortled; "with what delight I would have responded to the [students'] letters requesting 'arms & ammunition'—! There would instantly have been such an order for pop-guns & pluffers & poison berries & peas issued from 'Head Quarters.'" But, she concluded, humorless state officials had taken the students so seriously that they had allowed their "poor native State" once again to make "a Jack-donkey of herself."[7]

Sue, however, found little support for such lighthearted banter. When Carey North met the formidable Louisa Cheves McCord at the Virginia springs in the summer of 1851, she openly opposed the secessionist politics that South Carolina's preeminent bluestocking advocated. At first she had listened to her quietly. But when McCord demeaned those she scorned as submissionists and singled out James Petigru as particularly "queer" among them, Carey was not amused. She came to her uncle's defense and would not "give in." When McCord pressed her to say whether she shared his political persuasion, Carey affirmed that she was "staunch on the same side." Furthermore, she was proud that her Uncle Henry Lesesne had separated himself from other Southerners at Salt Sulphur Springs who openly snubbed President Fillmore when he was their fellow guest.[8] Like her Uncle James, Carey was both a Southerner and a loyal supporter of the American Union.

Undoubtedly Jane North, who deplored secession as a "madness . . . bequeathed by Mr Calhoun to his State," had shaped her daughter's opinions. But Carey proved that she was quite capable of assessing politicians and analyzing issues on her own when she visited Washington in 1851 and watched distinguished senators debate the American fisheries dispute with Great Britain. Because the fracas, although of principal interest to Yankees, had roused nationalist frenzy even in the South, Carey followed the speeches intently. At first Michigan senator Lewis Cass especially pleased her. Despite his Democratic politics and his unappealing "large, stout, coarse," red-faced, and puffy-eyed appearance, she found his remarks "strong & to the point." The next day, she was thrilled by Louisiana senator Pierre Soulé's speech. His "lively gestures, admirable management of voice and clear enunciation," and "fire and animation" were wonderful to watch. But she saw through them to a chauvinism she rejected. His contention that any American accommodation of foreign fishing vessels would be spineless surrender, like his denunciation of any "negociating under the British Cannon," convinced her that he had added "more mischief than truth" to the debate.[9]

But style was important, and Cass's "tame & tiresome" reply to Soulé disappointed her deeply. Much better was South Carolina's own Senator Andrew Butler, who effectively defused the oratorical bombast of the Louisiana senator. Carey almost burst with local pride. "How powerful is the sentiment which connects us with those who possess the same common interests, the same country or spot as home with ourselves." Her former prejudice against Butler for his long association with Calhoun melted under the strong "influence that the place or country, in particular one's home exercises over one's feelings."[10]

Carey's connection between place and political stance became even more marked after she married and moved to Bonarva. Her new "interest in foreign powers, ('the despots of Europe' à la Kossuth)" was "created & increased by . . . being a Planter's wife!" But in 1856 she discouraged Charles from accepting an invitation to run for Congress on the Know-Nothing ticket. Electioneering in the summer would exhaust him. Electoral victory would leave her alone at Bonarva with the children. So she was delighted when Charles, perhaps persuaded by the likelihood of a Democratic majority in his district, declined the nomination. Nonetheless, she followed public events with increasing attention. As she contemplated the future, she was sure that the country was headed straight for disunion. Charles's argument that Northerners "love[d] their dollars too much" to drive the South to secession simply did not convince her.[11]

Humanitarian concerns more than economic self-interest shaped Jane North's response to the Crimean War. To her, the misery of "our English Brethren in the Crimea" resembled the plight of "the suffering poor at the North." But Mary Petigru, who identified with neither starving Yankees nor English soldiers mowed down in the Charge of the Light Brigade, rallied "on the side of [Czar] Nicholas." Once again Carey measured foreign affairs against her identification with plantation interests. Any war in Europe would, she thought, inevitably threaten the exporting South with "utter ruin." Even her single-mindedness, however, had its limits. When it came to Italian liberation from foreign rule, she could not stifle her aesthetic passions. Her love of Italian literature triggered approval for Napoleon III's military support of Piedmont's campaign against Austrian rule over Lombardy. In fact, almost every family member enthusiastically supported Italian unification except Mary Anna Porcher, who was at that time traveling in Europe with friends who were "on the Austrian side."[12]

Perhaps because their interpretation of European events was largely shaped by their reading, the Petigrus were fascinated by foreigners who wrote about the United States. Several of them had enjoyed Fanny Kemble's *Journal* describing her travels in the United States in the mid-1830s. None approved of Frances Trollope's stinging indictment of American behavior in *The Domestic Manners of the Americans*. In later years, they discussed geologist Charles Lyell's blander descriptions of America in his *Second Visit to the United States* more dispassionately than they discussed either of those earlier commentaries. Still closer to home was Adèle Allston's response to Frederica Bremer's *Homes of the New World*. She had entertained the Swedish author when she toured several Pee Dee River plantations, and although she anticipated Bremer's attack on slavery, she had treated the distinguished visitor "without reserve." Her diary entry on the occasion reflects the defensiveness of a plantation mistress. She had shown Bremer "the condition of the negroes in all simplicity and truthfulness, not feeling that their condition is a reproach to us. They are well fed, well clothed and their great increase is proof that their government is lenient. Their labor not grievous."[13]

Although Bremer was at least impressed enough to write that slaves in the American South were treated better than those in Cuba, she predicted that emancipation was inevitable, even where slavery was relatively benign. Not surprisingly, therefore, the Honorable Amelia Matilda Murray's pronounced sympathy for the peculiar institution convinced Mary Petigru that Murray's *Letters from the United States* was more accurate, differing as it did from "Miss Bremers sentimentalism & folly, on the Slavery question." Murray's sound "judgement & candour" were borne out, Mary thought, by "how well she seems to understand the character of the negroes!" She "certainly does not describe them too favourably."[14]

The fate of their peculiar institution was the public issue that most troubled slaveowning Southerners. Throughout the 1850s, their politics focused ever more narrowly on its future and the destiny of their section as inflammatory rhetoric spawned physical violence elsewhere. In 1856 open warfare between slave- and free-state supporters led to mayhem on the Senate floor when Massachusetts senator Charles Sumner characterized proslavery violence in Kansas as rape and named South Carolina's Senator Andrew Butler as a perpetrator. Resenting both the sexual allusion and the political message, Butler's cousin, South Carolina congressman Preston Brooks, entered the Senate chamber two days later and beat Sumner into unconsciousness while several Southern senators looked on passively. He then resigned his seat, whereupon his constituents unanimously reelected him in a special by-election. Jane North had no sympathy with the hysteria that either Sumner's verbal attack or Brooks's physical response generated. That her state's representative was "to be a hero on one side & Sumner a martyr on the other" was contemptible enough. That the South Carolina legislature was at the same time debating a bill to reopen the international slave trade was still worse. On that, the whole family agreed as they rallied behind Johnston Pettigrew, whose resolutions opposing the trade cost him his seat in the next legislative election. Although the state never did legalize the trade, rumors of illegal landings of slave cargoes in remote Carolina inlets made Jane irate at the "ugly thing" that brought "out so much cupidity in the guise of humanity."[15]

Because every Petigru household relied on slave labor, the response to Northern attacks on the peculiar institution inevitably introduced private interests into discussions of public policy. But family members gave neither uniform nor unstinted allegiance to the institution. None so publicly upheld the right to challenge it as did James Petigru when he undertook the successful defense of an alleged Yankee abolitionist. Carey Pettigrew also felt free to criticize the institution. She challenged the premises of poet-planter William Grayson's "The Hireling and the Slave," which was, ironically, dedicated to his good friend James Petigru. In responding to his contention that Northern capitalists exploited their wage laborers unmercifully whereas Southern planters treated their happy slaves leniently, Carey doubted that "persons totally opposed" to slavery would be "convinced by his argument." Surely those who supported the institution must admit that the realities of plantation life subverted the poem's idyllic claims of slave-owners' paternalism. Even if one accepted its argument about industrial exploitation, Grayson's insistence on planters' universal benevolence rang false. "We rail back" at Yankees "about the misery of the poor at the North," Carey wrote, "but instances occur of horrible oppression & crime at the South, (& very, very often) that could only be in the midst of Slavery." A similar awareness made her mother and sister read Harriet Beecher Stowe's *Uncle Tom's Cabin* with reasonably open minds. Lou found it "engrossingly interesting and very natural" and could not understand the intensity of Southern attacks on it, for to her the book seemed "true."[16]

Whatever ambivalence about slavery such commentary implied, the Petigru women shared the racial attitudes common in both the North and the South. Racial stereotypes that justified slavery were only part—although a major part—of their stereotypical thinking. When Louise Porcher disapproved of Adèle Allston's hiring an Italian nursery governess, she elaborated on inherent deficiencies common to persons whose inferior European origins she deplored. "It is not the *niggers* only," she asserted, "who 'the less they have to do, the less they want to do.'" Not only Italians demonstrated such deficiencies. When, in 1850, Mary O'Shea, who had been the Allstons' nursery governess for several years, gave notice, Louise jumped to the conclusion that she must have done so because she was "tired of her quiet & *celibat*-state." Obviously it was "vain to expect to attach an irisher to one. They are a light & fickle people, whose feelings are evanescent but far more abiding & faithful to anger than kindness." Mary Petigru's assignment of ethnic stereotypes was even more heavy-handed. Her response to a series of suspected arsons in Charleston was a proposal "to send off or emprison all the idle disorderly foreigners Irish & German." And Caroline Carson described her fellow passengers aboard a ship on which she sailed to England in 1861 as "a collection of dirty S. Am[eric]an Spaniards with parrot like voices, long cigars, and quizzy little children who look like monkeys with their tails tucked into their trousers." Jews too were subjects of scornful ethnic modeling. When as a belle she visited the Virginia springs, Carey North felt uncomfortable in the company of a Mr. Thom, who fidgeted constantly and looked "like a Jew." Three years later, a Mr. Levin made her even more ill at ease because he was a "conceited, forward Jew, who pushes himself upon every one."[17] And when the Allston girls boarded at Madame Togno's school in Charleston, they were withdrawn from a dancing assembly when "common" Jews began to attend.

However demeaning such depictions were, none spurred private fears as much as those used to justify slavery. Whether based on the Old Testament curse on all of Canaan's descendants or on the contemporary pseudo-scientific ranking of races, racial differences were tools used not only to defend human bondage but also to reduce the enslaved to a subhuman species. But chronic fears of slave insurrection implicitly conceded a common humanity, a shared love of freedom, and even an understandable determination to seize it. The anxiety that Nat Turner's Virginia rebellion spread throughout the South in 1832 was intensified by the presumption of black bestiality. In Charleston, where tales of the rape and murder that Denmark Vesey had allegedly planned in 1822 still circulated, nineteen-year-old Harriette Petigru trembled at her impending fate. Louise Porcher, who spent the summer of 1832 in the isolated pineland village of Cordesville, felt "quite panicstruck" whenever "the dogs bark[ed] fiercely" at night. Fifteen years later, Jane North had much sounder reasons for anxiety after slaves killed a neighbor known to be a harsh taskmaster. Brother's response that "even the lowest people may be raised by despair to the commission of great crimes" scarcely offered much consolation.[18]

By 1850, rumors of revolt had become a chronic preoccupation. Adèle Allston, in anticipation of Robert's prolonged absence during the summer, wished she "understood the use of firearms, and weapons of defence." Her sense of vulnerability ballooned after she went to Pawleys Island, where a "number of runaway negroes" were rumored to be lurking in nearby woods. She fervently wished she was "capable of using fire arms."[19]

At Badwell, Mary Petigru was similarly alarmed two weeks later by the arrival of a "very free & impertinent" peddler, who displayed "great interest in talking to, & trading with the negroes." The longer he hung around, the more she suspected that he was "an abolition agent." But Carey, who was spending the summer with her Aunt Adèle on Pawleys Island, felt that Badwell was a far safer place to be without an adult white male protector. Although she did not explicitly contrast the Georgetown district's population, which was almost 90 percent slave, with that of the Abbeville district, where slaves comprised barely 61 percent, she clearly sensed a difference. Nevertheless, she insisted that the real issue was not slavery but rather Yankee attacks on the institution. "There is nothing to fear if the Northerners will let us alone and create no disturbance."[20]

Even when they were not openly admitted, fears of slave unrest were a subliminal constant. In 1856 Carey, as mistress of Charles Pettigrew's Bonarva plantation, scanned newspapers nervously for "accounts of insurrectionary movements." But when she read about rebelliousness elsewhere, she tried to reassure herself that it would remain at a distance. "Everything goes on well, there is no trouble or dissatisfaction of any kind," she wrote her mother in late November. But that reassurance conveyed doubts, as did her reiteration a month later that "every thing with us is quiet as usual, there are advantages in a remote situation, such as nonintercourse with the rest of the world for domestics." As Carey did at Bonarva that Christmas, Adèle made the Chicora festivities more elaborate than usual. Ostensibly they marked the master's election as governor. On his triumphant return from Columbia, he had ordered "many a stout glass of whiskey" to be added to the customary holiday pies and cakes. But at the same time, the overseers at both Chicora and nearby Waverly "brushed up their guns and ammunition chests &c. and observed and listened, but held their tongues." Adèle too remained tense, even though she observed "no signs of organization or of serious discontent."[21]

There were, however, disturbing signs elsewhere. In early February 1858, three slaves on a place near Bonarva killed their white owner, a man known to be "fretful & full of threats," although not a hard master. Later that year, Peter, a Pettigrew slave so trusted that he had been assigned to oversee a convoy of wagons carrying slaves and supplies on the ten- to twelve-day journey from Bonarva to Cherry Hill the previous summer, was suspected of villainy. After a visit to Bonarva, Joe Allston wrote that he had apparently left his pistol behind. No one located it in the search that Charles ordered. Only in response to his master's overt challenge did Peter finally produce the gun from a trunk that he had earlier said he could not open because he had lost the key but that he had, in fact, broken open while the search was under way. He expressed wide-eyed astonishment that the pistol happened to be there. Charles found the whole episode "most extraordinary, and capable of the most unfavourable construction." At the same time, he warned Carey, who was then at Cherry Hill, that she "had better give it the most favourable aspects" if she spoke of it before the servants, who would doubtless make their own surmises.[22]

Scarcely six months later, a Bonarva maid's dinner was salted with copperas, which turned the meat green. Grace, the cook, denied having anything to do with it. Although the misdeed apparently reflected a conflict among the servants, Carey was shocked by "an act on the verge of crime." She was little reassured by Charles's assessment of the incident. "The world," he wrote from New York, "is full of wretches and wretchedness. I think it is growing worse and worse."[23]

John Brown's raid on Harpers Ferry in October 1859 strengthened that analysis. It sparked numerous reports of nascent rebellions throughout the South. Carey trembled for her Badwell kin as word of a planned uprising in the Abbeville district spread. "How insecure is our situation" and how great the "fear for the Future." But at the same time, she ridiculed the cascade of rumors and the widespread discovery of "suspicious characters" who were being "warned to vamose." Harmless people became the victims of fear, but "call out 'Yankee' & it is like shouting 'thief,' every body gives chase."[24]

Less than a year later, Carey seemed more ready to join that chase. In September 1860 evidence that a slave rebellion had been plotted on a plantation only ten miles from Cherry Hill caused her "grave apprehension." A local man had "discovered concealed on his place a supply of arms & ammunition, with preparations for the concealment of more"; under interrogation, "negroes" confessed that there was "a plan to burn the dwellings in every direction, & a 'general rising['] in Oct." The alleged instigator was a white man who had been "wandering through the country for some months pretending to be a Fool." He was soon apprehended, but Carey, alone with her children at Cherry Hill, pressed Charles and Johnston to come up at once—and to come armed with good revolvers. No one could know "when, nor where the difficulty may begin." She assured her brother-in-law that she was not "foolishly frightened" or "looking pale with terror," but she also admitted that during the long nights she slept neither much nor well. That Mary Petigru insisted on staying alone at Badwell also worried Carey. Mary seemed impervious to alarm and convinced that her slaves were "innocent" despite prolonged contact with the "old miscreant," who had spent considerable time among them. Worst of all, local men were slow to organize slave patrols. When Charles finally arrived at Cherry Hill, however, the whole uproar seemed to him a matter of "foolish talking among the Negroes, for which the equally foolish talking of the Whites is partly responsible."[25]

He had barely made that observation when reports reached him that some twenty slaves had been apprehended in the woods near Bonarva plotting an attack on the nearby town of Plymouth. Allegedly, some 300 slaves were ready to kill all of the whites; seize their money, weapons, and ammunition; and then burn down the town. Intensive patrols were organized at once. As his sister Annie put it, "The tighter the reins the lesser the danger."[26]

PART TWO

The War Years

CHAPTER TWELVE

The War Comes

The 1860 presidential election precipitated a crisis that had fermented since Southern delegates stalked out of the Democratic nominating convention the preceding spring. Even before the convention assembled in Charleston on April 23, the city had pulsed with political excitement. As the delegates streamed into town, they were already jockeying for the candidates who would best represent their regions. After ten days of debate and fifty-seven ballots had produced no candidate acceptable to delegates from both North and South, tempers boiled over and the convention split in half. On May 3, Jane North, Adèle Allston, Mary Petigru, Caroline Carson, and Sue King watched from the crowded gallery of Institute Hall as the delegates from eight Southern states marched out. Six and a half weeks later, the Northern delegates reassembled in Baltimore and nominated Stephen Douglas of Illinois. On June 28, the Southern delegates, who also met in Baltimore, selected John Breckinridge of Kentucky as their presidential candidate.

Once again sectional loyalties, partisan commitments, and allegiance to the federal Constitution contended against one another as Petigru women watched election politics play out. Even before the nominations were made, Senator Charles Sumner of Massachusetts excoriated the "Barbarism of Slavery" in his first Senate address since Preston Brooks had beaten him senseless four years earlier. To Carey Pettigrew, his "wicked but able speech" portended "anarchy! bloodshed! confusion." But she thought little better of South Carolina senator James Chesnut's reply. The oratorical violence with which he denounced Sumner's argument as the "incarnation of malice, mendacity, and cowardice" seemed equally "atrocious." By November, Jane North doubted that the country could survive "the ultra Politicians" in both sections who were so obviously its "Bane and Scourge."[1]

As soon as Abraham Lincoln's election was certain, Louise Porcher contended that it announced the Union's collapse. Indeed, that collapse had already begun "when the two sections could no longer meet without such excesses that all lawmaking or statesmanlike views or actions were out of the question." Now Lincoln's election sealed the Union's fate. "We are," she wrote her son, an officer in the U.S. Navy, "in the midst of a *Revolution . . .* where the party now in power advocate the perpetration of every crime against us. They invoke the negroes to '*burn* & *poison*[']'" and even promise to "come to their aid." That very morning, in fact, the Porcher's coachman had hinted to thirteen-year-old Marion that she would not live to celebrate Christmas and had called her mother names that clearly portended more general violence.[2]

But few family members as yet shared Louise's dire anxiety. Carey, who had followed political developments as closely as any of her kinswomen, now largely ignored the political for practical economics. Because she and her children were in Charleston on their way from Cherry Hill to Bonarva, her first reaction to the election was to make sure that no matter what its aftermath, she would have enough money to get home. She headed straight to the Pettigrews' Charleston factors and drew as much gold as they would advance her. Hoarding that specie, she spent only the absolute minimum on essential supplies. But despite that practicality, she was tempted to fatalism. It seemed "hardly worth while to be so very careful, for if a crash comes all fare alike." And the implications of that crash included whites' observations that Charleston blacks were already convinced that "this election decides their freedom."[3]

Neither Lincoln's election nor South Carolina's swift adoption on December 20 of a secession ordinance united the family. Carey was sure that her native state had acted decisively to repudiate a president who was hostile to slavery. If only her adopted North Carolina would follow suit, "how strong the Southern States" would soon be. Her mother took a totally different tack. Jane North so loved the South that she grieved at South Carolina's "present course as one might lament for a prodigal." The whole South was plunging toward its own destruction so recklessly that her heart and her head sickened at "how many must suffer and be dragged along" into disaster. Therefore, she was almost alone in admiring Brother's refusal to remain in his pew when, the Sunday after the election, the rector of St.

Michael's Church omitted the customary prayer for the president's health and well-being.[4]

As South Carolina moved out of the Union, the political changes within the Petigru clan increasingly strained family relations. When Harriette Lesesne praised her state senator husband's proposal to delay secession until other Southern states joined their own, their eighteen-year-old son reproved his mother "really sharply." Louise Porcher, as much committed to secession as her nephew, heralded the "beautiful bright" dawn of "our Independence." In the same week that Louise trumpeted her readiness for the sacrifices it would demand—"modified *table*, plain wholesome food without *dainties* of any kind," not even "a Pudding on Xmas day"—Mary Petigru shuddered at her state's "critical position," its "very unenviable distinction . . . in being first to break the Union." Why this rush to disunion, she wondered. "What grievous wrongs has [South Carolina] to complain of more than all the rest!" Jane North was sure the result would be the North's having "the best in the end." She marveled at "the temerity which could break up this august government, and not recoil from an act involving the well being of millions, and the *glory* of the nation."[5] Jane's firmness only fed the conflicting personal and political loyalties that gnawed at Adèle Allston. Her opinions, as her daughter Bessie later recalled, lay with her secessionist husband, but her emotions drew her toward her brother, who considered the federal Constitution a nearly sacred text.

Differences of opinion did not impede the steady march toward disunion in the weeks before Lincoln's inauguration on March 4. By then, seven states had seceded and joined together as the Confederate States of America. They had also seized most of the federal forts within their boundaries. By March 4, so many Southern representatives and senators had vacated their seats that a Northern-dominated Congress had handily passed the Morrill tariff, which was more protective of Northern manufacture than the tariffs that had precipitated the nullification controversy. Republicans had also defeated all attempts by border-state politicians at compromise. As Carey assessed these actions, she compared them to those of the nascent Confederacy: "What a contrast is presented by the greedy crew & blk republicans" and "the dignified and able conduct of the Southern Congress." The only chance she saw for a reconstituted Union would be to exclude "those pestilent new England states," which she knew was impossible.[6]

Despite conflicting loyalties, family bonds remained strong, and discussions of political differences, civil. But civility could not mask tension. In a family overwhelmingly Confederate, Brother's open unionism was a constant irritant. Lou North, who thought him a "Black Republican," was appalled at her mother's praise for the "one man left who is free to hold his opinion." Jane Amelia flaunted her disagreement with her husband's politics. The Sunday after he had abruptly left church services, she publicized her secessionist fervor by arriving alone and at the last minute at St. Michael's for services she ordinarily did not attend. Casting her invalidism aside for the occasion and "attired finely, with as much gilt about her hat & head as was possible," she was ushered midway down the central aisle to the family pew. Then, lest her presence should somehow be overlooked, she sang all of the hymns "pip[ing] out in shrilly tones so as to attract the attention of all the congregation." Such an open show of family dissidence made the Porchers flee hastily after the service, "fearful of . . . some disagreeable, conspicuous scene."[7]

James's aversion to incivility prevented other such scenes. He continued to invite secessionist politicians to his famous Sunday dinner parties, at which his daughter Caroline Carson, as ardent a Unionist as he, presided. That prominent role made her unionism rather than her father's the principal target for their kinsmen's criticism. James Petigru, after all, was the clan's respected male head; Caroline was a woman whose style offended its social code. Moreover, she had lived in New York for most of the preceding year, and her allegiance seemed to lie as much with the North as with the Union. She had been reluctant to return to Charleston in the early spring of 1861. She had even made sport of Lou North's ardent Confederate patriotism and admitted that she could not possibly "share the opinions" of the South.[8] She had thus isolated herself not just from South Carolina politics but from her family as well.

Neither Caroline's unionism nor her kinswomen's secessionist enthusiasm could have much effect on the events playing out around them. Nonetheless, they all tracked public events more closely than ever before and probed them for their import. Minnie Allston pondered what President James Buchanan meant to signal when he sent the *Star of the West* to resupply Fort Sumter and reinforce the only federal troops remaining in South Carolina. Her sister Lou wondered why he had sent only a single unarmed vessel to accomplish that task. Neither sister could fathom the president's purpose. Was he, Minnie asked, a "*double dealer*," or was he simply unsure about what course he should pursue? Did he intend to maneuver South Carolina into firing the first shot? If so, what "horrors" might such a resort to force "usher in"? Would the "*whole South*" rally to South Carolina's support? If not, what then? Behind these questions lurked doubts "that So. Ca alone [was] equal to conquering actually, by force of arms, the Federal government."[9]

In any case, when the South Carolina batteries surrounding Charleston harbor fired on the *Star of the West*, forcing it to abandon its mission, outgoing President Buchanan's intentions became largely irrelevant. In his inaugural speech on March 4, the new president was no clearer. Then, a month after asserting that no violence need occur "unless forced upon the national authority," Lincoln notified South Carolina that he had ordered a federal naval force to resupply Fort Sumter.[10] In response, at 4:30 on the morning of April 12, 1861, South Carolina troops manning the forty-three batteries that commanded Charleston harbor began bombarding Fort Sumter while the federal vessels stood offshore. Vague perplexities vanished. Lou and Minnie, like most of their kinswomen, welcomed clear action. After a day and a half of constant bombardment, Major Robert Anderson and his ill-nourished troops, exhausted and without ammunition, struck the flag.

The easiness of South Carolina's victory exhilarated those who watched the battle from the shore. Awakened by the sound of exploding shells, sixteen-year-old Bessie Allston and fifty-eight-year-old Mary Petigru dressed hastily and rushed out to observe the action. From White Point Garden, only blocks from Ann Petigru's house on lower King Street where they were staying, they watched the shells rain down on the island bastion only four miles away across open water. Much to Bessie's surprise, Aunt Ann placidly ignored it all "until her usual hour of rising." Then she joined her sisters-in-law and nieces, who by that time had gathered to follow events from the top piazza of the Porchers' house, where they had a spectacular view of the harbor, the fort, and the batteries pummeling it. Bessie, the youngest among them, watched through her spyglass. The "deep interest" she showed impressed her elders with the "firmness in her opinions & actions."[11]

The shift from peace to war created a new unity of opinion. Aunt Mary abandoned her former equivocation to pledge allegiance to the new order. Although she had "never expected to see *war*" and found its actuality "a fearful thing," Carolina's decisive victory propelled her to the wholehearted pursuit of Southern independence. Sue King suddenly became "a violent patriot" and likened General P. G. T. Beauregard's attack on Sumter to "Joshua before the Walls of Jericho." For once, she was really proud of her husband, whose company had been heavily "engaged . . . at the batteries" and had "distinguished themselves by their zeal." She even bragged that Henry was "the only one of our connection who was *actually* engaged," a claim that gave short shrift to Ben Allston, Johnston Pettigrew, and Hal Lesesne, all of whom were on active duty in Charleston harbor. In fact, Hal's presence on Morris Island at the mouth of the harbor so tortured his mother that she was made "sick with excitement & trouble" as the firing went on and on and was barely able to celebrate victory when it came. Amid the excitement, Ann Petigru managed the rather unwarlike observation that Major Anderson must have been embarrassed at being the object of so much attention after his surrender when he had been "so long deprived of the comforts of the *toilet*."[12]

Only the "Old Whigs"—James Petigru, Jane North, and Caroline Carson—were, Mary Anna Porcher reflected, "incapable of keeping up with the impetuous spirit of the age." But, in fact, Jane had already begun to waver. It was simply "too much to hope that peace and adjustment" could follow the attack on Sumter. Her brother, who for thirty years had been a member of an unpopular and steadily shrinking political minority, now felt more isolated than ever before. Still, he wrote Jane that "the universal applause that waits on secessionists and secession has not the slightest tendency to shake my conviction that we are on the road to ruin." Caroline, who held equally firm, grew increasingly unhappy in an isolation much greater than her father's.[13]

Despite these tensions, nearly all of the family members then in Charleston gathered on May 10 for a dinner party at the Broad Street house to celebrate James Petigru's seventy-second birthday. Henry and Harriette Lesesne came. So did Sue, Henry, and Addy King; Adèle Allston and young Della; and Jane North and her daughter Lou. Even Ben Allston and Johnston Pettigrew got military leave to join them. As they all offered their congratulations, Henry Lesesne summed up their warm sentiments in his toast to his former partner, whom he praised as "the character wh[o] for integrity & purity shall command admiration when political distinction shall be forgotten," to which Caroline replied, "Spoken in good time."[14] Then they all drank to their state's most prominent Unionist.

Adèle revealed the depth of the chasm bridged by Henry's toast in a letter she wrote only days later advising her minister to leave South Carolina. Joseph Hunter and his wife were no longer welcome or fit to remain, for despite fifteen years in the South, they now sided "with the North in its present attitude of bitter hostility" to the Confederacy. Such insistence on uncritical conformity made other Petigru women equally hostile to anything that blocked Southern independence. They fumed at North Carolina's and Virginia's laggard pace toward secession. They deplored the opportunism of the border states that clung to the Union. They despised "the duplicity & cowardly sneaking" of the Lincoln administration.[15] They excoriated the North for the riots and crimes in which its citizens engaged.

Despite their loyalty to the cause, however, they were not blind to its flaws. They condemned the Confederate government as well as the states for the corrupt patronage that bred inefficiency. By September, Minnie even raised questions about its permanence. She was deeply grieved at "how sadly, & how soon, this glorious experiment of self government has failed." Still, she had never been "a great admirers of republican institutions," and the Richmond government's resemblance to the federal model only reinforced her doubt that it would last. But the North was even worse. "As far as the idea of the progress of the human race is conceived," support for Lincoln's despotic rule was " 'the saddest sight the world 'ere saw.' "[16]

Well before the war was a year old, the women, responding to the uncertainties that clouded their futures, relied ever more consciously on the mutual support that kinship ties had long provided. Thus they particularly resented the disruption of mail service, which began as soon as South Carolina seceded. Back in December 1860, Lou North had fretted that the next letter she received from North Carolina would probably "be from a foreign nation" but still trusted that "the mails will not be interrupted" and that she would still hear regularly from Carey. Trust was not enough. By mid-February, nearly two months before the fighting started, all postal service to Charleston was reduced to one delivery a week; by June, any letter successfully sent north from Charleston had become "an extraordinary event," and any letter received, "a welcome entertainment after a long fast."[17]

After Caroline Carson went north that June, maintaining any contact with her sympathetic father became a complicated affair and communication with the rest of her kin pretty much ended. Yet she was glad to have escaped from Charleston. Its hot, damp climate had long exacerbated her health problems. Its emotional atmosphere burdened her psychologically. Her efforts to avoid political discussion had not lessened her aunts' and cousins' hostility but instead had cut her off from most family discourse. Even Aunt Jane North's sympathy lacked fervor. She merely urged her daughters not to be "*ashamed*" of their cousin, for everyone was "entitled to her opinion," even if she did "not believe in either the glory or the profit" of secession. More positively, she commended Caroline for trying to adhere to Johnston's belief that political discussion "destroys femininity," noting that at least on that score Caroline was "wiser than her aunts."[18]

Caroline's leaving in June further intensified her aunts' and cousins' aggravation. They were outraged by her decision to visit her older son, Willie, in Germany, where he was studying for a commercial career. They deplored her borrowing $1,000 from her hard-pressed father to travel in first-class accommodations with a maid. The elegant hotels, the carriage she hired in Paris, the theater and the opera performances she attended galled them almost as much as did her politics. To Minnie Allston, her "selfishness" seemed "like the car of Juggernaut," destroying everything "tender & holy which lies in its path." No one gave any thought to Caroline's inner struggles with her own conflicting loyalties. As she sailed for Europe in July, she was both relieved to be out of the way and "very sad to feel it . . . a relief."[19]

The most hurtful treatment came from her mother. Jane Amelia, who now relied on brandy laced with laudanum to replace the morphine she could no longer obtain, was determined to punish Caroline for her desertion. Fully aware of how desperately her daughter missed the son whom she had had to leave with her parents, Jane Amelia destroyed most of Jem's letters to his mother, speciously arguing that they were too poorly written to be sent. Her malice was perhaps understandable, for she too was suffering grave personal losses. On the night of December 9, 1861, flames that had raced across the Charleston peninsula from an uncontrolled bonfire burned the mansion that had been her home for twenty-three years to the ground, destroying virtually all of its contents. James was in Columbia at the time. Henry King, who was in town, ignored Jane Amelia's orders to save clothing, furniture, and household linens first in order to rescue the paintings and books his father-in-law most valued. So in the gray ashes of the morning, Jane Amelia faced the future without "a *bed* a *chair* a *table* a *carpet* a *curtain* and but a few cotton blankets not a particle of crockery of any kind not a pot or pan."[20] It was bad enough that the house was miserably underinsured; its contents were totally uninsured. Her comfortable security was gone. In the wake of war, with his law practice nearly at a standstill, James Petigru lacked the funds to replace his loss. Indeed, he had little income other than a salary paid him to codify state law. Even that was due to stop the next year when his commission expired. Nor had his openhanded generosity and his family's perennial extravagance left him with significant savings from the rich proceeds of his earlier practice. As she looked into the bleak future, Jane Amelia derived little emotional comfort from her children. Politically at odds with Caroline and temperamentally at swords' point with Sue, she gained only minimally more satisfaction from her son, Dan. Before hostilities had begun, she had failed in her attempt to get him a commission and a safe staff position. So Dan, then thirty-nine, had enlisted as a private—and remained one.

Like her sister-in-law, Louise Porcher sought Confederate congressman William Porcher Miles's aid in securing a commission to shield a kinsman from the dreaded lot of a common soldier. In the first flush of secessionist patriotism, Hal Lesesne had left college to volunteer as a private in the forces guarding Charleston harbor. But when the ground war began on the

Virginia front, his aunt shrank "from the thought of the *moral* dangers, to one of his tender years."[21] Ironically, although Hal eventually did gain a commission, Louise's son Charley never did. He enlisted at seventeen to join Hampton's Legion and fought in Virginia as a private for four long years.

Adèle Allston, at least, never had to fear that her West Point–graduate son would serve in the ranks. Ben, who had spent three years in the U.S. Army and served as an officer in the state militia, accepted a major's commission in the Confederate army before he left for the Virginia front in June 1861. Three months later, he was promoted to colonel, in charge of an Alabama regiment whose commanding officer had just been killed in battle. His mother's fears for him had already been intensified by letters from his father, written when he visited Ben immediately after the first battle at Manassas (Bull Run), in which he described the horrors of the body-strewn battlefield.

It was no small wonder, then, that for the first time in her life, Jane North congratulated herself that "in the order of providence" all of her children were female. The irony of that abrupt change of opinion amused her daughters. But the humor of the situation dwindled as the thrill of the first Confederate victories abated. Soon Lou was convinced that "we must conquer or be subjected to the most awful fate that ever befell a people."[22] As she learned that their armies would inevitably endure retreats as well as triumphs, Carey contemplated the toll on civilians that those retreats would impose. She believed a scorched-earth policy would be essential wherever Yankee troops set foot on Southern territory—a scorching that might destroy all of her own and her relatives' prosperity. She voiced this awareness only six months after her kinswomen had cheered so heartily as they had watched shells batter Fort Sumter for two exciting spring days.

CHAPTER THIRTEEN

The Early War Years on the Home Front

Securing customary supplies for the table was the first real challenge that war presented to civilian households. Early in the first year, the issue was variety rather than quantity, and the Petigrus changed their diets accordingly. Less than two months after Sumter fell, Jane North observed "a general feeling that we must do without luxuries." In late June, Jane Amelia Petigru discovered that ice, which Charlestonians had long imported from New England, would soon be unavailable at any price. The increasing effectiveness of the federal naval blockade led the Badwell folk to experiment with coffee substitutes as dwindling supplies forced prices up. By the autumn of 1861, brews made from rye and wheat and even dried cranberries replaced the bean, and tea, except on special occasions, was steeped from sassafras bark. Long accustomed to seasonal scarcities, Jane readily substituted "batter cakes and muffins" when other supplies ran short.[1]

Wartime shortages pinched hardest in Charleston. As winter loomed, the prices of bacon, lard, butter, sugar, candles, soap, and starch, as well as of coffee and tea, all soared beyond the means of the poor. Nonetheless, Harriette Lesesne believed that "plain food" like bread, beef, rice, and hominy was still plentiful and reasonable, even though Sue King complained about the "pressure of high prices."[2] As a result, the long-established family practice of sharing supplies assumed greater importance. Butter, honey, and other provisions sent down from Chicora Wood kept the Allstons' Charleston kin in relative luxury. As prices rose, Adèle reorganized dairy work at

Chicora, churning all excess cream into butter, which brought a good return when sold in the city.

Even before a shot was fired, Jane North had prepared for another shortage. Fearing that cheap Northern textiles might soon become unavailable, she decided in January 1861 "to reinstate wheel & loom that the women may clothe themselves at least." Her foresight paid off. By May, the "scarcity of dry goods" made it imperative to "guide the spindles & direct the loom" if her slaves were to be kept clothed.[3] At Chicora, however, Adèle did not put her two looms back into operation until 1863. Like Jane, she had long since abandoned domestic manufacture of cloth as inexpensive rough cloth produced in the North or in England had eased the task of clothing the Allstons' constantly expanding work force. But after the federal blockade cut off imports, a return to the old ways became essential.

Public necessities also changed domestic work patterns as women volunteered to sew and knit for the troops. Louise Porcher and her daughters made socks for the lancers of Charley's Hampton's Legion. As Mary Anna jested, "the turning of the heel" had become a "great test of one's patriotism." Her Aunt Ann Petigru not only knit socks herself but also taught "the little nigs to knit!" Carey Pettigrew pressed that strategy still further at Bonarva when she "offered . . . to do any work" requested by making " 'the institution' . . . sew for the defenders."[4] In a single day in May, she boasted, her servants had sewn and washed fifteen pairs of drawers that she had cut out in the morning. She further taxed her slaves by contributing plantation supplies of blankets for the benefit of North Carolina troops headed to Virginia.

The Petigru women also proved their patriotism by venturing into new kinds of domestic production. Harriette Lesesne, Louise Porcher, and Lou North all stitched sandbags for Charleston's harbor fortifications. Other Petigru women joined groups of ladies organized to make clothing for the troops as earlier charitable societies had sewn for the poor and sick. Although the organizational structure was not new, many younger women like the teenage Porcher girls and their cousin Jinty Allston joined such groups for the first time. In rural areas, groups like these had formerly been rare. So the sewing group formed at Buffalo, nearly sixty miles from Badwell, of which Jane North was a "directress," was indeed an organizational innovation in the rural upcountry. But in the rice-growing low country with its still more widely scattered white population, similar arrangements were impossible. Adèle and her daughters, therefore, acted as individuals when they collected "flannels, socks and old clothes" from their neighbors along the

Waccamaw and Pee Dee Rivers to benefit wounded South Carolina soldiers hospitalized in Virginia after Manassas.[5] And when Adèle undertook to make uniforms for new companies being raised to fight in Virginia, she had to depend on a Charleston society to send up the yard goods and patterns she needed. Similarly, at Bonarva, Carey was constantly frustrated by the absence of any organized group through which she could order supplies and funnel completed garments.

Not all of the Petigru women, however, were equally enthusiastic about the demands of war work. Sue King showed no zeal in sewing or knitting, alone or in a group. Why should she? Domestic chores had always bored her. Now there were far more interesting and exciting things to do. Shortly after Fort Sumter fell, William Hurlbut, a New York journalist and long-time friend of Sue's, came to town. The fire-eating *Charleston Mercury* immediately alerted its readers to the presence of a reputed abolitionist, libeler, swindler, and traitor (for he was a Carolina native). At once, the local vigilance committee prepared to apprehend him.

It was a scenario worthy of Sue's attention. Hurlbut vanished suddenly in Charleston, only to reappear in Georgia, where he was arrested, then sent to Richmond, and, denied habeas corpus, jailed without trial. Rumor tattled that Sue had sheltered him in her home until he could escape, and she could not avoid the scandal this escapade produced. Her unsigned article defending Hurlbut as a Southern sympathizer who had returned home to help the cause only made matters worse. Its widely guessed authorship set tongues wagging. Aunt Louise sizzled at Sue's "perfectly horrid" behavior.[6] Adèle, long Sue's favorite aunt, broke with her completely. Her father-in-law thought her defense of Hurlbut, whatever she might say in her own defense, was indefensible. All of her close kin concurred that she had once again disgraced herself. Only her father tackled the problem head-on, finally convincing Sue to rein herself in lest she do further harm to Hurlbut's chances for release.

The federal seizure of Port Royal on South Carolina's southernmost coast and the invasion of the adjacent Sea Islands, however, soon drew attention away from the Hurlbut affair. On November 7, seventeen warships and twenty-five transport vessels loaded with 12,000 infantrymen and marines launched an attack on the forts surrounding Port Royal Sound, all of which fell within four hours. At once, federal troops spread out to occupy the rich plantations on the adjacent Sea Islands. Their owners, as unprepared for the attack as the Confederate military, fled inland, abandoning unharvested crops of valuable long-staple cotton and most of their slaves. In a trice, the myth of Southern invincibility was dead. Thereafter, no coastal Carolina community could feel safe.

As a result, James Petigru wrote Jane North, "consternation has reigned in town and country. The excitement has been awful and it does not abate, except imperceptibly. All the males are gone out of the city and the women, young and old, are in terror and alarm." From the relative safety of Badwell, Lou North considered the event's long-range implications. She was mortified that "our men did not behave well" and that the Confederate military had fallen "into the error of over confidence & when they were over powered they fled not retreated." Even more ominous, most of the Sea Island slaves had refused to flee with their owners. As knowledge that federal troops had allowed those slaves to defy their masters spread among upcountry slaves, who anticipated that Yankee occupation might bring their own liberation, Lou feared that she might well "live to see the extinction of slavery."[7]

Such anxiety fed a more widespread perception of servile unrest. From the time that Lincoln's election was sure, rumors of insurrectionary plots had burgeoned. In January some of the Porcher slaves were overheard planning to "knock [Philip] on the head" the day the Republican president took office. In early May Mary Anna Porcher was sure that "our enemies will do their *worst* to incite a revolt." Three weeks later, Annie Pettigrew passed on reports that poor whites living near her brothers' plantations had been discovered "exciting the negroes to *rise, calling* upon the *boys,* as it termed them . . . to be in readiness" as soon as locally stationed Confederate troops were sent to Virginia, leaving planter families defenseless. That August, Annie's sister-in-law Carey, whose access to the Northern press was now limited to items reprinted in Southern papers, denounced the "atrocious" schemes planned by "wild" Yankees. Excerpts from the *New York Times* and *New York Tribune* confirmed that abolitionist Wendell Phillips and many others had openly proclaimed that the North's "20 *millions* will never succeed against the South, until they call to *their aid* the 4 millions slaves!" If that happened, Carey concluded, "the horrors at home will render . . . defeat easy." Not even her refuge in New York spared Caroline Carson similar apprehensions. She too feared a repetition of "the insurrection of St Domingo on a larger & (if possible) more frightful scale!!"[8]

That October, evidence that a slave had murdered an old woman living near Badwell shook Jane North's customary self-confidence. This woman who for twenty-four years had headed a household with no resident white male now admitted that she slept better when there was a man in the house, even though the "man" was either sixteen-year-old Jem Carson or thirteen-year-old Charles Allston, five-day boarders at a nearby academy who spent most weekends with their Aunts Jane and Mary. After the Yankees seized Port Royal, Mary Petigru, who six months earlier had declared that she was happiest at Badwell "without any one but her servants," was set on tenter-hooks by her maid's report that "the negroes expect something." Her sister Jane, usually less perturbable than Mary, now took her major solace from the hope that nothing "but an invasion" would "start" the blacks. Should an invading army arrive, the Abbeville district was in such an "unprotected state" that a repetition of the shocking behavior of the Sea Island slaves seemed inevitable.[9]

Moreover, the protection that Abbeville's upcountry remoteness had once promised was fast eroding as a tidal wave of black and white refugees washed over it. Jane doubted that the coastal planters who attempted to save their slaves by moving them inland could succeed. Both soil and climate limited their agricultural options to crops that could never employ the large number of field hands that low country plantations kept busy. Even in her own home, she wondered how she was to feed and house the refugees who were almost swamping Badwell. Harriette Lesesne and her four young children, Louise Porcher's three daughters, and Ann Petigru all arrived from Charleston scarcely two weeks after Port Royal fell. This unexpected burden strained Jane's equipoise, for her scarce supplies were already taxed even before her white household tripled.

In addition, the servants Ann brought extended the low country black grapevine into Jane's immediate domain. Their "tales of the panic in Charles-ton," Lou North agreed with her mother, were likely to "wile away many a long evening" in the quarters. However much the longtime mistress of Badwell might reassure herself that "so far as we can learn many of the negroes are quite loyal," she was positive that, although they all now acted "perfectly well," some at least would "gladly go to the Yankees." That became increasingly likely as able-bodied white men were siphoned off by the Con-federate draft. It was clearly important to strengthen the armed forces, but it was downright dangerous to leave too few white men to keep the "black population . . . in check" just when slaves needed "very little encouragement" to become "perfectly insupportable." Jane ended her litany of real and anticipated troubles with a fervent "God help us."[10]

By comparison with Charleston, however, Badwell still seemed a secure haven. There, each evening, eight to ten women gathered around a table next to a "blazing fire on the hearth" while one of them "read Pickwick Papers or something else" aloud and "the rest . . . knit[ted] diligently." Between nine and ten o'clock, they dispersed, reasonably certain that the next day would resemble the last. But although they cultivated an air of contentment, troubling undercurrents occasionally surfaced. The candles they burned to light their evening's work became scarce as the army requisitioned tallow. Jane, Mary, and Lou lost the privacy they customarily enjoyed as their five-bedroom house was stretched to accommodate twelve residents, largely kept indoors by winter weather. And Jane's usual gracious calm was rubbed almost raw by the increasingly rigid ways of Ann Petigru, who, when she arrived in November, summarily announced that she expected to remain "for the winter at least."[11]

Then, on December 10, nineteen-year-old Louly Porcher came down with typhus. Eight days later, she died. Aunts and cousins had nursed the "insidious fever" to no avail as Ann Petigru watched "over the same scene again in the same room, same bed" where her daughter had died from the same disease six years earlier. The senior Porchers, who rushed up from Charleston, arrived too late to see their daughter alive. Devastated by the death of a second daughter within two years, Louise nonetheless bore up "with as much resignation as one could hope for." Louly's younger sister Mary Anna roused herself "to a sense of duty" and attended to Marion, the youngest, who became so upset and sick that she too almost died.[12]

By Christmas 1861, the euphoria of the spring had also died. Although hope for a conclusive military victory over the North remained strong and Mary predicted authoritatively that divine intervention would protect Charleston from Yankee destruction, personal grief and insecurity continued to press upon the family. Minnie Allston, who had been confined to her bed by rheumatism and perhaps a miscarriage the preceding spring, remained in precarious health. Nonetheless, she had stayed on either at her husband's Waverly plantation or at their beach cottage, both of which were within easy range of the blockading federal fleet, in her concern for Joe's troubled mental condition. Ever since early 1861, his behavior had swung mercurially between "animated & roused up" highs and "exceedingly irritable and disagreeable" lows. When Jane had visited them in March, she had diagnosed Joe's malady as "a habit of mind indulged in until it is in danger of becoming unmanageable" and had wondered "whether he will strive against & overcome it."[13]

Gradually, however, Joe began to improve as new activities diverted his attention from his failures as a planter. He raised a volunteer militia company and as its captain became so engrossed in his new military duties that he urged Minnie to go up to Badwell so he might be "more at liberty to do [his] part in the martial line thoroughly."[14] But she refused, fearful that he might suffer a relapse and need her help. So they spent the summer together at their beach house despite reports that runaway slaves were skulking in the surrounding woods and fears that federal vessels just off the coast threatened imminent invasion. As a result, Joe joined the special night watch to guard against insurrectionary violence and, on his return to Waverly, regularly drilled his company, which was mustered into the Confederate army early in the spring.

By February 1862, however, Minnie's refusal to leave Joe alone seemed validated when he developed pneumonia and a rheumatism "in the head" that needed her nursing.[15] More devastating to his ego, the men in his company in their May election of officers displayed their resentment of the planter elite by stripping him of his rank. Bitter that he, a Carolina rice planter and the nephew of Governor Robert Allston, was reduced to serving as a private while a man who was his social inferior became the new captain, Joe once again retreated into moody silence.

A similar social upheaval shocked the North Carolina Pettigrews. Following Lincoln's election, both William and Charles had left their old Whig-Unionist Party to become ardent secessionists. But when William ran for a seat in the North Carolina secession convention, he was defeated by a Unionist who had minimal ties to plantation interests. Although Charles and Carey were deeply troubled by the rejection, their attention was distracted by the new house they were building to replace the old Bonarva homestead, which had burned the previous Easter. Even though the unsettled state of things made them build somewhat more modestly than they had hoped, Carey was deliriously happy when the house was finished in May. She enjoyed laying out both flower and vegetable gardens as much as she delighted in planning new uses of interior space. The organization of the barnyard for the forty-cow herd engrossed as much of her interest as providing for future guests. Dreams of the profits to be made from selling garden and dairy surpluses momentarily replaced old worries and staved off new ones while she rejoiced in the promise of instructing her children, extending her reading, and playing her new piano in the wonderfully spacious house.

That summer, wartime reality overwhelmed euphoria. The federal blockade trapped the bumper crops that Charles had expected to sell in lucrative Northern markets. Shorn of income, Carey could not take the children to Cherry Hill for the summer, and for the first time, they all faced the threat of malaria at Bonarva. Nor did things improve in the fall. Corn and wheat were a drug on the local market. Beef and poultry sold no better. Despite these wartime circumstances that thwarted their hopes for prosperity, Carey became ever more patriotic. She accepted the loss of markets as a necessary price for Confederate victory. She was ready "to give up every thing, to accomplish our entire independence of those selfish, insolent" Northerners.[16]

By November, those Northerners increasingly threatened the violence she dreaded. In August they had seized the forts commanding Hatteras Inlet, which gave them strategic bases from which to launch attacks on the mainland. In November their occupation of Port Royal increased fears that the North Carolina coast was equally vulnerable. Moreover, the socio-economic gulf in Washington and Tyrrell Counties separating the poor majority from the small elite planter class created a tinderbox of potential unrest. The "swampers" (lumbermen and shingle weavers) and "agrarians" (proponents of land redistribution) had long resented the relative opulence in which planters lived. And the planters, who by 1861 had become solidly secessionist, now feared not only these dissenters' potential support for an enemy invasion but also their willingness to incite revolt among plantation slaves. So when the openly pro-Lincoln candidate won a militia election in October, class warfare threatened as unionism and populism merged. Behind it all, Carey saw a clique who supported "the Yankees because they assert, [that] they are the poor man's friends & wld only take from the rich."[17]

On February 8, 1862, when 7,500 federal troops landed on Roanoke Island, Carey was minimally surprised that neither the militia, the 300 Confederate troops who had been raised locally, nor the 2,500 Georgia men stationed there offered effective resistance. As she had believed for some time, planning and equipping the island's defenses had fallen victim to "culpable neglect, petty bickering, & mismanagement" within the Confederate command at Norfolk. Whatever its cause, the island's surrender opened the way for federal forces to seize all North Carolina ports north of Wilmington and stage raids inland along the rivers that flowed into them. Wherever federal troops landed—and they held Plymouth, the town nearest Bonarva, for much of 1862—slaves deserted in droves while local "low whites" were, as Carey put it, "not to be trusted at all" because "they wld betray or murder any gentleman."[18]

Carey, however, did not witness those repercussions. The morning after Roanoke Island fell, Charles gathered up Carey, then seven months pregnant, their five children, his sister Annie, and five servants and hustled them off to safety. Traveling at top speed, they covered forty miles the first day, getting as far as Williamston. There, Charles left them to continue the rest of the journey without him. In doing so, he broke with the gentlemanly obligation never to allow ladies to travel without a white male escort of their own class. But he felt compelled to return home to guard his 150 slaves and, should the Yankees actually reach Bonarva, to burn his crops.

Carey and Annie, who never before had traveled under such conditions, now made their way on their own. After 130 miles of rough roads, accidents, and unpredictable accommodations, they arrived at the comfortable home of Raleigh relatives. There Annie remained, but Carey and her flock, after only a single day of rest, pressed on. Eleven days after they had left Bonarva, they arrived in Hillsborough exhausted but welcomed by family friends who fed and sheltered them. George Collins, son of the Pettigrews' Somerset Place neighbors, arranged for Carey to rent a vacant house belonging to his father-in-law. Others lent her furniture. In that, Carey was a most fortunate refugee. Although the house was "not in the best repair" nor very "encouraging looking," it could be made "habitable."[19] The furnishings, although largely castoffs, were adequate.

It was not long, however, before these initial triumphs dimmed as Carey struggled to develop new strategies to support her family. As a first step toward garnering funds for daily expenses, she hired out several of the servants she had brought with her. Then she redistributed household chores so that she could still devote much of her time to teaching the children. None of this was easy. Keeping up her reputation as a "very brave woman" was hardest of all. She lacked the courage to "look ahead further than necessary" as she faced childbirth in a strange town with no adult family members on hand.[20] She took what comfort she could from Charles's insistence that she take refuge in Hillsborough, where good medical attention was available and he could visit her occasionally.

Exactly two months after the fall of Roanoke Island and her flight from Bonarva, Carey gave birth to her fourth daughter, Alice Lockhart. Luckily her sister-in-law Mary Blount Pettigrew had arrived in time to help at the birthing. She stayed on with Carey for the rest of a difficult year, filling in for the long-term nursery governess, Mrs. Armstrong, who had left the South for what Jane North now called "the enemy's land." Still, Carey was so anxious to settle down at Cherry Hill that only six weeks after Alice was born she left Hillsborough for Badwell. It was a wise decision, for there she would have other relatives close at hand. But Charles was determined to plant at Bonarva, ignoring both the Yankees at Plymouth and their poor white allies. During that spring and summer, only a few of his slaves deserted or refused to work. But as the year wore on, it developed into the most "unfavorable season for the cultivation of a crop" that Charles had ever experienced. His field hands showed less and less "disposition to labour."

And the short crop they produced did little to support his family, forcing him to reconsider how to deploy his slaves in the coming year.[21]

Meanwhile, Carey was left to cultivate Cherry Hill on her own after she, her children, and Mary Blount settled there in June. The place had stood empty for two years. The former ineffective overseer had quit in 1861 when Charles had tried to change his contract. His replacement, whom Jane North had hired, was not much better qualified, but he was the best she could find among the war-shrunken pool of employable white men. Moreover, until Carey arrived, his assignment was vague, for Charles had never tried to make Cherry Hill more than a self-sustaining summer home. Now Carey undertook to turn it into a productive plantation. In March, Charles had sent up Jackson, the head plowman at Bonarva, and a small force of field hands to do spring planting. By May, a few more slaves and several wagon-loads of supplies from North Carolina had arrived. Jane had sent substantial amounts of corn and fodder from Badwell. So when Carey first arrived at Cherry Hill that summer, she found an operating plantation, although one her mother doubted could ever achieve year-round self-sufficiency.

Undaunted, Carey set to work clearing more land for cultivation. By the end of June, she boasted that as a "planter!! for the first time," her hands were "very full." Her assertion that she was managing a plantation for "the first time," however, ignored the two years she had overseen the work at Bonarva during Charles's prolonged stays in New York. It was part of the ladylike deference that also made her tell her brother-in-law William that she had "no ambition to be a manager," although she did "*insist* upon . . . being very energetic" and appeared to know more than she really did.[22] But given the overseer's deficiencies, Cherry Hill would fail miserably unless she was an active manager. And given Charles's decision that September, after President Lincoln issued the preliminary Emancipation Proclamation, to move his remaining slaves inland, it was clear that the Pettigrews had only Cherry Hill to support them.

By then, Carey was desperate for her husband's help. Diphtheria had laid her and several servants low. Badly frightened, she wrote Charles a feverish letter begging him to abandon his futile attempts to recover some thirty-five absconding slaves and to bring those he still controlled to Cherry Hill at once. When he received her letter, however, he was already on his way to Salisbury, North Carolina, with most of Bonarva's remaining slaves, whom he hired out to a railroad contractor laying track in the vicinity. Only then did Charles act on Carey's letter, returning to Bonarva, collecting the few slaves he could still locate, and bringing them to Cherry Hill, which he reached in mid-November. Even with the addition of those slaves, the work force there was notably smaller than he had counted on since he had had "to leave a number at Bonarva, some of the best families . . . [who] were dropping from him so fast that the only chance was to cut for it" without them. Almost as grave a loss were "the great supplies & abundance for a store room, lard, butter, flour," which were "so much required at Cherry Hill" but which he had been obliged to abandon.[23]

During the first eighteen months of the war for Southern independence, federal forces had gained control of much of the North and South Carolina coast. Even before the Emancipation Proclamation, they had offered the chance of freedom to slaves within reach of their lines. In the North Carolina low country near Albemarle Sound, native Unionist agrarians and federal forces had dislodged the old elite. The coastal slaveowners, who had chosen secession and supported a war to defend slavery, had lost much of their ability to control their labor force. The men of the Petigru family, James alone excepted, had supported secession as the way to maintain the old order. The Petigru women who shared that conservative commitment now faced not the stasis they sought but a social and economic maelstrom that was destroying their former security. When fathers and husbands could no longer provide, wives and mothers assumed new responsibilities. It was not the autonomy that some of them had sought. Nor was it the future their privileged position had promised. Jane North was not alone when she pondered her grandchildren's fate: "The dear children! I think of them very often, and of the altered prospects of all the young."[24]

CHAPTER FOURTEEN

The Repercussions from the Battlefield

By 1862, the ugly realities of war had already tarnished the Petigru women's initial optimism about a swift and easy victory. By June, more of them had fled their homes than had not. By fall, they questioned whether the South could ever "get the better" of a seemingly "numberless" enemy.[1] Each military engagement drove home the dangers their men faced not just on the battlefield or at sea but also in hospitals and prisons.

Not all of the male Petigrus bore arms. Some were too young—but would not be if the war dragged on. Some were too old—but not for the home guard. Of those who did serve, only Johnston Pettigrew played a highly conspicuous role. Selected by President Jefferson Davis for quick promotion to brigadier general, he was assigned command of a brigade of North Carolina, Georgia, and Virginia regiments in the spring of 1862. By May 31, he was in the thick of Confederate resistance to General George McClellan's bloody peninsular campaign in southern Virginia. At the battle of Fair Oaks (Seven Pines), his insistence on leading his own Twenty-second North Carolina regiment into the fire zone nearly cost him his life. Severely wounded, he declined immediate help and was left on the field for dead when the Confederates retreated. The next day, he was picked up by Yankees and taken to a field hospital. Nursed back to health, he was later repatriated in a prisoner exchange. But before that good news reached his family, they spent five days mourning his death.

Although no other family member held as high a rank as Johnston, all of those who enlisted faced similar dangers and fed similar worries at home.

Charley Porcher, a private in Hampton's Legion throughout the war, fought in several of the numerous encounters that eventually checked the peninsular campaign. Charley's older brother, who had resigned his commission in the U.S. Navy, was serving in 1862 aboard a Confederate patrol vessel in the Gulf of Mexico. Although Phil was not anywhere near the Mississippi River in April when Admiral David Farragut skirted Confederate naval defenses, ran the forts south of New Orleans, and bombarded the city into submission, his family did not know that and feared the bad news the smashing federal victory might bring them. Phil wrote his mother at once to reassure her and to urge her not to despair. Louise, thus fortified, resolved to bear "her anxieties with as much patience as one could hope for."[2]

Like his cousin Charley, Hal Lesesne fought throughout the war in South Carolina's Hampton's Legion, although most of the time as an officer. His father, who was fifty when the war began, was a captain in the "Charleston Invincibles," which Mary Anna Porcher dubbed a "highly respectable corps of elderlies."[3] Organized in the first year of the war to protect the city in the absence of regular troops, they never saw battle. But in the late winter and spring of 1862, as federal troops marched northward along the Sea Islands from Port Royal, it seemed likely that Charleston would come under direct attack. Only after they reached James Island just south of the city were they stopped at the battle of Secessionville. There, on June 16, 1862, Captain Henry King was wounded. He was then carried into the city to his father's house, where he died the next day, the first of the Petigru kin to be mortally wounded in battle. His death made Sue the first and ultimately the only war widow in the family.

Henry's death, coming as it did only two weeks after the false reports of Johnston's, further darkened a year marked by other misfortunes. In early October, Private Joseph Allston, responding to another enemy probe of local defenses, was twice wounded, first at Pocotaligo and then at Coosawhatchie, villages about sixty miles west of Charleston. Although the wounds were superficial, Minnie increasingly worried that his military service would worsen Joe's mental difficulties. At almost the same time, Joe's cousin, Lieutenant Colonel Benjamin Allston, was wounded at Harrodsburg, Kentucky. Receiving little news from so distant a front, Adèle had assumed that her son's regiment was engaged in Generals Edmund Kirby Smith's and Braxton Bragg's unsuccessful Kentucky campaign and had waited in suspense for two weeks before she learned that her son was wounded and a prisoner but also reassuringly safe and well cared for in Lexington.

Despite her passionate support for the Confederacy, Adèle had always anticipated that the war would bring disaster. Even before Ben had been stationed near Manassas when the very first battle of the war was fought there, she had paled at "the awful prospect which lies before us" and believed that "the nature of the contest . . . is most serious, not to say *desperate.*" She worried almost as much about her husband as about Ben. His health had long been uncertain, and now it seemed more precarious than ever. Because of his political preeminence in the Georgetown district, the war placed new demands on his diminished strength. Throughout 1861, Robert Allston had voluntarily assumed much responsibility for local defense. Indeed, Adèle was sure that "he was the only man" in the district "who can be looked to as a leader," especially as doubts about the loyalty of small farmers and towns-folk arose. When "alarms about invasion" increased, Adèle doubted that local forces could beat off federal troops and concluded that their only hope lay with divine intervention. Only God could save the South from the "most wicked and desperate people" who were intent on imposing "great . . . suffering if they succeed." Twenty-one-year-old Della, who before the war had shown little interest in public affairs, now shared her mother's fears and prayers: "Heaven defend us . . . and give each of us the power & will to act wisely."[4]

Robert's accumulating financial problems, whose extent Adèle under-stood only much later, also eroded their security. The blockade that pre-vented his crops from reaching profitable markets drained his ability even to pay the interest on the huge debts he had incurred in the 1850s. Particularly burdensome was the mortgage he had undertaken to pay Ann Petigru for her Pipedown plantation and its field slaves. By November 1861, Robert could pay her nothing, and Ann refused his proposal to cancel the debt and return the slaves. He therefore sent the Pipedown crew along with a large part of the Chicora labor force far up the Little Pee Dee River to keep them safe from coastal raids. But on the minimally productive land he owned there, they produced no more returns than the slaves who had been con-scripted to build military fortifications around Georgetown's Winyah Bay.

Nonetheless, because he still planted at Chicora and operated a new salt-works at Pipedown, Robert refused to flee inland. In the spring of 1862, however, he sent his family to stay with friends near Kingstree until the summer cottage he was building for them in the pineland village of Planters-ville, ten miles inland from the coast, was finished. That fall, he sent Bessie and Jinty to Madame Togno's school, which had moved from Charleston to Barhamville, near Columbia. Their youngest Porcher cousin, Marion, was already enrolled there. And fourteen-year-old Charles Allston, who returned to his old school at Willington, would be nearby—even nearer after he transferred that December to the Arsenal Academy, a military school in

Columbia. For Adèle and Della, who had long since finished school, Robert rented a "very humble" and rather rundown country house at Croly Hill, near Society Hill.[5] So by the end of 1862, all of his dependents were well away from the coast, although only Adèle and Della were in any real sense refugees.

These moves relieved Adèle somewhat. Not only were her younger children safe, but they had all, as far as possible, resumed their customary peacetime occupations as students. Still, the paucity of neighbors at Croly Hill and the discomforts of living in a strange house depressed her. For a short time, Ben relieved her loneliness. Freed in a prisoner exchange, he came to Croly Hill in December to recuperate. For a few weeks, his mother basked in the pride he inspired. But when he recovered sufficiently to rejoin his brigade, she continued to worry about the bullet in his groin, which could not be removed safely, and wondered whether his having been wounded and captured once was a harbinger of worse things to come.

Henry King's family had at least been spared the agony of suspense after he was shot down at Secessionville. But his death left Sue torn by mixed feelings. She had, of course, donned mourning. Still, Henry's death formally ended a grievously unhappy marriage. Although in the early months of the war, it had apparently improved, by late 1861, the whole family knew that Henry and Sue had separated, probably as a result of her role in the Hurlbut affair. Throughout the spring of 1862, Mitchell King, who had long lamented Sue's inability to get on with people, filled his diary with cryptic entries criticizing his daughter-in-law's attitudes and behavior. Nonetheless, he continued to hope that his son's marriage might be put back together. On May 4 Sue seemed ready "to be reconciled." But in Columbia the month before, she had behaved so outrageously with an infatuated young soldier that Mary Boykin Chesnut, the wife of a prominent planter-politician and once Sue's schoolmate, thought her behavior had been "pitiful." Although Mary McDuffie Hampton, the wife of General Wade Hampton, wondered whether the gossip about her was accurate, William Trescot, a prominent intellectual, insisted that Sue was a "fast" woman about whose flirtations people talked avidly but whose "quarrelsome" company they avoided assiduously. Such reports compelled James to go up to Columbia and tell his thirty-eight-year-old daughter that she had stayed there "*long enough*."[6]

At his insistence, Sue returned with her father to Summerville, where he and Jane Amelia now lived. She was still there when Henry was brought from Secessionville to his father's Charleston home. But when, despite his rocky marriage, he gave "his last breath to the name of his wife & daughter," Sue was not present. Although she acted well enough on becoming a widow, her cousin Carey Pettigrew suspected that she had to "act considerably" in so doing.[7]

Sue's daughter, Addy, then eighteen, became "very forlorn" upon her father's death. Throughout her childhood, she had witnessed her parents' mutual antagonism, resentments, and hostility. Because Sue had determined early on that Addy would be her only child, the youngster had associated little with other children. Moreover, Sue had mocked her for being "affected & very absurd," even as a six-year-old. Aunts and cousins readily agreed that Sue had little sympathy with children and no talent as a mother. Her Great-aunt Adèle felt obliged to offer Addy moral instruction because her mother did not. And Della Allston, at fourteen, sympathized with her "poor little" cousin, who got into scrapes at Madame Togno's school because she had "not had the best opportunity to learn the great difference" between right and wrong. Grandpapa Petigru praised Addy when she was sixteen for "growing more like her aunts on the father's side" than like Sue, a thing that neither he nor Sue "ought to regret." And Grandpapa King noted in his diary Addy's complaints about her mother, doubtless opinions he shared. Sue thought she was "always right—whoever differs from her—must be wrong—mental hallucination—She thinks herself infallible."[8]

Although Henry had bequeathed Sue a lifetime income from his estate, the "disordered condition" of his affairs left her virtually nothing.[9] Only her father-in-law, still a wealthy man when he died in 1862, barely five months after his son, could provide Sue the financial independence she craved. But even his generosity to his daughter-in-law, to whom he left one-third of Henry's share of his estate, with the rest going to Addy, availed little. Henry's brothers and sisters insisted that his debts to his father be sub-tracted in full from it, and those debts consumed virtually all of Sue's and Addy's potential inheritance. In the end, Sue received only the $1,000 her father-in-law had bequeathed each of his daughters-in-law independent of her husband's share. A similar provision for grandchildren allotted Addy the same minimal portion.

Although Henry's death had released Sue from a frustratingly unhappy marriage, widowhood without the means to live comfortably left her little freer to follow her own preferences. For room and board, she must depend on the hospitality of her parents, her in-laws, and her friends. For everything else, she was on her own. She hoped she might support herself by her pen. But wartime constraints closed New York publishers to her as much as they closed New York markets to her planter kin. She had to search long and hard even for a Southern firm to bring out *Gerald Gray's Wife*, her best novel, which was almost complete when Henry died. When a Richmond house finally issued it in 1864, it paid her next to nothing. Furthermore, this novel drew the harshest denunciation of anything Sue had written as knowledgeable readers recognized the settings, recalled the incidents, and saw through the thinly veiled depictions of real-life Charlestonians.

Jane North, generally more appreciative of Sue's writing than most of her kin, thought the new novel was "written with more vigor than the predecessors and less portraiture perhaps."[10] But she was shocked by how much Sue's own experiences were reflected in her portrait of a marriage rooted in male deception and female self-deception and how deliberately she attacked prevailing social values. It would have been more prudent not to have published it. But prudence had never been Sue's style, and Henry's death left her so desperate for money that even the pittance her Richmond publisher offered was irresistible. It did not go far. Nor did her attempt to earn money by giving readings prove rewarding. So like many other impecunious Carolina ladies, she began to work as a clerk in the Confederate treasury office in Columbia.

Like her sister, Caroline Carson was also thrown on her own resources. When she had chosen to go north, she cut herself off from all direct contact with her family except for William Carson's sister and brother-in-law, who lived in New York. But unlike Sue, she kept her old friends and carefully cultivated new acquaintances. Each sojourn in the North had added to her list of friends there, and when she was exiled from the wartime South, they proffered aid. Indeed, in wartime New York, Caroline was welcomed as a representative of her father, whose outspoken loyalty to the Union many patriotic Northerners celebrated. Massachusetts Republican congressman Robert Winthrop called on her, as did Caleb Cushing, who had chaired the 1860 Democratic nominating convention. Historian George Bancroft expressed his admiration for the father directly to the daughter. And bon vivant George Templeton Strong entertained her, less because she was "conversable, agreeable, and handsome in a mature style" than because she symbolized Southern unionism.[11] Of more practical assistance, a former schoolmate who had married George Schuyler opened not only the highest reaches of New York society but also her home to her exiled friend. Likewise, Christian E. Detmold, a prosperous entrepreneur who had been somewhat of a protégé of her father's, was both endlessly hospitable and a font of sensible advice.

So Caroline felt comfortable living in New York. Indeed, at one time, it had seemed possible that she might marry a Northerner. After her husband's death, she had attracted many men. At her father's dinner parties, she met not only local politicians, lawyers, and intellectuals but also distinguished visitors in town to litigate or lecture. Among them was Edward Everett, a man only five years younger than her father, who in the past had been president of Harvard College; a Massachusetts congressman, senator, and governor; and American minister to England and secretary of state. In 1858 Caroline and her father entertained him at both family and formal parties when he lectured in Charleston and stayed in their home. Family members quickly perceived that this prestigious Bostonian paid Caroline a great deal of attention, and they speculated about what was going on. Jane North observed "a slight touch of sadness" in Everett's demeanor and attributed it to his wife's being insane and near death. The sadness, however, lightened whenever Caroline was present. Everett spoke to her "in the most paternal manner as my dear" and held her hand "a good deal." Jane speculated that "if he were to be freed from the matrimonial yoke there is no telling what he might propose."[12]

Even before his wife died in July 1859, he was addressing Caroline as his "dearest love" and pledging to her that he was "totus tuus." So when Caroline came home in December of that year sporting a new emerald and diamond ring, it was not surprising that Lou North thought it might be an engagement ring. Interest in the putative romance peaked in 1860 when Everett ran as the vice presidential candidate on the Constitutional Union ticket, headed by John Bell of Tennessee. Minnie Allston imagined the glory her cousin might enjoy should Everett be elected, marry Caroline, and give her the opportunity to "eclipse the Presidentess." But soon after the Bell-Everett ticket went down in resounding defeat, Everett broke off whatever his commitment to Caroline had been. As she explained it to her Aunt Jane, all was "over between Mr Everett and herself" because "his health & fortune both failing makes the sacrifice necessary."[13] So by 1861, when Caroline arrived in New York as an exile, the romance was finished.

Part of Caroline's loss was the economic security that marriage to Everett would have brought. Since 1859, the purchaser of Dean Hall had paid nothing on his mortgage. After the federal blockade cut off profitable rice markets in 1861, he stopped planting altogether. So in 1862 he rented the place to a Sea Island planter eager to move his slaves inland. Although James Petigru hoped the new arrangement might be "good news for Caroline," none of the rent money ever reached her. As a result, for the first time in her life, she had to count every penny she spent. Even so, she was so much in debt by June 1862 that she begged her father to send her $1,100, which she knew he could ill afford. For more than a year, she had subsisted "nearly on the charity of friends," paying month-long visits to those with Southern Unionist connections like the Lowndeses, to old New York friends like the

Schuylers, and to new acquaintances like Mrs. Starr Miller of Rhinebeck, a "Lady Bountiful" who befriended her solely as a tribute to her father.[14] By the end of the year, some of her New York friends put together a kitty of $2,100 so she could rent her own apartment in the city and enjoy a measure of stability.

Now, however, Caroline worried increasingly about her sons. Willie was not doing well in his commercial studies in Europe. Neither the Swiss school he first attended nor the Berlin and Dresden businesses in which he was subsequently apprenticed spurred him to make much effort. Even the salaried position he landed in Frankfort that in 1862 promised to make him self-sustaining lasted less than nine months. Without a steady job to occupy him, he cultivated an enthusiasm for the Southern cause that horrified his mother. She had "counted on that boy as safe" but now feared that Willie might return to South Carolina and join the Confederate army.[15]

Caroline's younger son, Jem, who "tug[ged] most at [her] heart strings," caused her even greater anxiety. Because he was sick when she left South Carolina in 1861, she had reluctantly left him behind under her father's guardianship. He was, at sixteen, still enrolled in the Willington Academy near Badwell, where she hoped he would be sheltered from wartime hysteria. He was not. Although the wrenching separation from his mother made him "very grave, almost amounting to gloom," it had not converted him to her politics.[16] As soon as he turned seventeen in April 1862, he wanted desperately to get into the fight. His mother, desperate that he should not, pressed him to join her in the North. Jem refused, with some backing from his grandfather, who declined to force him to leave his native state. When his grandmother wrote triumphantly of Johnston's urging Jem to seek a commission in the cavalry, the letter spurred Caroline to yet more frantic strategies for luring him north.

In truth, Caroline's campaign mixed parental love and maternal fear with a modicum of self-interest. "My friends provide most generously for me now," she explained to Jem, and she counted on earning something by her art. But surely he and Willie "would not have me all my life dependent on other people, while you are having yourselves consumed for the rage of S C."[17] She was, however, also fearful that her sons might stagger to alcoholic deaths in their father's footsteps. In her eyes, life in the Confederate army, fighting for no principle she thought worthy of respect, would surely destroy the self-control she had tried to implant in them.

Jane North was just as concerned that Jem might fall "into low & dissolute company" among enlisted men. Still, she could not condone Caroline's insistence that her son come north. It would have been far better for her niece to have stayed "among her own people" instead of joining "those transcendental progressionists." Carey Pettigrew, even less tolerant of her cousin's choices than her mother, regretted that she had "decided to cast her lot with the enemy" and resented the letters she wrote her father begging him and her mother to come north. Mary Anna Porcher concurred that Caroline's letters were a public embarrassment to all of her kin since they were doubtless opened and read during their devious routing from New York to Charleston. Jane Amelia found her daughter's carryings-on not just treasonable but a clear indication that she "must be mad." Jem, caught in the torments of emerging manhood, felt shamed by his mother's advice that there would be "no dishonour" in his seizing the "only chance" to avoid Confederate military service by making a run through the lines.[18]

Both her Southern kin and her Northern friends overlooked the ambivalence in Caroline's loyalties. In June 1862 she condemned the blind folly of Southerners, who, in launching a war to defend slavery, had instead "overthrown it." Four months later, she read Lincoln's preliminary Emancipation Proclamation as a device to entice slaveholders to end the war at once by promising that if they did so the proclamation would be "restricted to its narrowest bounds" and "the extreme of Emancipation [would] not be insisted upon." Except for this underlying acceptance of slavery, however, she consistently endorsed federal war goals. She celebrated General Ulysses Grant's victory at Fort Donelson because it "revive[d]" her hopes that the nation might yet be restored to the grandeur it had enjoyed when she was born. She praised George Bancroft's 1862 Washington's birthday address, which placed Chief Justice Roger Taney and his *Dred Scott* decision "where he deserve[d] to be" and "set up" Jeff Davis "in a pillory before the world."[19]

Having thus cast her lot with the North, Caroline had to make her own way there. Gradually she realized that her pride if not her survival demanded that she begin to support herself by her own efforts. In a conventional, ladylike way, she had long dabbled at sketching and painting. So when she finally had a settled base of her own in New York, she enrolled in drawing classes at Cooper Union and took private lessons in pastel and watercolor techniques as well. She hoped she could make her living as a portrait painter but all too soon realized that, although her friends might buy her drawings for $20 apiece, strangers would not. So she turned to "the only lucrative business open" to her and learned to tint photographs.[20]

All told, the events of 1862 made great demands on both men and women but in different ways. Boys aspired to the manhood that military service represented. Young men learned to endure both the tedium of camp and hospital life and the life-threatening demands of battle. Older men, long settled in comfortable lives, scrambled to provide protection and basic necessities for their traditional dependents. Women learned to be more self-sufficient. Public events intruded on their domestic life and shaped their emotions more than ever before. They feared for the lives of their soldier kin. They feared invasion and its repercussions on their slaves' behavior and their own safety. They feared the loss of their homes and mourned up-heavals in how they lived. But they did not surrender to those fears, even when military defeats inflicted private loss. In differing degrees, almost all of them found new ways to replace or supplement their traditional dependence on men. It was not an autonomy they sought consciously. It was a wartime necessity.

CHAPTER FIFTEEN

The Roof Tree Falls

The more public events impinged on their lives and the more visions of a swift and sure triumph faded, the more critical the Petigru women became of their political and military leaders. Early on, the shock of the Yankee triumph at Port Royal had made Mary Anna Porcher suspect treason on the part of the Confederate general who surrendered there, for his brother had remained an admiral in the U.S. Navy. Similarly, when the defenders of Roanoke Island made only a feeble stand against the federals, Carey Pettigrew attributed the disaster to a Georgia colonel's overconfidence that he need do nothing to block an attack because "he cld whip the Yankees when they landed." As for broader failures in strategic planning, General Benjamin Huger, who commanded the whole Norfolk district and was said to drink so much that he was "often . . . entirely unfit for business," bore responsibility for the "frightful curse" the war had already become. Surely only "inexplicable" mismanagement or deliberate "treachery" could explain what had happened.[1]

Minnie Allston was similarly outraged by the Confederate military deficiencies that opened the door to federal victories in Tennessee in early 1862. Mary Anna shared her cousin's conviction that official malfeasance and cowardice lay behind "the disasters in the West," for although "the ranks appear willing to fight, . . . the miserable officers prefer a retreat always to the risk of being shot." Like Carey, she suspected that the "boasted generals" who caved in so easily had "taken to *drink!!*" Indeed, she had heard that there was "not one sober officer in the whole Army."[2]

If drink was not the explanation, then treason must be. Or if treason was not responsible, then complete military incompetence must be. What else could explain Grant's victories at Fort Donelson and Shiloh? What else could have opened the way for Admiral Farragut's gunboats to steam up the Mississippi, circumvent the many riverine fortifications south of New Orleans, and take the city by surprise? Even Jane North suspected either that "treachery" lay at the bottom of these western defeats or that the South was "dreadfully out generalled." Either possibility bore out her conviction that war was always "a dreadful game—and never without untold misery."[3]

In response to these defeats in the West, even ardent supporters of the Confederacy became critical of the civilian government in Richmond. Mary Anna was baffled by its "stupor" in meeting naval and ground attacks. Moreover, she blamed the spiraling inflation and food shortages that were acute by 1863 on politicians who lacked the will or skill to govern. Her Aunt Jane, who admitted that her faith in Jefferson Davis "was never much," commented wryly that his early supporters only now understood "how prosperous the country was before [being] ruined by politicians." But there could be no turning back. "Alas! for our country, & alas for ourselves."[4]

In 1863 no Petigru faced starvation. But as the price of corn shot up from $2 a bushel in 1862 to $3 in 1863 and other prices rose similarly, even those in the country faced malnutrition. At Cherry Hill, the high price of meat drove Carey to experiment with a vegetarian diet. But when Charles arrived there in December 1862, he was so appalled by his wife's gaunt appearance and his children's pinched faces that he insisted on a return to more nourishing fare even though they could ill afford it. Necessities other than food were equally scarce and expensive. Jane North found that she could not buy "a shoe for [her] people, except three mean pair" that she had "picked up by chance." When, the next month, she located twenty-five pounds of shoe leather to be cobbled at home, the excessive price made her wonder whether things would "ever find their level again." The following spring, Charles failed to find even the cotton yarn that Carey needed in the cotton-producing North Carolina piedmont. There was, he reported, "nothing but extortion among the factory men."[5]

Far worse than shortages and high prices were the deaths that ravaged the family in 1863. Private Dan Petigru, then not quite forty-one, died not from battle wounds but from the "nauseous disease" he had contracted in an army camp south of Charleston. Because it left him with a severely ulcerated throat, he was furloughed home for treatment. For the next six months, he lived with his parents in Summerville and went down to Charleston for medical attention. After staying in the city for the long New Year's weekend,

Dan died suddenly on the morning of January 5. His father got the news an hour or so later on his way to town and immediately sent a note to Jane Amelia before he continued on to the city to make funeral arrangements. Her grandson, Jem Carson, was with Jane Amelia when she opened the note, "fell back & schreamed hysterrically a ½ doze[n] times." Within minutes, however, she calmed herself, reflecting briefly on how much her wastrel son's behavior had improved in his last year. Throughout the day, she swung back and forth between extreme grief and compensatory consolations, and that night, Jem heard her groans echoing throughout the house. The next day, still in a state of high tension, she opened a newly arrived letter addressed to Dan. "Dear husband," it began and went on so full of "various endearing epithets" that Jane Amelia guessed her son might have been secretly married. Notwithstanding the "terrible shock" it gave her, she wrote the letterwriter, Miss McDowel, at once, telling her that "if it was so she was ready to receive her as her daughter and the sooner it was made known the better for her character." Apparently, McDowel did not respond. When he next wrote to Caroline, Dan's father referred neither to the mysterious lady nor to her letter, but he said enough to cast doubts on his son's reformation. Dan's features, he reported, had remained handsome enough even in death to remind him again of the "encouragement from ladies on whom he made a favorable impression" that his son had regularly encountered.[6]

Few family members other than his parents grieved much for Dan, whose shiftless ways and distressing misconduct the family had long lamented. Still, his parents mourned the death of their only surviving son. For Jane Amelia, it added to the woes of her invalidism. For James, its timing was critical, for it sharpened his awareness of his own decline. As of January 1863, his only significant source of income ceased with the termination of his commission to codify South Carolina statute law. But well before then, his failing health had roused his sisters' concern. At seventy-three, he was overweight, short of breath, frequently hampered by severe chest pain, and often depressed. He hinted at the extent of that depression in a letter to a friend written in July 1862. He had just "lost Henry King," and Johnston Pettigrew was held "a prisoner and wounded . . . in Fort Delaware. My house," he continued, "is burnt & I live at Summerville, and Mrs Petigru suffers from nervous debility as much as usual."[7] Even so, he refused to give in. Throughout late 1862, he commuted almost daily to Charleston in order to complete the code on schedule. In December, when he became too sick to commute, Ann Petigru invited him to stay in her empty town house. In January, convinced that he needed personal attention, Adèle reopened her Charleston house and cared for him there. Within weeks, however, General

Beauregard ordered women and children to evacuate the city, and James had to be moved to the King mansion, where Henry's brother still lived.

By February 21, the old lawyer knew he was dying and called on Henry Lesesne to add a codicil to his will. Shocked by his brother-in-law's condition, Henry notified the rest of the family. Jane North and daughter Lou managed to get down from Badwell on March 7, the same day that Harriette Lesesne reached Charleston from her upcountry refuge. But Adèle got to the city only on March 9 a few hours after Brother had died. Jane Amelia never came.

James's death left "so terrible a void" in the Petigru clan that his sisters could barely write about it. Adèle tried to compensate by beginning to call her fourteen-year-old son Charles by his middle name Petigru. For Louise Porcher, her brother's death sharpened the pain she still suffered from the recent deaths of her two oldest daughters. Minnie Allston found no words to express the "magnitude" of the family's grief. But Jane North came closest to doing so when she grieved that the family's "roof tree has fallen."[8]

Perhaps somewhat blinded by his grandmother's vagaries, Jem reported that Jane Amelia "wasnt so much affected as was expected."[9] Her husband had done all he could to ensure her future support. She was to have the lifetime use of all of the income his estate produced, and if that was not enough to keep her in comfort, the capital, with the exception of Badwell, which could not be touched as long as Jane North or Mary Petigru lived, was to be tapped for Jane Amelia's support. The war, however, largely negated the will. Henry Lesesne, its executor, sold the empty Broad Street lot and with the proceeds purchased Confederate bonds, which within two years were worthless. In 1863 the slaves James had left brought only a small return. No buyers offered to purchase his law office or his valuable collection of legal books. Other assets left after his debts were paid were valued at little over $8,000. As a result, most of Jane Amelia's income came from the Bank of Charleston, whose directors honored its longtime solicitor by pledging to support his widow. In the old days, family members rather than a public institution would have been Jane Amelia's ultimate safety net. Accordingly, Ben Allston wrote his father from his military post authorizing him to contribute an appropriate sum in his name. But by 1863, even Robert Allston had no money for such purposes.

Ironically, it was Sue King who, in addition to her Uncle Henry, most helped Jane Amelia. She had been visiting Summerville before her father died and stayed on for almost a year. But living with her mother again was, as her father had predicted it would be, a "severe trial." Only her daughter

Addy's presence for much of the year made the tensions bearable. Sue was too mercurial. She felt trapped in an arrangement she never would have chosen voluntarily. She chafed at the restraints her own "peculiar" life experiences imposed. But she had no place else to go. Her remaining friends were few. Madame Togno no longer offered her a refuge in Columbia. Living with her in-laws was hardly a comfortable alternative. Even the few friends on whom she could pay calls from Summerville generated self-pity: "I am obliged to shut my eyes & ears to the most glaring things, or else live in total solitude—for between the supercilious neglect of one half & the covert slander of t'other, my couch of life has *many crumpled rose leaves*—& I really have to be *grateful* to those who *only* abuse me behind my back, & are not impertinent to my helpless face. And then for my as-yet-unexploded-in-any-way acquaintances—not only is their number very small, but like the sieges, it is a mere matter of time."[10]

Jane Amelia was just as full of self-pity. She wrote long, incoherent letters to Henry Lesesne in which she complained about his stinginess. But he had done everything he could to assure her a yearly income of almost $3,000. He had even persuaded the Bank of Charleston to forgive James's outstanding debts. Still, the widow's income would not buy the delicacies this sixty-eight-year-old invalid demanded or the opiates that her pains and her thirty-year addiction required. Without them, her "nervous debility" soared. Because the blockade had made morphine virtually unobtainable, she had recently been dosing herself with a combination of laudanum (a tincture of opium) and brandy. But as prices for everything skyrocketed, that too threatened to evade her reach. Without a quart of laudanum a month, which cost over $15 when she could get it, she fell into "spasms" and "convulsions."[11] So in pages and pages of incoherent ramblings she pressed her brother-in-law for more money. In similar style, she pleaded with George Trenholm to have his blockade-runners bring her morphine. And to everyone she complained that living in the summer cottage James had rented in Summerville was killing her.

Behind her peevish complaints lay miseries complicated by James's death. Jane Amelia was stalked by the hallucinations common to recent widows. She imagined that James was physically present and was "constantly looking round to see him." Returning from her afternoon carriage rides, she would glimpse him "at the top of the steps in the Piazza," where he would "hold out his hand and say well Jane [where] have you been, and who have you seen." When the apparition vanished, there was "no one to sit with" her. Sue laughed at such nonsense: "Poor Mamma! she has been accustomed to have

Papa make believe he thought her dying whenever she went on so." But although Sue would not "perform such comedies" as her father had, Jane Amelia would not "give up the dodge."[12]

Even though Caroline Carson was spared her mother's demands, she was more profoundly affected by her father's death than Sue was. Because direct communication with the South had become rare by 1863, she learned that her father had died not from a friend or relative but from a newspaper. Facing a future without his advice and sympathy made Caroline feel more desolate and insecure than ever before. Sympathetic Northern friends could not compensate for the absence of kin. Edward Everett realized this, as he also grasped the practical consequences for a lady with neither father, nor sons, nor property available to support her. Attempting to bridge the coolness that the end of their earlier intimacy had created, he now reached out: "Allow me, who am old enough to be your father, to take your father's place, in this respect. I ask it of you as an act of kindness to me, assuring you that you could do me no greater."[13]

In part conscience salving, the offer was also generous. But it stung Caroline badly. The emotional wounds he had inflicted still chafed. That this man who had once promised so much and then retracted should intrude on her new grief abraded her pride, and Caroline rejected his offer with unusual bitterness. "There was but one person who might have shielded me through the accumulated sorrows of the last two years. . . . But he was not equal to the trust, and I must bear all this alone." She claimed that the kindness, charity, and tender concern of her many other friends was all she needed. "I want nothing that you have to give," for "having nothing I possess all things." With cool assurance she closed her letter: "I would have you feel no disturbance on my account, . . . and I remain as always yours with perfect sincerity."[14]

That same gritty independence provoked her to attempt to return south. Although doing so would endanger her personal security, diminish her income, and challenge her newfound autonomy, her concern for Jem overcame her doubts about doing so. She had heard nothing from him or about him since the previous December. When news of her father's death arrived, she was plagued by fears that her son would soon join the Confederate army—if he had not already done so. So before the month was out, she began to pull the strings that would allow her to travel to Charleston. Her father's friend, General Winfield Scott, wrote on her behalf to Secretary of War Edwin M. Stanton, making the most of her plan "to smuggle away a Son who is about attaining the age that will subject him to be drafted into the rebel army." Almost immediately, the War Department forwarded the documents allowing Caroline and her maid to travel to and from New Bern, North Carolina, on a military vessel. But it took another month before she received authority to pass through Union lines. Never, despite her direct appeal to General Johnston Pettigrew, did she receive permission to pass through Confederate lines. But that was of little consequence, for by the time she had received all of her papers from Washington, she was too sick to travel.[15]

It was then that she received the devastating letter her mother had written with the intention of making Caroline the scapegoat for all of the miseries the war had inflicted. In it, Jane Amelia deliberately lied to her, telling her that Jem had joined the Confederate army as Johnston Pettigrew's aide-de-camp and predicting that "Willy will come as soon as he hears this." That was, she concluded, only just punishment for Caroline's treasonable association with an enemy fighting not "about the Blacks or the Union . . . [but] to crush us only from malice."[16]

The rest of her kin were not much more forgiving. Henry Lesesne concluded that his niece would have been mortified by her reception in the South had she come. Even her father had discouraged an earlier, short-lived plan on the grounds that such a visit would be "painful" for her and "serve no good purpose." Less kindly, Lou North thought that Caroline's 1863 plans betrayed her cousin's "usual unhappy want of judgement to go away when she should have remained & return when it is detrimental to her in every way to do so." Johnston, who had never lost his fondness for Caroline, probably ignored her request for a Confederate pass to shield her from the "bitterness & enmity" she would undoubtedly meet in the South.[17]

By not going, however, Caroline reaped benefits she might otherwise have lost. Everett was among several anonymous "gentlemen of Boston" who, at his initiative, raised $10,000 as a "*testimonial*" to James Petigru's "great merits" and invested it in U.S. bonds for his daughter's benefit. Despite her refusal of Everett's early offer to help, Caroline surely needed a reliable source of income and replied that she was "honoured" to accept "the monument which they raise[d] up to my Father."[18]

That monument was the only substantive repair of the family's fallen roof tree and the past it represented. The clan's greatest hope for an equally luminous future died when Johnston Pettigrew, already wounded in General George Pickett's famous charge at Gettysburg, took another bullet while commanding the rear guard protecting General Robert E. Lee's retreat. Rather than risk being taken prisoner again, he insisted on being carried by his troops into Virginia, where he died on July 17. When she first heard of his role at Gettysburg, Carey Pettigrew had "such faith in a kind Providence" that she could not think that "anything so sad is in store for us as hearing of [his] being again desperately wounded." But on July 21 news of his death reached Cherry Hill. This time, there was no reprieve. Jane North lamented, "Our brightest hope gone . . . all our hopes for the future of this frail life put out." As they had in the past when the deaths of young people had severed glowing anticipations, his kin sought strength in submission to God's will. Because His will now seemed to favor the enemy, those earlier appeals for God's intervention on the South's behalf gave way to increasing secular hopelessness. Confronted with Johnston's death, Minnie Allston embraced the despair of Calvary: "My God, My God why has thou forsaken us." Her mother, borne down by the loss of "a man of so much genuine genius and capacity," had to struggle to subdue previously unthinkable doubts, doubts that "must be put down, for they cannot be answered without uttering discontents unlawful for a Christian."[19]

Carey was the only one to respond more in anger than in despair. So much battlefield carnage, the loss of so many men made her bemoan women's impotence to enter the fray more actively, and Johnston's death only deepened her frustration at the gender-defined role that left women "only as hitherto [to] work & pray for their defenders." Adèle Allston laid bare the seeming inutility of faith when human endeavor failed. Like her elder sister, she saw "nothing to cheer" by July 1863. "If this war lasts two years longer," she predicted, "African Slavery will have ceased in these states." "If we had had a great general to command our forces in Penn," she continued bitterly, "we could have gone any where and put an end to the war. Such was not the will of God." "All that we dreaded has thus far happened."[20]

When Caroline Carson heard the news of Johnston's death, she thought at once of Jem. Her mother had written that Johnston had asked him to be his aide-de-camp. Had Jem then shared his cousin's fate? She pressed the many federal officers she knew to ascertain whether her "poor boy has fallen, is a prisoner, or among their wounded." From lieutenant to general, these officers and their friends searched hospitals and prisons and scanned lists of the dead for his name. None found any trace of Jem. After a month, Caroline concluded that he was probably safe. But the episode left her on edge, more furious than ever that her mother had "felt no reluctance to inform me of that which she knew would fill the measure of my sorrow."[21] Sue King didn't even bother to write her sister that Jem was relatively safe in Charleston serving in the Confederate Signal Corps. But at least rumors that Willie was trying to join the crew of a Confederate raider never reached her before he arrived in New York in December 1863 aboard a Cunard packet. And within a month, Caroline's friend Samuel Blatchford had secured him a clerkship in the New York office of the Illinois Central Railroad.

Because of that same isolation in New York, Caroline learned that Jane North had died only months after it happened. The decline and death of Badwell's doyenne threatened the Petigru network as fundamentally as had James's and Johnston's. Her health had deteriorated steadily during the late 1850s when she had acted as her own overseer, constantly exposed to the weather and subjected to a series of accidents. Her stamina had been further strained by the trials of accommodating the wartime refugees who flocked to Badwell. Finally, the shock of Brother's death when she was sixty-three completely broke her health. Pressed by her daughters to take the waters at South Carolina's Glenn Springs, she spent most of the summer there. But she only grew worse. The food was almost inedible—"sour and wretched" bread and no butter.[22] She fretted constantly about leaving family members to cope with a leaky roof. She had ample time on her hands to worry about the many young men—the sons of friends as well as family members—likely to be killed or mangled on the battlefield. She despaired that Charleston would not survive an anticipated Yankee attack.

Back home in early September, she was sicker than when she had left. She suffered "dyspepsia in its most violent form, violent burning in her chest & vomitting after eating anything however slight."[23] The loss of her wheat, rye, and oat crops to a vicious hail storm and her field peas and sweet potatoes to searing drought obsessed her with fears for her dependents. Unwilling to surrender the burden of Badwell, she did her best to carry on. But nothing could ease the pain in her swollen stomach as the tumor she felt there grew steadily.

By the end of October, Jane's daughters and all of her sisters except Adèle were at Badwell to see her through her last days. Their vigil ended on November 5 when she died, "her mind . . . at perfect peace." But her "distressed afflicted family" faced an "awful blank," for as a schoolmaster neighbor put it, she had "filled the position of 'head of the family' as thoroughly as any man ever did." Now Mary, by the terms of Brother's will, took over the homestead. And "poor dear Sister Mary" was, at least in Harriette Lesesne's eyes, "by nature & habits most unfit." Moreover, she and Louise Porcher were such "combustible elements" that they were unlikely "to control themselves sufficiently to enable them to get on in the same house."[24]

By the time she died, Jane's religious faith had been severely tried. She was convinced that only God could turn around the tragedies of the war, but she doubted that He would. Her letters, like those of her kinswomen, reverberated with litanies drawn from the Book of Common Prayer. It was not a novel recourse. Except for Mary, who was a Presbyterian, the Petigru women were all Episcopalians and had often used the same ritual phrases to comfort each other as they had mourned the death of a young child. But as the war dragged on, public events propelled them to use those phrases as a counterweight to their loss of secular hope. At first their confidence in an easy Confederate victory had seemed to confirm Louise's assurance that a benevolent God smiled on them. But as mounting defeat cast increasing doubt on that divine blessing, their appeals for God's mercy, expressed in phrases from both communion and Lenten services, reflected helplessness instead of hope. Recognizing the extent of human vulnerability that the Confederate collapse at Port Royal had revealed, Lou North was newly compelled to understand "that submission to God is the great lesson in Life." Overwhelmed by private grief at Brother's death, Lou's mother responded similarly to public "disgrace and defeat." "Nothing but the influence of Religion can keep down bitter sorrow & sad repining," because religion required sufferers "to take up [their] cross and bear it with courage & constancy." When as "a pilgrim & wayfarer travelling home" Jane faced her own death, she mingled grief for both public and private losses. "The love of country" and the "love of friends" were alike "temporal and temporary."[25]

If Jane's faith gave her strength to endure, Louise Porcher sought from hers the power to set the terms of that endurance. Ever since 1835 when she had embraced the evangelical mode William Barnwell had injected into traditional Episcopal ritual, she had put her trust in an implicit contract with the divinity. She believed that "continual Prayer" and "such good works as the times seem to call for" would win God's mercy. But faced with the disasters that war brought, her faith nearly failed. Acknowledging that "without God[']s help our case is desperate from every point of view" now only drove her to doubt God's immediate oversight. Although she tried to put aside "all vexing thoughts & trust in God with a feeling of submission," actually doing so was a severe challenge.[26]

Adèle Allston had never shared either Jane's resigned submission or Louise's evangelical optimism. Her prewar diaries record a tormented struggle with a feeling of spiritual unworthiness. So great was her "sinfulness of . . . heart, love of the world, covetousness, envy and all uncharitableness" that she could scarcely hope for the "God of mercy [to] forgive us our sins, and purify our hearts." She had accordingly accepted her personal trials and losses as well-deserved punishment for her own iniquity. But extending that understanding to public events produced an unease that undermined her faith more severely than the war disrupted either Jane's or Louise's. The defeat at Gettysburg tempted her to heresy. Pray as she would "for resignation, perfect resignation," to God's will, it did not come. And Harriette Lesesne, who had seen in South Carolina's victory at Fort Sumter "the wonderful interpositions of God" that protected "our brave men" and sent "storm & wind . . . to serve our cause," fell absolutely silent about religion as she became preoccupied with the personal deprivation that war inflicted.[27]

Among the second generation, religious responses varied even more widely than they did among the first. Doubtless the least committed of them all before the war, Sue King had spoofed high-church ritual and cut short a brief flirtation with Methodism. But immediately after Sumter, she startled the whole family when, at the age of thirty-seven, she was confirmed in the Episcopal church. Minnie Allston doubted the sincerity of this "conversion," and there is little evidence that it lasted, for Sue apparently did not seek religious consolation either after Henry's death or after her father's. To Johnston's demise, she responded more patriotically than piously by allowing that heavenly mercy would ultimately prove stronger than "Yankee engines" and "Yankee doggedness."[28] But Caroline Carson, who had read widely in religious literature since she was in her mid-twenties and was a consistent churchgoer, never gave up her quest for a mystical union with the divinity. While she lived in New York, she considered various religious alternatives. She toyed with the conservative Unitarianism of Orville Dewey. She found in Ernest Renan's 1863 *Vie de Jésus* a believable historical Christ who preached a moral revolution that would ultimately ameliorate the human condition. It is likely, however, that her secular identification with the victorious North as much as her religious studies made it easier for her than for her kin to continue believing in a benevolent God.

Certainly for the rest of the family, the events of 1863 nourished disbelief in divine benevolence. The year that began with the Emancipation Proclamation, reached its nadir in defeat at Gettysburg, and concluded with the sweeping federal victories that cut the Confederacy in half could scarcely do otherwise. And the deaths of kin that deprived the Petigru clan of the two who had most cemented the family in the past and of the one who had most promised it a distinguished future induced a spirit of desperate futility. Some replaced hope with Job-like resignation. Others were denied even that consolation.

CHAPTER SIXTEEN

Life Goes On

On June 24, 1863, just nine days before the Confederate defeat at Gettysburg, Della Allston married Major Arnoldus Vanderhorst in her parents' Charleston home. The event was extraordinary. Three years earlier, when Arnoldus was already courting her, it would not have been. Then, with the country at peace, her mind was filled with memories of a glorious social season and anticipations of a relaxing summer. Not yet twenty, Della could "afford to be very quiet" after the nineteen balls and many more small parties at which she had shone that winter.[1] Even the season's end did not end the courting. On balmy early summer afternoons, the same young gentlemen who had been her dancing partners all winter escorted her on long rides out of the city. Although Pinckney Alston soon became her most persistent suitor, Arnoldus Vanderhorst was her apparent favorite. And family gossip already speculated that a match was in the offing.

The son of Elias Vanderhorst, a large-scale planter on the Combahee and Ashepoo Rivers who also owned Kiawah Island and a major Charleston wharf, and Ann Morris Vanderhorst, a native New Yorker with extensive property in the North, Arnoldus seemed an appropriate suitor to the elder Allstons. Robert had made no secret that he expected his daughters to marry, marry early, and marry well. Lou North certainly thought that Arnoldus met Robert's prescriptions for a suitable husband. He was "a good young man," and, she reminded her sister Carey Pettigrew, "you know the Gov's views about women marrying." But Della, like so many other belles, enjoyed being the center of attention too much to be lured into an early marriage. Lou, still unmarried at twenty-seven, sympathized, allowing that if Della did "not feel like it certainly no one would think she should."[2]

But a year later, when the war drew so many of her old flames into the army, Della assessed the situation rather more soberly as she wondered what the future held in store for her beaux—not just Arnoldus but Grimké Rhett, Julius Blake, and especially Pink Alston, whom she singled out as a friend "I am truly sorry to lose." Then she added, "I will think of him," only to cross those words out as revealing too much even for her diary. Mr. Chisolm, however, was quite another matter. That summer, Della turned him down abruptly. She had no doubt that he was an "excellent person," but she simply did not even want to think about marrying. Her reservations then seemed less a preference for life as it was or a recognition that wartime was no time to marry than a sense of her own deficiencies. If her suitors knew "all that passes within, out of the reach of every human eye," they would certainly not propose to one as little "amiable" as she.[3]

Nevertheless, Arnoldus's departure for the Virginia front caught her emotions unprepared. Her "really . . . warm friendship" with him would make her "miss him very much." Later, as the first reports of Manassas reached her, she feared for his safety. For several days, she found it hard to conceal her feelings for the young officer. It was then that her Aunt Jane North guessed that Della would eventually "smile" on Arnoldus. Although he was "not all we could wish," still, "a good temper, a good fortune & a good character" went "far to recommend a man." Yet Della's apparent coolness in his presence made her question the match, for "if the little God does not light the torch it is a poor business." One Georgetown neighbor even suspected that Arnoldus had been "driven to the point of the bayonet from hopeless love."[4]

Her Aunt Jane's two-pronged observation probably came closer to the truth than Della herself realized. But she was pressed toward marriage by wartime conditions. In 1862 the threat of invasion and the necessity of moving to Croly Hill eroded her former sense of security. The death of her nineteen-year-old cousin Louly Porcher had laid bare her own mortality. And the enemy's proximity to Charleston closed that onetime center of her social life. Moreover, there was Arnoldus's constancy. So early in 1862, she promised to marry him. But no sooner had she given her word than she drew back. Writing in her diary that "this is no time for engagements," she wished she "had not yielded to his entreaties thinking [she] could make him happier than he was." Consequently, acting on her parents' advice, she refused to set a date for the wedding until the war was over. Because Arnoldus was still optimistic about a speedy Confederate victory, he at first consented to wait for the "blessed peace" that would allow him and his bride "to live in uninterrupted pleasure."[5]

For much of the year, the young couple exchanged frequent letters full of romantic love, male chivalry, and womanly nobility. Della wished she were "a man to take part in this war," but Arnoldus was "delighted" on his "own selfish account" that she was not. "What would we do," he asked, "without the women of our country?" Lacking their "spirit, and bravery," the cause would already "have fallen through." Why? Not because of the uniforms they sewed or the nursing they did, but because Southern men fought for "woman[']s love," and "every man in the army knows that the brave women at home would despise them if they behaved badly in the great battle." But as McClellan's army besieged Yorktown and then drove up the Peninsula toward Richmond, Arnoldus's view of war became less romantic. Facing his first battle that June, he was "anxious to be through" with it. Even though McClellan's army was turned back, his optimism about a speedy and definitive Southern victory vanished. He therefore resumed his own personal campaign, pressing Della to set an early date for their wedding. By December, further delay seemed intolerable. "It is a long time to wait for the end of the war . . . quite too long for one who was four years in gaining his object."[6]

Military defeats and Lincoln's preliminary Emancipation Proclamation also took their toll on Della's plans for the future. In October 1862, at a plantation near Chicora Wood owned by Francis Weston, the head carpenter and "18 others of his finest, most intelligent and trusted men had taken his family boat . . . at an early hour after dark and made their escape to the enemy."[7] At once, Robert Allston took preemptive action, buying a 1,900-acre plantation at Morven, North Carolina, some ninety miles up the Great Pee Dee River from his South Carolina plantations. That winter, he transported inland those slaves who had not been hired out for railroad construction or impressed by the government and who were not essential to operating his saltworks or maintaining his own, Ben's, and Joe's plantations.

Since Morven was little more than twenty-six miles from Croly Hill, where Della and Adèle continued to live, they saw Robert regularly as he traveled back and forth between Morven and the coast. But only during the summer, when the women joined Robert in their recently constructed cottage at Plantersville, did the family live together. After their return to Croly Hill in the fall, Adèle twice ventured to Charleston with Della—in January 1863 to care for her ailing brother and in March to attend his funeral. As Della's life grew less settled, Arnoldus's pleas for an early wedding gained ground. On a March visit to Croly Hill, he spoke so eloquently for an April wedding that Della almost gave in. Finally, in April, she set a June date.

The prospective wedding provoked conflicting responses. Della's brothers openly doubted its wisdom. Bessie was grimly silent. And Jinty, the youngest sister, said outright that June was "entirely too soon." On the other side, Arnoldus's insistence that he would "not hear to its being put off any longer" gained support from the bride's father. Meeting peacetime expectations as closely as conditions allowed, Robert followed the social rituals prescribed for a planter father. When Arnoldus asked his permission to marry Della, just as he had sought parental permission to court her before the war, Robert responded punctiliously: "You had permission to win my dear daughter's affections, if you could. If you have succeeded in this, and can make her happy as she deserve[s] to be, I will not withhold my consent." But in his absence, when Arnoldus presented himself for the customary conversation about the groom's finances, it was Adèle, not Robert, who had to be convinced that he had the resources to "take care of his wife while he lives, and make provision for his widow if he should be so unfortunate as to be taken from her."[8]

Having concluded that this was so, Adèle, facing "the first wedding in our family," determined to make it "a great event."[9] In the middle of the war, that required infinite ingenuity. The Vanderhorsts insisted on its taking place in Charleston despite the nearness of federal troops just south of the city. The Allstons, however, had removed all of the good furniture from their Charleston house to protect it from damage by enemy shells. So Adèle ordered furniture shipped down from Chicora Wood. With fine fabrics almost unavailable at any price, she ransacked her own wardrobe for the trousseau. Similar inventiveness and the resources to pay the exorbitant prices blockade-runners asked enabled her to fashion a wedding that closely resembled the one she had dreamed of when she had contrasted the humble circumstances of her own with the most elegant of prewar nuptials.

The Vanderhorsts, as parents of the groom, had less-demanding roles to play, but they too met traditional expectations. A week before the wedding, Elias presented his future daughter-in-law with heirloom jewelry as a promise that Della would always find in him, "when a certain event takes place, a kind and affectionate parent."[10] Early on the wedding day, both fathers signed the marriage contract by which each pledged to place $10,000 in trust for the couple's benefit. Finally, on the evening of June 24, 1863, Della descended the steep, elliptical stairway of her parents' house, radiant in a dress of Brussels net and white silk smuggled through the blockade and a lace veil made from her mother's most treasured shawl. There she took her father's arm, only to relinquish it when he gave her in marriage to Major Arnoldus Vanderhorst. At the reception that followed, the guests were astounded by an array of food that defied wartime shortages and, still more remarkable, the sufficient, if not copious, supply of French champagne that Robert had somehow secured. Except for Della's older brother and three of Arnoldus's, the immediate families on both sides were present. Those absent were all on military duty. But beyond the bride's immediate family, only Henry Lesesne, Carey Pettigrew, and Lou North graced the ceremony—a marked difference from Carey's peacetime wedding ten years earlier. The absence of so many of Della's kin was mute testimony to how the realities of war shaped even this apparently idyllic moment. Only two weeks later, the Yankees resumed their bombardment of Charleston. It continued with little remission until the end of the war. Della's nuptials were thus a brief, almost surreal interlude.

Even so, she and Arnoldus began life together under far more favorable conditions than did most Southern couples married in 1863. Because he was assigned to General William Whiting's headquarters in Wilmington, North Carolina, they could actually live together, albeit with accommodations and a way of life markedly different not only from their prewar expectations but also from Arnoldus's earlier fantasies of a wartime domesticity in which his future wife would be "as nice and as neat a little housekeeper as any in the land." The rooms he was lucky enough to rent were small and cramped. He was unable to give this daughter of a great rice planter "all the advantages a young wife should have." And Della was just as deficient in managing her urban household. Neither as a Charleston belle nor as a plantation daughter had she ever shopped for food, and her first trip to Wilmington's market revolted her. She could not stomach the "small dirty place with meat vegetables & fruit indiscriminately piled" in a fashion that was "eminently disagreeable particularly before breakfast."[11] She vowed never to return.

The newlyweds' housing was only slightly less depressing than the market. Its limited space and facilities for storing and preparing food gave little scope for the chores necessary to keep three servants occupied. "We have little to cook, soup being the principal thing but if Jack is sent out for any thing or called off from the kitchen in the least, John immediately takes his stand in the vacated domain 'to see after the soup' as he always says on inquiry." Inept as a manager and disgusted with the resources available to her, Della distanced herself from the domestic chores Arnoldus had so romanticized. With little else to keep her busy, she found that time passed very slowly indeed. Her first fortnight in Wilmington seemed "the longest two weeks" she had ever spent.[12] Only Arnoldus's regular return for midday dinner and his limited office duties, which allowed him to spend most afternoons with her, eased the tedium. But their long walks together relieved her boredom only minimally, and when unfamiliar people called, she was stiff and uncomfortable.

After only a month in Wilmington, Della snatched the chance to visit her mother for six weeks at Croly Hill, ostensibly to recover from a rheumatic attack. While she was away, Arnoldus managed to rent a six-room house to provide better living arrangements and give Della more to do on her return. But that return also marked the end of the honeymoon. November 22 was, so she wrote in her diary, the "first evening Arnoldus has passed away from me since June of his own accord."[13]

Della's marriage did not leave Adèle alone at Croly Hill. That fall, Bessie and Jinty stayed on to study under their mother's tutelage and that of a Dr. Read, who taught Bessie German and Latin and gave piano lessons to both girls. In addition, Bessie, now eighteen, gave French lessons to a neighbor's child. Although their social life was a far cry from that of prewar Charleston, both girls enjoyed the novelty of the covered dish suppers and country dances with which their neighbors amused themselves. Still, those rural pastimes also bothered Jinty. She had never seen "more regular-cracker-dancing than they have here" and thought that a dancing " 'professor' would be the greatest blessing to the place."[14] A few months of such complaints convinced Adèle that her thirteen-year-old daughter still needed the systematic teaching that Madame Togno's school continued to offer in Columbia. So early in 1864, Jinty accompanied her brother Charles, now almost sixteen, when he returned to his military academy in the state capital.

During the early months of 1864, therefore, Adèle had a slim household at Croly Hill. Even Bessie was away for much of March visiting Della in Wilmington. And Robert made only brief stops on his monthly trips between Morven and the low country. Luckily, Bessie had returned by the time Adèle received the message from overseer Jesse Belflowers that Robert was desperately sick. Although his chronic ill health had worsened under wartime strains, he had refused to shed any of his responsibilities. While Adèle worried about his physical decline, Robert fretted most that "in moving about" he would "neglect something, overlook many things & perform [his] duty imperfectly." He constantly worried about his enormous debt burden and what would happen to his family when he could no longer attend to his complicated business affairs. He prayed that God would grant him "health & memory for [his] duties." In February 1864, aware that both were failing, he left the relative safety of the Plantersville cottage for the comforts of Chicora Wood's big house.[15] So it was to Chicora that Adèle and Bessie hastened.

By the time they arrived, Robert was bedridden. As committed as ever to salvaging his family's future, he could do little now except wonder about what lay ahead for Ben. With no news from his son in the western theater, he took to musing about whether Ben would ever return to take up life as a rice planter. If he did, he would surely need a wife to make life on an isolated Georgetown plantation rewarding and, just as important, to assure the family's continuity. But as far as his family knew, Ben at thirty was still unmarried. He had had his "tender passion[s]" but had been unfortunate in love. More positively, he had escaped entanglements with women of whom his father could never approve, "the Ladies (however beautiful, accomplish'd & agreeable)" Ben had met in his peacetime army service.[16]

Just two days before Christmas in 1863, Ben was in Eagle Lake, Texas, visiting the wonderful woman he had met the previous month in Houston. In a letter they received several months after it was written, Ben assured his parents that she was "very bright, intelligent," and pretty, with "natural" and "unaffected" ways. Indeed, she "interested" Ben more than any other woman he had "met with for a long time." The indirection with which he wrote virtually acknowledged that she fell far short of his parents' expectations. Although pretty, her appearance was marred by very bad teeth. Her "natural" ways bespoke a minimum of social polish. All told, Ellen was "a wild flower of the prairies, never having known much restraint, or been much taught." But it had been love at first sight. He asked, "How would you all be pleased with me to bring home . . . a companion from the 'wilds['] of Texas?"[17]

Ben did not wait for an answer. On February 24, 1864, he and Ellen Stanley Robinson were married. He had admitted to his mother the month before that his army pay was insufficient even to support himself as a bachelor and would surely fall far short of supporting a wife. He did not remind her that he had already drawn on his father for $5,000 just to cover his own expenses. But he did recall that she had once promised to treat his wife like a daughter even if he should marry a "squaw"—although he also recalled her belief that his own good sense would preclude such a mésalliance. Nonetheless, the deed was done. So when word of Ben's marriage to his "wild flower" reached Chicora Wood in early April, Robert wanted Adèle to have Ben send Ellen to South Carolina, where "we will take care of her."[18]

Robert spoke those words from his deathbed with Adèle and Bessie at his side. Although he was furious that Belflowers had summoned them without his permission, he welcomed his wife and daughter when they arrived on March 27 and was grateful for their nursing. But neither they nor his physician could halt the progress of his congestive heart failure. On April 11 Robert Allston died. As she watched her husband of thirty-one years fade, Adèle was horrified "to see his manly & noble form, his able head & strong arm all prostrate & powerless. Warmth gradually decrease. Coldness. Silence insensibility take the place of warmth Love tender emotion." Now she must try to replace him as the family's head. Bessie wrote Ben that their mother was resolute, "very calm," and "wonderfully supported in this sore affliction."[19] But she was wracked by self-doubt as she faced managing the family's finances. She dared not look ahead. She recognized as never before how much Robert's prudent management had provided her and her family security. As a widow responsible for three minor children, she must now cultivate the very prudence and self-restraint that had made her husband seem so cold, so resolute, so distant.

Adèle's first weeks of widowhood were eased by her kinswomen's condolences. Lou North, still grieving for her mother and so many others who had died recently, mourned "that never has a family had to pass through such ordeals of suffering & loss as we are called on to endure." Carey Pettigrew lamented that "one blow ha[d] fallen after another, since Uncle's death little more than a twelvemonth. How many have been taken from our family; all in the midst of their usefulness, & never more important to those who are left to mourn." Sue King, reviewing the deaths that had riddled her own generation and thinned the generation of her parents, concluded that "this unholy, wicked War has killed many besides those the Yankee bullets have struck." Nor did Robert's death end the deadly procession. That same month, Louise Porcher got the news that her son's ship had been sunk and that Phil was among the missing. It was Jane Amelia Petigru, however, who most directly expressed the grief of widowhood that she shared with Adèle: "Your time has too soon followed mine of the greatest trial a woman can have to bear and to lose so kind and good a man. I dont pretend to try to give any consolation, that is out of the question. . . . You have great cares on your shoulders, and children to look up to you for protection and *aid*, and of course I who know you so well, am sure you would never be so foolish as to sit down mourning, when you have so much of duty to perform."[20]

Her new duties drove Adèle through the next decade. Happily, Robert's will did not, as she had feared it might, favor some of their children— presumably the sons—over the others. Each child was to receive a plantation and an equivalent number of slaves for its operation. Adèle herself was bequeathed the Charleston house, whatever servants she might need, $50,000 worth of stocks and bonds, and all of the silver, furniture, carriages, and horses she chose. She was also responsible for managing all of the property since her coexecutor, her brother-in-law Henry Lesesne, was only minimally available. Therefore, her initial efforts were directed toward keeping the estate intact until the war ended and a final distribution could be made under peaceful conditions.

Her life as a plantation mistress had taught Adèle much about management. She had run the house, gardens, and barnyard as well as all domestic manufacture at Chicora Wood. During Robert's many absences, she had undertaken general oversight of the home plantation. Never before, however, had she assumed full responsibility for all of the Allston plantations and their labor force, which in 1860 had numbered over 600 slaves. By 1864, their number had diminished, but the supervision of those remaining had grown ever more difficult. One hundred of them were up at Morven. They and those in South Carolina working on the five Allston plantations and at the saltworks were her immediate responsibility. Those who had been hired out to build railroads or work in government shipyards also required much attention if she was to derive any income from their hire. Those conscripted to build military fortifications were worrisome chiefly because inadequate shelter or rations endangered their health. Keeping track of them all had strained even Robert's skills, many of which Adèle lacked. Moreover, for the first time in her life, Adèle faced financial responsibilities for business operations about which she knew little. Often Robert's accounts gave her no guidance. Where were the funds to pay the interest on outstanding mortgages? How was she to meet the exactions of regular and special wartime taxation? How was she, with Henry Lesesne's legal advice so distant, to verify Robert's holdings, his outstanding mortgages, and the property on which his estate might legally be taxed? How should she judge what bills were legitimate and, of them, which should be paid first? How could she make those indebted to Robert pay up their obligations so that she had the cash she desperately needed? Often this tangled thicket of competing necessities thwarted her. Nonetheless, she grappled with it all as best she could.

When the crops were harvested in the fall of 1864, marketing them presented additional difficulties. How could Adèle shield plantation produce from military requisition so that she could get a fair price for it from civilian buyers? Once, because there was no domestic market for it, she evaded the blockade to smuggle a bale of cotton to Nassau. But the price it brought barely paid expenses. Thereafter, she concentrated her efforts on selling rice. When the price seemed right, she negotiated sales in either Charleston or Columbia. But even making such traditional arrangements required time and effort. She had to write innumerable business letters. She traveled frequently from Croly Hill to Morven and to the home plantations near Georgetown. Often her best efforts were frustrated. Sometimes there was no alternative to accepting defeat. When a War Tax Office bureaucrat insisted she sell him some property at a price Robert had earlier refused, she knowingly caved in to extortion.

Equally resistant to her control, as it lately had been to Robert's, was the fast-shrinking labor force. Since early 1863, when news of the Emancipation Proclamation reached them, Allston slaves had asserted their independence ever more boldly. Soon after Robert's death, Belflowers reported rumors "of a Party giting up to Go off," although at present he thought "the People all Seames to be Quiet With the exception of Some 4 or 5 of the younge People which is suposd to be in the Party Consernd." As Confederate troops left nearby bases to go to the front, the early trickle of deserters swelled to a flood. In July 1864 Adèle suspected that Maum Mary, previously one of her most trusted house servants, was behind "all these plans for escape," even concealing her runaway son in Chicora's big house. She was sorely perplexed about what action she should take. Were she a man, she wrote her teenage son Charles, she would have Mary and her husband "removed & put in confinement." But she was not a man and so concluded it was best "to let things remain as they" were. But not entirely. She wrote Belflowers to "take the keys at once" from Mary and James, for it did not seem "reasonable or right to leave negroes in the enjoyment of privileges and ease and comfort, whose children go off in this way."[21]

At Ben's Guendalos, where there was no white overseer, the driver who had been left in charge was apparently slaughtering Ben's hogs and distributing the meat liberally. Food supplies at Nightingale plantation were reportedly similarly confiscated. In a vain effort to stem further liberation of persons and supplies, Adèle petitioned Colonel Francis Heriot, the commander of the remaining Confederate forces in the Georgetown district, to halt the continuing "abstraction" of able-bodied white men from the area.[22] He complied to the extent of forwarding her request to Governor Andrew Magrath, who in turn sent it on to President Davis. There the matter died.

Fending off impending disaster at home only added to Adèle's perplexities about Ben. As the eldest son, he would, in normal times, have assumed many of his father's responsibilities that now fell to her. But as a Confederate colonel on duty in the West, he could do little. Moreover, without his father's driving ambition and competence in practical matters, his presence might not even prove helpful. Nonetheless, Ben was torn between the competing demands of family and military duty, with little guidance from his mother's letters, which took one to two months to travel between South Carolina and Louisiana. Indeed, their letters often crossed on the way, compounding Ben's confusion. The letter that Adèle wrote in late May reminding him that his dying father had refused to send for him did not reach Ben until he had received leave to go home to aid his widowed mother. Almost simultaneously, a letter from his brother arrived describing their mother as "very much distressed, & very much worried about the affairs of the estate" and much in need of help but also containing Adèle's ambiguous message that Ben "ought not to leave to come over, although she would be very glad to see" him. Charles, an unusually astute observer for his sixteen years, realized, as Ben did not, that neither course would satisfy their mother, for if she "were to be deprived of the privilege of being anxious," she "would not be at all happy."[23] Meanwhile, Ben equivocated between his desire to fill the patriarchal role to which he believed his father's death entitled him and his desperate need for his mother's approval.

Then things got even worse. Early in June, his Shreveport office desk was looted of his official papers and some $12,000 in government funds for which he, as a purchasing agent, was responsible. When this catastrophic news reached her, Adèle wrote Ben two puzzling letters. On July 2 she informed him that without Robert's prudence and resources, finding $12,000 to cover Ben's loss would be nearly impossible. But only three days before, she had written that there was "no comparison between the loss of fortune and the loss of *honour*. Fortune; property we must all lose to a greater or less degree. We may be reduced to poverty, and have to live by our work, gain our daily bread in the sweat of our brow; but Oh! let no reproach rest on our name, our good and honourable name."[24]

Baffled by this ambivalence, Ben was also perplexed by Adèle's response to his marriage. Having learned of it while her husband lay dying, her grief at both events intermingled. Pressed by Robert's dying wish, she felt obliged to welcome Ellen as a daughter. Nonetheless, Ellen sensed coolness in her mother-in-law's communications. In turn, her letters to Adèle displayed a distant and defensive edge. She always referred to her husband as Colonel Allston. In her first letter to his mother, she asserted that he was "perfectly content with his choice" and that she therefore expected that the expressions of goodwill his family had so far made would not be "weakened" when they met her in person. That she intended to be a "good wife," Ellen thought, was sufficient ground for Adèle to be "more than satisfied" with her new daughter-in-law.[25] Adèle reserved judgment.

Ellen's pregnancy further complicated Ben's dilemma about coming to his mother's aid. If he and his wife were to go to South Carolina, they must leave his Shreveport post by September, for the baby was due in November. Because his mother's wishes were still unclear, he canceled his intended leave

THE WAR YEARS

in August, and Ellen went back to Texas to stay with her recently remarried mother. So it was in Austin that Adèle Allston's first grandchild, the third Adele Allston, was born. Thereafter, nothing went well. Ellen missed Ben horribly in a town where she knew almost nobody and in a house where her stepfather made her uncomfortable. Childbirth had left her physically miserable, troubled by back pains. Nursing made her nipples sore. And because her milk was inadequate, the baby was fussy. When little Adele came down with thrush, tending her drained Ellen's remaining strength. Remembering the days of her courtship and the first months of marriage was her only relief from sadness. On the first anniversary of their engagement, she recalled their mutual satisfaction as Ben's love and her "own deep affection" mingled. "All then was bright no hard realities, nothing but a long dream of happiness." But within a year, her life had become burdened with "the cares and sorrows of womanhood."[26]

War had not blocked Della's and Ellen's marriages. Nor could Robert's death and Adèle's widowhood be attributed to it. But it had shaped the nature and circumstances of each. Neither young woman, each the wife of an officer on active duty, entered into the life of comfort and luxury that as a plantation mistress she might otherwise have expected. Robert's 1860 will leaving 100 slaves and a plantation to each of his children and the requisites for a sophisticated urban life to his wife was already a hollow mockery when he died in 1864. Instead of plentiful leisure, Adèle faced demanding challenges to the family's economic survival that made her appreciate at last the relentless drive, self-control, and steely work ethic of the patriarch she had so resented even as she had valued the security of being his wife. Widowhood did not bring the autonomy for which she had so long yearned.

CHAPTER SEVENTEEN

The War Drags to a Close

By late 1864, the Confederacy's fate was sealed. Military demands had already drained the South's material and human resources. Ongoing warfare generated only more casualties, more defeats. Severe shortages propelled soaring inflation. And the enemy's rapidly expanding control of Southern territory narrowed the support the Richmond government retained. To the extent that they did so, the Petigru women escaped the acute depression common to refugees largely because most of them had moved inland in family units. The Porchers, Minnie Allston, and Ann Petigru at Badwell lived close to the Pettigrews at Cherry Hill. The Allstons at Croly Hill and the Lesesnes in rented homes near Spartanburg were farther removed. But by mid-1862, they had all found refuges that remained relatively safe until the last months of the war. After Jane North's death, however, significant changes occurred at Badwell. Louise and her two daughters returned to their family's Goslington plantation just north of Charleston. Minnie and her two daughters left for Dryslope, the 133-acre farm close to Cherry Hill that Joe bought for them, leaving only Ann Petigru, Mary Petigru, and Lou North at the old homestead with Jack and Tempe nearby in the China Grove house. Although these moves eliminated much of the friction at Badwell, her sisters worried that living with her two admittedly eccentric aunts was hard on Lou, who nonetheless did "her duty bravely, however irksome, however trying."[1]

More deeply disturbing to them all was the fear that outright resistance to slavery would spread inland. After the Confederate draft had removed most able-bodied white men from upcountry farms, Jane, who for twenty-five years had confidently headed a household devoid of white males, rejoiced when Brother won an exemption for her overseer, who was now "the only man capable of keeping things in order should the blacks take it into their heads to be unruly in this part of the country." Things were little better at Cherry Hill. The slaves who arrived from Bonarva could report how much the nearby presence of federal troops had diminished planter control. Doubtless they also were aware that those left behind at Bonarva were "dropping off one or two at a time," with "young prime fellows" leading the way. Possibly they knew that the Emancipation Proclamation had cleared the way for the commander of federal troops in Washington and Tyrrell Counties to free all remaining slaves and encourage them to plunder the big house and commandeer all plantation supplies. Even Charles's decision to move most of Bonarva's laborers inland and to hire them out to a railroad contractor proved disastrous because the railroad contractor who employed them paid pitifully small wages, worked them unmercifully hard, and fed them appallingly little. Surely the "black ruin" Jane had prophesied in 1862 had descended on the Pettigrews.[2]

Cherry Hill offered little consolation as Carey found that running it became ever more difficult. At first neither house servants nor field hands gave her "the slightest trouble." But they began to engage in passive resistance as soon as the 1862 crops were planted. Carey detected "a certain slackness . . . [although] otherwise every thing [was] as usual." Consequently, with help from her mother and her neighbors, she succeeded reasonably well in running Cherry Hill year-round as a self-sufficient farm. The complexity of her tasks, however, gradually undermined her self-confidence. Was she really competent to manage completely on her own? Her newly hired overseer threatened to leave. When cold weather came on and Carey could find no leather for shoes, the field hands refused to work unshod. And when she contemplated hiring out some of the slaves to bring in a cash income, she hesitated to do so because she had "no confidence" that they would not seize the opportunity to run away.[3]

By mid-1863, mere slackness was giving way to overt sabotage and worse, especially since Charles, despite his residence at Cherry Hill, was often absent trying to protect his interests elsewhere. Only if he stayed there constantly would Carey feel "satisfied the negroes will not recklessly destroy the corn in the field." Only his steady presence would make the slaves curtail their woods meetings, whose loud singing and "great 'carryings on'" she heard nightly from her bedroom. Carey was frightened by their leader, Africa, and sure that despite his deceptive veneer of deference, he would "pervert every negro on the place if he goes on so." He would most certainly "join the Yankees & commit every enormity if he has a chance."[4]

These trials were made the more bitter by the fact that Johnston left his entire estate to William Pettigrew. He had long openly deplored Charles's poor management and spendthrift ways. Still, to leave his older brother not even his part ownership of Cherry Hill rankled. But although Charles and Carey knew nothing of William's will, which would ensure their children's full ownership of the plantation, they held no grudge against him as their inviting him to live with them testified. And when William declined, it was largely because he wished to remain close to the slaves he had hired out in Chatham County, west of Raleigh.

As a result, William was nowhere near Cherry Hill when Louise Valerie was born in July 1864, although he was among the first to send congratulations. For Carey, the birth of her seventh child was less a source of joy than an occasion for resignation. Two years earlier, when her Uncle James had commended her for almost equaling Queen Victoria's proliferation of progeny, she had shot back that she had no "desire to emulate her Majesty!" Still, with five daughters and two sons born in only eleven years of marriage, she was fast approaching her majesty's amazing fertility. Once again, however, the rest of her family found that the baby's only fault was being "another little *girl*." But the child's Great-aunt Louise quipped that no one had ever considered the five sisters who comprised the first generation of Petigru women "too many." And Mary Anna Porcher cheerfully observed that the child's sex would make her "much more of a comfort than a boy could ever be."[5]

But for Carey, the addition of another child was no comfort. She was already overwhelmed by too many claims on her resources. Tallow for candles like leather for shoes had become almost unobtainable. Her efforts to manufacture much-needed cloth were thwarted by servants who loafed as much as they spun and broke looms, for which she could find neither spare parts nor material to repair old ones. Food was so scarce that ten-year-old Charley's emaciation was only partly explained by his secretly sharing his dinners with his dog. And fewer adults were available to help her meet multiplying crises. Her mother was dead. Mary Blount Pettigrew left for Richmond in March 1864 to assume duties as the chief matron of a military hospital. And Armstrong had not returned.

Unlike her sister, Minnie Allston had had no previous preparation for managing an agricultural operation before she lived at Dryslope. At first, she employed an overseer. After he quit, she relied on Charles Pettigrew's farming advice and Charles Allston's reassuring presence when he lived with her while he attended nearby Willington Academy. At least until he left to attend school in Columbia, this teenager reinforced Minnie's authority. Most of all, however, it was Carey on whom Minnie depended for both psychological and material support. Their houses were near enough to allow them to visit frequently, exchange produce from their gardens, and lend each other servants when special skills were needed.

Nothing, however, assuaged Minnie's worries about Joe. After the wounds he received in 1862 at Coosawhatchie healed, he returned to active duty, first at various posts along the South Carolina coast and later in Virginia. His transfer far from home to a more active war zone multiplied Minnie's anxiety. In June 1864 he was wounded again and furloughed. When he returned from South Carolina to Virginia in early 1865, he was wounded a third time and then taken prisoner. Through it all, Joe's personality changes continued to haunt Minnie as his constant criticism undermined her composure. "How unwise in a man," Carey reflected, "to thwart [his wife] at every turn, & for every mistake or failure, see no fault in the servant but aloud always blame the wife who has to gain every thing from them by contending." His nagging eroded mistress-slave relations so that by 1864 Carey believed that Minnie's servants had become "utterly ungoverned, & nearly ungovernable." Carey attributed the problem to Minnie's weak organizing and management abilities. But Minnie blamed her chaotic household, as well as Joe's mental deterioration and the ill health of her two remaining daughters, on the "awful war" whose end she could not see.[6]

Like her sisters, aunts, and cousins, Minnie no longer looked for relief from a Southern victory but simply awaited the war's end. So too did Louise Porcher, whose son Charley was wounded in the late spring of 1864. In June she was still lambasting General Grant as a most "dangerous enemy," but she no longer hoped that either Confederate leadership or divine intervention would save the Confederacy. Indeed, she had become so fatalistic that she spent that summer in Charleston, choosing to take her chances amid Yankee bombardment of the city rather than spend the malarial season at her husband's plantation. Even in the city's northern reaches, she and her daughters heard the whistling of shells coming so near that Satan himself seemed to have sent "his chosen servants . . . to enlarge the borders of desolation beyond what we thought possible." After the first frost, they again opted for Goslington, where, until January, they felt notably safer. But when General William Tecumseh Sherman's army swarmed into South Carolina from Georgia, no place was safe. Mary Anna, who feared their time was at hand, tried to cultivate a "trust" that invasion and surrender might still somehow be "averted."[7] Nobody, however, believed that they would.

Although Caroline Carson welcomed Union victories as the just dispensation of a benevolent God, even she was appalled by the destruction that war continued to unleash on the South. From May 5 to May 12, 1864, the "dreadful carnage" in the Wilderness and at Spotsylvania drove home the incomprehensible cruelty of the war. "Who ever heard of seven days battles before? The best plea the Southerners ever offered for separation was that we were different peoples. But the battles show we are of one blood. None but Americans have ever so fought." Despite her horror at the casualties, however, she still prayed for Grant's success and praised Sherman's long march through Georgia to the sea. The destruction they wreaked must surely open Southern eyes and "unseal" the Southern common sense needed to bring these bloody scenes to a close.[8] But not yet.

Despite being "suffocated" by these events, however, her Southern kin still harbored an "intense detestation of the enemy," which Grant's policy of "unconditional surrender" continued to inflame. Yet more than ever before, death and the fear of death hung over them. By the time her sixteen-year-old son was drafted in 1864, Harriette Lesesne's alarm for her eldest son's safety had already made her question the reason for more fighting. Stationed then at Fort Sumter in the very emplacements from which he had helped drive federal forces three years earlier, Hal had so far survived a vicious Yankee bombardment for infinitely longer than the Carolina attack that had launched the war. But how long could his luck last? Harriette wondered whether continued resistance was of any utility. How "many of our bravest and best must fall even if we are able to repel the enemy?"

When Charles Allston turned sixteen the same year, Adèle, like Harriette, contributed her second son to the war. Both of the Porchers' sons had been on active duty ever since the war began. They had escaped harm until Phil was among the missing and Charles was wounded in 1864. It was then that the Porchers' stoicism amid "terrible . . . calamities" began to waver. At first they knew nothing more about Charley than they knew about Phil and lived "in a state of fearful suspense not knowing from hour to hour what blow may fall." Louise never saw "Mr Porcher come in without an awful thumping at the heart & every ring at the bell causes the same. I try to be still & know that it is God—'not a sparrow falleth &c.' "[9] Finally, however, word came that Charley's wound was superficial and that he was being so well cared for by a Richmond family that he was back in action almost at once. Three months later, he was wounded again and again he survived.

Each time his family had waited only days to learn Charley's fate, but Phil's remained unknown forever. That spring, the *Juno*, on which he was an officer, had been overdue in port for a month before word reached Charleston that it had been sunk. Of the vessel's two well-stocked lifeboats, only one, with but two sailors aboard, was found. As soon as he heard that news Phil's father accepted the fact that his son was in all probability dead. But his sisters continued to hope, prolonging their "agony of suspense and doubt." For almost a year, "every day seem[ed] of an unnatural length" as they waited for their brother's return. His mother wavered between denial and acceptance, desperate to know definitely one way or the other. The indecisiveness doubled her melancholy. "What is so dreary as suspense! alas I know from experience all the slow agony it inflicts!!" As was her wont, she turned to religion but found little comfort. Like Adèle, who wrote Louise as soon as news that the *Juno* was missing reached her, not knowing tried her faith even more than knowing the worst. They both prayed "that God will not abandon us. That He will in his good time help us and that He will give us grace not to fall from Him, neither for the pains of life or death."[10]

Although neither of her sons was even wounded, Caroline Carson for a while faced fearful premonitions unknown to her kin. In the year following his grandfather's death, Jem had refused to write his mother. Consequently, her first direct news of him in more than a year came in letters Jem wrote in March and April 1864. Until then, she had imagined battlefield scenes endlessly repeating those that news of Johnston's death had first sparked. That was bad enough. But at the same time that she learned definitely that Jem was a private in the Confederate army, federal draft law that had previously exempted a son who was the sole support of his widowed mother was changed. Now she confronted visions of Willie's being conscripted and facing Jem as an armed enemy. Jem virtually wallowed in the prospect. Enraged that Willie, whose sympathies must lie with the Confederacy, might fight for the Union, Jem angrily wrote his brother two scathing letters. To his mother he wrote a minimally more gentle one, conceding grudgingly that a Southern woman had the right to choose a Northern residence, especially if, like Caroline, her health suffered in warm climates. Southern chivalry made him proclaim that it was "nobodys dam[ned] business in what place she chooses to live, her honor is the same & after the war [if] any one criticises her course if a lady I cut her acquaintance if a man I fight him." But to his brother, he made no such concessions. It was possible for a Southern man to be loyal to his section but not spend his entire life in the South. He might even leave it permanently, once the war was over. But to absent himself in wartime was treason. Willie's post was now in his native region and "not with Lincoln." Until Willie should act on that premise, Jem threatened what his mother most dreaded: "If ever I got a commission & were to meet you in battle, Id shoot you as I would a dog."[11]

Caroline was stunned at the unbridled vitriol her younger son unleashed.

Jem ranted that he would rather never have been born than face the disgrace with which his mother and brother now tainted his life. Then he stopped lest he "say something which is unbecoming of a son." Caroline answered both letters with a mixture of maternal love and reprimand. Defending Willie, she reminded Jem that "in a civil war it is surely no dishonour for a son to espouse the cause of his mother, to stand by her and put himself in the way of maintaining her by his labour." Still, she feared that her Abel might slay her Cain. She was appalled by "the possibility of having to send the one son to meet the other perhaps in deadly combat. Every day 'the pale hand draws the dark foldings of the eternal curtain closer & closer round me.'"[12]

Only Sue managed to defy that enveloping gloom. When she left her mother's Summerville home in December 1863, she went straight to Columbia, where, as her cousin Mary Anna Porcher put it, she undertook "to make herself notorious during the sitting of the Legislature." She succeeded. War widow or no, she appeared "in brilliant colours and carried off all the finery she could collect." When she first arrived, her old schoolmate, the prominent socialite Mary Boykin Chesnut, interpreted her "scarlet facings" as a signal that she had "hauled down the flag of distress (widow's cap) and run up a Union Jack." Although her meager purse obliged her to live at Mrs. Rutger's boardinghouse, Sue found excitement in the drawing rooms of various hotels. Chesnut was shocked on entering one of those rooms to see "some of the men, *whose wives I knew*, dr[a]w away an inch or two from the sirens by whom they were lolling on sofas. . . . The degree of familiarity and the intimacy between our noted legislators and some of these women whose names are in everybody's mouth was unconsciously and frankly exhibited."[13]

That kind of dalliance thrilled Sue. But she was still sufficiently respectable to be invited even to Chesnut's parties. She appeared at one affair "gorgeously" arrayed in what one guest called "the unenclothesed common." Playing her seductive role to the hilt, she "went for Captain James, straight as an arrow." A little later, when Chesnut urged her to put on the shawl she had earlier discarded, Sue snapped back, "Why?" Her hostess replied, "'Such shoulders &c &c—bare &c &c—makes you look *that* willing—too willing, you know.' 'Willing for what?' 'Another husband.'" But Chesnut dared go no further. She feared Sue as she feared death.[14]

No other Petigru indulged in such gay parties, which became common in Columbia and Charleston in 1864. But all of them needed respite from the war-born tensions that ruled their lives. So they staged family get-togethers; called on friends and relatives; and, more constantly, sought relief in reading about times and places far distant. But their wartime exertions left them little opportunity for diversion. They wrote fewer letters. They made fewer diary entries. They read less, and what they did read was less instructive than escapist, "amusement" intended "to divert the mind from sadder thoughts."[15]

But nothing could divert Carolinians' minds in early 1865 as Sherman's armies stormed across South Carolina, punishing the state that had first fired on federal troops. By February 26, 1865, the federals were in Georgetown. By March 5, naval vessels carried marines up the Pee Dee River to seize control of the land and free those who were still enslaved. The plantation owners they encountered made no resistance. But at Chicora Wood, the federals found no owner, for not a single Allston was there or at any other Allston plantation. Adèle and Bessie had fled on February 24, going first to Morven and then to Croly Hill, where Della and Jinty joined them. At Croly Hill, the four white women and their three black female servants experienced Yankee occupation. Anticipating the worst, Adèle, aided by her butler, Nelson, and her soldier son, Charles, had buried the wine and the silver. Before the Yankees arrived, Charles left to rejoin his unit; Nelson hid in the woods lest he be forced to reveal where the intoxicants and valuables were hidden; and Daddy Aleck, the elderly coachman, joined Nelson with the horses. So as federal soldiers searched the house and grounds but did not find the buried trove, the seven women stood by terrified with no man, black or white, to protect them. None of them was harmed.

Only after those troops passed on to the north did Adèle receive the letter her neighbor, Jane Pringle, had written her on March 2. It assured her that the federal commander at Georgetown had promised safety to those whites who remained on their Pee Dee and Waccamaw plantations. But Adèle had not remained at Chicora Wood. In opting for Croly Hill, she and her daughters had avoided the celebrations and looting that followed the arrival of federal troops. As an Allston cousin described it, federal officers told the freedpeople "to take what they wanted." White planters, male and female, watched in a "fearful state of Alarm" lest worse follow. "For four days no one could eat & few undress or sleep at night." Although no assault was made on any white woman, Jesse Belflowers warned Adèle that at Chicora Wood "the Pople have behaved Verry badly" and that he feared they might do bodily harm to their former mistress and her daughters. When they had forced him to give them the keys to the barn, the freedpeople had treated him roughly. The situation was similar on all of the Allston plantations. The smokehouses and storerooms had been broken open and their contents commandeered. Livestock and farm equipment had been confiscated. And at Chicora, the freedpeople had taken all of the furniture from the big house and "Puld down the mantle Pieces Broke them to Pieceses, taken of all the doors & windows, Cut the Banisters & sawd out all such as wanted."[16]

Faced with that report, Adèle hesitated to return until she had some guarantee of her personal safety and property. When she wrote to ask for official aid from the occupying troops, however, she demonstrated just how little she understood the revolution that had overtaken her world and altered her standing in it. She claimed privileged treatment as "the widow of R. F. W. Allston." She said she acquiesced "entirely in the freeing of the negroes" but insisted that "our other property ought not to be taken from us."[17] Moreover, she expected to receive rent from the freedpeople who remained on her family's land, for, as she explained, that would be her only source of livelihood.

No one replied. Instead, Adèle received a private warning from Jane Pringle. Because she had fled from the Georgetown district according to her "instincts" instead of following Pringle's advice to stay at Chicora Wood, Adèle was barred "for the present" from any claim to the property she had left behind. Should she try to return, she would find the freedpeople at Chicora "perfectly insubordinate" and those on the other Allston plantations behaving "like devils." Compared to them, Pringle concluded, the Yankees were almost benign. "As to a protection for Bessie & you . . . as far as the Yankees are concerned You do not run the slightest risk."[18]

Girding up her courage with that minimal reassurance, Adèle did return, accompanied by fourteen-year-old Jinty and Bessie, who was now nearly twenty. As a precaution, they first stayed at Pringle's White House plantation. To that extent, at least, Adèle heeded Belflowers's warning against going directly to Chicora Wood, where he himself no longer dared go. On the day after she arrived, she and Jane Pringle went to Georgetown, where both took the oath of allegiance to the United States. The very next day, in her newly certified status as a loyal citizen, Adèle turned her efforts to reclaiming her family's property. She had learned in Georgetown that President Lincoln had ordered that property belonging to any Petigru be given special protection. That remarkable recognition of James Petigru's unionism, however, did little to ease her task. Her request that a soldier accompany her and Bessie to the Allston plantations was denied. So escorted by only their coachman, Adèle and Bessie set out for Nightingale Hall. As soon as they arrived in an open carriage, they were recognized. Surly black folk immediately surrounded them as Adèle demanded the keys to the storehouse. Her former minions refused. She persisted. When her direct demands failed, she played on sentiment. She stressed family ties. She prodded the women to press their men to comply. Finally Mack was persuaded to surrender the keys that had always been symbols of authority. To that extent, his old mistress retained her power.

The same process was repeated at Chicora Wood the next day, although it took longer and required more patience. When their old mistress arrived, "our people," as the Allstons had been pleased to call them, responded angrily. They adamantly refused to give up the keys that had so recently come into their possession and now represented their right to control their own lives. Again Adèle persisted, using the themes that had worked at Nightingale Hall, until finally Daddy Primus, the head carpenter, got the keys and handed them over.

Guendalos was a still tougher challenge. Because it was Ben's plantation and Adèle had never spent time there, she had no personal ties with individual freedpeople. Furthermore, during the war, there had been no white person resident. Jacob, the driver, had managed the place since Ben had left in 1861, and he was still its head man, with the self-assurance gained by de facto authority. His fellows, more than those on the other plantations, had similarly experienced four years free from white control. Therefore, when Adèle asked for the keys and Jacob refused, there was no dormant pool of support for her to tap. Fearing physical violence, she sent her coachman for help while she and Bessie paced back and forth on the road waiting for him to return. As they paced, black women chanted a defiant serenade: "I free, I free! / I free as a frog! / I free till I fool! / Glory Alleluia!"[19] Although their jeering was hardly an indication of subservience, the women were notably less threatening than the men, who brandished pitchforks and hoes and vowed that no white man would be allowed on the place. No white man came that day, and when Daddy Aleck returned alone with the carriage, Adèle and Bessie went straight to their Plantersville cottage, to which they had already moved from White House. There, for reasons unexplained, Jacob appeared the next day and handed over the keys to Adèle.

At Goslington, the Porcher women also awaited the enemy without any white male protector, for Philip had been conscripted into the militia in early February. As Louise later admitted, staying on was "all we cd do, as no way of escape was left." She hoped, however, that the fact that they remained would be taken as "a mark of confidence" and would gain "some respect" from the enemy. On the morning of February 21, when retreating Confederate troops passed through, they announced the imminent arrival of the conquering army. The Confederate soldiers "behaved very kindly," took nothing from the Porchers, "showed much sympathy" for their situation, and instructed Louise to "conceal food & any valuable[s]." She had just completed that task when two federal officers rode up and "tried to scare us by threats of the *black troops*." Feigning a boldness she did not feel, Louise replied that she was "not afraid of negroes." Actually, as she admitted three months later, she was shaken to the core when those troops arrived. "*It was a sight to strike terror*," she recalled; "wild hidious figures naked to the waist brandishing their arms & pointing their guns as if to shoot us as we stood on the Piazza." After their commander, a white New Yorker, ordered the troops to ransack the storerooms and smokehouses, he announced his mission. "I am come," he told Louise, "to liberate your people." He then addressed them, saying "that all there belonged to them, had been made by their blood & that the house servants must show where 'that *woman*' had hid her valuables." But, at least in Louise's eyes, the house servants "were faithful to us & more frightened than we were, [and] insisted the n[egro] troops were 'wild Africans' wd not at first believe they spoke the same language, & did all they cd to protect us, even when they called us names, contradicted them."[20] Together, mistress and servants watched the soldiers consume the supplies intended for their own use, saw all of the poultry killed, all of the livestock slaughtered, all of the horses, mules, and carts seized for use by the troops. It was only the Union commander's decision to make the house his headquarters that saved it and its furnishings from complete destruction. That, however, gave little comfort to the Porchers, who remained virtual prisoners in their own home for seventeen days until finally they were escorted to the railroad, where they took the train to Charleston.

When they arrived on March 11, they entered a city that had been occupied for three weeks. Indeed, the Charleston to which the Porchers returned seemed a reprise of Goslington. Within its urban confines, they could not avoid the troops, both black and white, whose constant presence fed the smoldering hatred war and defeat had left. In a scalding letter to her cousin Carey, Mary Anna let loose her bitterness. If Carey Pettigrew wished to prepare her "children to live as *equals* with our conquerors," she must teach them "that a well stuck to lie is always preferable to a plain truth, that any thing obtained by a cunning trick" is something to " 'boast on,' that cheating is 'smart,' stealing & pilfering . . . a splendid opening for a clever young man." In sum, the ten commandments were "played out." Those with old standards were destined to live, like the Porchers, "poverty stricken." It all proved that white Southerners had been "right in making the effort to free ourselves of a union with a people who only represent the devilish part of human nature."[21]

Louise, although equally seared by scorn and hatred, was less defiant than her daughter. For her, Charleston had become the "vally of humiliation," in which "ingenious tormentors" left "nothing undone that can distinguish them as a *'peculiar people.'*" The occupying Yankees and their black cohorts represented "the last phase of mans total degredation, & the obliteration of that 'Likeness['] in which he was originally made." Once again, she turned to religion to sustain her "in a trial that seems to take from us all hope as regards this World." Somehow enemy occupation, like the death of children, must be met with resignation.[22]

Still, by August, a glimmer of hope for "this World" pierced the gloom. President Andrew Johnson's reconstruction plans promised a return to an acceptable life. Confiscated property would be given back to its original owners. All but those most active in the Confederate cause would be granted amnesty. All that was required of the rebellious states to resume their full place, privilege, and power within the Union was official recognition that the Confederacy and slavery were at an end. Taken altogether, it gave Louise "reason to hope that the worst is over."[23] It was not, as she and her kin would soon discover. The social upheaval triggered by the war had only just begun.

PART THREE

The Long Years After

CHAPTER EIGHTEEN

The Despair of Defeat

Five days after the Porchers fled from Goslington to Charleston, Captain Hal Lesesne was killed at Averasboro, North Carolina, in a futile battle to stem Sherman's northward march. Three weeks later, General Lee surrendered to General Grant at Appomattox. Hal's death so near the end of the war devastated his mother. Even the solace of knowing where he was buried was denied her. Her "brave & noble hearted son['s]" unidentified body probably was interred somewhere on or near the battlefield, but no one knew where. So like Louise, who had sustained false hopes when Phil was lost at sea, Harriette lived for months in uncertainty. "If I were a man & had the strength, I would go to that battleground & to the neighborhood around & try to learn something more—but," she concluded, "all this is useless & vain." Somehow she must steel herself to accept the fact that her twenty-two-year-old son had died fighting for a cause that had become "perfectly hopeless" while he still lived.[1]

In the first months of her mourning, she had little contact with her kin, for she remained upcountry in Spartanburg. In late 1864 Henry had planned to buy a farm near Badwell so she could live closer to them. But Harriette had such "lugubrious apprehensions" about making another move that he gave it up. When the war ended five months later, returning to Charleston was blocked by the fact that Henry had sold their house on Tradd Street in 1863 and invested the proceeds in Confederate bonds, which were now worthless. That was one more factor in the "frightful convulsion" that made

Harriette's life an ongoing nightmare—a nightmare that in various guises stalked most of her kin.[2]

The Porchers, however, despite being "utterly ruined" financially, could return to their South Bay home, which had somehow escaped major damage during the long Yankee bombardment of the city.[3] It was there that Charley Porcher rejoined his parents. Joe Allston, emaciated and deeply depressed by the months he had spent as a prisoner of war in a Washington camp, came back to Minnie and their children at Dryslope. Even though he still owned Waverly plantation, his exhaustion and its accumulated debts deterred his return to planting. Della's husband, the only one of Elias Vanderhorst's four sons to survive the war, came home physically and mentally intact. Although he could not provide her luxuries, he was able to meet his own and his wife's immediate needs. But at first even his parents were so short of cash that they could barely find the $50 they recognized Arnoldus and Della needed immediately. But their cash shortage was only temporary. Arnoldus's mother could still draw on her extensive Northern investments. And almost immediately Arnoldus began repairing his father's Charleston wharf and restoring his several plantations, which, without a burden of debt, promised significant income in the near future.

Something closer to Joe's misfortune than to Arnoldus's good luck confronted Ben Allston when he came home. Like Joe, he was burdened with a heavily mortgaged plantation and commanded few financial resources. Unlike Arnoldus, whose father was determined to give his son the full benefit of his estates, Ben's mother was intent on using his father's estate to maintain and educate her three youngest children. Even their personal lives differed sharply. In 1865 Arnoldus and Della excitedly awaited the birth of their first child just when Ben and Ellen mourned the death of their firstborn. Sickly from birth, baby Adele had died even before her parents left Shreveport for South Carolina. Ellen, whose postpartum illness had interfered with the development of a strong maternal attachment, was more relieved than sorry.

Not surprisingly, when they first met as sisters-in-law, the two young wives found they had little in common. Nonetheless, Della greeted Ellen more warmly than did her mother or her younger sisters. She thought the young Texan was "a truly attractive person clever & amiable," despite her poor health and her many missing teeth. The rest of the family demurred. They found Ellen neither clever nor amiable. They were put off by her irritating manners, which they attributed largely to her undistinguished origins. Her frosty mother-in-law offered Ellen none of the psychological support she herself had received from Aunt Blyth when she had arrived as a young bride destined to live on a remote rice plantation. Isolated in an alien place amid constant rumors that freedmen were shooting and killing their former owners, Ellen was terrified more than Adèle had ever been by the overwhelmingly black population among whom she now lived. Nor did it help that federal officers, from General Rufus Saxton on down, refused to investigate the "possibility of an insurrection."[4] All that, added to the traumas of bearing her second child, Mary Duval, in February 1866, ravaged Ellen's health. Desperate to alleviate her miseries, Ben sent for his cousin Lou North, who came up from Charleston to help out.

Ben coped little better than his wife. Short on planting experience and pressured by family pride, he strove futilely to put Guendalos in working order. Still more challenging to his manliness was contesting for power with his fifty-five-year-old mother, whose thirty years of plantation experience outweighed his two and whose commitment to her minor children's interests limited his claims as his father's successor. Denied the mantle of family leadership that he had expected, Ben was no match for a woman determined to preserve the authority she had exercised since her husband's death. Calling up Robert's ghost, Adèle protested that she could not understand Ben's conduct when he reversed long-standing orders about plantation management at Chicora: "You act with great precipitation, and feel no hesitancy in undoing regulations made by your father, and that had worked well." She emphasized that she had never "rescinded an order or regulation of your fathers except when the circumstances which called it forth were changed." Pitting civilian experience against military, she asserted that Ben had "a very inadequate view" of the family's present condition because he had been away while the old order changed. Even so, he exceeded the bounds of good sense and common duty. Precisely because his "education was military," he "ought to know how serious a matter" it was to countermand established orders without due consideration. Although he probably had no "*design* to do wrong*," he had broken the cardinal rule that "wise men, when at a loss, not knowing the bearing of things, . . . *do nothing* until informed." Even when he sought her advice, she had "no hope of making any impression" on him because he "*consider[ed]* nothing."[5]

Clearly, Adèle's reproofs signaled an older person's scorn for youthful rashness. Just as clearly, Ben's training to accommodate ladies, respect parents, and be loyal to family clashed with his desire to assert manly authority. So he turned to Henry Lesesne, the coexecutor of his father's will, for support. But his uncle, whose generational loyalty was, in this case, stronger than his gender bonding, refused to back Ben's claims. In lawyerly fashion, he responded that if Robert had wished his son rather than his wife to administer his estate, his will would have indicated it. It did not. So he warned his nephew not to try to circumvent Adèle's authority.

Even in administering his own property, Ben's proud defiance of the new order astounded his mother. She was appalled when he refused to talk to two Freedmen's Bureau representatives who called on him at Guendalos, telling them that he was too busy to do so. Although she had a disposition no meeker than her son's, Adèle had learned that present necessity demanded accommodation. Even if Ben had been too busy at the time, he could have invited the officers into the house and requested them to wait until he was free. His brusque refusal would doubtless have harmful repercussions since all local freedpeople obeyed "the officers of the Freedmens bureau implicitly." Thus, Ben's rudeness would probably lead to trouble not only with his field workers but also with hers.[6]

Because both Ben's and Ellen's rash behavior irritated her, Adèle increasingly turned to Della for filial understanding and to Arnoldus for business help. She valued her son-in-law's advice because of the abilities he displayed in bringing Vanderhorst property back into profitable productivity. What she failed to understand was how heavily Arnoldus's responsibilities weighed on Della. During planting and harvesting seasons, he was away for weeks at his father's Ashepoo River plantation, in whose damaged house they could not yet live, and when he was in Charleston, all of his time and energy went to rebuilding the Vanderhorst wharf and revitalizing its trade. With Arnoldus either absent or preoccupied, Della spent more time with the elder Vanderhorsts with whom they lived than with her husband. She appreciated how much Arnoldus benefited from his father's resources and advice. She realized her own good fortune in sharing the amenities and ample supplies of the undamaged Vanderhorst mansion. And she acknowledged that her father-in-law doted on her, urging his son to value her as "a comfort & a treasure . . . through life." But often that atmosphere smothered her. Because Della was the elderly couple's only hope for heirs to carry on the Vanderhorst name, they petted and fretted over her lest any mishap threaten that hope. So when she caught her hoop on a raised tack on the stairs and sprawled down the last few steps in her eighth month of pregnancy, panic, luckily unnecessary, ensued. Elias's distress made Della feel guilty and inadequate. The whole episode made her so "terribly nervous" that she begged her mother to come down from Chicora to take charge of her confinement.[7] Adèle did come and was present when, on October 11, 1865, a third-generation Adele was born. The baby was not the male heir for whom the Vanderhorsts had hoped. Perhaps that explained why they

THE LONG YEARS AFTER

acceded so readily to giving the child an Allston rather than a Vander-horst name.

Despite her relative comfort and prosperity, Della yearned for the "Happy Past." Only occasionally did she peer "forward to catch a glimpse of the Future as it comes stealthily but swiftly on," a future whose uncertainties frightened her so much that she determined to "live from day to day allowing the 'Morrow' small space." But for her seventy-year-old Aunt Jane Amelia, present prospects were far more appealing than a glance backward. After James Petigru's death, she had lived the pinched life of a widow with steadily decreasing means. Ironically, Confederate defeat returned her al-most to prewar luxury, for her late husband's conspicuous unionism ensured that she, despite her conflicting views, would receive the goods and services available only from the federal military. At first her sharp and imprudent denunciations of the conquering army had made her grandson Willie Car-son warn her that although the U.S. government would do "everything in their power for Mr Petigru's *widow*," it would do nothing "*for a Secessionist*." If she wanted the official "help and support" Washington was prepared to offer, she must control her "treasonable talk." In an unexpected burst of common sense, she did so. It paid off. On the specific orders of General Sherman, whom her husband had befriended when he was a young officer stationed near Charleston, she was lodged in a confiscated Charleston man-sion and given full rations for herself and her servants. Glorying in this new plenty, she boasted that she needed only "signify a wish for it to be gratified at once." When Bessie Allston called on her, she marveled at her aunt's open delight in living "in luxury, when every one else is almost in want" and in having federal officers "at her beck and call." Indeed, their bounty enabled Jane Amelia to make up "baskets from her stores" for less fortunate friends and relatives. Although she insisted privately that she "did not in any way sympathize" with her husband's unionism, Charleston gossip tattled that "Mrs. Petigru has fraternized with the Yankees, & rec'd the best house in Charleston" in return. Still, her complaints that her income was insufficient for the comforts her invalidism required did not stop until she died from cancer on January 12, 1868. As Lou North sighed, no one could expect her aunt to exert a "self control she has never acquired."[8]

If her Charleston acquaintances scorned Jane Amelia's apparent frater-nization, they damned the conspicuous way in which "Mrs. H. King follows suit." By August 1865, Sue, who only nine months earlier had claimed a special relationship with Confederate general Pierre Gustave Toutant Beau-regard, was gallivanting about town with Yankees. One Charleston aristocrat who glimpsed her riding in a carriage near the Battery growled, "There goes

Mrs K driven by a Yankee thief in my uncles Stolen Buggy."[9] Nonetheless, Sue soon left for New York to earn money and revive her literary career by giving public readings. There, for a few months, she did well enough. But in small towns, she attracted few auditors. On her return to Manhattan, her following had shrunk so much that she soon lacked funds even to pay her hotel bill. Desperate for money, she went to Washington, where she capitalized on the political pull of her father's admirers to obtain a job as a clerk-translator in the Post Office Department.

Her sister Caroline Carson's greater reliance on her father's friends had long eased her way. She continued to live with Willie in the small house at 149 West 26th Street that they had purchased for her. She enjoyed an assured income from the $10,000 annuity his Boston admirers had established for her. And Willie's salary in addition to her own earnings from tinting photographs provided other comforts. Moreover, by May 1865, she was back in touch with Jem through the good offices of General Sherman, who had promised "to catch" her son for her and "send him" on.[10] Three months later, Jem joined his mother in Lenox, Massachusetts, where she was vacationing with friends.

Ambition for her sons propelled Caroline to exploit her contacts for their benefit. In February 1866 she went to Washington to find a job for Willie in the federal bureaucracy since his railroad clerkship offered little promise of promotion. While she was there, she also lobbied to save her kin's estates from confiscation. Looking to her mother's needs, she arranged to sell her father's law library to the Library of Congress. But the meager $5,000 Congress allocated to pay for the collection, admittedly much damaged by federal soldiers while it was stored, disappointed her and thoroughly displeased Jane Amelia. Finally, Caroline maneuvered a federal judgeship for a Unionist protégé of her father's who she hoped might assist her in legal matters when he returned to Charleston.

Although she was reasonably successful in helping others, Caroline had little luck in regaining control of the property she had left in the South. As soon as the war ended, Henry Lesesne made her coexecutor of her father's estate. But as long as her mother lived, she derived no benefit from any Petigru property. Thus, the only increase in her income came from the payment of interest on some $9,000 worth of South Carolina bank and railroad stock, which had paid her nothing during the war. Nothing could be done to redeem her other liquid assets, which the executors of her husband's estate had, without her knowledge or consent, reinvested in Confederate bonds. So although she had no intention of ever returning to South Carolina, her only hope for a substantial increase in either capital or income lay in Dean Hall. The man who had bought William Carson's Cooper River rice plantation in 1859 had sold it in 1863 and paid off his mortgage in depreciated Confederate currency. Because his contract with the Carsons had specified payment in U.S. dollars and Caroline had not been consulted about the mortgage settlement, she ordered her lawyer to challenge its validity and began a legal battle to regain the plantation that continued for the rest of her life.

Badwell was another matter. As long as Mary Petigru lived there, it could not be sold. After Lou North and Ann Petigru left for Charleston in 1866, Mary became Badwell's sole white resident. She got on "pretty well," finding that living alone was "not unpleasant," although she enjoyed long summer visits from the Porchers and Lesesnes. Rather than solitude, it was her responsibility for Jack and Tempe that burdened her. By 1868, Jack had become "helpless and infirm," incontinent and unable to dress himself without help.[11] Tempe somehow managed to cook for them, although she was almost blind. But, as the rest of the family thought, she had always been too lazy to clean house or mend clothes. When Mary visited them, as she did regularly, she was almost overwhelmed by the stench and disorder of the place. But she felt unable to do more than provide them minimal amounts of food while their clothing and bedding became increasingly tattered. She was therefore more relieved than troubled when in May 1869 a final stroke killed Jack and then the next year Tempe died.

If meeting Jack's and Tempe's needs had exceeded Mary's resources, providing for herself proved almost as daunting. She undertook Badwell's agricultural management for the first time after Jane's death in 1863 and for four years farmed the land with the labor of those freedpeople who decided to stay on. After the first year, her new responsibilities weighed so heavily that she decided to rent the land to a white farmer. But the freedmen balked, fearing that the arrangement would strip them of their claims on Badwell even though Mary had stipulated that the tenant must hire them. The outcome was exactly what her family would have predicted: she canceled the lease. For Louise Porcher, who was visiting at the time and had advised her otherwise, this proved once more that Mary was "peculiarly independent," conceding to no one the "*right* to interfere with her arrangements[,] a monopoly of power she highly enjoys." But those arrangements, her sister went on, were influenced "by persons of colour."[12]

Whether or not that was true, after 1867 Mary turned inward while Badwell's productivity deteriorated precipitately. Louise thought her older sister's crotchety solitude had distorted Mary's perception of the world and turned her disposition nasty. She now dealt harshly with her white neighbors and was so "impolitic" in dealing with the freedpeople who had earlier helped her that they became "insolent & lazy." Family members believed that Mary was dominated by her principal servant, Diana, who since the early war years had been a "continual irritant," disrupting the household with her manipulative ways.[13] It was too much for Lou North to bear. Even before Jane North had died, she had bitterly resented the misery that mistress and maid had bred in her once happy childhood home. Later she tried to forgive their behavior but realized that she could never forget the woe they had inflicted on her mother. When at last Mary died on a rainy, windy February day in 1872, few mourned her passing.

By then, Badwell was no longer central to the Petigru family. The aging and gradual demise of the first generation probably made that inevitable, for the second generation had long made Charleston its most frequent meeting ground. But postwar conditions diminished even the lure of Charleston. Those who remembered its social whirl in earlier years found it so "greatly changed" that "social intercourse, social feeling seem[ed] things of the past, almost." But to those who were too young to remember that special excitement, it still offered opportunities to flirt and court that rural life did not. Young people made do with what was available. Because black people now made South Battery and White Point Garden their own on Sunday, young white ladies and gentlemen strolled—for few now had horses and carriages—to the west end of Tradd Street. Instead of gazing across the harbor to Fort Sumter, they looked out on marshes and rice mills. Bessie Allston loved walking out to Chisolm's mill, where, sitting on piles of logs and lumber, she and her escorts could watch the sun set over the Ashley River. There, "many a momentous conversation was murmured . . . with the strong, pungent smell of the marshes borne . . . by the brisk, fresh breezes." There, she later mused as she recalled her first proposal of marriage, "it was easier to speak freely."[14]

On weekdays, however, the Battery and White Point Garden reverted to the city's white elite, both young and old. Appearances there constituted a conspicuous social bulletin board on which the progress of courtship was recorded. Adèle encouraged both Bessie and her sister Jinty to enjoy the sea air as they walked out with their many beaux, for despite her financial troubles, she wanted her daughters to have "frivolous fun" as well as "thoughts of serious purpose." But when her frivolous fun threatened serious consequences, Bessie, who turned twenty-two in 1867, had to end her many pleasant strolls with Herbert Sass. Rumors about them "had become so numerous & were so generally believed" that she thought that was "the only way to put a stop" to gossip about a serious engagement.[15]

THE LONG YEARS AFTER

That same year the first postwar St. Cecilia balls illustrated that, although the externals had changed, underlying attitudes had not. This reincarnation of the social season's traditional high point offered the stage from which eighteen-year-old Marion Porcher, who only two years earlier had accepted the charity of a calico dress, was launched as a belle. For Bessie, to whom the war had denied a debut at the customary age, the second St. Cecilia that year saw her belated introduction to society. She had hoped to come out at the first ball. But she had hesitated to burden the family budget with the cost of a proper ball dress. So without consulting her mother, she bought a length of white alpaca, rather scratchy but relatively inexpensive, from which she fashioned a dress, which she trimmed with the thirteen-year-old scarlet silk-velvet ribbons that had once adorned an opera cloak made in Paris for Della's debutante years. A few days before the ball, Bessie proudly displayed her handiwork. Adèle was appalled. No daughter of hers would ever appear at a St. Cecilia ball so inappropriately dressed. Throwing financial prudence to the winds, she called in an accomplished dressmaker to make a real ball dress, one of white tulle over white silk. Because it was finished too late for the first ball, Bessie postponed her debut until the second, at which she shone gloriously in her traditional finery. The next year, Jinty was similarly dressed for the ball that constituted her social debut. And when Leila Lesesne, the last girl of the second Petigru generation, reached eighteen and attended her first St. Cecilia ball, she wore a dress of white tarlatan trimmed with white satin.

However much the social season fed youthful good spirits, it seldom lifted the gloom oppressing the oldest kin. The elderly mostly devoted their minds and energies to strategies for survival. The ailing Ann Petigru, a childless widow of seventy-four, was better off financially than most of her generation. But like them, she focused on her substantial losses. Her heavy investment in Confederate bonds was worthless. The $40,000 mortgage she held for Robert Allston's purchase of Pipedown and its slaves was equally worthless. Yankee shells had so damaged her Charleston house that when she returned to the city in early 1866, she, like the Lesesnes, was reduced to renting a room from the Porchers, whose sole income then came from taking boarders. Without the assistance that the federal army extended to all Petigrus, her own home would probably have been repaired much more slowly, if at all. When it was made livable, Ann rented it out for the income. But in November 1866, when family frictions made living with the five Porchers untenable, she evicted her tenants and pooled her resources with the Lesesnes' to enable them all to move into her house. Seven people, however, also crowded her six-room house. The Lesesnes occupied the third floor, the parents sharing its two chambers with their three youngest children, aged nine, eleven, and thirteen. Ann occupied her old room on the second floor and gave the chamber across the hall to Lou North in exchange for her help in managing the house. The first floor drawing room and dining room were common space for them all.

Such limited quarters probably would have proved difficult under the best of circumstances. In this case, having two boisterous young boys underfoot sorely tried their increasingly "excitable" aunt, and the adults, accustomed to running their own households, soon clashed over expenditures. Lou North, whose age placed her midway between the house's senior and junior occupants, was caught in the middle. Initially, she had hoped that Ann would calm down enough to allow them to "work well together." But Uncle Henry grossly exaggerated the quality and quantity of what his contributions to the household purse ought to buy, and Aunt Ann managed the house purse so laxly that the agreed-upon Lesesne contributions ran short well before Lou thought they should. After only six months, Henry moved his family to a rented house in Summerville, leaving Lou alone to cope with her Aunt Ann's rapidly deteriorating health. As a thirty-five-year-old spinster, Lou might at any time have been expected to care for an elderly relative in return for subsistence. Now, with almost no financial resources of her own, she concluded that she must put up with her aunt's "peevish & unreasonable" behavior, which played itself out in "the tyranny of old age." She felt trapped within "prison bounds" that were scarcely loosened when Uncle Henry told her that Ann's will would benefit her. In fact, that only tightened the moral obligation Lou already felt. So she continued to care for Ann, who by late 1867 was "mentally . . . extremely feeble" and whose "arbitrary, & over exacting" expectations made her suspect that Lou was somehow cheating and taking advantage of her.[16]

When Ann died in January 1869, Lou did indeed inherit the house on King Street. But that was all. And without some other source of income, she could not afford to live there. Forced, therefore, to sell it despite the prevailing slow market, she consigned it that August to Henry Lesesne, who paid her a mere $6,000. He made a down payment of $2,000 and gave his niece a mortgage note bearing 7 percent interest for the rest. It was a meager reward for years of unpaid service to a rich widow who bequeathed $11,000 to each of the two LaBruce nephews, who had never helped and seldom visited their aunt. To all of the other Petigrus, Ann made only token bequests amounting in all to no more than $2,500. And to Adèle Allston, she explicitly left nothing as retribution for the debt Robert Allston had owed her but never paid. In death as in life, Ann subverted the harmonious goodwill her sisters-in-law and nieces had striven to maintain with this singular and, to their minds, difficult woman. In the end, she remained a LaBruce despite her forty years as part of the Petigru family.

Lou's personal sacrifices to Ann's comfort had involved surrendering the independence that earning wages as a clerk in the Freedmen's Bureau's Charleston office might have given her in the immediate postwar years. Caring for her increasingly demanding aunt had compelled her to turn down the bureau's offer of a full-time job. But even working there periodically, she tasted the autonomy it promised. Hired when the great "press of work" of registering black voters led to the massive employment of temporary workers, she had at first viewed the job as demeaning. But earning $2.50 a day for exertions she found minimally taxing added to her self-confidence and gave her money she could actually spend at her own discretion. Simply being able to send a gift to her godson Charley Pettigrew from her "own earnings" lifted her spirits as little else did in those grim years.[17]

Still, class feelings against earning daily wages persisted. Her association with other ladies (Ravenels, Middletons, and Pinckneys) who, like herself, had been reduced from formerly comfortable lives was agreeable. But the untutored wives and widows of Yankee soldiers as well as the "vulgar" local women with whom she also worked gave her pause. Nonetheless, Lou consciously determined to treat all of her coworkers with that "universal kindness and Charity" her mother had implanted in her daughters.[18] But when Major Judd and his undistinguished Charleston-born bride invited her to join them in a carriage ride around the Battery and Lou accepted, she burned with shame to be seen in public with them.

Whatever its complications, working at the bureau fed Lou's determination, once Ann died, to support herself by her own exertions. But just when her "anxious efforts to make a little go a great way" tried her patience more than ever, employment opportunities in the federal offices were sharply reduced. For a time, she considered opening a school somewhere in South Carolina, believing that "every one is poor but everyone strives also to be educated."[19] Louise Porcher even suggested that Lou and Carey Pettigrew join forces to open a school in Baltimore. In the end, however, only Lou went to Baltimore, but to take a teaching job, not to establish her own school.

Carey, although she was also desperate to "make a little money," was too essential to Charles's operations at Bonarva to leave home. For a brief time, she dreamed of writing and selling short stories. But after she wrote just one story and faced the complications of getting it published, she lost heart, doubting that it was worth as much as $5. And "nobody wld give such a price" as the $15 or $20 she then needed to buy Charley a new suit. So instead of trying to live by her pen or to undertake a school in Baltimore, she gave piano lessons to the children of her Bonarva neighbors, much as she had done at Cherry Hill when she had taught the schoolmaster's children music in exchange for Charley's tuition. Minnie Allston, who needed money just as much as either of her sisters, lamented that she had wasted the educational opportunities given her as a child. If only she "were qualified," she "might set up a school" and "succeed." But she was held back by "a pang of positive terror" that she did "nothing well."[20]

Of all of the Petigru women, therefore, only Adèle Allston possessed the resources, resolve, and necessary skills to open her own school. A distinguished woman of fifty-five, she conjoined the entrepreneurial experience she had gained at Chicora Wood with an intellectual acuity derived from a lifetime of serious reading to open a school in the stylish Charleston mansion that Robert had bought at the peak of their glory. Its location on fashionable lower Meeting Street made the house ideal for a girls' school. And as the widow of Governor Allston with extensive contacts throughout the state, she was a mature lady to whom parents could safely entrust the moral and social training as well as the mental development of their adolescent daughters. By the time her school opened in January 1866, ten boarders and twenty day pupils were already enrolled. Within a year, the number of day students had doubled and included the daughters of Christopher Memminger, former Confederate secretary of the treasury, and of wealthy rice miller Jefferson Bennett. In her second year, she built on that initial success. Instead of her niece Mary Anna Porcher, who had been her first French teacher, she employed Mademoiselle LePrince, who had taught the Allston girls at Madame Togno's school. Similarly, she engaged Mr. G. W. Alexander, also formerly at Madame Togno's, to be the principal English teacher. For the most advanced students, Professor Lewis Gibbes came down from the College of Charleston to teach mathematics and Latin. Adèle herself continued to teach history, and Bessie both supervised the younger pupils and gave music lessons.

For such fare, Adèle charged substantial fees. In 1866 tuition, board, and room for a nine-month term came to more than $450. Lessons in piano, dancing, drawing, and painting were extra, as were washing and pew rental. Unfortunately, however, it soon became clear that even formerly wealthy planters, professionals, and businessmen could no longer afford such fees. As one father wrote Adèle, "Schools must suffer from the pressure of the times," pressure that made the erstwhile elite "feel ruin." That prediction was all too true. By July 1867, Adèle was struggling with the many parents who had fallen badly behind in paying their daughters' bills. Former Confederate general W. W. Harlee was exceptional only in making no apology for his inability to pay. "It is utterly out of the power of our most reliable and wealthy people formerly," himself among them, "to raise a few dollars in anyway whatever."[21] Still, as payments proved ever more elusive, other impoverished Charleston ladies opened new schools that competed with those already struggling in a diminishing market. It was clear that the situation had become serious when LePrince, sensing Adèle's financial problems, quit without notice to join the faculty of a newer school.

In addition, Adèle had not helped herself by giving private lessons to the daughter of Yankee general Dan Sickles, whose reputation was tainted both by his having killed his wife's lover in a duel and by the couple's subsequent reconciliation. When she further offended public opinion by admitting the child of another Northern general to regular classes, Southern parents started withdrawing their daughters. By October 1868, enrollment had decreased so drastically that Adèle gave up advertising in the local press. The following June she closed the institution she had described as one "designed to be a Comfortable and Cheerful home for Young Ladies, where every care will be extended to the moral, intellectual, and physical training of the pupils," where French was the language of instruction, and where the best teachers were "employed in every branch."[22] That July, Adèle exercised her widow's dower right to one-sixth of Robert's estate by claiming not the house his will had left her but Chicora Wood.

Nonetheless, the thought of facing plantation life once again so depressed her that her youngest daughter concluded she must stay with her mother to bolster her spirits in a lonely existence on the Pee Dee. Jinty betrayed just how hard that sacrifice taxed a nineteen-year-old girl when on Sunday, June 6, 1869, she wrote on a letter she had received from a beau eager to marry her that in leaving the city for good she was doing something she might "regret for many a long day."[23] Adèle never recorded her regrets at leaving so explicitly. But it had been in Charleston, while lawyers and creditors disputed the settlement of Robert's estate and wrangled over his debts and assets, that she had created an independent financial footing for herself. In choosing at last to return to the isolation of Chicora and the social values it represented, she demonstrated her belief that her younger son's efforts to continue his family's plantation traditions were more important than her own quest for autonomy. Here too continuity overshadowed change.

CHAPTER NINETEEN

The Return to the Plantation

When Adèle Allston returned to Chicora Wood, she had committed herself to salvaging as much of Robert's estate as she could. Already, emancipation had wiped out more than two-thirds of his prewar capital while leaving his debts intact. The Meeting Street house, when it sold in 1870, brought only half of what the governor had paid for it in 1857. The value of agricultural land had plummeted even more sharply. Thus, the property that Adèle claimed as her dower right was critical not just for her own survival but also for her children's future. Had she chosen the Charleston house, she would have owned the property outright. By opting for Chicora Wood, valued at one-third of the total estate, she was entitled only to its lifetime use. So she was torn. When she chose Chicora, she had to make it pay.

It would not pay, however, if Ben were left in charge, as he had largely been during the three years she kept her school in Charleston. The short crops he produced had confirmed her initial assessment that he was, at best, an inept planter. Her efforts to guide him had fed his resentment at being treated as though he were "still a child,—and would always be."[1] His delays in sending their rice to market when prices were highest, especially his procrastination with the 1869 crop that had jeopardized the negotiations with the estate's creditors that were essential to saving Chicora for the family, drove Adèle nearly wild. More long-lastingly, they could not agree on how the labor force should be treated. Ben refused to alter prewar discipline rooted in slavery. His mother believed change was imperative.

Her attitude represented enlightened self-interest. When Adèle had returned to the Pee Dee in 1865, she had made her determination to remain in control of Chicora's land and assets clear. She had acted pragmatically. She had immediately taken the loyalty oath that allowed her to reclaim the Allston plantations. She openly wished that "the divisions of our land could be healed and that our southern people could act and think with moderation."[2] She had had enough of chaos and violence. She deplored the planters who tried to reestablish their former authority by flogging their workers and reneging on the labor contracts they had made under Freedmen's Bureau regulations.

Adèle had been among the first Georgetown-area planters to sign the standard Freedmen's Bureau contract, which sanctioned a disciplinary system reminiscent of slavery. To her, its provisions, which severely limited the liberties of her newly freed employees and bound them to work for her profit, seemed reasonable. For Ben, acting as her agent, the very idea of a contract proved so problematic that he applied it inconsistently. At times, he gained the workers' resentment by holding them exactly to the line; at other times, he angered his mother by trying to bribe them into compliance. When field hands challenged his authority, he sometimes denied them the food, clothing, and housing that Adèle had contracted to provide. On those occasions when he actually had no supplies to distribute, that tactic only made his explanations less credible. His mother constantly reprimanded him for letting the workers do as they pleased, for handing out excessive supplies just because he happened to have them, and for failing to enforce the rules of behavior she had established. But if Ben failed to change his ways to embrace the spirit of the new order, so too did Adèle. She ceased calling her workers "our people" and ever more frequently referred to them as "the nigs." She once wrote her son that they should accept "the triumph of the negroes" only if they could turn it to their own advantage.[3]

Just as Ben's assertion of patriarchal claims clashed with his mother's tough-minded pragmatism, so too did it cloud his relationship with his wife. When they were apart, their letters revealed their strong sexual attraction. But when they were together, Ellen's wish not to *have any more* babies ran at cross-purposes to that attraction. After the prolonged illness that followed the birth of her first child, she concluded that babies "evidently dont agree with me, dont suit my constitution." But in appealing for the only form of birth control she knew, she sent a mixed message. Acknowledging her own passion and recognizing that Ben would have difficulty governing his, she nonetheless expected him to restrain himself. "What do you say darling? Now dont think I am serious in my question for I know you say 'you leave it to me' but that wont do."[4]

Later, in response to either Ben's expectation of marital gratification or his desire for a son and heir, Ellen reluctantly dropped her pleas for abstinence or coitus interruptus: "So as far as babies are concerned I am resigned although life does not appear 'couleur de rose' from that point of view." Because the rosiness of their life together was constantly dimmed by the ill health that followed each childbirth, the sexuality that bound them together continued to come between them. Ellen admitted her own irresistible desire for physical intimacy but blamed Ben for those pregnancies. He was unable to control himself "even under very ordinary temptations," and she could not "help caressing" him in ways that made him "give way."[5] So in eleven years of marriage, Ellen bore six children, three of whom died in infancy.

Their marriage was further strained by Ellen's intense dislike of the South Carolina low country. She had hated it from the day she arrived. Again and again, she begged Ben to cut his ties and move back to Texas with her. He steadfastly refused, and in 1867, she went west alone to spend the winter. After less than four years of marriage, Ben sensed they were drifting apart. He had never liked the distance implicit in her always calling him Colonel Allston: "I wish my dear one you would accustom yourself to call me Ben while you are away. . . . We should be and I believe wish to be nearer & dearer to each other than any other may be and if you continue to call me Colonel, it may seem formal and produce reserve and formality between us."[6] Unfortunately, Ben admitted in the same letter that his mother had criticized her use of that stilted form of address.

Incensed by her husband's letter and a disapproving one from Adèle, Ellen replied with a "scorcher." Ben responded not with a love letter but with an ardent defense of his mother. Adèle's "fretted" letter, he insisted, was not intended to wound her daughter-in-law. But the tone and content of Ben's letter made Ellen even less willing to return to the neighborhood where her mother-in-law ruled supreme. Ben, in turn, was so angered by her request that he leave his troublesome family to settle in her native Texas that he suggested the possibility of a formal separation. Almost anything would be better than living in South Carolina with a wife who took "no interest in it, sharing with [him] neither hope nor pleasure nor pain as relating to the home life." He had seen such marriages in the King and Carson households, where "brilliant women" had made their homes "more a Hell than a Heaven."[7] He wanted none of it.

The letters that followed conveyed Ben's disapproval of Ellen's life in Texas, which comported ill with his "ideal of a Christian wife & Mother." He disdained the frivolity she shared with her friends and family there. He deplored her dancing at parties, which she had not done since their courting days. He condemned her having taken a job clerking in an Austin office, which made her financially independent. But he still hoped to save their marriage. He urged self-restraint. He wanted both of them to try "more zealously and faithfully to please each other," to learn to "yield," to be "less intent upon selfish ends or plans." He pledged himself, if she did return, to sire no more children until they were "settled for good."[8] In May Ellen came back. She had been in Texas for six months and looked forward to a full year free of childbearing. By October, she was visibly pregnant.

That was not the only ill omen. The Allston clan welcomed her no more warmly than they had in 1865. Indeed, as time passed their frostiness turned frigid. Because the cottage on Pawleys Island was unlivable in 1869, the Guendalos and Chicora Wood folk still had to share the summer cottage in Plantersville. Ellen and Ben moved there early. Adèle, Bessie, Charles, and Jinty arrived in July. But after a month of resenting Ellen's arrangements, the younger Allstons rebelled and Ellen surrendered all domestic responsibilities to Adèle. Only then did Bessie end her partial hunger strike against Texas menus.

By this time, Adèle was thoroughly exasperated with both Ben and Ellen. She therefore turned her full attention to her younger son's future. In the last year of her school, she had scavenged the funds to send Charles to the College of Charleston. But when Robert's wealthy and childless Northern cousin, John Earl Allston, gave Adèle $10,000, the time was opportune for Charles to begin his practical education as a planter, using that money to improve and cultivate Chicora Wood under his mother's supervision. That arrangement doomed Ben's remaining hopes of being a rice planter, for he had just lost Guendalos in bankruptcy proceedings. So in March 1870, soon after the death of their first son, born the previous year, he and Ellen set out for Austin, where he proved to be no better at business than he had been at planting. While he dabbled in a variety of enterprises and sold insurance, Ellen bore another daughter who died in infancy. Less than two years after they arrived in the West, Ben's business failure was so complete that he moved Ellen and their only living child, five-year-old Mary Duval, back to South Carolina. When he arrived, his mother gave him Exchange plantation, a minor Chicora adjunct, to provide him a residence and source of income. Ellen, somewhat chastened, gave in to her mother-in-law's expectations enough to enable both households to spend the summer of 1871 together on Pawleys Island in the double cottage that, for the first time since 1861, was safe and livable. That, at least, seemed to signal a better future.

So did Ellen's giving birth to two healthy children: Charlotte, born in either late 1871 or early 1872 and named for Ben's paternal grandmother, and

Robert Francis Withers, born in 1873, a son and heir deserving his grandfather's given name. But bearing and nursing those children drained what was left of their mother's health. So as damp winter weather descended in late 1874, Ellen went home to Texas for the third and last time. Shortly after she arrived, she began coughing up blood. Within a few months, it was evident that she was dying of consumption. Ben went out to be with her and was there when she died that summer.

In many ways, Ellen's unhappy years as a married woman mirrored Adèle's first years as Mrs. Robert Allston. She was pregnant almost half the time. Several times childbirth brought her close to death. She watched three children die. And she hated the isolation of the alien low country. But the difference in the two women's circumstances was just as marked. Adèle had mastered her sense of isolation with the moral and practical support of kin who lived nearby. She had arrived at Chicora Wood at a time of economic growth, and despite subsequent years of panic and depression, her husband's fortunes had prospered. Finally, Adèle herself possessed the gritty willpower and survival instincts that drove her to adjust, at whatever personal cost, to the demands her husband, his plantations, and their children made on her. Ben's Texas "wild flower" never enjoyed those advantages.

The economic distress of the postwar years was, by itself, grim enough to try even Carey Pettigrew's strong personality and happy marriage. Unlike the Allston holdings, Charles's plantations had never generated much prosperity in her time. During the first postwar crop year, while Charles began to restore Bonarva, Carey and the children remained at Cherry Hill. Not only did she miss him sorely, but she wished he were with her for practical reasons. Her remaining field laborers resisted all of her efforts to impose a work discipline reminiscent of slavery. They were, she complained, uppity, rude, lazy, uncooperative, presumptuous, and given to endless demands for shorter hours and more generous supplies. All told, she found them "a heavy burden," clinging "to the idea of making us do every thing possible for them."[9] Not surprisingly, when she gave orders but offered few rewards, many of them simply drifted away.

Mulling over her frustrations, Carey dreamed of restoring a mythic past that in hindsight seemed almost perfect. She imagined herself working again side by side with Charles, whose mere presence would sustain her authority. But then more realistic memories intruded. She questioned her husband's managerial abilities. She doubted that his health would bear up under the strain. Was he not undertaking too many projects? Was their outcome not more likely to produce disaster than improvement? Her letters balanced requests for Charles's approval of what she was doing at Cherry Hill with warnings against his overly ambitious operations at Bonarva, especially his plan to erect and operate a steam saw- and gristmill in a town some fifteen miles distant. She praised the "energy, & the struggle" he displayed. But were not "milling, fishing, planting [and] shingling" too much for any one man? Would it not be better to "*concentrate*" his efforts?[10]

Careful never to challenge him outright, Carey tried both to restrain and to help Charles without discouraging him. She wanted to share his burdens and thought they could "arrange better, as far as aiding one another goes," if she had an equal role in planning their economic activities. She conceded that his unsettled prewar debts had to be paid off and that until they were, they would constitute a "gulf" into which everything he made or sold "must go—justly."[11] Still, she believed that if they planned well, they would at least be able to give all of their children a good education. But their present financial straits made even that uncertain.

Weighing Charles's chances of success amid Bonarva's swampy miasmas against Cherry Hill's more healthful climate, she would have preferred to remain in her native South Carolina near friends and relatives. But Charles had pinned his hopes and his family's future on Bonarva. And more than anything else, Carey wanted to be with her husband. Although doubting the wisdom of doing so, she joined him there in October 1866, despite the open hostility of white agrarians and freedpeople about which Charles's letters had warned her. As Carey wrote Minnie Allston, her return was propelled mainly by her "sense of right & duty."[12]

That return proved more painful than her worst expectations. The house she and Charles had built and furnished in 1861 had been stripped bare and badly damaged. For two months, she and her family lived with their Collins neighbors while Carey gathered whatever furniture and equipment she could find. The tableware and kitchen utensils Mary Collins gave her were a sad reminder that Somerset Place was about to be auctioned off to pay Josiah Collins's debts. Once Carey moved back into the minimally equipped Bonarva house, which had been built for a large staff but now employed only three servants, she rattled around in its unfamiliar emptiness. All of her old domestics were gone, and as she moaned to Minnie, her new free servants required "more *observation* than formerly" if she was not to "pay them while they use time for themselves." Fortunately, they proved reasonably satisfactory. Tony, a "dining room servant," was both "respectful" and "obliging." Ayme competently prepared three meals a day for all of the Pettigrews, including Mary Blount, as well as for Mary Armstrong, who had returned as nursery governess, and Armstrong's son. Laura, the chambermaid and washwoman, however, was "frightfully slow, & poking."[13]

Outside the house, things were notably less satisfactory. The field hands worked only when watched and did their best only when their employer worked with them. Charles's poor health precluded his setting an example and made even supervising them difficult. In the first full postwar crop year, his harvest of corn and other grains was poor, and his new lumber business produced even fewer profits. In 1868 endless spring rains flooded the fields and clogged the canal linking Lake Phelps to Albemarle Sound, making it unusable for boats large enough to carry bulk grain to market. After Charles abandoned his traditional crops for truck farming, in 1869 the first crop brought in less than $3,000. By 1870, Bonarva seemed almost hopeless, and Charles's debts remained a "bottomless swamp swallowing up everything."[14] His family faced real want.

As their income contracted, so did Carey. Always thin, even skinny, she lost weight steadily. Mary Johnston's birth in 1867 had tried her physique so severely that she joked that should she live long enough, she would become "a shadowy sort of creature, approaching the grasshopper species."[15] The quality of her life grew slimmer too. In 1869 she was forced to sell the piano that had long been her major emotional outlet and more recently the source of a small income from teaching. More drastic in its physical effect was the miscarriage that led to her severe illness that fall.

By then, Carey's bitterness at the public circumstances shaping her life knew no bounds. She had first met the revolutionary changes in her domestic staff by trying to rely on the soft but compelling style of the old paternalism. When that failed, she pleaded and wheedled. Finally, she became a threatening scold. As no style produced the dutiful compliance she expected, her old good humor faded. The sharp shift away from white dominance and black deference eroded her former self-assurance. Managing a house filled with eight children, an ailing husband, and visiting family frequently destroyed her equanimity.

Carey was the more embittered because, in the immediate postwar years, she had tried to build new bridges between the big house and the quarters— albeit always on her own terms. She and Mary Blount established a Sunday school in which they intended to teach basic literacy to Bonarva's black residents. They started out with a confidence born of their success in providing a thorough home education for Carey's children. When the black children, instructed only once a week, lagged far behind the young Pettigrews, who were taught daily, the women grew discouraged. The even slower advance of adult literacy tried Carey's patience still more. Ayme, who was motivated by an ardent desire to read the Bible, made visible, although "*very little*," progress. But it seemed "hopeless" to try to "hammer a few ideas on the subject of letters into Laura's brain." For her as for Tony, "the darkness of their intellects remain[ed] undisturbed."[16]

At bottom, Carey showed little tolerance for the preferences of the freedpeople. She was galled when black women demanded time off to attend to their own homes and children. She resented those women who refused to work for her but lived at Bonarva because their men were housed and employed there. She clung to the belief that the older—and better—servants shared her assessments. When Maum Sue died of old age in 1867, Carey asserted that the longtime Badwell servant knew "in her heart" that her race was unfitted for freedom "unless *controlled*." Insisting that she herself did not "object to their being free" because she had "always thought slavery had many evils, & was bad for the whites," Carey nonetheless complained that having "no laws, no control over the negroes" was "a wretched business." As time went on, her conviction grew that all blacks were lazy, dirty, sexually lax, and "hard to get on with." But as she looked at the local timber workers and tenant farmers who constituted most of Bonarva's white neighbors and had largely aided the Yankees during the war, she proclaimed that they were "not much better, unreliable, grasping & false."[17]

There were now few barriers between kitchen politics and public politics. Like many other Southern women, Carey connected all of the evils affecting her life, whether at home or in the neighborhood, at the state or at the national level. She blamed all Northerners for holding the South in even tighter economic thrall than they had before the war, angrily agreeing with the male Pettigrews that "the yankee[s] somehow get all our money." In 1867 she hoped that President Andrew Johnson's vetoes of the second Freedmen's Bureau bill and the civil rights bill would shelter the white South from radical attempts to give freedpeople equal status with whites. When Congress overrode those vetoes, it only confirmed "how hateful those Radicals are in their course, & how natural!"[18]

Resolutely hostile to all of the changes going on around them, the Pettigrews rejected the pragmatism that had allowed Adèle Allston to make the shrewd concessions that self-interest demanded. Carey indignantly scorned the loyalty oath required of high-ranking Confederate activists (which neither Charles nor his brother William had been) before they could retrieve their confiscated property or be allowed to vote. "No decent man," she railed, could possibly "take the oath those monsters prescribe." She would even go without postal service rather than approve of a Southern postmaster who took the required oath. Somewhat later, when the House of Representatives began to debate impeaching President Johnson, Carey prayed the process would boomerang. "Shld the mad Radicals carry their point, . . . the hot broth they are stirring so vigorously will be a scalding mess for themselves." Surely they were no less than "the curse of this unhappy country," even "of the World."[19]

The closer radicals were to home, the more menacing they appeared. In the summer of 1867, when Washington County freedpeople held political meetings to form a Union League, rumors that they were actually plotting racial violence spread like wildfire. Because the son of a Pettigrew servant had come, with his mother's encouragement, from nearby Edenton to lead the drive, Carey was put doubly on guard. That someone from her own household could so conspire convinced her that no white person was safe as long as "the negro is master as far as he chooses to assert his 'rights'!" That assertion of rights was made more terrifying by its resemblance to the rights white agrarians had demanded when, during the war, they had directly attacked the property of the plantation elite. The anxiety all of this created played itself out in Carey's response to state politics. In 1868 she believed that her own and her family's safety depended on defeating Republican governor William Holden. If he were reelected, she was sure he would "gladly set the negroes to cut the throats of all the *even decent* people in the country."[20]

Although Governor Holden was in fact defeated, nothing assuaged Carey's dismay over the whole democratic process. "What a tiresome government with continual elections recurring to upset the minds of the people. The nigs wld really work & behave, but for the low white men who make their profit by agitating them." In the past, she had feared slave insurrection. Now she was sure that the open collaboration of free blacks and "low" whites in an inflammatory political process made North Carolinians of both races and all classes not only discuss the likelihood of race war "quite freely" but also prepare for it.[21]

Perhaps influenced by the political turmoil but also lonely at isolated Bonarva, Mary Blount Pettigrew, who had remained single for forty-two years, decided to marry a physician she had met while working at a Virginia military hospital. But only weeks after their June 1868 wedding, she realized that Peter Fielding Browne had aspirations quite different from her own. A widower twice over, he was a crotchety, ailing man who, despite earlier promises to the contrary, refused to move from the home on Virginia's remote Outer Peninsula that he had shared with his first two wives to an inland town near Richmond where Mary Blount would enjoy agreeable neighbors and the amenities of urban life.

Almost three years into a disappointing marriage, Mary Blount perversely found new hope in her brothers' financial problems. William, because he was mired in the same agricultural and marketing difficulties as Charles was, declared bankruptcy in 1871. That in turn produced an upheaval in the Pettigrew family's intertwined property arrangements. William's creditors demanded that Charles repay the debts he owed his brother, thereby forcing him to turn Bonarva, his principal asset, over to them. Then, because Mary Blount was one of William's creditors, her brother could no longer act as trustee for her share of their father's estate. Browne thereupon seized the opportunity to assert his marital claim to all of his wife's property and, in negotiating with other creditors, gained control of Bonarva. William's Belgrade plantation was similarly transferred to Neil McKay, not only a creditor but the longtime friend who had married Annie Pettigrew in 1863. When Annie died the next year, the terms of their marriage contract gave McKay all of her property. Able to buy off other claimants to Belgrade and acquire it well below its market price, he then sold it to Charles well above the market price. Those maneuvers both doubled Charles's mortgage debts and forced Carey, in the light of Mary Blount's openly expressed desire to live at Bonarva, to move from the home she had again made comfortable to the decrepit old house at Belgrade.

The financial implications of these shifts were dire. Browne, despite Mary Blount's wishes, had no intention of moving to his new plantation. During the first year he owned it, he hired it out to tenant farmers. Charles, who at the time of McKay's and Browne's marriages had suspected that they were more attracted by his sisters' property than by their personal traits, sensed at once that Browne planned "to make a living without . . . the trouble of working for it" and to gouge maximum profits as an absentee landlord. He was right. Browne at first thought he could pluck the fruits of his third wife's "very nice fortune" by making only occasional inspections of resident tenants who would pay him dearly to till his fields for his profit.[22] But when they did not, he conceived the even more unrealistic plan of dredging the old canal to Albemarle Sound to make it navigable for ships large enough to transport bulk grain to lucrative markets. Browne further fantasized that he could raise huge crops at Bonarva, and Mary Blount encouraged his unrealistic projects as she fantasized an escape from a house haunted by memories of her predecessors.

Meanwhile, Carey struggled with the dilapidated Belgrade house. The roof leaked badly, but Charles lacked the means to repair it. Her new neighbors were the very populists whose wartime activities had contributed so much to the Pettigrews' downfall. For a while, she seriously considered returning to Cherry Hill. But the tenants there had eked out so little from its cultivation that it offered no better prospect. So she stayed on at Belgrade, where her despair grew steadily as she watched seventeen-year-old Charley support the family as Browne's and McKay's overseer at Bonarva and on former Pettigrew lands adjacent to Belgrade. His grinding manual labor and long hours were almost futile as the tenant farmers resisted his efforts to produce a big crop that would profit the new owners but do little for either tenant or overseer.

Most of Carey's efforts in the first years at Belgrade were given to nursing Charles, who by 1873 was too sick to do any work. Still, throughout the spring, she somehow also managed to teach the younger children and supervise planting the large vegetable garden and orchard she hoped would provide most of the family's food. By April, Charles was too sick to be left alone even for a short time because he was too weak to "obtain assistance" on his own.[23] His death on November 20, 1873, left Carey emotionally bereft and overwhelmed by complex business affairs as executor of his will. Until his debts were settled, her claim to any of his property was at best tenuous. She had neither capital nor income of her own. The future of her eldest son, who was just nineteen, seemed as dark as her own, for Browne's and McKay's schemes threatened to burden him with the same load of debt that had weighed down his father. But if he was to support his mother and seven siblings, what were the alternatives?

The person to whom both mother and son turned for help was William Pettigrew. Although he had entered the Episcopal ministry after he had given up planting, he had advised Carey on business matters throughout Charles's long decline. Unfortunately, his minimal (and often unpaid) clerical salary limited his ability to offer much financial support. But his celibate life and prudent ways allowed him to place the little he did earn largely at Carey's service. He had already paid most of the tuition while his oldest niece, Jane, completed her two-year course at the Virginia Female Institute in Staunton. When eleven-year-old Caro displayed considerable musical talent, he had enabled Carey to replace the piano she had been forced to sell. Four years later, he paid most of Caro's tuition at St. Mary's school in Raleigh as well as Tom's at Lehigh College.

In truth, few Southern families in the 1870s paid as much for their children's education as Carey did. Even with William's help, doing so taxed her purse so severely that she sometimes fell a year or more behind in paying their school bills. The girls still at home went without so that the one then attending school might have the clothes, books, and other requisites to complete her education. All of this, together with Carey's struggles to pay off Charles's debts, left the family nearly destitute. One by one, she tapped every possible resource. In 1874 she offered to trade Cherry Hill for the

$6,000 mortgage note Charles had given McKay for Belgrade and its adjacent Lakeside plantation. When McKay insisted that Cherry Hill was worth no more than $3,000 and turned her down flat, Carey became suspicious. When McKay began to demand repayment of debts of which Charles's incomplete financial records made no mention, Carey nearly foundered. As she struggled to meet each claim, McKay produced another, until he had upped the ante from the initial $3,000 to an incredible $25,000. With that, even William, who had once believed that his college classmate was a good friend, suspected him of deliberate fraud. And when this Presbyterian cleric resolutely refused to review the entire debt record with Carey and him, his suspicions were confirmed. Even more ominous, Charley believed that honor compelled him to assume responsibility for the alleged $25,000 debt in order to keep at least one Pettigrew plantation in the family. At this point, his Uncle William warned the young man against doing so. It was unlikely he would ever have the necessary money. It was almost certain neither McKay nor his heirs would display any "mercy" or "liberality." Nonetheless, Charley did assume full responsibility for all that McKay claimed his father had owed. But when McKay unctuously insisted that the Pettigrew children "call him Uncle," he met his match in eighteen-year-old Tom, who looked the reverend "full in the eyes" and bade him a frigid "goodbye DR." After he left, twenty-one-year-old Jane almost shrieked that "our Aunt [Annie] is dead, Dr McKay is married again. . . . I wish he wld let it alone."[24]

But he left nothing alone. Nor did he cease pressing for more until 1886, when Charley, by then thirty-two, gave up planting to practice law, which he had been studying in off-seasons. With his new legal expertise, he defeated one last McKay scheme in which the preacher colluded with another creditor in an attempt to drive down the price for which Belgrade sold. But it was an empty victory, for that sale alienated the last acre the Pettigrews owned in North Carolina. It also ended Carey's life as a plantation mistress. For thirty-three years, she had struggled to "keep the old plantations, & strengthen the old influences & the family name." Despite her best efforts, she was finally defeated. "Usurious interest, & many years of poor, or bad crops, have wound us up."[25]

The following January, Carey, three of her daughters, and Mary Blount, who since Browne's death in 1880 had again lived with her sister-in-law, moved into a small house in nearby Plymouth. With contributions from Charley, who shared that home when he was not riding circuit, the five women lived respectably, although not luxuriously. William continued to help Carey pay for the children's education. As her daughters, one by one, completed their studies, they began to support themselves. Jane, the oldest, who had studied voice and piano in Baltimore after she had graduated from Virginia Female Institute in 1871, taught school for six years prior to her marriage. Unlike her mother, she made no social debut and never enjoyed the life of a belle. Nonetheless, she did not lack suitors, and in 1878 she finally consented to marry Miller Williams.

Carey was of two minds about Jane's decision. On the one hand, young Williams was successfully cultivating cotton on his uncle's Mulberry plantation in the midlands of South Carolina. On the other, it was evident that he would never fall heir to Mulberry. Thus, the young man's future was certain only as long as his uncle, former U.S. senator James Chesnut, lived. So Carey held back. She "wld certainly never wish [her] daughters to marry *for money*." But she was also "opposed to their marrying without . . . being assured they will not be obliged to undergo hardship & great privation." She certainly liked Miller, but she doubted the wisdom of Jane's committing herself to him.[26] Nonetheless, when Jane accepted him, Carey so disapproved of long engagements that she encouraged a speedy wedding. Within a month, Jane and Miller were married at Belgrade and on their way to Mulberry, where Miller's aunt, Mary Boykin Chesnut, who lived nearby, helped them settle. In April 1879 Jane bore her first child, Serena Chesnut. The next year, she gave birth to a second, who died at once. Then in December 1881, Charles Pettigrew was born.

Although their children's names recognized ties to both Jane's and Miller's families, the Pettigrew tie tugged harder, especially after 1880, when Miller bought Bonarva from the recently widowed Mary Blount. Recalling her own painful experiences there, Carey had tried to discourage him. But it took three years of fruitless effort to convince Miller that he, like his predecessors, could not make the place pay. The price for which he sold it barely covered the debts he had contracted in buying it. So when James Chesnut died in 1885 and Miller lost the use of Mulberry, he left the Carolinas to engage in a series of unsuccessful business ventures in Kentucky and Indiana while Jane bore three more children, one in 1883, another in 1885, and the last in 1887. Exhausted by childbearing and poverty, she died in 1890. She was only thirty-five.

Carey did not live to grieve for Jane's death, for she had died after a brief illness on March 8, 1887. Nor had she seen any other daughter marry. But she had enjoyed the satisfaction of knowing that all of her daughters were sufficiently educated to support themselves in a world that would offer them none of the luxuries she had tasted in her youth. As her mother had done before her, she had prepared them as well as she could for whatever roles they might have to play. Similarly, although her efforts to secure her sons

The Pettigrew family cemetery at Bonarva, where no monuments commemorate those who died after 1863. William H. Pease photograph, 1992.

their plantation heritage had failed, she had encouraged Charley to read law on his own and had sent Tom to college to learn engineering. It was their mother's death even more than the sale of Belgrade the year before that marked the end of the Pettigrew era in the North Carolina low country. All of her children had been born when their father and his brother owned three major plantations and a number of minor ones there. But after nearly a century of planting in Washington and Tyrrell Counties, the Pettigrews lacked funds even to erect simple tombstones over the graves of their father, their mother, and their Aunt Mary Blount, who outlived Carey by only three weeks. The last permanent marker in the family burial plot was the monument erected to General Johnston Pettigrew after his death in 1863.

Carey's legacy, therefore, was not what she left to her children but her children themselves. Despite the turmoil that had riled her world, she had turned out daughters who were, as their Great-uncle Henry Lesesne once observed, "such young women as she was herself," women prepared to face an uncertain future with competence and composure. Nevertheless, at the birth of each daughter, Carey had lamented the child's sex. And her last two pregnancies, when she was over forty, had induced a sense of guilt at her maternal failings. In 1869 she had been "so impatient, so violently disturbed" at being once more with child, that when she miscarried and became gravely ill, she understood it as "a punishment" for her *"really sinful"* anger at being again pregnant. The following year, when her last confinement ended in the premature birth of a short lived daughter, she accepted that too as a punishment, which she took "humbly, & tho' very sorry," bore patiently as her "repentence."[27]

Carey's Cinderella-like emergence from her widowed mother's strained household and her marriage to a great planter never produced the security and luxury both seemingly promised. But despite Charles's debts and cancer, her first eight years of marriage had at least held out the possibility of future prosperity. But the four war years and the twelve that followed placed such hope almost beyond imagining. All told, her twenty-four years of married life had increasingly demanded that she attend to plantation and business affairs. In her last years, others sensed that she grew "hard" and "very severe." But in her own mind, she had failed to drive hard enough. In a fit of introspection some six years before she died, she wrote that she did not "desire riches for riches sake" but longed only to "pay the debts, & live without the searching cares of very narrow means." Trying to come to terms with her defeat in doing even that much, she echoed Hagar's prayer: "Thou God seest me. . . . Have I also here looked after him that seeth me?"[28]

CHAPTER TWENTY

The Return to the City

The Porchers' economic and social descent was both steeper and deeper than the North Carolina Pettigrews' decline. Their Goslington plantation, primarily a vacation home, had never provided more than a supplement to Philip's business earnings. After the war, so many of its farm workers were lured to nearby Charleston that serious plantation cultivation became almost impossible. At the same time, emancipation had destroyed Philip's brokerage business, which in the past had generated most of its profits from the slave trade. Nor was there much of a market for real estate despite record low prices. So simple survival forced Louise to turn their old home into a boardinghouse, an arrangement that replaced Philip as the principal support of his family and weakened his claims as head of his household.

Blinding themselves to the full import of the North's military victory, Louise and her daughters blamed their woes on the freedpeople. Even as newly liberated folk flooded into the city, the women could not accept either the permanence or the broad significance of emancipation. Mary Anna, then twenty-five, defied reality, insisting, "We shall never proclaim them emancipated," as though "we" had such power. She really believed that the black population would "remain in bondage and reap the reward of their voluntary servitude!!" To prove it, she pointed to the Porchers' own "liberated slaves" who had stayed "true" to their former owners and had become a "tower of strength" in time of need. As for the rest, they would soon recognize that their lives were "worse . . . than ever before." Every day, Mary Anna beheld the proof right outside her front door. "Horrible looking creatures"—men, women, and children—"destitute of food & every comfort" lay about in the streets with their "filthy bundles," the very "picture of misery & squalor." Surely no respectable white person would take "any interest in them any more than in so many dogs."[1]

The officers of the Freedmen's Bureau, however, did take interest in them, aiding the ex-slaves rather than the supporters of the defeated Confederacy. White Charlestonians' fury at their own destitution and the comparative plenty given former slaves boiled over when they observed federal officers in social intercourse with the government's black beneficiaries. Louise and her daughters fumed when they glimpsed a "mixed crowd of blacks & whites" aboard an excursion boat in the harbor. They shuddered at the sight of white men and black women driving together in carriages while they had to walk. But open contempt could not mask their own humiliation. Sheer necessity made seventeen-year-old Marion Porcher accept a pair of shoes and a calico dress from a Northern society organized to provide "destitute *ladies* with clothes, shoes, stockings &c &c." Even portraying that transaction as a "contribution" that white Southerners had forced on Yankees did not conceal her discomfort. Similar pride hindered her mother's ability to attract boarders. When the Northern general and his wife who were her first tenants left after only a few months, Adèle Allston guessed that Louise's attitude of social superiority would severely impede her efforts to replace them. The lady turned landlady would not grovel to her potential clientele. "When War has wrought the ruin of a people," she contended, "it is the higher classes who feel the reverses."[2]

Although Louise could bolster her self-confidence by dwelling on her former social status, Philip could not. Like so many of his class whose ability to support and protect his family had been shattered, he sank into depression and alcoholism. He had always been a heavy drinker, but faced with defeat and humiliation, he became a drunkard. Driven by fits of anger and delirium tremens, he sometimes exploded in physical violence that terrified his wife and daughters. Lou North reported one especially severe outburst in January 1868: "a very sad week to our dear friends at S. Bay" ended when "the poor father became very very violent & apparently dangerous, so that it seemed as if he must be sent to some asylum." Moreover, Aunt Louise's "positive misery" had already been stretched almost beyond endurance by her son Charley. After four years of fighting in Virginia, he sought no steady employment and became "nothing but a flaneur of the idlest sort," who threatened to follow in his father's footsteps.[3]

That summer, Louise took Philip to Badwell. There, where he had "no resources but books," he improved. But when he returned to Charleston, it became clear that only Badwell's isolation had kept him from the bottle. It was more than Louise could bear. Weakened by chronic malaria and the victim of nearly every epidemic that swept the city, she died at age fifty-five in May 1869. Little more than two years later, Philip followed her. With both parents dead, Mary Anna and Marion moved into the Lesesne house in Summerville, where they helped care for their Aunt Harriette, whose health had become "very delicate."[4] Four years later, Mary Anna, thirty-five and still a spinster, died. Two years earlier, Marion, the youngest of Louise's four daughters, had married Arthur Peronneau Ford. She was the only one to bear children—two daughters, one named Mary Anna and the other, Louise Petigru, and a son, Robert.

Although the senior Lesesnes outlived the senior Porchers, they experienced a parallel deterioration. In the immediate postwar years, Henry had enjoyed a brief period of professional and political success. Having served as a state senator throughout the war, he was appointed chancellor in 1865 over the South Carolina Court of Equity for three years. But once the radicals gained control under the new 1868 state constitution, his political career ended. He lost his judicial appointment and that same year was defeated in his bid for the Charleston mayoralty. Thereafter, his physical health, which had never been good, declined, and his bouts of depression became ever more severe as manic-depressive cycles ruled his life. Everyone who lived with him found him "a constant source of anxiety & trouble." In his view, however, it was Harriette who was the problem. He refused to take her "ailments" seriously despite one doctor's diagnosis that she was suffering from congestive heart failure.[5] After the family moved back to Ann Petigru's old house in Charleston, which he bought from Lou North in 1869, he largely left her care to their daughter Leila until 1877 when Harriette died. By the time Henry died nine years later, both of his younger sons had perished in accidents; his oldest, who had long maintained professional ties with his lawyer father, had broken with him completely; and Leila had married Robert Smith and moved to Savannah. Not surprisingly, after Harriette's death, Henry's depression deepened. He became a hopeless alcoholic, selling everything he owned to keep himself in drink. Because her father had sold even the house he had promised her, Leila, after her husband's death in 1888, which left her with an annual income of only $500, had to undertake paid work as a companion to an elderly couple.

Unlike the Porchers and Lesesnes, Sue King not only escaped near destitution but even regained many of the material comforts of prewar life. Snaring a job as a foreign-language clerk in the Post Office Department in Washington was only her first step in a campaign against genteel poverty.

Susan Petigru King Bowen. Photograph in Caroline Carson photograph album.
Courtesy of the South Carolina Historical Society.

For a while, her daughter's marriage to John Middleton in December 1865 overshadowed all of Sue's prospects. The only son of J. Motte Middleton of Cape plantation and Elizabeth Hamilton, the daughter of a onetime South Carolina governor and U.S. senator, John had read law with Sue's father after graduating from Harvard. His years as a Confederate officer left him more ready to marry than to settle down, so despite the war's inroads on his family's wealth, he whisked his bride off to Europe on a yearlong honeymoon, during which he supposedly combined business with pleasure. In Switzerland, Addy's first child, Elizabeth, was born but soon died. Shortly after they returned home in the spring of 1867, the Middletons' first son, Henry King, was born.

Sue was delighted to play grandmother on a brief trip she made to Charleston that fall. But she had no intention of limiting herself either to that role or to clerking. She had already resumed her writing career and had sold a short story, "My Debuts," to *Harpers Magazine*, the proceeds from which paid for the trip south. Its Southern heroine had gone north to live by her pen but had married a wealthy gentleman—just the scenario Sue had in mind for herself. Indeed, she told her relatives that she had that year been engaged to marry a California millionaire who backed out only because "their political views were too much opposed for peace." Whether or not this was as much a fiction as the *Harpers* story, Sue cultivated her image as "a lady of society—a leader of the ton," whose "woman-of-the-world-ly" manner attracted universal attention.[6] In so doing, this onetime ardent Confederate used her father's reputation as well as her own assets to construct a social life within Washington's highest Republican circles. Like her sister, she made the most of their father's friendship with William Tecumseh Sherman and found ways to attract the attention of President Ulysses S. Grant. She battened as well on associating with the lesser politicians who also cultivated those wartime heroes, partying and flirting as she always had.

But whatever her Carolina kin may have known of Sue's Washington adventures, they were totally unprepared for her marriage to South Carolina Radical Republican congressman Christopher Columbus Bowen. Only her Carson nephews, out of all of her relatives, attended the early evening wedding on August 17, 1870, at which, the invitation to Jem stated, "Gen'l Sherman hands me over & 'gets a receipt.'" Presumably their mother also knew about it in advance. But the rest of the family first learned of it in the papers. "Sue's last & most horrid escapade" positively appalled Minnie Allston. She had "*actually married* Bowen the Radical M C from Charleston," a man of the "worst character" who was "said to have deserted the Confederate Colours, & is a Murderer & a blackleg."[7] Minnie was not far from the truth. Chris, as Sue called him, was a native Rhode Islander, eight years her junior, who had gone south when he was eighteen and kicked around at many things—itinerant mechanic, Georgia farmer, Florida faro dealer, and, when conscription threatened, organizer of a Georgia volunteer cavalry company. Bored while stationed far from battle, he had forged the signature of his commanding officer on a pass extending a leave he had sought to gamble in Charleston and Savannah. He was caught, court-martialed, stripped of his officer's rank, and dishonorably discharged. In revenge, he arranged the murder of the commanding officer. For that crime, he was arrested and jailed by civil authorities. But with a gambler's luck, he and the slow-witted private who had actually pulled the trigger were still awaiting trial when federal troops occupied Charleston and released all prisoners. At once, Bowen began a new job as a Freedmen's Bureau agent, from which he was dismissed a few months later for irregularities in his accounts. Nonetheless, he had learned just enough law by then to act as a lawyer for freedpeople, whose cases he took pro bono, and thus to enter South Carolina's Reconstruction politics.

In 1868 Bowen was elected a Republican delegate to the state constitutional convention, where he secured an electoral base as a strong advocate for black civil rights, including suffrage. When the constitution that emerged enabled South Carolina to rejoin the Union that year, Bowen was handily elected to represent its first congressional district. Then, in Washington, he met Sue. Whether she knew about his previous marriages before their wedding is unclear. Probably she had at least heard gossip about the woman with whom he had been living in Charleston. In any case, right after the wedding, the legal tangle of her husband's marital past became public when Tabitha Park (or Parke or Parkes) brought suit against Bowen for divorce. Initially, she charged Bowen with deserting her in 1867 to live in "open adultery with another woman, and in an extravagant and luxuriant style." In response, in January 1871 Bowen offered to settle for $1,000 and an uncontested divorce. But Tabitha, "a large, masculine looking woman" who had kept brothels in Macon and Columbus, Georgia, and who some years later would be convicted of murdering several subsequent husbands, sought revenge. Bowen's marriage to Sue gave her ideal leverage. In the bigamy trial that followed, which was marked by much creative maneuvering, Sue was listed as a witness for Bowen. But just before she was summoned, she became so "very ill in the witness room" that she had to be discharged.[8] Whether any performance in the witness box could have been more dramatic than being dismissed as a delicate lady too fragile to withstand a public appearance is an open question. In fact, neither was necessary. Christopher Columbus Bowen was saved from conviction by one juror who refused to find him guilty as charged. Reports suggest the likelihood that the juror had been well rewarded beforehand for agreeing to hang the jury.

Chris's legal troubles, however, were not over. While he was fighting Tabitha's charges, Frances Hicks appeared before a federal grand jury with solid evidence that she had married Bowen in 1852. His second bigamy trial hung on the validity of an altered and unrecorded New York State certificate of divorce, which the jury entirely discounted when it reached a guilty verdict in only twenty minutes. This time, Sue played a more active role. Addressing the presiding judge of the District of Columbia Supreme Court on her husband's behalf, she pleaded that there were extenuating circumstances. As the *Washington Patriot* reported, Mrs. Bowen "in a feeling manner, said, in a firm, yet gentle voice: 'If he did it, I did it. If he is to be sentenced, please sentence me.'" She confessed that it was she who had procured the marred divorce document. "It was obtained in good faith. If irregular, if invalid, we are not in fault. . . . I cannot part from him! He is too pure, too good! You know him not; I do know him."[9] Unconvinced, the judge sentenced Bowen on June 13, 1871, to a two-year term in the Albany penitentiary and a fine of $250.

Even then, Sue did not give up. Why did she have powerful friends if she could not turn to them for help? She went straight to the White House. After President Grant declined to see her, she followed the Grants to their summer home in Long Branch, New Jersey, where she prevailed on Julia Dent Grant to convince her husband to hear Sue's pleas. Her persistence paid off. On July 8, 1871, Grant pardoned Bowen. That same day, the *New York Times* reported, Christopher Columbus Bowen, freed by a "full and unconditional pardon . . . walked out of jail in company with Mrs. PETTIGRU-KING-BOWEN."[10]

The next year, whether Chris was a congressman became as doubtful as whether Sue was legitimately married. After a yearlong investigation, the House of Representatives ruled that the campaigns of both candidates in the 1872 election had been too corrupt for either to be seated. Inconvenient as that was, it did not put Bowen completely out of office, for he had also been elected to a two-year term as sheriff of Charleston County. As a result, Sue came back to live in Charleston. Even before she arrived, her disgraceful present and Chris's tawdry past had tortured her kin. Now they scorned all contact with the Bowens, who regularly entertained "negro visitors" in their home. But that was nothing compared to the shame they felt at Sue's open letter to the press appealing to her father's memory in defense of her husband's conduct. How dared she invoke the name of James Louis Petigru, "whose life was a lesson of nobleness and duty; whose time belonged to the oppressed of every sex" and race, to defend Bowen from "vile persecution" and allegations of "murder, arson, forgery, burglary," and "bigamy"?[11]

But even then, her Aunt Adèle and sister Caroline tried to shield her. Adèle was so "greatly distressed" at the "awful . . . position" in which her "miserable and unfortunate niece" found herself that she offered her a temporary refuge at Chicora simply because Sue was "near to [her] in blood."[12] When Sue refused, however, Adèle joined virtually all of the rest of the family in avoiding all contact with her. Only Caroline still reached out to her sister. She had plundered her scanty funds so that Jem could stand by Sue in Washington during Chris's first bigamy trial. Not until Sue held back her sister's share of the final settlement of their father's estate did Caroline limit herself to maintaining only the appearance of family peace.

The Bowens had no financial reason for not passing on the small sums they owed Caroline. They lived on fashionable Bull Street in relative luxury in a large, well-furnished house of which Sue boasted to her sister. They employed five servants to keep the establishment running smoothly. When summer came, Sue and Chris moved to a newly built eight-room house on Sullivans Island. The ingenious Bowen could probably have sustained this style of living with the profits he reaped from a local phosphate-mining venture and the $20,000 he derived annually from legitimate fees paid the sheriff of Charleston County. But the *Charleston News and Courier* charged that he took in an additional $40,000 or so a year from "the systematic practice of gross and palpable frauds."[13]

Despite her plush material surroundings, Sue was not happy. Polite Charleston society, which had long condemned her abrasive personality and defiant behavior, now shunned her absolutely. And to the few individuals who tried to welcome her on her return to the city, she put up a defensive shield of witty repartee. Greeted by one former colleague of her father's, she inquired whether he was afraid to be seen talking to a woman of her notorious reputation. When the startled gentleman retorted that he had been seen talking to much worse women, Sue vowed that she had "never been seen talking to a worse man." Either unwilling or unable to hold her tongue or modify her behavior, Sue watched her social circle shrink to Chris's political cronies and a few impoverished gentlewomen. After the excitement of Washington, the "deadly loneliness" of her life oppressed her. "Of what constitutes 'society,' I have none. My parties are all given by myself: my guests are, for the most part, old & poor & forlorn—less friendless perhaps than I, but a great deal more destitute than I ever was." Worst of all, even her own daughter would have nothing to do with her. To her mother's sorrow, Addy had become her "worst enemy," her "bitterest foe," who refused even to allow her son to visit his grandmother.[14]

Addy's life, however, was little happier than her mother's. Her marriage to John Middleton was so joyless that for most of 1867 she lived with her grandmother. When Jane Amelia died in January 1868, Addy joined her husband in Georgia, where their third child, John, was born in April. When her husband died later that year, having squandered most of his inheritance and earned virtually nothing, his widow and children had no alternative but to live with her relatives. For the next nine years, she spent winters with the Lesesnes and summers with her King aunts in Flat Rock. Her older son died shortly after his father, the younger in 1874.

In 1875 her mother died. From its start, 1875 had been a bad year for Sue. In April the *Charleston News and Courier* printed verbatim the proceedings of a libel trial that revived all of the past charges against Chris, from his war-time court-martial and indictment for murder to his conviction on bigamy charges. Although Chris achieved a technical victory, probably by again bribing a juror, his triumph was brief. A grand jury, acting on evidence presented in the libel trial, immediately indicted Bowen for the wartime murder of his commanding officer. That indictment, however, never came to trial because the key witness, the private who had actually gunned down the colonel, vanished, never again to be found. And the corruption disclosed by an official investigation into the sheriff's accounts led to another detailed airing of Bowen's unsavory activities, printed in full in the *News and Courier.* Neither Sue nor her kin could ignore that record.

So Sue's relatives were relieved when she died of typhoid pneumonia that December. Caroline Carson suggested that even Columbus, as she scorn-fully called Bowen, might be "secretly glad to be rid of an uneasy compan-ion." Although she prayed that "poor Sue" find peace "where all scandal ceases," she contemplated how unlikely it was her sister "could have lived out a long life with Bowen without some explosion worse than all the rest."[15] But despite the many embarrassments that Sue's more than thirty years of scandalous behavior had caused them, the Petigru clan presented a remark-able front of family unity at her funeral. All of those resident in Charleston were present for the service in St. Michael's Church and her burial in its churchyard.

In making the funeral arrangements, Chris ignored Sue's recent consider-ation of converting to Roman Catholicism. The Sisters of Charity had nursed her during her last illness. A Catholic priest had attended her on her deathbed, although Caroline believed he could not have given absolution to a non-Catholic. Yet although Chris himself embraced Catholicism shortly after Sue's death, he chose to bury her next to her parents and brothers in the prestigious St. Michael's Episcopal churchyard. It was also he who composed her epitaph: "Her Soul,—bruised, not crushed—Undismayed, / Won a crowning Grace— / Brave—Trusting—Unshaken— / WIFE-HOOD."[16]

On the day of Sue's death, all of her jewelry as well as her will, if there was

Adele King Middleton Kershaw. Pen sketch from a photograph.
Courtesy of Mrs. Donald McK. Allston, Jr.

one, disappeared. It was a scenario that later made a probate judge question her husband's testimony and motives. Chris may have been worried by Addy's claims as her mother's heir-at-law. He had notified Addy when it became clear that Sue was near death. He did so, he later explained to Caroline, because "Sue had tried hard to reconsile her and had always said she would come when it was to late." When it was almost too late, he had written, "Mrs A Middleton the darkest sadist hour of my life is fast approshing. My Wife, Your Mother is dying if you wish to Come the house is open. C. C. B." Less than an hour before Sue died, Addy did come. Bowen said he offered her whichever pieces of her mother's jewelry she wished, but Addy took only a single ring. Neither then nor later did Bowen offer Addy anything else. "If Mrs Middleton hat treated her mother deacently I would be vary glad to make her Comfortable."[17] Within the year, Christopher Columbus Bowen made himself comfortable by marrying the eighteen-year-old daughter of the Radical Republican governor of South Carolina.

Addy remarried in 1877. After her June wedding, she went west with George Trenholm Kershaw, a South Carolinian then planting in Mississippi. The next year, she gave birth to her first Kershaw son, George Jr., and two years later, to a daughter, Frances. Her new life was little more propitious than her former one. George's plantation did not flourish. In 1880 he was arrested for shooting and killing a black trespasser. Thereafter, he held a series of ill-paying jobs at various places in Georgia where their remaining children were born: Adele Petigru in Atlanta in 1882 and James Petigru in Macon in 1883. Still, theirs was apparently a warm marriage, sadly shattered when Addy, age forty-five, died in childbirth on April 8, 1889.

Mourning the irony that Addy had weathered so much adversity only to die just when her life was becoming reasonably comfortable, her Aunt Caroline observed sadly that nothing had come "easy to her but death." Then she posited a mythic past as she extended her lament to embrace the whole Petigru clan: "Indeed all our lives were spoiled by the War."[18]

CHAPTER TWENTY-ONE

The Luck of the Allstons

On August 31, 1872, Henry Lesesne, acting as executor of James Petigru's will, notified all living family members that Badwell was for sale. It could not be sold until Jane North, Jack Petigru, and Mary Petigru had died, and now its sale was limited to Louise Pettigrew's direct descendants so that the old homestead would continue to cement the Petigru clan. Instead, however, it became a bone of family contention. Jem Carson, with a brand new engineering degree from Columbia College, saw his opportunity to convert Badwell into a profitable mining operation. Consequently, although he had no interest either in farming or in living there, he tried, with his mother's consent, to secure its mineral rights before the rest was auctioned off. If that strategy failed, he planned to buy the whole and then sell off all but the mineral rights to a buyer who might or might not be a relative. If that strategy failed, at least he would have bid up the price that James's residual heirs—his children and grandchildren—would receive from the sale. When Carey Pettigrew realized his intentions, she was indignant. Because all of the residual heirs had authorized Jem to act for them, he had "greatly the advantage" in bidding since the residual heirs, acting as a group, would not need to pay the whole sum bid while other family members would.[1] More-over, Jem's plan to defy his grandfather's intentions should he become Badwell's owner and then resell the homestead outside the family simply infuriated her.

At the auction, nearly all of the family backed Lou North, who was represented by her lawyer cousin, James Petigru Lesesne. He opened the

Louise North. Photograph.
Courtesy of Mrs. John H. Daniels for Mulberry Plantation.

bidding at $3,000, a sum believed to be a fair market price. But because Jem, like the rest of Lou's kin, knew that Lou had $6,000 in cash and notes at her disposal from her Uncle Henry's purchase of the house Ann Petigru had left her, he felt safe in forcing the bid up to $5,500. Even so, Lou would not be satisfied until she owned the house in which she had grown up. So she thought it worth "the increased amount" she was "so wantonly compelled to pay" to avoid "the digging and 'projicking' of such a cub" as Jem Carson.[2]

At first owning Badwell satisfied Lou, by then a thirty-nine-year-old spinster, giving her the "space & privacy" she had wanted since adolescence. Only after both of her sisters had married had she been "exalted" to the "dignity" of having a room of her own. But during the war, even that private space was usurped by refugeeing kin. After the war, Lou always lived in "other people's houses": first Aunt Louise's, then Aunt Ann's, and finally Aunt Harriette's. Now Badwell promised her not only a "comfortable house" in which to live independently but also enough farmland to support that life.[3] She also dreamed of making Badwell once again a family center for older kin on long summer vacations and the younger folk who would absorb family traditions on briefer visits.

Soon, however, the burdens of farming and the isolation of living alone made her view Badwell less enthusiastically. Charles Lesesne, whom she first engaged as her overseer, had no more success than most of those who had earlier tried to make the place profitable. Furthermore, other family members, even her sisters, failed to visit as postwar poverty and new living arrangements put Badwell out of reach. Finally, living there alone reduced her already dim marital prospects to zero. Even as a young woman, her wretched complexion and poor posture had made her so shy and had attracted so few beaux that her mother had believed her unmarriageable. But Lou yearned for male companionship and never gave up hope. When she heard of forty-two-year-old Mary Blount Pettigrew's marriage to Dr. Browne, she wished that she might find "some satisfactory M.D. or any other M—a trousseau looks so nicely."[4] For all of those reasons, she rented out the land and lived at Badwell only occasionally, spending most of her time with one or the other of her sisters.

Until 1882, her offers of marriage were nil. Apparently, the only man Lou had ever attracted was her cousin Ben Allston, and her Uncle Robert had absolutely forbidden his children's marrying their cousins. When Robert could no longer say nay, Ben had already married Ellen. As a result, Lou played the traditional role of a maiden aunt to her sisters' children. She had even helped out at Guendalos after Ellen's little Mary was born, for Ben had known he could count on his cousin when his sisters failed him. Still, it was not until seven years after Ellen's death that he asked Lou to marry him. It took the long winter visit that she paid to her Aunt Adèle in 1882 to foster the renewal of Ben's old affection that led to a June wedding. By then, Ben was forty-nine and Lou was only a year younger, an age at which she was unlikely to bear a child. So, at last, this marriage of first cousins was not only tolerated but approved.

Adèle, who had long lamented her son's lonely life and wished that he "had a good wife," was greatly pleased. Although her niece was "not strong in appearance," she was "very gentle and sweet," so any reservations about the marriage of cousins quickly disappeared. Others in the family were not quite so positive. Della Vanderhorst wondered why, after having "had so much of her own way and lived independant so long," Lou would want to marry at all. On the other hand, Caroline Carson was sanguine that having "an

Exchange plantation, home of Benjamin and Louise North Allston.
William H. Pease photograph, 1992.

interest of her own" at long last would free her cousin from being a "servant of the whole family." Carey Pettigrew, who was losing that service, was not "quite satisfied," although it did seem likely that Lou's marriage would be "wise for her in many respects." Even Ben had misgivings about "all it involves."[5] Nonetheless, the wedding took place on June 2, 1882. For the first five years of marriage, Lou struggled to make do as the wife of an unsuccessful small planter. Then, after Ben sold Exchange plantation, took holy orders, and became the rector of an impoverished Episcopal church in Georgetown, she scrimped harder still as the wife of an ill-paid minister. Nor did their income improve much when he was called in 1890 to a slightly larger parish in Union, South Carolina, whose chief appeal was its proximity to Badwell, even though it was still about seventy miles away.

However pinched Lou's circumstances, her marriage was far happier than Minnie's. A year after the war ended, Joe Allston, like Ben, had attempted to resume rice planting but was defeated by old debts and new labor problems. The law practice he opened in Georgetown at the same time was equally unpropitious, for his clients were local planters no more prosperous than he. Even so, in their first months back in the low country, Minnie's life was eased by Joe's decision to live not in the old house at Waverly but in the comfortable house he bought in Georgetown, where, in May 1866, their first and only son, Joseph North, was born. By the end of the year, Minnie was so optimistic about their future that she threw a big dinner party in the best prewar fashion. The feast was so bountiful that the whole family "lived on the remains . . . for over a week."[6]

Unfortunately, her optimism was soon dashed as it became apparent that Joe's law practice, although it occupied much of his time, paid virtually nothing. The following summer, Minnie came down with typhoid fever and nearly died. By the fall of 1867, Joe was already bankrupt, unable to pay off his debts for Waverly or to earn a living from the law. Deciding to try his luck elsewhere, he left for Baltimore in 1868, while Minnie, after packing and storing all of their belongings, took the children to Bonarva to stay with Carey until Joe established an office and found housing. Never adventurous, Minnie trembled at "the great risks of moving, *again*, this time to succeed or starve." She feared "the confinement of a pent up city life for the children, . . . the heavy espenses attendant upon moving to such a distance[,] the change from a southern to an almost northern climate, the absence of 'sweet' air[,] the thought of living in 'rooms' and moving probably every season, the sundering of all the ties which bind us to this dear old unhappy country, as home." Their future confirmed her forebodings. She, Joe, and their three children spent their first Baltimore summer in two hot upper-story rooms of a boardinghouse. Thereafter, they moved from one small rented house to another. No domicile was permanent. They lived as transients in places that forever seemed alien. The "unwholesome repressed atmosphere for children to grow up in" depressed her spirits. Just as hard to handle was Baltimore's urban economy. High prices for every necessity seemed to compress the minds and bodies of city dwellers to make them selfish and inconsiderate. "Perfectly aware" of the effect of these pressures on herself, Minnie most feared their "results upon the children."[7]

Two more pregnancies tightened the Allstons' circumstances. Frances, who was born in the summer of 1869, lived little over two years. In 1872, at age forty, Minnie delivered her sixth and last child. Caroline lived and was much loved, but her needs taxed already tight resources. By then, Joe's recurrent bouts of illness, which made him unable to work, deepened the gloom that pervaded their lives. On a visit in 1869, Lou had been shocked by the swift progression of his manic-depressive cycles and the mental lethargy that left him, even on his calmer days, with no energy to work. "God only knows what is before his family," she warned Carey; his mood swings alone were "enough to destroy them."[8]

As family concern mounted, other relatives were consulted. In 1871 Ben found Joe "for the most part in an abstracted condition" that made it clear he would never have a legal practice sufficient to support his family in even minimal comfort.[9] Nor did he have other sources of income sufficient to do so. He had been forced to sell Waverly for a price so low that it provided little long-term improvement in his finances. As a result, Minnie realized that she must rear her children in a poverty that she had never experienced, even during her mother's worst years at Badwell. In 1870 she could not even afford to buy them simple Christmas presents. Still worse, she lacked funds for their education. But in that area, at least, her sisters helped. Frequently, two or three of Minnie's children lived with their Aunt Carey, who taught them along with her own offspring. Periodically, their Aunt Lou lived with the Allstons so that she could teach all four children at home. By the time of Ben's 1871 visit, however, Minnie's ability even to feed, clothe, and shelter them was uncertain. And when Lou North and Henry Lesesne arrived a little later, they found Joe so confused that he got lost just walking around in his own neighborhood.

The short-term solution was to send Joe, Minnie, and their children to Bonarva, where the quiet of rural life might turn Joe around. In fact, it did for a time. After little more than three months in the country, he was sufficiently recovered to return to his Baltimore law practice. When Charles Allston visited him there in February 1872, he found that, although Joe could not attract many clients, his mind seemed "to be awake which is a great point." Unhappily, it did not stay awake. The next year, Minnie took the children to Badwell, where Lou promised to give them a home and an education while her sister returned to Baltimore to be with Joe. Remaining with her husband was "the only course" open to a wife, whatever the personal cost. But "what a life" that meant for Minnie, and, Carey sighed, "what anxieties every day must bring."[10]

In 1876 the couple's only source of funds came from selling the remainder of their real estate for $12,000. Notwithstanding, that year Minnie brought the children back to Baltimore, where, again with her sisters' aid, she somehow managed to finish their education. Even before she turned twenty in 1878, Jane, the eldest, had a steady teaching job that provided her parents' and siblings' principal support. The other children worked as they could but contributed notably less. Lucy taught on and off when she could find employment. Young Joe's earnings were limited to his pay as a seasonal farm hand. And Caro, the youngest, was only sixteen and still in school when, in 1882, Jane suffered the mental breakdown that left her unable to work. As Minnie saw it, the only option that remained for her and Joe was to leave Baltimore and settle permanently at Badwell, which Lou, now married to Ben, no longer occupied. After three years in a Baltimore asylum, Jane was well enough to join her parents there. Even so, her double cousin Bessie cringed that she was still "insane! poor child poor child. . . . She was working so hard to help the family and it was all lik[e] pouring water into a bottomless bucket." Still, until her death in 1890, Jane did what she could to help, embroidering articles that could be sold in Baltimore. Joe also brought in a small salary as the local postmaster, a job that left him lots of time to write. Lucy, who married William Nelson Meade in 1887, lived elsewhere, as did Caro, who supported herself as a teacher. But Minnie, despite the sanctuary that Badwell again provided, never shook herself free from the "intolerable" anguish inflicted by the illnesses of both her husband and her eldest daughter.[11]

Adèle Allston's daughters fared far better than her nieces. Of the three, Della came closest to fulfilling Adèle's aspirations for them all. During most of her financially secure married life, she lived in the fourteen-room Vanderhorst mansion on Charleston's northern edge. After 1870, when the main house at Chickesee, the family's Ashepoo River plantation, was restored, she and Arnoldus spent each planting season there. During those warm spring months, she became the plantation mistress. A little later, the old summerhouse on Kiawah Island, all of which the Vanderhorsts still owned, provided her and her children vacations that resembled those she had spent as a child on Pawleys Island. Following her mother's pattern, she gave birth at roughly two-year intervals to much-loved children, four of whom—Adele Petigru, Frances Allston, Elizabeth, and Robert Withers Allston—bore Allston names, while three—Anna Morris, Elias, and Arnoldus—were named for their Vanderhorst progenitors.

Della did not, however, replay her mother's life. She escaped the life-threatening illnesses that had so often accompanied Adèle's pregnancies and deliveries. She refused to nurse any of her children, being a "firm believer" in feeding infants "by the bottle." More burdensome, for eleven years she reared her numerous, closely spaced children in a three-generation household in which her in-laws, although "as kind as possible," were a constraint on mother and children alike. So Della lacked the home of her own for which she yearned. She welcomed the freedom that spending the spring at the plantation and the summer on Kiawah provided. Managing those establishments efficiently with the help of the children's nurse, a cook, and one maid fed her self-confidence. Furthermore, the informality of those months relieved her of constantly cautioning her children lest their noisy play disturb their grandparents in the four-story house they all shared in the city. By contrast, the winters in town began to seem "very dull." The old folks were "so queer." Arnoldus was so often absent attending to business. And Della's

The Vanderhorst mansion on Chapel Street, Charleston.
William H. Pease photograph, 1995.

quick temper spilled over when it should not. Still, although her older brother criticized her for such displays, Lou could only admire her for doing her part so "courageously & sweetly."[12]

It was not until Arnoldus's father died in 1874 that Della finally convinced her husband to move their growing family into a Charleston home of their own. No sooner had they done so, however, than his mother pressed them to return to the old mansion on Chapel Street. Elias had wanted it to remain his son's home. His widow now promised Della its management if doing so would save the house and Elias's plans from "destruction."[13] So after only three years on their own, Arnoldus and Della moved back to the mansion where they had already spent nine of their fourteen years of married life. For two more years, their children lived under their grandmother's watchful eye until Ann Morris Vanderhorst died at eighty-five.

By then, with seven children to rear, Della employed a governess, for, like her mother, she intended to educate her daughters rigorously and thoroughly. She also followed social practices of the older generation by introducing her girls to social proprieties as they paid calls, attended parties, and promenaded around the Battery together. In addition to the customary emphasis on musical performance, she encouraged their participation in sports that she had not even known about as a child. In 1880 her budding adolescents roller-skated with other young people of their class, and her oldest daughter was an eager archer. Also a phenomenon of changing times, mother and daughters often rode public streetcars rather than taking the family carriage to go shopping or calling. And for a short while in 1880, both fifteen-year-old Adele and thirteen-year-old Anna Morris attended a public school.

Such innovations were, however, only superficial variations on the upbringing their parents had known. The young Vanderhorsts observed Charleston's social rituals just as their mother and grandmother had. They enjoyed the material comforts provided by their father's prospering businesses, now concentrated in his thriving wharf and various newer enterprises. In 1881 he spared little on a general refurbishing of the Chapel Street mansion to make it as "comfortable and desirable" and as "fine [a] house and groun[d]s" as his means would allow.[14] Most unconventionally, he also conveyed all of his property to Della that fall.

Three weeks before Christmas, Arnoldus hosted a large deer-hunting party on Kiawah Island. On the morning of December 1, his guests spread out to occupy their stands on his vast estate, agreeing to meet again at the house by the end of the day. As dusk approached, Arnoldus still had not appeared. After a period of uncomfortable waiting, his friends fanned out to look for him. A group that included his servant Quash found his body near his shooting blind. By then, it was too dark to leave the island, so they waited until dawn to take the body back to Charleston. Fortunately, Jinty learned of the catastrophe just in time to be with Della when Arnoldus's body arrived. Later that day when Bessie heard the news, she hurried down from Chicora to stay with her sister for as long as there was need. It was she who broke the news to her twelve-year-old nephew, Elias, away at boarding school. His father, she wrote, had apparently just been "in the act of crossing a log, when evidently he had used his gun as a support, like a stick in crossing and the jar of placing it suddenly on the ground in that way had caused the right barrel to go off. It seems that had been in a dangerous condition for some time & he had warned Quash about it the night before when handling the gun."[15] Nothing more was said about the accident before Bessie went on to describe how bravely Elias's mother was holding up under the shock.

Della was forty-one when Arnoldus died. She had been his wife for eighteen years. She lived the next thirty-four as his widow. Initially, she was totally unprepared to cope with the business arrangements essential to governing the extensive Vanderhorst property. Unlike her mother, who was not widowed until she was sixty-three and who had learned much about the business of planting in her forty-two years as the mistress of Chicora Wood,

Della lacked any managerial experience beyond what her home and children had required. Nonetheless, after the first few weeks, when she was sustained largely by emotional support from her mother and sisters, she directed her efforts toward mastering the new responsibilities placed upon her as the head of a large family and the proprietor of extensive and varied commercial property. With unexpected grit and perseverance, she soon became a competent businesswoman. Unsure at first even about how to write a check, she gradually mastered the arcana of bank accounts and business ledgers. And although she never managed their day-to-day business, she supervised the leasing and other proprietary concerns of the wharf, the plantation, and the Kiawah lands. On her twenty-fifth anniversary and seven years after Arnoldus's death, her brother Charles Allston reflected on the "long lifetime [that] seems to have passed" since that wartime wedding.[16] For Della, that lifetime embraced a fundamental transformation from vapid incompetence to the hardheaded strength of character needed by the widowed parent of seven children and the guardian of all of their assets.

However prematurely Arnoldus's death ended Della's married life, Bessie's days as a wife were startlingly fewer. Because she was two years older than Della had been when she was married and had always shown a marked streak of independence, Bessie came to matrimony with not only different expectations but different qualities. She had few illusions about her appearance, describing herself as "small and very thin," with a nose and mouth she "would never have chosen" and a complexion with a "great disposition to blush at every word and look." Nonetheless, Julius Pringle had decided when she was barely seventeen and he was only twenty that someday he would marry her. But that took him seven years—three as a Confederate officer and four struggling to restore his Brookville plantation. So slow was his courting that Ellen Allston deemed her sister-in-law simply perverse for resisting all efforts to encourage the romance. Adèle gave it no encouragement at all. Although her mother admitted that Bessie could do worse, she wanted her daughter to marry a "man of more animation, and intellectual elasticity." Julius's mother openly opposed the match. Her other son, Lynch, was already engaged to a young woman with neither beauty nor fortune to commend her, and, as Minnie Allston quipped, Mrs. Pringle believed she "really . . . ought to have satisfaction in at least one of her children's marriages."[17]

In the end, however, maternal opposition did little to discourage the young people's mutual attraction. When Julius finally proposed in August 1869, Bessie accepted on the spot. His mother's consolation lay, as she boasted to outsiders, in having delayed her son's proposal for three years.

But when the deed was done, both mothers concentrated on making the April 1870 wedding as much like the old days as possible. They came close. Bessie "looked lovely in white muslin with illusion veil & orange blossoms." Her younger sister and bridesmaid wore "white with pink sash & pink flower in her hair." Their widowed mother, who never gave up her mourning, was handsome in "black velvet & lace." The reception at Chicora was in the same tradition as the triumphs that had produced an extravagant dress for Bessie to wear to her first St. Cecilia ball and cakes and champagne for Della's wedding festivities. Although this time there was no champagne, the abundant ice cream that topped "the usual supply . . . of good things" brought the reception to a sumptuous end. The next day, Jane Pringle entertained the wedding guests at her White House plantation with an equal display. During these festivities, neither family allowed its opposition to the event to show. But it had not disappeared. Della's praise of the "beautiful presents" Bessie received "from all her friends and some of [Julius's] relations" made that clear.[18]

Bessie, however, was determined that the remaining friction should not mar her marriage. When Adèle first visited her at Brookville the following month, she praised her for following the biblical prescription to make "her husbands true interest her pursuit." Jane Pringle still entertained doubts. She feared that Bessie's intense dislike of Lynch Pringle might "lead to something dreadful between the brothers." But Bessie's brother Charles concluded that the difficulty lay "entirely between Julius & his mother" and that Bessie was wise just to "keep quiet & let [Julius] do what seems best to him."[19]

Rather than Jane Pringle, it was the restricted circumstances of their everyday lives that tested the bonds between Bessie and Julius. Despite the elegance of their wedding, they faced the same hard times common to most planting families. Saddled with large debts, Julius worked long hours in the fields despite "scorching sun" and inclement weather to raise the crops that might repay his creditors. In the evenings, exhausted by such hard physical labor, he often fell asleep in his chair. Although his lively wife understood the cause and sympathized with his weariness, she found it hard to excuse the Pringle "family trait to spend all the evenings at home in slumber." She supposed that when she grew old, she too might doze off, but at thirty-one, having "to sit & watch a snoring figure" provoked "very rebellious & unwifelike feelings after a long day alone." It was downright disillusioning "to discover all the unloveliness in face & form to wh[ich] at other times" she was "blind." But such irritations were minor abrasions in a marriage whose only real sadness was that Bessie and Julius seemed likely to remain "settled married people without children."[20]

In mid-August 1876 Julius left home to travel to the Democratic state nominating convention in Columbia. On the way, he stopped in Charleston. There he suffered a massive stroke. As soon as the news reached Brookville on that August 21, Bessie caught the next train to Charleston. But when she reached Kingstree, the northbound train brought a message that Julius was dead. She went on in a state of shock. By the time she reached town, she had determined that she alone would sit with his body throughout the night. The next morning, just as firmly, she watched his coffin sink into its Magnolia Cemetery grave, refusing to leave until "every clod of earth was put, & it smoothed over & leveled."[21] Julius had died when he was thirty-four. Bessie, three years his junior, would live for forty-five years as his widow.

At first she was in a state of denial. She cried little and spoke less. But inside, she almost choked on rage. Linking her husband's premature death to the poverty that war and defeat had brought, she was firmly convinced that if Julius "had had the smallest competency without debt," he "wd have lived to be an old man in all human probability." So she dressed as though she were an old woman. She donned a "little old lady's widows cap" and shrouded her body in deep mourning. She gave away all of her pretty clothes. Although doing that was voluntary, giving up the home she and Julius had shared was not. Her tiny inheritance from his debt-ridden estate forced her to abandon Brookville and return bitterly to her childhood home. She had thought she "had left the nest forever and lo at the end of a few short years" she was "back again," her "wings broken & bleeding."[22] She resumed the role of an unmarried daughter or maiden aunt. Until Ben remarried, she cared for his motherless children. For the rest of her life, she was always on hand to nurse a sick child, console a troubled sister, assist an aging mother.

Gradually, however, Bessie constructed an independent life. In 1880 she spent all that Julius had left her and took on a hefty mortgage to buy out her brother-in-law's interest in the Pringle family's home plantation. For the first few years, her brother Charles managed White House for her, but when he failed to make the profits needed to pay off her mortgage, Bessie decided "to relieve him and try it" herself.[23] Remarkably good weather that year gave her the bumper crop that cleared the mortgage. She also revived her interest in music, renting a piano in 1880 as a first step. She became active in the Charleston Women's Memorial Association, a group organized to commemorate the Confederate dead but that later contributed mightily to the Lost Cause myth. She traveled frequently. She spent a number of winters in New York studying art. And she began to write, at first for her own amusement and later for publication.

Elizabeth Allston Pringle and an unidentified servant. Photograph reproduced in
Elizabeth Waties Allston Pringle, *Chronicles of Chicora Wood*
(New York: Charles Scribner's Sons, 1922).

In 1893 Bessie looked back over the twenty-three years since her wedding.
Gone was the "enthusiastic, pleasure loving, intense, rebellious, headstrong
girl" who had married Julius Pringle. At forty-eight, Bessie deemed herself
"a quiet, hum-drum, docile middle aged woman, who is almost incapable of
very strong feeling, who is perfectly content to go on from day to day doing

the day's duty however irksome and uninteresting it may be and quite ready to find plenty of enjoyment in the quiet things that surround her and make up her life." But that resignation was partly self-deception. Her stays in New York sharpened her awareness of the "weary rote of the southern condition" that condemned her to the "dreary" life of the "much less interesting" woman she had become.[24] But would she have been any more interesting had she continued the life she shared with Julius for a brief six years?

Her life, in any case, contrasted sharply with that on which her brother Charles and his bride embarked in December 1874. The Allstons welcomed Emma Rutledge Lowndes into the family with a warmth they had never bestowed on Ben's Ellen. Bessie even pronounced their marriage a "great blessing." In the following seven years, Emma had four healthy children. None of them bore a Petigru name, and the only Allston namesake was Robert Allston's little-known Northern cousin John, whose financial generosity had enabled Charles to establish himself as a planter. If that unusual naming pattern attached more value to cash than kinship, it also marked the distance that never closed between old ways and new, between Adèle and Emma. No intimacy developed between them, and Charles was pulled into the Lowndeses' entrepreneurial orbit more than Emma was drawn into the Allstons' family network. His ability to purchase Windsor plantation shortly before he married reflected his participation in a prosperity that set him apart from his kin who planted at Exchange, Chicora, and White House. He was, as Lou described him, "a successful man—of cool judgment, cautious and clearsighted, and with a certain charm which so often belongs to self contained non-commital persons."[25] Charles was, in short, his father's son.

Adèle's youngest child was the last of her daughters to marry. At twenty-seven, Jinty was also the oldest on the day she became a bride. Eight years earlier, however, she had teetered on the brink of becoming the youngest bride of her generation. But she had rejected Henry Williams then not because he could offer little of the financial security parents still expected but because her mother, if left alone at Chicora after Bessie's impending marriage, seemed likely to sink into depression.

In the six years before Henry gave up and married another woman, Jinty spent most of her time on the plantation with her mother. Their days were often dreary in a house that was often "fearfully cold" in more ways than one. Adèle regretted that Jinty was "very solitary and without associates of her age" but nonetheless thought her daughter had been "right to come [home] and [be] a great comfort" to her. Yet Jinty and Henry continued to correspond. Moreover, she spent enough time in Charleston to be courted by numerous scions of the old elite. She danced, walked, and rode with James Pringle, Jr., John LaBruce, Herbert Sass, St. Julien Jervey, and Edwin Frost. But it was to a stranger that she eventually linked her fate. She first met Charles Albert Hill, an English businessman who was very much "out side of the old crowd," in 1874. At first she scorned him. When he asked her to go riding, she supposed that "it will be a very absurd sight," for, she warned her mother, "Mr Hill is certainly no whip."[26] Nonetheless, his wealth and his English connections apparently balanced such deficiencies. On April 25, 1877, Jinty married a man almost as foreign to Carolina as Ellen Robinson had been.

During the first ten years of their childless marriage, Albert provided his wife beautiful clothes, European travel, a well-furnished mansion on Charleston's South Battery, and a "very large comfortable house" in Flat Rock where they spent the summers they did not travel abroad. Then, suddenly, ill health brought their fashionable life to an abrupt halt. Charles, only six years his wife's senior, became an invalid. As a result, they left Charleston to live year-round in Flat Rock. Thereafter Jinty saw little of her family and old friends and lost the urban amenities she so valued. Once again Caroline Carson lamented the ill luck of the Petigrus. Jinty, who had "seemed the one prosperous one," now shared their common decline, made worse by the "penalty of having no children to provide for or to love her." Nonetheless, Adèle took this too in stride. She regretted her daughter's loss, but after so many sorrows and upheavals, this latest one seemed "nothing."[27]

Adèle, who was then seventy-seven, had seen her own life continually stripped down. Only Chicora and its immediate dependencies were still hers. The 1873 depression had forced her to sell the stocks and bonds that had previously tided her over bad crop years. Her only reliable cash income now derived from the $5,000 annuity John Allston's will had provided her. Early in the 1880s, she was cutting expenses wherever she could. But she clung to those things that meant most to her emotionally. She considered but rejected giving up summers on Pawleys Island because she treasured the family get-togethers that still occurred there. But after deciding to keep that nonessential property, old age curtailed her willingness to make other financial choices. A few years later, she asked Della to take over even her most routine banking transactions.

As her property shrank, Adèle became ever more preoccupied with its eventual distribution. She drafted one codicil after another to ensure that her will would treat all of her children equitably. Having used most of the $10,000 John Allston gave her in 1870 to launch Charles's planting career and

Jane Allston Hill. Photograph.
Courtesy of Mrs. John H. Daniels for Mulberry Plantation.

the rest to assist Ben, she juggled her remaining property to compensate her daughters as best she could. Still, it would be hard to divide Chicora and the land and houses on Pawleys Island unless they were sold. And it had been to save those properties for her children that she had sacrificed so much else. As a result, her efforts to make a fair will that would strengthen the bonds among her children never ceased. It was her "earnest desire" that they share the little that remained of the Allston heritage with neither greed nor rancor and continue to "live in the exercise of mutual love and confidence towards each other."[28]

As for her grandchildren, Adèle worried most about their moral and ethical inheritance. Like Jane North, who had combined the joys of grand-mothering with practical instruction of the children and pointed advice to the mothers, she used both avenues to mold Ben's and Della's children to her own standards. Only when they were toddlers had she dared display the unrestrained delight she took in Della's youngsters. She adored her "dear little name child." She commended Anna and Elias as "fine children." And Elizabeth absolutely "won [her] heart." As they grew, she continued to relish their company but also advocated the strict discipline with which she had reared her own children. She suggested that Elias's parents needed to exert "a little firmness" in governing the six-year-old boy. And when Elias reached nineteen, his grandmother advised his mother to make sure he used his time wisely and filled "his mind with history, or other useful things." She pressed her grandchildren at every age to exercise greater self-control and their parents to employ more consistent discipline. Only when children were "pliable" enough to be set straight could "the germs of evil" be rooted out.[29]

Adèle's role in rearing Ben's children was even greater. Between Ellen's death in 1875 and Ben's marriage to Lou North in 1882, she assumed the major responsibility for their upbringing, although Bessie undertook much of their day-to-day care and instruction. When their grandmother took charge of ten-year-old Mary, four-year-old Charlotte, and two-year-old Robert, she was determined to undo Ellen's erratic child-rearing practices. Unfortunately, Mary, her favorite, died only two years later. Charlotte, who was unmanageable when she arrived, after three years had "much improved in behaviour" and begun to assume "the subdued look that dear Mary had." Robert, who as a boy spent more time with his father and by the time he was nine could "trot and gallop a horse, and do many boyish things," was taught by his grandmother to do them "without losing his gentle" manners.[30] Because she derived real pleasure from her grandchildren, Adèle was sad-dened that she saw Emma and Charles's children so seldom. They lived near enough to visit Chicora frequently, but Emma apparently resented her mother-in-law's assertive interventions and was far less willing than either Della or Ben to share her children with their grandmother.

Despite her joy in the young people, Adèle became increasingly preoc-cupied with her own aging. She had resolved "to plod on in the path of duty," but she wearied of the burdens Chicora Wood imposed. She longed for the mythic peace she associated with her Badwell childhood and of which visits to Flat Rock reminded her. "How happily," she mused, "a family might live in these fastnesses if only they had outside means to pay for grocery and clothes and they could do good among the poor people who are ignorant and consequently helpless." But she lacked the means. She was tied to Chicora. And as her physical strength drained, her self-confidence waned. She grew "so timid" about her "ability with horses" that she hesitated even to drive the two miles between home and church. She vacillated about visiting Della and the grandchildren because Charleston seemed so far off. But her daughters made sure she did not become a recluse. Once or twice Bessie took her to the Virginia springs. In 1885, when she was seventy-four, Jinty and Della took her to New Orleans on a trip she described so gleefully that Lou concluded she was enjoying "a very satisfactory and happy old age."[31]

But at home, keeping up her spirits was hard. The world seemed to close in on her. The weekly mail became the principal event to which she looked forward. She reviewed the sad incidents of the past, especially the deaths of her own and her sisters' young children. She immersed herself in "the memory of all [her] sorrows." She missed her grandchildren when they went away to school and embarked on independent lives. Her "increasing infirmities" made it "more and more difficult" for her even to write letters to them.[32] As she wrote less, the weekly mail brought her fewer responses. But rather than blame others for her miseries, Adèle blamed herself for letting her own shortcomings propel her into the periods of depression from which she had long suffered. She did what she could to fend them off, but without her former physical vigor, it was hard to counteract them.

Still, she kept on. On November 15, 1896, Adèle attended church as usual. The next day, she and Bessie drove over to Plantersville to do errands and call on friends. It was "a long drive," Bessie recalled, "but very very pleasant, the air so fresh & Mama so full of enjoyment." When they got back to Chicora at dusk, Adèle lay down and "took a good rest in her room." It had been "a happy day."[33] Nine days later and just two weeks after her eighty-fifth birthday, Adèle Allston died.

The Pain and Joy of Autonomy

In the prewar years, no one but her sister Sue rivaled Caroline Carson's drive for autonomy. By the time the war ended, Caroline had been a widow for nine years, more than five of which she had lived on her own in New York. Her separation from her sons had cut short her maternal role. The death of her father had so cut her off from her Southern kin that she had been forced to rely on Northern friends for needed assistance. To free herself from complete dependence on them, she had begun a career as a professional artist. Never, however, did she overcome her deep-rooted anxiety about her own and her sons' futures. Without a solid financial base, she was trapped on an emotionally charged roller coaster, soaring in periods of artistic accomplishment and social success, plunging as her sons' minimal achievements and her own futile efforts to regain Dean Hall tinged even her best years with dark premonitions.

Like many of her kin, Caroline had put her faith in education to ensure her children's future well-being. The settlement of William Carson's estate had, even before the war, foreclosed the likelihood that either son would support himself as a planter. So she had sent Willie abroad to prepare him for a mercantile or banking career. Once she had reclaimed Jem at the war's end, she sold her diamonds to send him to Columbia College to study engineering. Whatever her sons' subsequent failings, neither could blame his mother for not having provided him a vocational education at considerable personal sacrifice. Even while Caroline was bedridden with a prolonged life-threatening illness when Jem was in college, she contributed to his support by knitting garments that she sold to wealthy New York friends.

Happily, by the time the young man graduated, Caroline had recovered her health. Once again, she was the poised and charming woman who, all of her life, had attracted admiring followers. In 1872 one of them, T. Walter Langdon, a wealthy New Yorker, asked her to chaperone, at his expense, his two nieces on the customary European grand tour. Although he subsequently canceled the trip, he paid Caroline $1,300 for the time and effort she had devoted to planning it. Suddenly, she had money in hand to fulfill her long-standing dream of traveling and painting in Europe. So in early July she sailed from New York to Liverpool for a five-month tour that ended in Rome, where she planned to pursue an artist's life. First, however, she explored the rich museums of northern Europe. The force and beauty of the Alps exhilarated her. Long stays in Turin, Milan, and Florence strengthened her fascination with Italian culture. Her ability to absorb it all was enriched by lifelong language study and serious reading that prepared her to live in Europe. When she arrived, she was already fluent in Italian, which she had begun to study in the 1840s. Ever since, she had read widely in Italian literature. Her knowledge of European history, which she shared with most of her Petigru relatives, allowed her to root her traveler's observations in a past she knew well. So by the time she arrived in Rome at the beginning of December, Caroline, confident that technical instruction from some of the city's many resident artists would free her talent, was ready to settle down and get to work. She rented a furnished apartment in the tourist quarter just above the Spanish steps and began her new life.

Grateful for the practical assistance of Julio Posi, who had taught her Italian in Charleston and had just resettled in his native city, Caroline reveled in being on her own in the place she most wanted to be. "All my life my great desire was to go to Rome—and here I am—And though a woman and fifty years old I find myself [as] full of enjoyment as any body I see, and more than most." Almost at once, she made friends among the expatriate community. Within a month, she was sharing frequent expeditions and meals with Mary Mason Hooper, the estranged wife of Massachusetts senator Charles Sumner. She met Crowninshields, Sturgises, and other elite Bostonians. They in turn introduced her to friends who were passing through the city as tourists. Her list of prominent Boston acquaintances eventually included Congressman Abbott Lawrence's widow and poet-professors James Russell Lowell and Henry Wadsworth Longfellow. She revived her acquaintance with old New York friends, among them Gus Schermerhorn,

Caroline Petigru Carson in Rome. Photograph in Caroline Carson photograph album.
Courtesy of the South Carolina Historical Society.

who "follow[ed] the hounds" with the Italian crown prince, and with Julia
Ward Howe's financier brother, Sam Ward.[1] She also renewed ties with Robert Bunch, who had been the British consul in Charleston, and expanded her
circle of English friends to include people like actress Frances Kemble.

More immediately attuned to her painterly aspirations, Caroline thrived
in the Anglophone circle that centered around the Boston sculptor William
Wetmore Story. Story's studio and apartment in the Palazzo Barberini were
prized meeting places for those who shared his artistic interests. Mrs. Story,

who made clear distinctions between those she found socially acceptable and those who were only her husband's professional colleagues, welcomed Caroline so warmly that the following fall Caroline moved into an apartment on the Via delle Quattro Fontane, almost opposite the Barberini. Pleased to be included in Mrs. Story's social circle, where she met "all the big wigs," she found it even more rewarding to encounter the artists who gathered in Story's studio.[2] Landscape painter John Rollin Tilton, sculptor Luther Terry, and painter Henry Greenough, all Americans who lived in or near the Barberini, became her good friends, as did a partly overlapping group of women artists, among whom the portrait painter Lizzie Boott was prominent.

Caroline's Anglophone associations, however, did not obscure the Rome of the Romans. She was thrilled by the physical remains of the ancient city she had learned to venerate as a child. Now the republic and empire to which her father had introduced her came alive. Her artist's eye reconstructed the imposing buildings whose ruins marked where they once stood on the Palatine Hill. Similarly, she relived the saga of Christian Rome when she visited the Vatican. Despite her Protestant background, she rejoiced in the marvelously costumed and staged dramas of Catholic ritual. Nor did she let her keen interest in the past blind her to the present for she followed both the pageantry and the political maneuvering of King Victor Emmanuel's government as it attempted to construct a secular state in newly united Italy.

Then there was the rest of Italy. Only four months after her arrival in Rome, she explored the mezzogiorno when her old and very rich friend Annette Hicks invited her to Naples. From there, she took side trips to Pompeii and Vesuvius. She soaked up the natural beauty of the Amalfi peninsula, delighted in the scenery around Sorrento, and gazed back at the Bay of Naples from the heights on the Isle of Capri. In June she went north to avoid Rome's sweltering summer heat. She stayed several months at Bagni di Lucca in the hills northeast of Pisa. On her way home, she revisited Florence and Siena before she reached Rome in early December with a collection of sketches to develop during the winter months. The first year of her Italian residence established a summer travel pattern she followed in later years, going to spas for her health and to the cultural centers and scenic locations that constantly furnished new material for her art. Over time, it was the coolness and scenery of the mountains that most satisfied both interests. At Lake Como or in the Swiss or Austrian Alps, she sketched and painted while at the same time she enjoyed associating with the many English-speaking vacationers the mountains attracted.

During her winters in Rome, she developed contacts with the exclusive

Roman aristocracy. Her knowledge of their language and culture was essential to her doing so. But her entrée was also facilitated by wealthy American women who had married into that aristocracy. Caroline's most immediate connection with the old nobility, however, was her friendship with Michaelangelo Caetani, Duke of Sermoneta. A liberal senator in the new government and a Dante scholar of international repute, the Duca, as she usually referred to him, had first met her as her maid's patron.

Although he was nearly seventy and totally blind, the Duca and Caroline got on so well together that, for a time, the possibility of a romantic attachment flitted through her mind, as perhaps it did through his. But although she dallied with its possibilities, she evaluated the situation pragmatically. "Were it not for [Caetani's] wonderful use of his beautiful language, and the irrepressible wit of his discourse, he would be but a dull companion." In fact, even with his wit, he was a bore when he rambled on, criticizing his wastrel king and bemoaning his country's tax structure. But when they discussed Dante, whose poetry Caroline had studied for many years, the Duca fascinated her—even thrilled her as he recited the passages with which he made his points. On most other topics, their interests were more likely to diverge. And although he was at "the very top of the Roman nobility," his blindness and consequent aversion to crowds meant that he was unlikely to expand her social world.[3] So she confined her genuine affection for the old scholar to admiring his mind and enjoying his intellectual companionship.

In any event, it was the lure of art, not the glitter of nobility, that had attracted Caroline to Rome. Although she began her hunt for a suitable teacher soon after she arrived, it took her several months before she found one she could afford. Gustavo Simoni was "poor & little known to fame," but his paintings, which she first saw in a shop window, were "excellent" and his ability to teach her "just what [she] . . . so long wanted to learn" about watercolors made him an ideal instructor.[4] Later, after she developed that technique, she studied other media—sometimes with formal instruction, more often simply by watching her colleagues at work. Before long, she was selling her paintings to American and British travelers.

When she left New York, Caroline had expected to live very comfortably in Rome on the income generated by the trust fund established for her in Boston, the South Carolina stocks and bonds of her own that she had recovered after the war, the few securities she inherited from her father's estate after her mother's death, and the sale of her New York house. But her income never quite supported the style of living she so valued. So she instituted weekly receptions in her apartment-studio at which, although they were ostensibly social affairs, she displayed her work to potential buyers. With an eye to business, she encouraged friends and acquaintances who bought her paintings to invite their friends and acquaintances to her open houses. She also cultivated her downstairs neighbor, Anna Brewster, who puffed her work in a column that appeared regularly in the *Philadelphia Bulletin*. It was doubtless Brewster's praise of this "charming aquarelleist" that led a planning committee of the 1876 Centennial Exposition in Philadelphia to appoint Caroline to its Roman subcommittee, charged with selecting works by resident American artists for display.[5]

So this self-exiled Southern lady began to earn significant sums for her paintings. Although her botanically accurate watercolors of flowers most attracted buyers, she also catered to tourists who wanted mementos of places they had visited or copies of paintings they had admired. She also did decorative work, painting fans, trays, screens, and even hangings. In 1875 she almost doubled her income from American sources with the $1,600 she made from sales. Although she never earned quite that much again, she averaged, while she was active, between $600 and $700 a year. But because sales varied sharply from one year to the next, she could not count on any set sum. Her market was "always a sort of chance." And her desire to paint oil portraits conflicted with market imperatives. By 1875, "flower painting" had already begun to seem "very monotonous." Still, it was her watercolors that won recognition. In 1876 she was the only foreigner and the only woman to be elected to the newly formed Società degli Acquarellisti in Roma. That honor was significantly enhanced by Princess Margarita's praise for the "Fiori di Madame Carson" that were displayed at the society's first annual exhibit.[6] And it was watercolor paintings of flowers that Caroline was invited to show elsewhere.

After she concluded that her flowers were "pretty nigh perfection," Caroline was drawn more and more to oil painting and portraiture. Her first ventures in this line were miniatures and pastel sketches by which she had attempted to make money even before she left Charleston in 1861. Now she addressed the basics that had earlier daunted her. She took formal lessons from Onorato Carlandi, Otto Brandt, and Jim Pole and visited the studios of other artists who generously shared their live models. Although her skill in oils never matched her mastery of watercolor, by the mid-1880s, she was no longer "afraid to face any public" with her portraits.[7] Her need for the more extensive studio space that painting in oils imposed, as well as her desire to entertain more extensively, led her to rent a larger apartment and to hire her maid's new husband as cook and general factotum. But these added comforts also brought added worries.

She was so haunted by the possibility of poverty that she doubted whether even prudent management would permit her to live so comfortably for long. She had for years accepted the fact that her prewar luxuries were a thing of the past, but she still longed for costly conveniences like keeping her own carriage. As a result, she became ever more preoccupied with salvaging any American property to which she believed she had a claim. Conducting that campaign from Rome involved months of waiting for business letters to go back and forth. Too often she discovered only after the fact that her agents and lawyers were not following her directions. The sale of her New York house was botched when her agent accepted $2,000 less than the minimum price she had authorized. Her Charleston lawyer never pressed her claim to the lot on which her father's Sullivans Island beach cottage had stood. When Lou North bought Badwell, Caroline waited years for her lawyer-cousin James Lesesne to send on her $2,111.78 share of the proceeds. Nor did he as executor of Mary Petigru's estate ever forward the $150 her aunt had bequeathed her. And Sue held back the dribs and drabs of income that trickled in from their father's estate. Although, except for the Badwell proceeds, the sums due were small, they were large enough to have provided some of the luxuries she could not otherwise afford.

With her capital significantly less than she had counted on when she went abroad and her dividends from stocks and bonds notably diminished by the panic of 1873, Caroline's fixed income consistently fell short of the $2,000 a year she considered essential for living in Rome. During her twenty years there, her annual income from American sources averaged less than $1,800. In good years, sales of her paintings carried her. When sales did not, she taught young American ladies to paint, coached Italian diplomats in English, or sold the works of other artists on commission. But her style of living, which in her youth had bordered on the extravagant, was always limited by her uncertain income.

Caroline had believed that the sons she had educated for well-paying careers would contribute to her support. Neither Willie nor Jem ever did so significantly. In fact, they asked for her help more often than they gave her any. In her early Roman years, she missed them, especially Jem, her favorite, more than their material support. She wrote during her first year in Italy: "It often comes over me that all the bounties of art and nature are as nothing to the company of my children, and it seems impossible to hold out on this side of the Atlantic. Often times I am so hungry to see you that I have a great pain in my heart and go sighing all day." But occasionally she also sought Jem's material aid, reminding him how freely she had "literally coin[ed her] blood" to send him to Columbia.[8] During her first year in Rome and while he held his first job, Jem did send his mother several $100 gifts. After that, he almost never even offered to help.

Jem disappointed his mother again and again. He drifted from one job to another, never advancing, always either quitting in anger or getting fired. Often he was unemployed. Although Caroline sensed the nature of her son's problem early on, she refused to face it for a long time. When she did, she had no success in moderating his behavior, whether it was his aversion to taking orders from superiors or his proclivity to hang "round doing nothing" in the long intervals between jobs.[9] Willie did only somewhat better. He too went laterally from one job to the next, either in government bureaus or railroad offices. But at least he drew on his mother's resources far less frequently than did his brother. The more she watched their disappointing work lives, the clearer it became to Caroline that the only hope for either son's prosperity lay in his marrying money. But both brothers were constant losers in romantic affairs as well. Neither ever married.

What had been true in 1877 when Caroline had confessed to her diary that "every body's sons" were "better off" than hers continued to be true.[10] In later years, in fact, Caroline dipped so often into her capital to meet Jem's frequent and Willie's occasional requests for money that the trustee of her Boston trust fund warned her against thus endangering her own security. Clearly embarrassed that others recognized her sons' financial shortcomings, she covered for them by insisting that these withdrawals were only loans, not gifts. None of these "loans," however, was ever repaid, nor did her sons respond when, in the late 1880s, Caroline, weakened by age and illness and living on less that $1,600 a year, begged them to "pull the ends together by a wise economy" in order to give her some assistance.[11] On the single occasion in her twenty years in Italy that Jem visited her, she not only paid all of his travel expenses but sat at home alone while he spent most evenings out on the town. And Willie, who with far less urging visited her twice at his own expense and was very companionable while there, never helped his mother financially.

Yet Caroline continued her costly legal battle to regain Dean Hall for her sons' ultimate benefit. She spent sizable sums on the suits and countersuits that moved glacially through the courts. As in her other efforts to control how her claims on American property were handled, she found herself powerless to oversee and direct her lawyers—and she resented it. But what could she do from far-off Italy? Year after year, one suit after another ricocheted between state courts in South Carolina and federal courts and between lower courts and higher as every decision was appealed by the losing party all the way to the U.S. Supreme Court and, just as frequently, referred back to a lower court.

For one illusory year, Caroline thought she had regained Dean Hall and began its restoration. Like her cousin Carey Pettigrew and her Aunt Adèle Allston, she was sufficiently wed to the plantation tradition to want her sons to be planters. In cultivating Dean Hall, they would, she trusted, be able to provide her additional income. Willie, who had never outgrown ill-founded fantasies, took up the task at once, although he had not lived on a plantation since he was eleven and knew precious little about Dean Hall in particular or planting in general. But when he admitted to these deficiencies and begged Caroline to join him there to instruct him and keep him company, she refused outright. Not only did the low country climate make her physically sick, but life at Dean Hall had brought her only "disappointment and humiliation."[12] Despite her own hostility to Cooper River life, Willie's ineptitude, and Jem's failure even to visit Dean Hall, she shouldered most of the responsibility for planning and financing its cultivation. She borrowed money from friends. She advised Willie about planting, right down to specifying how much mulch each field would need. She developed a long-range plan to substitute mulberry trees and silk cultivation for the old cash crops of rice and cotton. She even toyed with importing Italian laborers to replace local freedpeople.

Evidently, she did not foresee that Dean Hall would produce more trouble than crops. Before anything was harvested that year, another suit in a South Carolina court produced a decision that again clouded the Carsons' title. Her head splitting from "this last blow," Caroline wondered whether it would not be wiser just to "cut down all the timber pay ourselves—set fire to Dean Hall and come away."[13] Nonetheless, she launched an appeal that resumed the legal wrangling and resulted in three more unfavorable decisions between 1886 and 1891. By then, however, Caroline was too old and sick to pursue the struggle.

Her failure to regain the plantation, like her sons' failure to fulfill her ambitions for them, drove her to introspection about the meaning of her life. Almost a half century earlier, when she had first grappled with the circumstances of her disastrous marriage, she had hoped to gain "the sad satisfaction of knowing by what mistake" she had thrown away her own happiness. In an acrostic sonnet on her name, which she wrote in January 1853, she probed the personal failing she believed had sealed her fate. In trying to grasp "each passing toy in reach / Owning, the while, each but a worthless prize," she had become a "wav'ring woman," internally torn between her compulsion to seek pleasure and her "*Conscience*," which warned her against that frantic quest. What conscience had failed to do, war had done by cutting off the means that had made her sybaritic life possible. Now, as she looked back, she nearly welcomed that "dreadful change we all underwent by the war—breaking up our old lives and compelling us as it were to begin all over again when we were already weary and looking for rest." It had launched her into a life as an independent woman and expatriate artist. But as stimulating as her new life was, it never filled the emotional void left by Everett's abandonment and her father's death. Certainly her children did little to compensate for that aching emptiness. Nor, in all likelihood, would marriage to her Duca have done so, for it would have made her still "more positively unhappy if he had turned out unmanageable," although attending to him would at least "have been something to do."[14]

By 1889, however, all possibility of marriage had vanished. Several months before her seventieth birthday, she insisted that although she did not "feel the weight of years," she did feel her "isolation, and the weariness of time dragging on."[15] Her childhood friends had all died. The friends she had first made in Rome were either dying or moving to Florence as both artists and tourists sought out that Renaissance mecca. Had she been financially able, she too might have deserted the eternal city. But she was stuck there with few amusing or interesting companions. And so she mulled over the men in her life whom she either had loved or might have loved.

At the very end, one last person whom she loved unreservedly entered her life. He was little Giacomo Carlo Angelo Pizzuti, born to her maid and her cook in 1886. She became his surrogate grandmother, whom he called "Toto." And Toto responded by finding him no more trouble than a dog "and much more amusing." Even the antics of "terrible two" failed to annoy her since, she now believed, it was "old people," not young parents, who had the patience "to take charge of the children."[16]

Without Giacomo's frolics and his obvious affection for Toto, Caroline's last years would have been unremittingly bleak. But even he could not dull the pain her cancer inflicted. In 1890, when she had eleven polyps removed from her nose, neither she nor her doctor realized that the growths had already metastasized. By April 1892, a "hard angry looking" tumor that flared up on her arm, burning "like a coal of fire" and sending "darting pains" to her heart, made the finality of her disease clear. When Willie arrived in Rome on July 15, he found his mother, as his grandmother had been for much of her life, subjected to the "miserable pass" of "life under the influence of morphine injections."[17]

Exactly one month later, Caroline Carson died. The next day, August 16, 1892, she was buried, as she had wished to be, "beneath the cypresses" of Rome's Protestant cemetery. Her entire estate, amounting to less than $25,000 and her claims to Dean Hall, was bequeathed equally to her sons. Only one possession went elsewhere. She had made sure her love letters from Edward Everett, which she had lacked the "resolution to burn" herself, would be destroyed by her banker.[18] Her other highly prized correspondence, her father's letters, went to Jem, who, almost thirty years later, published many of them in a biography of his grandfather, which he dedicated to his mother. It was Willie, however, who first commemorated her life. He ordered the epitaph cut on her simple tombstone: "Caroline Carson / Born at Charleston / South Carolina / January 4 1820 / Died at Rome / August 15 1892." Years later, Jem ordered an addition: "Daughter of / James Louis Petigru / The Union Man / of / South Carolina / Resurgam."

No one thought to add "Artist."

In the eighty years between 1816, when the first of Louise Gibert Pettigrew's children married, and 1896, when the last of them died, her descendants had enjoyed the prosperity and then suffered the decline of their region in a pattern that suggests a version of "shirtsleeves to shirtsleeves in three generations." But what did "shirtsleeves" mean for the Petigru women? Louise Pettigrew's daughters had grown up on a medium-sized upcountry farm where their brothers had worked in the fields beside the family's few slaves. As adults, however, two of the three brothers married the daughters of low country planters, and, building on the connections thus opened to them, four of the five sisters married well-educated men who planted rice and cotton on low country plantations, practiced a learned profession, or did both. Consequently, by 1840, this first generation of Petigru women enjoyed economic prosperity and social privileges well beyond those of their mother.

Their daughters did likewise until the Civil War and its aftermath revolutionized the Petigrus' world. By war's end, their menfolk's largest capital investment had been wiped out, but the huge debts they had contracted to buy land and slaves remained. Without an assured labor force to work the land, they saw the value of their real estate plummet. And the thoroughness of their military and political defeat rendered Confederate bonds and money completely worthless. Worst of all, the men themselves were mauled and damaged. Five of those from the Petigru family who had gone to war did not return. Those who did came back so much altered that their physical and psychological wounds scarred the rest of their lives. Of the men who had remained at home, the elders who had most guided family affairs, James Petigru and Robert Allston, succumbed to stress and the illnesses of old age. And the rest who had remained civilians or served only in the reserves watched their manly power to protect and provide for their families dwindle almost to nothing.

The women endured parallel changes. Long before Sherman reached the Carolinas, the threat of invasion had driven most of them from their peacetime homes. While they were gone, their houses and many of their belongings were destroyed or badly damaged. When they returned, it was to a world that compelled them to do much of the domestic work that slaves had formerly done for them. In the years that followed, finding black women who would wash clothes or cook meals proved so trying to Adèle Allston that she predicted a gloomy future in which "white people will have all such work to do."[1] And in 1896, when this widow of a great rice planter died, only one of her mother's descendants was a plantation mistress, although another did own a large agricultural estate, and the wife of one grandson continued the plantation tradition. Adèle's only consolation was that all three were Allstons. But of that lucky trio, the only one whose husband still lived had married a man too young to have seen battle. The other two were widows of Confederate veterans whose premature peacetime deaths had vested their property in their wives.

Those were the realities that drove most of the third generation toward self-sufficiency. In their childhood and adolescence, they watched their mothers shoulder responsibilities previously thought to be men's. Indeed, of Louise Pettigrew's married daughters, only Harriette Lesesne never attempted to earn money by her own exertions during those years. Those who did, whether by planting and home manufacture or by urban occupations, made sure that their daughters were educated not only to improve their own and their children's minds but also to support themselves. Whether that shift in emphasis came about as the result of the mothers' wartime and postwar experience or their awareness that the war had diminished the likely pool of eligible young men, it served well the eighteen of Louise Pettigrew's great-granddaughters who lived to adulthood. At least twelve of them would earn their own keep for a significant period, and at least ten never married. Measured by the traditional belief that a woman's success lay in attracting a desirable husband, bearing and rearing children, and presiding over her family's home, that bold statistic suggests a marked decline in status for the third generation of Petigrus.

Still, one must ask whether the lives of the third generation represented a return to or a departure from the lives of their predecessors. Although Louise Pettigrew had owned a few slaves as well as agricultural land, the Badwell of her time had been an upcountry farm on which her growing daughters had worked in the house, the dairy, the poultry yard, and the garden. As adults very much on the rise, they had not considered such work demeaning. As she expanded Badwell into a modest plantation, Jane North taught her daughters and their visiting cousins to perform many of the domestic tasks she had learned there as a child. At Chicora Wood, Adèle's children were introduced to at least some of those tasks. So for those of the first generation and a significant number of the second, keeping house in the postwar world, even with few or no servants, was little worse than cycling back to the lifestyle that Louise Pettigrew had known. Remaining single and earning one's own living outside one's home, however, did not constitute a return to the old ways.

In this respect, the third generation differed markedly from Adèle Allston, who in the immediate postwar years conducted her school in her Charleston home, and Louise Porcher, who ran a boardinghouse in her family's home on South Bay. These older women's activities were, in many respects, a continuation of their prewar lives, during which they had taught their own children and managed their own households. What was new, therefore, was less what they did than that they did it to support themselves and their families. Previously, that responsibility had fallen solely on widowed Jane North. Of the rest, only Sue King and Caroline Carson had broken ranks before the war to earn money by their own personal exertions. And both of them had used their earnings to supplement rather than replace the income they derived either directly from male kin or from the capital males had bequeathed them. So the postwar innovation was either the decision to achieve the independence from men that earning one's own living implied or, conversely, the necessity to work for pay that resulted from being single. Surely Louise Pettigrew's great-granddaughters were well aware that while only one of the five sisters in the first generation and only two of that generation's eleven adult daughters did not marry, more than half of the third generation remained single. Consequently, the reason those women became self-sufficient is intimately connected to why they did not marry. Was it a matter of personal choice? Was it a recognition that the wartime slaughter and postwar deterioration of so many men made finding a suitable husband unlikely? How much of that gender imbalance was caused by ambitious Southern men migrating out of the South to escape their section's dismal economy in ways that women could not? Or did women's failure to marry reflect a new social milieu at home?

For the two previous generations, courting had gone on largely in the social arena that Charleston provided even for those who lived in the country. More specifically, it had occurred within the circle of young men whose varied contacts with Petigru fathers, uncles, and older brothers introduced them to the drawing rooms, dining tables, and family parties at which they met resident or visiting daughters, sisters, nieces, and cousins. All of James Petigru's sisters had married within his social or professional circle. So did his daughters and his one granddaughter. And his nieces who married before the war had found their husbands among either his or Robert

Allston's acquaintances and kin. By contrast, when Carey Pettigrew's and Minnie Allston's daughters came of age, they had neither a father nor an uncle capable of providing them such advantages. Only the Vanderhorst girls, who benefited socially from living in Charleston, were more likely to marry than remain single.

Just as crucial to changes in the lives of the Petigru women and how they viewed their place in the world were their shifting attitudes about race. While slavery lasted, mistress-servant animosity was contained within the clear-cut boundaries the peculiar institution mandated. When blacks breached those boundaries, they could be punished swiftly by their white owners or supervisors. With emancipation, however, racial hostility played itself out more openly in the kitchens, parlors, and private chambers of the white women. When a servant defied an employer, the mistress could no longer assume that her will would prevail. Now she was more likely to be met with a black woman's assertion of personal independence than with externally compliant servility. White women, resenting their loss of power, strove vainly to restore it. Black women, resenting any infringement on their new liberty, acted to protect it. Out of that clash, a racially defined kitchen politics emerged.

If they wished service, therefore, white women had to curb their anger at home and vent their frustration elsewhere. This loss of control at home inescapably fed their wrath at race-based civic disorder. In a sense, Caroline Carson's denunciations of striking laborers in the American North or rebellious peasants in Ireland paralleled the class hostilities her Southern kin expressed. But there was a major difference. Hers was intellectualized and expressed at a distance. Theirs was expressed primarily in racial terms and revealed a passion rooted in direct personal experience.

Unremarkably, that private wrath begot an intense observation of public politics. Having contested black power in their homes, the Petigru women were as fully incensed as the Petigru men by biracial political organizations, election riots, and demonstrations against segregated streetcars. Before the war, they had generally relied on men to protect them whenever they felt threatened by servile unrest. But during the war and especially in its closing weeks, they had witnessed white men's inability to quell black defiance, and after the war, they watched as their husbands and brothers were rendered almost as impotent politically as they themselves had always been. Just as their own lives linked kitchen politics and public events, their men's loss of prewar power to make and enforce their political preferences subverted traditional male claims to dominance within their own homes.

Still, neither the men's visible loss of control over others nor the women's postwar gain in control of their own lives was rooted solely in the Civil War, for patriarchy had never ruled supreme and unchallenged. The degree of autonomy that individual women had enjoyed in earlier years had varied from the dutiful passivity of Harriette Lesesne to the bold assertiveness of Sue King. Generally that autonomy was negotiated between spouses with unequal resources. In Robert Allston's household, Adèle customarily confided her rage at her husband's dominance only to her diary, while outwardly she conformed to his firm rule in exchange for the generous material benefits he provided her and her children. It is unlikely that Robert ever seriously considered the possibility of sexual equality except perhaps by planning to give each daughter, as well as each son, a working plantation at her coming of age or her marriage. At the other extreme, Caroline Carson defied and then left her planter husband, taking their sons with her but losing any benefit from his property until his death entitled her to life use of the widow's third. Carey Pettigrew molded an entirely different kind of autonomy as she clung loyally to the debt-ridden and ailing husband who cooperated with her to reshape their marriage along companionate lines. And Jane North was obliged by her husband's early death rather than any personal choice to rear her three daughters on a plantation devoid of any resident white male. Thus, although patriarchy may have been the prevailing model before the war, it was not a ubiquitous reality.

Indeed, the Petigru women, like so many others in both North and South, had persistently approached marriage cautiously, ever reluctant to give up the freedom they enjoyed as young women. But the first and second generations had simply assumed that they would someday become wives and mothers. Except perhaps for Mary Petigru, they grieved when they found no husband before they reached thirty. Nonetheless, they delayed their weddings as long as they dared, while their mothers generally withheld full approval of a daughter's engagement, disappointed that she had not waited for a better mate. Thus the more than half of the third generation who failed to marry reflected not just a realistic acceptance of the difficulties that impeded making good marriages but also a continued reluctance to be caught in an onerous one. Of their pool of suitors, many were financially insecure; others were scarred by the war. And the large family circle and social atmosphere that had encouraged courting in their mothers' and grandmothers' time had shrunk in size and resources.

Even without the war, family ties would doubtless have contracted as the first generation, who had consciously cemented them, died off. The deaths of James Petigru and Jane North eliminated the family's magnetic central figures and diminished the pull of Badwell. The war itself sharply reduced the frequency of their personal contacts and their ability to render each other mutual aid. Neither during the war's last years nor afterward did Chicora Wood and Bonarva produce excess food to be shared with urban kin. Nor could city dwellers so easily accommodate young relatives to enable them to attend school as day pupils after the war. As a result, family cohesion stretched little beyond the limits of individual households or the closest blood ties. Mother-child bonds remained the firmest. Adèle Allston as a widow and Carey Pettigrew as the wife of a dying man both fought tenaciously to retain their husbands' plantations to ensure that at least one son would enjoy a planter's life. They could not anticipate that, ironically, a daughter would fall heir to Chicora and that all of the Pettigrews, sons and daughters alike, would leave North Carolina after their mother's death. The bonds among sisters held almost as firmly as those between mother and child, at least among Jane North's, Louise Porcher's, and Adèle Allston's daughters. But the ties among cousins and between aunts and nieces languished. They had less time to write letters and visit each other, and even if they had the time, they generally lacked the money to travel. As for receiving the guests who used to stay for weeks, the new paucity of supplies and servants constricted the hospitality that Bonarva and Chicora had once offered unsparingly. Even though Jinty Hill and Della Vanderhorst maintained large fully staffed houses in Charleston, they did not own them until the late 1870s. Thus, the cousins met and mingled far less frequently than had young Norths, Porchers, Allstons, Lesesnes, Petigrus, and Pettigrews in times past.

It was, however, the death or disability of a husband rather than loosening family ties that most affected married women and pushed them into unsought autonomy. It was their husbands' deaths that transformed Della Vanderhorst into a businesswoman and Bessie Pringle into a planter, just as a generation earlier, her husband's death had forced Jane North to farm Badwell. It was their husbands' disabilities that drove Carey Pettigrew and Minnie Allston to be both master and mistress in their own homes. Their daughters absorbed all of this and learned firsthand the wisdom of having skills and talents that would enable them to live without the support of men. Consequently, their mothers met little opposition as they steered them all toward the teaching careers for which they were so consciously and conscientiously educating them. Despite being financially strapped, both Carey and Minnie managed to send the daughters they and their sister Lou had so painstakingly taught at home to boarding schools in Virginia and North Carolina for one or two years. They even provided an additional year of professional music study for two of them. And Della, whose relative

Jane Pettigrew (second from the right) and schoolmates at the Virginia Female Institute. Photograph. Courtesy of Mrs. John H. Daniels for Mulberry Plantation.

prosperity enabled her to employ a governess for her children when they were young, sent her older girls to day schools in Charleston until they were ready and willing to attend boarding schools in New Jersey and Maryland.

Here, too, although they altered its specific purpose, the later generations built on family tradition that had from the first stressed education. Louise Pettigrew had understood it as a tool to prepare her children to rise in the world. Her great-granddaughters used it to cushion family decline. But Jane North had recognized its income-producing potential for women all along. She had made Badwell an academy for her daughters and their cousins because she valued knowledge and because she wished to prepare the girls to shine in society and, later on, carry out their duties as mothers. But she had also foreseen that if they failed to marry, that same education might enable Carey and Lou to support themselves as governesses. Still earlier, when she herself had contemplated opening a school in Abbeville, she had grasped its potential for giving her a better life. Thirty years later, when her daughter Lou reflected on Jane's failure to open that school, she reconstructed the event in an inaccurate but revealing framework. "How different would our

Mother's life & ours have been had her brothers & sisters not felt themselves at liberty to oppose & discourage her having a school."[2] Had Jane been alive to correct her daughter, she would have told her that Brother had, in fact, encouraged her. It was the school's potential patrons who had wrecked her plans. But the world had changed enough by 1867 that both the public and all of her kin, except her eldest son, had welcomed Adèle Allston's decision to open her school and to employ a daughter and a niece as teachers. In the following years, Jane's daughters met financial crises by working as part- or full-time teachers. Still later, as they came of age, at least seven of her eight granddaughters started their adult lives as well-prepared full-time teachers.

The story of the Petigru women is no simple narrative. Sometimes it moves steadily forward. Sometimes it turns back on itself. It is not a story about patriarchy or women's autonomy, although each plays an important part in its telling. It is first and foremost what the title of this book says it is—the story of a family of women. At first the society in which these women moved seemed fair and promising; their sorrows and disappointments, largely personal. But as war destroyed the economic basis of that society, public events increasingly drove their private lives. As their world changed, the women's responses to it changed in a complex interweaving of private and public. At times, they were merely acted upon; at other times, they moved in response to external pressures; occasionally, they initiated changes they consciously sought. Although they held many values in common, neither their personalities nor their ambitions for themselves were uniform.

The story of the family they comprised is a more straightforward one, rising and falling with the passage of time. The Petigrus emerged from Louise Pettigrew's Badwell to set themselves apart from all other Pettigrews with the name that honored their brother James's centrality. Their marriages, rather than weakening Petigru ties, strengthened them as the women maintained continual contact with each other and were able to render the mutual aid that sustained initial affection. Moreover, their passion to maintain the distinction with which James had first endowed their family nurtured their willingness to assume responsibility for each other's children because collectively they embodied the future of all of the Petigrus. The war years, therefore, became a pivotal factor as public events destroyed both the material resources that had facilitated mutual aid and the continual personal contact that sustained affection. Although not directly caused by the war, the deaths of family elders weakened the force of the past at the same time that the deaths of younger men diminished hopes for future distinction. Finally, the failure of more than half of the third generation of women to marry eroded the driving centrality of rearing a next generation to maintain a family prestige that had, in any case, already largely vanished. By the time Adèle Allston died, the Petigru connection had become more a genealogical reference than an organizing force. In short, the women survived individually. The family that once bound their forebears together faded into memory.

Genealogical Charts

Genealogical information for the first three generations of Petigrus comes from many sources, some of which contradict each other. We believe, however, that information for the first and second generations and at least the births of the third generation is accurate and full. Marriage, progeny, and death dates of the third generation are most complete for those born before 1875. We have made no systematic search for genealogical data from the twentieth century.

CHART I

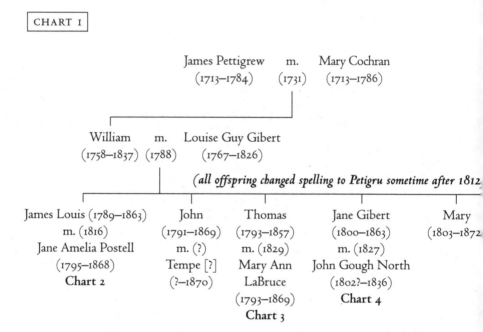

James Pettigrew m. Mary Cochran
(1713–1784) (1731) (1713–1786)

William m. Louise Guy Gibert
(1758–1837) (1788) (1767–1826)

(all offspring changed spelling to Petigru sometime after 1812

James Louis (1789–1863)
m. (1816)
Jane Amelia Postell
(1795–1868)
Chart 2

John
(1791–1869)
m. (?)
Tempe [?]
(?–1870)

Thomas
(1793–1857)
m. (1829)
Mary Ann
LaBruce
(1793–1869)
Chart 3

Jane Gibert
(1800–1863)
m. (1827)
John Gough North
(1802?–1836)
Chart 4

Mary
(1803–1872)

arles	Louise	[Adeline] Adèle Theresa	Harriette
—1835)	(1809–1869)	(1811–1896)	(1813–1877)
	m. (1829)	m. (1832)	m. (1836)
	Philip Johnston Porcher	Robert Francis Withers Allston	Henry Deas Lesesne
	(1806?–1871)	(1801–1864)	(1811–1886)
	Chart 5	**Chart 6**	**Chart 7**

CHART 2

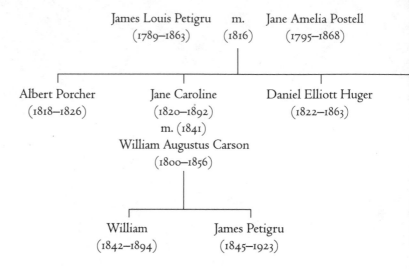

James Louis Petigru   m.   Jane Amelia Postell
(1789–1863)   (1816)   (1795–1868)

Albert Porcher   Jane Caroline   Daniel Elliott Huger
(1818–1826)   (1820–1892)   (1822–1863)
                m. (1841)
     William Augustus Carson
         (1800–1856)

William   James Petigru
(1842–1894)   (1845–1923)

Susan Dupont
(1824–1875)
no. 1 m. (1843) Henry Campbell King   no. 2 m. (1870) Christopher Columbus Bowen
(1819–1862)   (1832–1880)

Adele Allston
(1844–1889)
. 1 m. (1865) John Middleton (184–?–1868)   no. 2 m. (1877) George Trenholm Kershaw
(1851–1924)

CHART 3

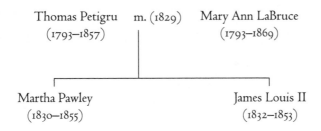

Thomas Petigru   m. (1829)   Mary Ann LaBruce
(1793–1857)   (1793–1869)

Martha Pawley   James Louis II
(1830–1855)   (1832–1853)

CHART 4

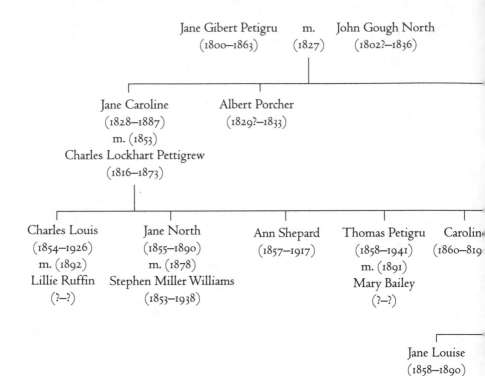

Jane Gibert Petigru   m.   John Gough North
(1800–1863)   (1827)   (1802?–1836)

Jane Caroline   Albert Porcher
(1828–1887)   (1829?–1833)
m. (1853)
Charles Lockhart Pettigrew
(1816–1873)

Charles Louis   Jane North   Ann Shepard   Thomas Petigru   Caroline
(1854–1926)   (1855–1890)   (1857–1917)   (1858–1941)   (1860–819
m. (1892)   m. (1878)   m. (1891)
Lillie Ruffin   Stephen Miller Williams   Mary Bailey
(?–?)   (1853–1938)   (?–?)

Jane Louise
(1858–1890)

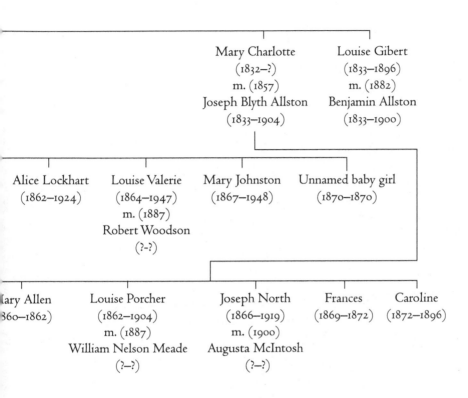

Mary Charlotte
(1832–?)
m. (1857)
Joseph Blyth Allston
(1833–1904)

Louise Gibert
(1833–1896)
m. (1882)
Benjamin Allston
(1833–1900)

Alice Lockhart
(1862–1924)

Louise Valerie
(1864–1947)
m. (1887)
Robert Woodson
(?-?)

Mary Johnston
(1867–1948)

Unnamed baby girl
(1870–1870)

Mary Allen
(1860–1862)

Louise Porcher
(1862–1904)
m. (1887)
William Nelson Meade
(?–?)

Joseph North
(1866–1919)
m. (1900)
Augusta McIntosh
(?–?)

Frances
(1869–1872)

Caroline
(1872–1896)

CHART 5

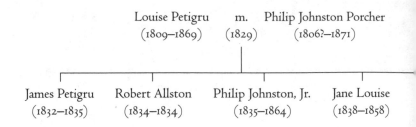

Louise Petigru   m.   Philip Johnston Porcher
(1809–1869)   (1829)   (1806?–1871)

James Petigru	Robert Allston	Philip Johnston, Jr.	Jane Louise
(1832–1835)	(1834–1834)	(1835–1864)	(1838–1858)

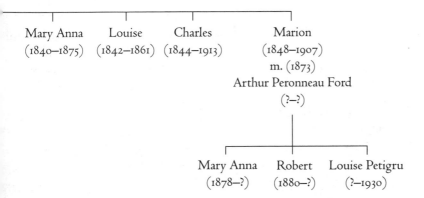

Mary Anna	Louise	Charles	Marion
(1840–1875)	(1842–1861)	(1844–1913)	(1848–1907)

m. (1873)
Arthur Peronneau Ford
(?–?)

Mary Anna	Robert	Louise Petigru
(1878–?)	(1880–?)	(?–1930)

CHART 6

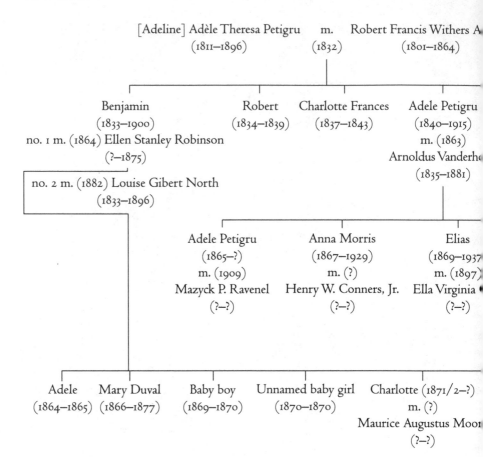

[Adeline] Adèle Theresa Petigru   m.   Robert Francis Withers A
(1811–1896)   (1832)   (1801–1864)

Benjamin   Robert   Charlotte Frances   Adele Petigru
(1833–1900)   (1834–1839)   (1837–1843)   (1840–1915)
no. 1 m. (1864) Ellen Stanley Robinson   m. (1863)
(?–1875)   Arnoldus Vanderh
no. 2 m. (1882) Louise Gibert North   (1835–1881)
(1833–1896)

Adele Petigru   Anna Morris   Elias
(1865–?)   (1867–1929)   (1869–1937
m. (1909)   m. (?)   m. (1897)
Mazyck P. Ravenel   Henry W. Conners, Jr.   Ella Virginia
(?–?)   (?–?)   (?–?)

Adele   Mary Duval   Baby boy   Unnamed baby girl   Charlotte (1871/2–?)
(1864–1865) (1866–1877) (1869–1870)   (1870–1870)   m. (?)
Maurice Augustus Moor
(?–?)

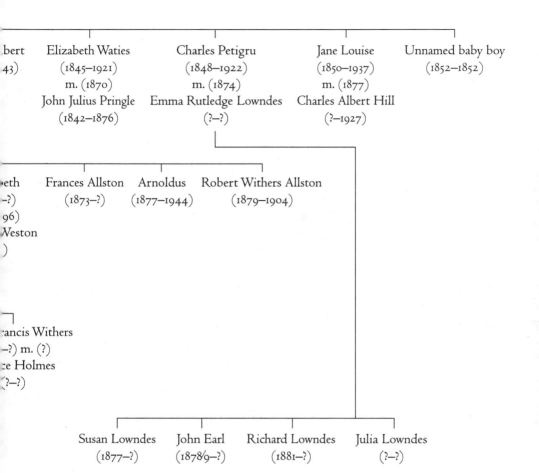

bert
43)

Elizabeth Waties
(1845–1921)
m. (1870)
John Julius Pringle
(1842–1876)

Charles Petigru
(1848–1922)
m. (1874)
Emma Rutledge Lowndes
(?–?)

Jane Louise
(1850–1937)
m. (1877)
Charles Albert Hill
(?–1927)

Unnamed baby boy
(1852–1852)

eth
–?)
96)
Weston
)

Frances Allston
(1873–?)

Arnoldus
(1877–1944)

Robert Withers Allston
(1879–1904)

ancis Withers
–?) m. (?)
te Holmes
(?–?)

Susan Lowndes
(1877–?)

John Earl
(1878/9–?)

Richard Lowndes
(1881–?)

Julia Lowndes
(?–?)

CHART 7

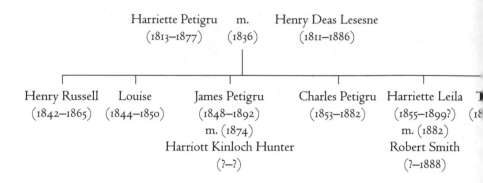

Harriette Petigru   m.   Henry Deas Lesesne
(1813–1877)   (1836)   (1811–1886)

Henry Russell   Louise   James Petigru   Charles Petigru   Harriette Leila
(1842–1865)   (1844–1850)   (1848–1892)   (1853–1882)   (1855–1899?)   (18
                    m. (1874)   m. (1882)
            Harriott Kinloch Hunter   Robert Smith
                  (?–?)   (?–1888)

The following abbreviations are used throughout the notes. Abbreviations of personal names are followed by the person's full name with the maiden name in parentheses. A hyphen preceding a final initial indicates a second marriage.

ABSPM	Ann Blount Shepard (Pettigrew) McKay
AFP-Car-USC	Allston Family Papers, South Caroliniana Library, University of South Carolina, Columbia, South Carolina
APAV	Adele Petigru (Allston) Vanderhorst
APHP-SCHS	Allston-Pringle-Hill Papers, South Carolina Historical Society, Charleston, South Carolina
ATPA	Adèle Theresa (Petigru) Allston
AV	Arnoldus Vanderhorst
BA	Benjamin Allston
Car-USC	South Caroliniana Library, University of South Carolina, Columbia, South Carolina
CLouP	Charles Louis Pettigrew
CLP	Charles Lockhart Pettigrew
CLS	Charleston Library Society, Charleston, South Carolina
CNP	Jane Caroline (North) Pettigrew
CPA	Charles Petigru Allston
CPC	Jane Caroline (Petigru) Carson
CPo	Charles Porcher
EE	Edward Everett
EP	Ebenezer Pettigrew
ESRA	Ellen Stanley (Robinson) Allston
EWAP	Elizabeth Waties (Allston) Pringle
HCK	Henry Campbell King
HDL	Henry Deas Lesesne
HPL	Harriette (Petigru) Lesesne
JAPP	Jane Amelia (Postell) Petigru
JBA	Joseph Blyth Allston
JCJ	James C. Johnston
JGPN	Jane Gibert (Petigru) North
JJP	James Johnston Pettigrew
JLAH	Jane Louise (Allston) Hill

JLP	James Louis Petigru
JNPW	Jane North (Pettigrew) Williams
JPC	James Petigru Carson
LGNA	Louise Gibert (North) Allston
LPPo	Louise (Petigru) Porcher
MALP	Mary Ann (LaBruce) Petigru
MAPo	Mary Anna Porcher
MBPB	Mary Blount (Pettigrew) Browne
MCNA	Mary Charlotte (North) Allston
MJPoF	Marion Johnston (Porcher) Ford
MK	Mitchell King
MKP-SHC-UNC	Mitchell King Papers, Southern Historical Collection, Wilson Library, University of North Carolina, Chapel Hill
MP	Mary Petigru
PC-LC	Petigru Correspondence, Manuscripts Division, Library of Congress, Washington, D.C.
PFP-NCDAH	Pettigrew Family Papers, Division of Archives and History, North Carolina Department of Cultural Resources, Raleigh, North Carolina
PFP-SHC-UNC	Pettigrew Family Papers, Southern Historical Collection, Wilson Library, University of North Carolina, Chapel Hill, North Carolina
PJPoJr	Philip Johnston Porcher, Jr.
PoFP-Car-USC	Porcher-Ford Papers, South Caroliniana Library, University of South Carolina, Columbia, South Carolina
RFWA	Robert Francis Withers Allston
RFWAP-SCHS	Robert Francis Withers Allston Papers, South Carolina Historical Society, Charleston, South Carolina
SDPK-B	Susan Dupont (Petigru) King Bowen
VFP-SCHS	Vanderhorst Family Papers, South Carolina Historical Society, Charleston, South Carolina
WC	William Carson
WPoM	William Porcher Miles
WPoMP-SHC-UNC	William Porcher Miles Papers, Southern Historical Collection, Wilson Library, University of North Carolina, Chapel Hill, North Carolina
WSP	William Shepard Pettigrew

PROLOGUE

1. Among the recent works that have challenged, elaborated, or refined Anne Firor Scott, *The Southern Lady: From Pedestal to Politics, 1830–1930* (Chicago: University of Chicago Press, 1970), the following contain interpretive assessments of how privileged women lived and how they thought in the nineteenth-century South. Those who lived with their families on plantations are addressed in Catherine Clinton, *The Plantation Mistress: Woman's World in the Old South* (New York: Pantheon Books, 1982); Jane Turner

Censer, *North Carolina Planters and Their Children, 1800–1860* (Baton Rouge: Louisiana State University Press, 1984); and Steven M. Stowe, *Intimacy and Power in the Old South: Ritual in the Lives of Planters* (Baltimore: Johns Hopkins University Press, 1987). The interaction between mistress and enslaved servant is explored in Elizabeth Fox-Genovese, *Within the Plantation Household: Black and White Women of the Old South* (Chapel Hill: University of North Carolina Press, 1988); Marli F. Weiner, *Mistresses and Slaves: Plantation Women in South Carolina, 1830–80* (Urbana: University of Illinois Press, 1998), carries the analysis of those relationships beyond the end of slavery. The lives of ladies in town and city are elucidated in relevant sections of Suzanne Lebsock, *The Free Women of Petersburg: Status and Culture in a Southern Town, 1784–1860* (New York: W. W. Norton, 1984); Jean E. Friedman, *The Enclosed Garden: Women and Community in the Evangelical South, 1830–1906* (Chapel Hill: University of North Carolina Press, 1985); and Jane H. Pease and William H. Pease, *Ladies, Women, and Wenches: Choice and Constraint in Antebellum Charleston and Boston* (Chapel Hill: University of North Carolina Press, 1990). The impact of the Civil War on Southern women is weighed in George C. Rable, *Civil Wars: Women and the Crisis of Southern Nationalism* (Urbana: University of Illinois Press, 1989); Catherine Clinton and Nina Silber, eds., *Divided Houses: Gender and the Civil War* (New York: Oxford University Press, 1992); Drew Gilpin Faust, *Mothers of Invention: Women of the Slaveholding South in the American Civil War* (Chapel Hill: University of North Carolina Press, 1995); and, the only one to carry the story beyond the war's end, Lee Ann Whites, *The Civil War as a Crisis in Gender: Augusta, Georgia, 1860–1890* (Athens: University of Georgia Press, 1995). The other pioneering assessment of the later period is Jane Turner Censer, "A Changing World of Work: North Carolina Elite Women, 1865–1885," *North Carolina Historical Review* 73 (January 1996): 28–55.

CHAPTER ONE

1. EWAP, *Chronicles of Chicora Wood* (New York: Charles Scribner's Sons, 1922), 58–59.

2. JLP to JGPN, August 31, 1827, PFP-SHC-UNC.

3. JLP to ATPA, November 15, 1851, December 21, 1858, RFWAP-SCHS.

4. The name of the plantation was changed from Matanzas to Chicora Wood in 1853. For simplicity, we have used Chicora Wood throughout the text.

5. RFWA to ATPA, January 30, 1832, in Joel H. Easterby, ed., *The South Carolina Rice Plantation as Revealed in the Papers of Robert F. W. Allston* (Chicago: University of Chicago Press, 1945), 65.

6. EWAP, *Chronicles*, 60; JLP to [?], April 28, 1832, typed fragment, VFP-SCHS; JLP to ATPA, April 23, 1832, RFWAP-SCHS.

7. EWAP, *Chronicles*, 78, 60; JLP to ATPA, April 23, 1832, RFWAP-SCHS.

8. JLP to ATPA, March 31, 1836, RFWAP-SCHS; CPC to JGPN, February 7, 1837, PFP-SHC-UNC; HPL to ATPA, June 12, 1837, RFWAP-SCHS.

CHAPTER TWO

1. JAPP to ATPA, September 9, 1834, RFWAP-SCHS.

2. LPPo to ATPA, June 27, [1850]; ATPA, Diary, November 23, 1837; and RFWA to ATPA, December 15, 1838, all in RFWAP-SCHS.

3. RFWA to ATPA, December 8, 1850, RFWAP-SCHS.

4. LPPo to ATPA, January 9, [1845], and JGPN to ATPA, [April 1853], RFWAP-SCHS.

5. JAPP to ATPA, December 20, 1833, RFWAP-SCHS.

6. ATPA, Diary, January 1, 1852, and HPL to ATPA, July 30, 1850, RFWAP-SCHS.

7. JLP to ATPA, February 6, 1843, RFWAP-SCHS; CNP to JGPN, August 6, 1850, PFP-SHC-UNC.

8. JGPN to LPPo, July 15, [1859], RFWAP-SCHS.

CHAPTER THREE

1. JJP to JCJ, May 29[?], 1849, PFP-SHC-UNC.

2. JGPN to ATPA, February 13, 1839, RFWAP-SCHS.

3. JLP to JGPN, January 29, 1838, in JBA, "Life and Times of James L. Petigru," scrapbook compiled from serial in *Charleston Sunday News* (1899–1900), CLS, 8, 9.

4. JGPN to CNP, April 23, [1841?], PFP-SHC-UNC.

5. Ibid., January 16, 1849.

6. Ibid., February 20, [1849?], February 19, 1849.

7. JGPN to ATPA, September 3, November 12, 1850, January 8, 1849, RFWAP-SCHS.

8. JGPN to ATPA, August 27, 1850, RFWAP-SCHS; ABSPM to WSP, July 8, 1853, PFP-SHC-UNC.

9. JGPN to ATPA, January 22, 1855, RFWAP-SCHS.

10. JLP to JGPN, February 27, 1855, in JBA, "Life," 28; JGPN to ATPA, December 26, 1856, RFWAP-SCHS.

11. MP to ATPA, April 20, 1837, RFWAP-SCHS.

12. JGPN to ATPA, November 1, [1837], and LPPo to JGPN, July 20, 1832, RFWAP-SCHS.

CHAPTER FOUR

1. JLP to ATPA, September 9, 1839, and JGPN to ATPA, June 22, 1848, RFWAP-SCHS.

2. EWAP, *Chronicles of Chicora Wood* (New York: Charles Scribner's Sons, 1922), 110.

3. ATPA, Diary, March 15, 1850, and RFWA to ATPA, November 29, 1838, RFWAP-SCHS.

4. JGPN to CNP, March 30, 1840, April 7, October 6, 1843, PFP-SHC-UNC; JGPN to ATPA, June 20, 1850, RFWAP-SCHS.

5. WSP to ABSPM, August 8, 1853, PFP-SHC-UNC; JGPN to ATPA, July 31, 1849, RFWAP-SCHS.

6. ATPA, Diary, February 26, 1850, RFWAP-SCHS.

7. CNP to ATPA, December 9, 1850, RFWAP-SCHS.

8. JGPN to CNP, February 20, [1851], PFP-SHC-UNC.

9. CNP to MP, February 20, 1851, PFP-SHC-UNC; ATPA to Mrs. Hamilton, May 19, 1853, RFWAP-SCHS; EWAP, *Chronicles*, 124–25.

10. ATPA to Jane Lynch Pringle, [July 1849], RFWAP-SCHS.

11. CPC to ATPA, August 16, 1834, January 10, 1835, RFWAP-SCHS.

12. Ibid., January 10, 1835; JLP to JGPN, August 4, 1835, copy, PC-LC.

13. SDPK-B to ATPA, August 28, [1837], RFWAP-SCHS.

14. CPC to ATPA, November 19, 1838, RFWAP-SCHS; JLP to [JGPN], May 21, 1839, copy, PC-LC; SDPK-B, *Lily: A Novel*, ed. Jane H. Pease and William H. Pease (1855; reprint, Durham: Duke University Press, 1993), 72.

15. JGPN to CNP, March 30, December 8, 1840, PFP-SHC-UNC.

16. LPPo to ATPA, January 24, 1851, RFWAP-SCHS.

17. [LPPo] to MCNA, [December] 18, [1853], PFP-SHC-UNC; LPPo to ATPA, November 25, [1853], RFWAP-SCHS.

18. R. Acelie Togno to ATPA, [January 31, 1855], RFWAP-SCHS.

19. APAV to ATPA, January 20, 1856, RFWAP-SCHS.

CHAPTER FIVE

1. JLP to Hugh Swinton Legaré, April 6, 1838, Miscellaneous Manuscripts, Car-USC; JLP to JGPN, May 21, 1839, copy, PC-LC.

2. JLP to ATPA, August 5, 1837, RFWAP-SCHS; JLP to JGPN, May 21, 1839, copy, PC-LC; MP to ATPA, March 8, [1839], RFWAP-SCHS.

3. JLP to ATPA, November 3, 1841, RFWAP-SCHS.

4. Ibid.

5. LPPo to ATPA, August 28, 1843, June 18, 1842, RFWAP-SCHS.

6. RFWA to ATPA, November 25, 1840, RFWAP-SCHS.

7. [SDPK-B], "Gossip," in *Sylvia's World: Crimes Which the Law Does Not Reach* (New York: Derby & Jackson, 1859), 210; LPPo to ATPA, [March/April 1841?], RFWAP-SCHS.

8. [SDPK-B], "A Marriage of Persuasion," in *Crimes*, 225.

9. JPC, *Life, Letters, and Speeches of James Louis Petigru: The Union Man of South Carolina* (Washington, D.C.: W. H. Lowdermilk, 1920), 226; LPPo to ATPA, June 18, 1842, RFWAP-SCHS.

10. JLP to JGPN, February 26, 1843, in JBA, "Life and Times of James L. Petigru," scrapbook compiled from serial in *Charleston Sunday News* (1899–1900), CLS, 10; LPPo to ATPA, July 26, June 24, 1841, RFWAP-SCHS; JLP to JGPN, May 19, 1842, in JBA, "Life," 9.

11. HPL to ATPA, November 5, 1842, and JLP to ATPA, February 6, 1843, RFWAP-SCHS.

12. JGPN to ATPA, July 29, 1843, RFWAP-SCHS.

13. LPPo to ATPA, January 9, [1845], RFWAP-SCHS; HCK to MK, October 15, 1845, MKP-SHC-UNC.

14. SDPK-B to CNP, December 2, 1844, copy, PFP-NCDAH.

CHAPTER SIX

1. JGPN to CNP, April 23, [1841?], PFP-SHC-UNC.

2. ATPA to JJP, May 28, [1858], PFP-SHC-UNC; EWAP, *Chronicles of Chicora Wood* (New York: Charles Scribner's Sons, 1922), 165–66.

3. APAV to ATPA, May 29, June 29, 1857, RFWAP-SCHS.

4. CNP to JGPN, January 17, 1851, PFP-SHC-UNC.

5. MCNA to PJPoJr, February 8, 1857, PoFP-Car-USC.

6. CNP to MP, February 20, 1851, PFP-SHC-UNC.

7. JGPN to ATPA, January 24, 1851, RFWAP-SCHS; JGPN to CNP, January 24, 1851; CNP to CLP, March 31, 1851; and CNP to JGPN, February 19, [1857], all in PFP-SHC-UNC.

8. LPPo to ATPA, [March/April 1850], RFWAP-SCHS; MP to CNP, February 7, 1857, PFP-SHC-UNC.

9. SDPK-B to ATPA, January 28, 1846, RFWAP-SCHS.

10. JGPN to CNP, February 8, [1849], and JGPN to CNP, n.d. [1847–49?], PFP-SHC-UNC; JGPN to ATPA, August 21, [1849], RFWAP-SCHS.

11. SDPK-B to ATPA, August 26, 1849, RFWAP-SCHS.

12. LPPo to ATPA, March 10, [1850], RFWAP-SCHS.

13. ATPA, Diary, March 5, 15, 1850, and LPPo to ATPA, [March/April 1850], RFWAP-SCHS; CNP to JJP, March 1850, PFP-SHC-UNC.

14. CNP, Diary, August 8, 1851, PFP-SHC-UNC.

15. Ibid., September 16, 26, 1851.

16. Ibid., October 7, 1851.

17. CNP to JGPN, October 25, 1851, PFP-SHC-UNC; ATPA, Diary, February [?], 1852, and RFWA to ATPA, March 1, 1852, RFWAP-SCHS.

18. CNP, Diary, August 12, 1852, PFP-SHC-UNC.

19. Ibid., September 2, 1852.

20. Ibid., September 10, 1852; CNP to JGPN, September 15, 1852, PFP-SHC-UNC.

21. CNP to HDL, September 24, 1852, PFP-SHC-UNC.

22. JJP to JCJ, February 5, 1849, copy, PFP-SHC-UNC.

23. CNP to JGPN, March 5, 1849, and MBPB to JJP, March 25, 1849, PFP-SHC-UNC.

24. MBPB to JJP, March 25, 1849; CNP to MP, March 26, 1849; and CNP to JGPN, April 2, 1849, all in PFP-SHC-UNC.

25. JGPN to ATPA, June 22, [1849], and MP to ATPA, October 8, [1849], RFWAP-SCHS.

26. CNP to JGPN, October [10?], 1852, and CNP to MCNA, September 19, 1852, PFP-SHC-UNC; LPPo to ATPA, December 4, 1852, RFWAP-SCHS.

27. CNP to [JJP], December 31, 1852, PFP-SHC-UNC.

CHAPTER SEVEN

1. JLP to JGPN, November 24, 1847, copy, PC-LC; LGNA to ATPA, July 19, [1849], RFWAP-SCHS.

2. LPPo to ATPA, [August 1, 1849?], October 15, 1849, RFWAP-SCHS.

3. JLP to JGPN, June 29, 1852, in JBA, "Life and Times of James L. Petigru," scrapbook compiled from serial in *Charleston Sunday News* (1899–1900), CLS, 24; JLP to JGPN, October 5, 1855, in JPC, *Life, Letters, and Speeches of James Louis Petigru: The Union Man of South Carolina* (Washington, D.C.: W. H. Lowdermilk, 1920), 315; JAPP to HDL, August 7, 1854, VFP-SCHS; JAPP to WPoM, July 7, 1860, WPoMP-SHC-UNC; JLP to SDPK-B, September 5, 1856, copy, PC-LC.

4. LPPo to ATPA, [August 1854], RFWAP-SCHS; JAPP to Mary Baber, September 9, 1840, Baber-Blackshear Collection, Hargrett Rare Book and Manuscript Library, University of Georgia, Athens, Georgia.

5. JLP to EP, September 5, 1843, in Sarah McCulloh Lemmon, ed., *The Pettigrew Papers* (Raleigh: North Carolina Department of Cultural Resources, Division of Archives and History, 1988), 2:592; ATPA to BA, November 30, 1849, RFWAP-SCHS; JLP to SDPK-B, May 11, 1843, copy, PC-LC; LPPo to ATPA, June 9, 1854, RFWAP-SCHS.

6. CPC, Commonplace Books, 1:25, 31, Car-USC. The pages in these Commonplace Books are unnumbered but are indicated here consecutively for each volume.

7. *The State ex rel. A. Ottolengui et al. v. G. W. Anker et al.* (Charleston: Samuel Hart, 1844), 26; CNP to MP, March 26, 1849, PFP-SHC-UNC.

8. CNP to JGPN, April 2, 1849, PFP-SHC-UNC; LPPo to ATPA, October 15, 1849, January 20, 1850, RFWAP-SCHS.

9. LPPo to ATPA, January 20, 1850, RFWAP-SCHS.

10. Ibid., July 11, 1850, and RFWA to ATPA, October 22, 1850, RFWAP-SCHS.

11. ATPA to BA, November 4, 1856, RFWAP-SCHS.

12. JLP to SDPK-B, July 12, 1849, copy, PC-LC; SDPK-B to ATPA, January 28, 1846, RFWAP-SCHS; CNP to CLP, March 31, 1851, and JGPN to CNP, June 23, 1858, PFP-SHC-UNC.

13. LPPo to ATPA, August 1, [1849], and SDPK-B to ATPA, October 3, 1849, RFWAP-SCHS; HCK to MK, October 11, 1849, MKP-SHC-UNC.

14. JGPN to ATPA, January 11, 1850, and LPPo to ATPA, January 20, 1850, RFWAP-SCHS.

15. MK, Diary, November 19, 18, July 12, 1853, MKP-SHC-UNC; HPL to ATPA, July 22, 1853, RFWAP-SCHS.

16. HPL to ATPA, March 6, 1854, RFWAP-SCHS.

17. LPPo to ATPA, August 17, 1854, RFWAP-SCHS. The toasts, enshrined as family lore, were called to our attention by Sally Simons, March 19, 1994.

18. LPPo to ATPA, [December 1854], RFWAP-SCHS.

19. Lucy Baxter, "Introduction," in *Thackeray's Letters to an American Family* (New York: Century Company, 1904), 13–14, quoted in J. R. Scafidel, "Susan Petigru King: An Early South Carolina Realist," in *South Carolina Women Writers: Proceedings of the Reynolds Conference, University of South Carolina, October 24–25, 1975*, ed. James B. Meriwether (Spartanburg: Reprint Company, 1978), 104.

20. LPPo to ATPA, February 20, [1856], and APAV to ATPA, March 9, 1856, RFWAP-SCHS.

21. MK, Diary, June 30, July 3, 1856, May 21, 14, 1857, MKP-SHC-UNC.

22. CNP to JGPN, January 10, 1858, PFP-SHC-UNC; JLP to JGPN, June 15, 1860, in JBA, "Life," 33; JLP to SDPK-B, January 12, 1858, copy, VFP-SCHS.

23. JLP to SDPK-B, January 12, 1858, copy, VFP-SCHS; JLP to SDPK-B, November 18, 1853, copy, PC-LC; JJP to JCJ, November 20, 1855, and LGNA to CLP, January 11, [1858], PFP-SHC-UNC.

24. CNP to JJP, December 22, [1855], PFP-SHC-UNC; SDPK-B, *Lily: A Novel*, ed. Jane H. Pease and William H. Pease (1855; reprint, Durham: Duke University Press, 1993), 12; SDPK-B, "Old Maidism vs. Marriage," in *Busy Moments of an Idle Woman* (New York: Appleton, 1854), 252; SDPK-B, *Lily*, 260.

25. SDPK-B, "Old Maidism," 253; SDPK-B, "Everyday Life," in *Busy Moments*, 158.

26. The exchange between Thackeray and Sue King is reconstructed in Scafidel, "Susan Petigru King," 103.

27. MK, Diary, December 1, 1853, MKP-SHC-UNC.

28. LPPo to PJPoJr, January 17, 1859, PoFP-Car-USC.

29. ATPA, Diary, March 8, 1839; MP to ATPA, March 8, [1839]; and LPPo to ATPA, November 25, [1853], all in RFWAP-SCHS.

30. JGPN to ATPA, March 6, 1856, RFWAP-SCHS.

31. JLP to ATPA, April 4, 1857, RFWAP-SCHS.

32. MP to ATPA, August 4, [1854], and [JGPN?] to ATPA, December 28, 1854, RFWAP-SCHS.

33. JGPN to CNP, June 20, 1856, PFP-SHC-UNC.

CHAPTER EIGHT

1. LPPo to ATPA, July 28, 1832, RFWAP-SCHS.

2. HPL to ATPA, May 31, 1832; JAPP to ATPA, September 20, 1832; and HPL to ATPA, January 6, 1837, all in RFWAP-SCHS.

3. SDPK-B to ATPA, January 28, 1846, RFWAP-SCHS.

4. CNP to LGNA, January 17, 1858, and LGNA to CNP, January 8, 11, [1858], PFP-SHC-UNC.

5. SDPK-B to ATPA, January 28, 1846, RFWAP-SCHS.

6. JLP to JGPN, April 22, 1851, in JBA, "Life and Times of James L. Petigru," scrapbook compiled from serial in *Charleston Sunday News* (1899–1900), CLS, 21.

7. MP to ATPA, January 21, 1856, RFWAP-SCHS.

8. RFWA to ATPA, November 11, 1860; Elizabeth Frances Allston Blyth to ATPA, September 5, [1836?]; and HPL to ATPA, August 27, 1834, all in RFWAP-SCHS.

9. RFWA to ATPA, November 11, 1860, RFWAP-SCHS.

10. JGPN to ATPA, June 13, 1854, June 10, 1853, RFWAP-SCHS; CNP to CLP, July 14, 1854, and JGPN to CNP, November 16, 1857, PFP-SHC-UNC.

11. LGNA to CNP, May 25, [1858], and CNP to CLP, October 17, 1859, PFP-SHC-UNC.

12. CNP to CLP, June 13, 1854, and MBPB to WSP, August 15, [1859], PFP-SHC-UNC.

13. CNP to JGPN, February 7, 1858, PFP-SHC-UNC; JGPN to ATPA, April 6, 1837, RFWAP-SCHS; JGPN to CNP, December 3, 1860, PFP-SHC-UNC.

CHAPTER NINE

1. JGPN to CNP, July 5, 1850, PFP-SHC-UNC.

2. JGPN to ATPA, January 11, 1850, RFWAP-SCHS.

3. CLP to CNP, March 13, 1851, PFP-SHC-UNC.

4. CNP to MCNA, September 19, 1852, and CNP to JGPN, October [10?, 1852], PFP-SHC-UNC.

5. CNP to CLP, February 1, 1853, PFP-SHC-UNC.

6. WSP to [JCJ], April 23, 1853, PFP-SHC-UNC.

7. LPPo to CNP, May 11[?], 1853, and JGPN to CNP, May 11, 1853, PFP-SHC-UNC; JGPN to ATPA, [April 1853], RFWAP-SCHS; [JGPN] to CNP, May 4, 1853, PFP-SHC-UNC.

8. CNP to LGNA, April 23, 1853, PFP-SHC-UNC.

9. WSP to [JCJ], April 23, 1853, PFP-SHC-UNC.

Notes to Pages 83–97

10. WSP to CNP, August 1, 1853; MBPB to WSP, June 5, 1853; and CNP to JBA, June 10, 1853, all in PFP-SHC-UNC.

11. CNP to JGPN, November 2, 1853, PFP-SHC-UNC.

12. CNP to CLP, June 13, 1854, and CLP to CNP, all letters in folders 343 and 344, PFP-SHC-UNC.

13. LPPo to ATPA, June 8, 1854, RFWAP-SCHS.

14. HPL to ATPA, June 8, 1854, RFWAP-SCHS; CNP to CLP, July 24, [1854], PFP-SHC-UNC.

15. CNP to JJP, December 22, [1855], and MCNA to CNP, August 31, [1858], PFP-SHC-UNC.

16. CNP to CLP, June 19, 1854, PFP-SHC-UNC.

17. Ibid.

18. [MCNA] to CNP, October 30, [1854], PFP-SHC-UNC.

19. CNP to MCNA, February 10, [1855], and CNP to CLP, July 14, 1854, PFP-SHC-UNC.

20. CNP to CLP, July 3, 1857, and CNP to JGPN, April 2, 1857, PFP-SHC-UNC.

21. CNP to CLP, March 4, 1853, and JJP to CLP, January 25, 1854, PFP-SHC-UNC.

22. CNP to CLP, August 3, 1854, and CNP to LGNA, February 1, 1855, PFP-SHC-UNC.

23. JJP to WSP, November 28, 1855, and CNP to JJP, December 22, [1855], PFP-SHC-UNC.

24. CNP to CLP, October 17, 1859, PFP-SHC-UNC; WSP to ABSPM, March 15, 1860, PFP-NCDAH.

25. MALP to CNP, June 6, 1860, and CNP to CLP, October 29, 1858, PFP-SHC-UNC; JLP to ATPA, October 20, 1859, RFWAP-SCHS.

26. CNP to CLP, October 13, April 21, 1859, PFP-SHC-UNC.

27. JJP to CNP, September 22, 1857, PFP-SHC-UNC.

28. CNP to LGNA, July 27, 1857, PFP-SHC-UNC.

29. CLP to CNP, March 10, 1859; CNP to CLP, March 10, [1854]; and CLP to CNP, March 11, April 14, 1859, all in PFP-SHC-UNC.

30. CLP to CNP, [Summer 1858?], fragment, PFP-SHC-UNC.

31. Ibid., September 1 [2?], 1860.

32. CNP to CLP, April 17, 1859, and CLP to CNP, April 27, 1859, PFP-SHC-UNC.

33. CNP to CLP, November 16, 1859, PFP-SHC-UNC.

34. WSP to JLP, May 1860, copy, and [CNP] to JGPN, May 8, 1860, PFP-SHC-UNC.

CHAPTER TEN

1. RFWA to ATPA, March 17, 1859, RFWAP-SCHS.

2. RFWA to ATPA, December 16, 1849, in Joel H. Easterby, ed., *The South Carolina Rice Plantation as Revealed in the Papers of Robert F. W. Allston* (Chicago: University of Chicago Press, 1945), 99.

3. RFWA to ATPA, March 11, 1851, RFWAP-SCHS.

4. JGPN to CNP, February 25, 1857, PFP-SHC-UNC; RFWA to ATPA, [April/May 1857], RFWAP-SCHS.

5. RFWA to ATPA, [November 29, 1851], RFWAP-SCHS.

6. ATPA, Diary, April 5, 1841; RFWA to ATPA, December 10, 1842, October 1, 1843; and ATPA to RFWA, [December 1846?], all in RFWAP-SCHS.

7. ATPA to Jane Lynch Pringle, [July 1849], August 14, 1849, fragment, RFWAP-SCHS.

8. Ibid., August 14, 1849; ATPA, Diary, February 28, March 12, 1850, RFWAP-SCHS.

9. RFWA to ATPA, May 14, 1849, May 7, 1854, RFWAP-SCHS.

10. CNP to CLP, July 24, 1854, PFP-SHC-UNC; RFWA to ATPA, June 2, 1856, RFWAP-SCHS.

11. ATPA to LPPo, October 17, 1856, RFWAP-SCHS.

12. Ibid.

13. ATPA to BA, September 30, 1849, and BA to ATPA, January 30, 1853, RFWAP-SCHS.

14. JLP to ATPA, January 28, 1856, RFWAP-SCHS.

15. ATPA, Diary, August 7, 1838, RFWAP-SCHS.

16. Ibid., January 16, 1850; ATPA to JGPN, February 1, 1851, RFWAP-SCHS.

17. ATPA to LPPo, January 28, 1851, and BA to ATPA, October 12, 1851, RFWAP-SCHS; JLP to JGPN, July 16, 1857, in JBA, "Life and Times of James L. Petrigru," scrapbook compiled from serial in *Charleston Sunday News* (1899–1900), CLS, 3; EWAP, *Chronicles of Chicora Wood* (New York: Charles Scribner's Sons, 1922), 166; LGNA to CNP, May 25, [1858/59?], PFP-SHC-UNC.

18. APAV, Diary, June 20–21, 1860, VFP-SCHS.

19. JGPN to ATPA, March 22, 1850, RFWAP-SCHS; JGPN to CNP, April 23, [1841?], PFP-SHC-UNC; RFWA to ATPA, October 3, 1856, and ATPA to BA, August 29, 1849, RFWAP-SCHS.

20. JBA to BA, December 27, 1850, RFWAP-SCHS.

21. JGPN to CLP, June 25, 1857, and CNP to CLP, July 14, 1857, PFP-SHC-UNC.

22. CLP to CNP, October 29, 1857, PFP-SHC-UNC.

23. JGPN to CNP, January 3, [1859], March 10, 1859, May 13, [1860], PFP-SHC-UNC; JBA to JJP, July 1, 1860, PFP-NCDAH; LPPo to PJPoJr, November 6, 1860, PoFP-Car-USC.

24. BA to ATPA, December 7, 1860, RFWAP-SCHS.

25. MCNA to CNP, April 26, [1860], PFP-SHC-UNC.

CHAPTER ELEVEN

1. LPPo to ATPA, September 18, 1832, and JGPN to ATPA, December 17, 1844, RFWAP-SCHS.

2. SDPK-B to MK, September 29, 1848, MKP-SHC-UNC.

3. JGPN to ATPA, March 12, 1849, RFWAP-SCHS.

4. CNP to JJP, March 1850, PFP-SHC-UNC.

5. RFWA to ATPA, May 24, 1850, and ATPA to RFWA, June 4, 1850, RFWAP-SCHS.

6. LPPo to ATPA, July 11, August 10, 1850, RFWAP-SCHS.

7. SDPK-B to ATPA, December 19, 1850, RFWAP-SCHS.

8. [CNP] to MCNA, September 12, 1851, PFP-SHC-UNC.

9. JGPN to ATPA, January 24, 1851, RFWAP-SCHS; CNP, Diary, August 11, 1852, and CNP to LGNA, August 13, 1852, PFP-SHC-UNC.

10. CNP, Diary, August 12, 1852, and CNP to LGNA, August 13, 1852, PFP-SHC-UNC.

11. CNP to CLP, July 28, 1854, and CLP to CNP, June 22, 1856, PFP-SHC-UNC.

12. JGPN to ATPA, January 22, 1855, RFWAP-SCHS; CNP to JGPN, April 22, 1855, PFP-SHC-UNC; JGPN to PJPoJr, May 16, 1859, PoFP-Car-USC.

13. ATPA, Diary, May 26, 1850, RFWAP-SCHS.

14. MP to ATPA, March 22, 1856, RFWAP-SCHS.

15. JGPN to CNP, June 20, 1856, PFP-SHC-UNC; JGPN to ATPA, September 7, 1858, RFWAP-SCHS.

16. CNP to JJP, December 2–[?], [1856], and LGNA to CNP, February 15, 1858, PFP-SHC-UNC.

17. LPPo to ATPA, July 26, 1841, January 20, 1850, and MP to ATPA, July 11, [1850], RFWAP-SCHS; CPC to JPC, July 2, 1861, VFP-SCHS; CNP, Diary, August 14, 1852, and CNP to JGPN, September 3, 1855, PFP-SHC-UNC.

18. LPPo to JGPN, July 20, 1832, RFWAP-SCHS; JLP to JGPN, December 29, 1847, in JBA, "Life and Times of James L. Petrigru," scrapbook compiled from serial in *Charleston Sunday News* (1899–1900), CLS, 16.

19. ATPA to BA, May 12, 26, 1850, RFWAP-SCHS.

20. MP to ATPA, June 10, 1850, RFWAP-SCHS; CNP to JJP, September 7, 1850, PFP-SHC-UNC.

21. CNP to JGPN, December 25, November 25, 1856, PFP-SHC-UNC; ATPA to BA, January 1, 1857, RFWAP-SCHS.

22. CNP to LGNA, February 4, 1858, and CLP to CNP, October 28, 1858, PFP-SHC-UNC.

23. CNP to CLP, March 5, [1859], and CLP to CNP, March 10, 1859, PFP-SHC-UNC.

24. CNP to CLP, October 30, 1859, and CNP to MCNA, December 19, 1859, PFP-SHC-UNC.

25. CNP to JJP, September 12, 1860; CNP to WSP, September 17, 1860; and CLP to WSP, October 10, 1860, all in PFP-SHC-UNC.

26. ABSPM to WSP, November 16, 1860, PFP-SHC-UNC.

CHAPTER TWELVE

1. CNP to LGNA, June 5, 1860, PFP-SHC-UNC; David Herbert Donald, *Charles Sumner and the Coming of the Civil War* (New York: Alfred A. Knopf, 1961), 356; JGPN to WSP, November 1, 1860, PFP-SHC-UNC.

2. LPPo to PJPoJr, November 9, 1860, PoFP-Car-USC.

3. CNP to CLP, November 20, 17, 1860, PFP-SHC-UNC.

4. Ibid., November 17, 1860; JGPN to CNP, November 19, 1860, PFP-SHC-UNC.

5. CNP to CLP, November 26, 1860, PFP-SHC-UNC; LPPo to PJPoJr, [December] 21, 1860, PoFP-Car-USC; MP to ATPA, December 27, 1860, RFWAP-SCHS; JGPN to CNP, December 20, 1860, PFP-SHC-UNC; JGPN to ATPA, December 29, 1860, RFWAP-SCHS.

6. CNP to JGPN, March 28, 1861, PFP-SHC-UNC.

7. LGNA to CNP, January 21, [1861]; JGPN to CNP, November 19, 1860; and CNP to CLP, November 20, 1860, all in PFP-SHC-UNC.

8. CPC to LGNA, February 8, 1861, PFP-SHC-UNC.

9. MCNA to LGNA, January 14, 1861, PFP-SHC-UNC.

10. David Herbert Donald, *Lincoln* (London: Jonathan Cape, 1995), 283.

11. EWAP to ATPA, April 13, 1861, and MALP to ATPA, April 16, 1861, RFWAP-SCHS.

12. MP to CNP, April 12, [1861], PFP-SHC-UNC; MAPo to CNP, April 16, 1861, PFP-NCDAH.

13. MAPo to CNP, May 6, 1861, and JGPN to [CNP], April 16, 1861, PFP-SHC-UNC; JLP to JGPN, April 16, 1861, in JBA, "Life and Times of James L. Petigru," scrapbook compiled from serial in *Charleston Sunday News* (1899–1900), CLS, 38.

14. JGPN to CNP, May 15, 1861, PFP-SHC-UNC.

15. ATPA to Mrs. Joseph Hunter, May 15, 1861, in Joel H. Easterby, ed., *The South Carolina Rice Plantation as Revealed in the Papers of Robert F. W. Allston* (Chicago: University of Chicago Press, 1945), 175; CNP to MCNA, April 13, [1861], PFP-SHC-UNC.

16. MCNA to CNP, September 13, 1861, PFP-SHC-UNC.

17. LGNA to CNP, December 17, [1860], PFP-SHC-UNC; JLP to CPC, November 23, July 5, 1861, PC-LC.

18. JGPN to CNP, June 3, 1861, PFP-SHC-UNC.

19. [MCNA] to CNP, June 5, 1861, PFP-SHC-UNC; CPC to JPC, July 2, 1861, VFP-SCHS.

20. JAPP to ATPA, December 18, 1861, RFWAP-SCHS.

21. LPPo to WPoM, May 1, 1861, WPoMP-SHC-UNC.

22. JGPN to CNP, August 15, 1861, and LGNA to CNP, August 7, 1861, PFP-SHC-UNC.

CHAPTER THIRTEEN

1. JGPN to CNP, May 30/31, 1861, PFP-SHC-UNC; JLP to CPC, August 22, 1861, PC-LC.

2. HPL to ATPA, October 25, 1861, RFWAP-SCHS.

3. JGPN to CNP, January 31, May 15, 1861, PFP-SHC-UNC.

4. MAPo to CNP, September 6, October 30, 1861, and CNP to JGPN, May 9, 1861, PFP-SHC-UNC.

5. RFWA to ATPA, July 15, 1861, RFWAP-SCHS.

6. LPPo to PJPoJr, June 22, 1861, PoFP-Car-USC.

7. JLP to JGPN, November 14, 1861, in JBA, "Life and Times of James L. Petigru," scrapbook compiled from serial in *Charleston Sunday News* (1899–1900), CLS, 40; LGNA to CNP, December 4, 1861, PFP-SHC-UNC.

8. ATPA to BA, January 16, 1861, RFWAP-SCHS; MAPo to CNP, May 6, 1861; ABSPM to [WSP], May 28, 1861; and CNP to LGNA, August 8, 1861, all in PFP-SHC-UNC.

9. JGPN to CNP, May 7, 1861, PFP-SHC-UNC; JGPN to ATPA, November 19, 1861, RFWAP-SCHS.

10. LGNA to CNP, November 18, 1861, and JGPN to CNP, November 21, 1861, PFP-SHC-UNC; JGPN to ATPA, December 10, 1861, RFWAP-SCHS.

11. JGPN to CNP, November 28, 1861, PFP-SHC-UNC.

12. Ibid., January 6, 1862; MP to ATPA, December 26, [1861], RFWAP-SCHS.

13. LGNA to CNP, March 12, [1861], and JGPN to CNP, April 22, 1861, PFP-SHC-UNC.

14. JBA to JJP, June 22, 1861, PFP-NCDAH.

15. Ibid., March 5, 1862.

16. CNP to LGNA, August 8, 1861, PFP-SHC-UNC.

17. CNP to JGPN, November 12, 1861, PFP-SHC-UNC.

18. CNP to JJP, January 27, 1862, and CNP to LGNA, February 24, 1862, PFP-SHC-UNC.

19. CNP to LGNA, February 24, 1862, PFP-SHC-UNC.

20. Ibid.

21. JGPN to CNP, May 1, [1862], and CLP to WSP, June 17, 1862, PFP-SHC-UNC.

22. CNP to WSP, June 27, [1862], PFP-SHC-UNC.

23. JGPN to ATPA, December 4, 1862, and MALP to ATPA, December 3, 1862, RFWAP-SCHS.

24. JGPN to CNP, May 1, [1862], PFP-SHC-UNC.

CHAPTER FOURTEEN

1. CNP to JJP, October 13, 1862, PFP-SHC-UNC.

2. JGPN to CNP, May 1, [1862], PFP-SHC-UNC.

3. MAPo to CNP, September 6, 1861, PFP-SHC-UNC.

4. MCNA to CNP, May 8, 1861, PFP-SHC-UNC; ATPA to RFWA, June 3, 1861, in Joel H. Easterby, ed., *The South Carolina Rice Plantation as Revealed in the Papers of Robert F. W. Allston* (Chicago: University of Chicago Press, 1945), 177; ATPA to CPA, September 12, 1861, RFWAP-SCHS; APAV, Diary, September 6, 1861, VFP-SCHS.

5. Sarah C. Williams to ATPA, October 17, 1862, RFWAP-SCHS.

6. MK, Diary, May 4, 1862, copy, MKP-SHC-UNC; Mary Boykin Chesnut, Diary, April 15, 1862, in C. Vann Woodward, ed., *Mary Chesnut's Civil War* (New Haven: Yale University Press, 1981), 324–25; JLP to CPC, May 10, 1862, PC-LC.

7. JLP to CPC, July 4, 1862, PC-LC; CNP to CLP, June 19, 1862, PFP-SHC-UNC.

8. CNP to CLP, June 19, 1862, PFP-SHC-UNC; SDPK-B to ATPA, June 7, 1850, and APAV to ATPA, February 6, 1854, RFWAP-SCHS; JLP to SDPK-B, August 16, 1860, copy, PC-LC; MK, Diary, July 28, 1862, copy, MKP-SHC-UNC.

9. HCK, Will, March 7, 1861, copy, Works Progress Administration transcript, Book 49, 988, Charleston County Library, Charleston, South Carolina.

10. JGPN to JLP, February 3, 1863, PFP-SHC-UNC.

11. George Templeton Strong, Diary, November 23, 1860, in Allan Nevins and M. H. Thomas, eds., *The Diary of George Templeton Strong* (New York: Macmillan, 1952), 3:64–65.

12. JGPN to CNP, April 11, 21, 1858, PFP-SHC-UNC.

13. EE to CPC, May 7, 1859, VFP-SCHS; MCNA to CNP, June 18, [1860], PFP-SHC-UNC; JGPN to ATPA, December 29, 1860, RFWAP-SCHS.

14. JLP to [JJP], November 29, 1861, PFP-SHC-UNC; CPC to JLP, September 7, 1862, fragment, October 29, 1862, VFP-SCHS.

15. CPC to JLP, November 25, 1862, VFP-SCHS.

16. Ibid.; JGPN to ATPA, June 22, 1861, RFWAP-SCHS.

17. CPC to JPC, October 21, 1862, fragment filed with December 5, 1862, VFP-SCHS.

18. JGPN to JLP, December 4, 10, 1862, and CNP to JJP, October 6, 1862, PFP-SHC-UNC; JAPP to ATPA, January 2, 1862, RFWAP-SCHS; CPC to JPC, October 29, 1862, VFP-SCHS.

19. [CPC to JLP], June 17, October 29, 1862, and CPC to EE, February 23, 1862, VFP-SCHS.

20. CPC to JLP, November 25, 1862, VFP-SCHS.

CHAPTER FIFTEEN

1. CNP to MCNA, January 30, 1862, and CNP to JGPN, March 4, 1862, PFP-SHC-UNC.

2. MAPo to PJPoJr, March 13, 4, 1862, PoFP-Car-USC.

3. JGPN to CNP, May 1, [1862], PFP-SHC-UNC.

4. MAPo to APAV, May 10, 1862, RFWAP-SCHS; JGPN to CNP, August 15, 1863, and JGPN to JLP, January 13, 1863, PFP-SHC-UNC.

5. JGPN to JLP, November 13, December 4, 1862, and CLP to CNP, April 15, 1863, PFP-SHC-UNC.

6. CNP to CLP, June 19, 1862, PFP-SHC-UNC; JPC to CPC, January 6, 1863, VFP-SCHS; JLP to CPC, January 8, 1863, in JPC, *Life, Letters, and Speeches of James Louis Petigru: The Union Man of South Carolina* (Washington, D.C.: W. H. Lowdermilk, 1920), 467.

7. JLP to W. H. Trapman, July 7, 1862, Petigru and King Letterbook, Car-USC.

8. JGPN to WSP, April 2, 1863, and MCNA to JJP, March 22, 1863, PFP-SHC-UNC.

9. JPC to CPC, March 28, [1863], VFP-SCHS.

10. JLP to SDPK-B, January 22, 1863, copy, PC-LC; SDPK-B to ATPA, August 28, 1863, RFWAP-SCHS.

11. JAPP to HDL, May 10, 1863, VFP-SCHS.

12. Ibid., June 7, 1863; SDPK-B to ATPA, August 28, 1863, RFWAP-SCHS.

13. EE to CPC, March 13, 1863, copy, VFP-SCHS.

14. CPC to EE, March 28, 1863, VFP-SCHS.

15. Winfield Scott to Edwin M. Stanton, March 27, 1863, PC-LC.

16. JAPP to CPC, June 14, May 31, 1863, VFP-SCHS.

17. JLP to CNP, December 16, 1862, PC-LC; LGNA to APAV, April 21, 1863, VFP-SCHS; JJP to JGPN, May 19, 1863, PFP-SHC-UNC.

18. Thomas G. Appleton to CPC, September 23, [1863], and CPC to Thomas G. Appleton, September 25, 1863, VFP-SCHS.

19. CNP to JJP, July 1, 1863; JGPN to [ATPA?], July 21, 1863; and MCNA to LPPo, July 21, [1863], all in PFP-SHC-UNC.

20. CNP to JJP, July 11, 1863, PFP-SHC-UNC; ATPA to CPA, July 16, 8, 1863, AFP-Car-USC; ATPA to APAV, July 31, 1863, VFP-SCHS.

21. CPC to EE, July 23, August 14, 1863, VFP-SCHS.

22. JGPN to ATPA, August 31, 1863, RFWAP-SCHS.

23. LGNA to CPC, September 8, [1863], VFP-SCHS.

24. MP to ATPA, November 10, 1863, RFWAP-SCHS; Octavius T. Porcher to JPC, December 28, 1863, VFP-SCHS; HPL to ATPA, December 8, 1863, RFWAP-SCHS.

25. JGPN to ATPA, August 31, 1863, RFWAP-SCHS; LGNA to CNP, January 3,

1862, and JGPN to WSP, April 2, 1863, PFP-SHC-UNC; JGPN to ATPA, September 3, 1861, RFWAP-SCHS.

26. LPPo to ATPA, September 20, 1861, September 2, 1864, RFWAP-SCHS.

27. ATPA, Diary, March 21, 1839, RFWAP-SCHS; ATPA to CPA, July 31–August 1, 1863, AFP-Car-USC; HPL to ATPA, April 16, 1861, RFWAP-SCHS.

28. MCNA to CNP, June 5, 1861, PFP-SHC-UNC; SDPK-B to ATPA, August 28, 1863, RFWAP-SCHS.

CHAPTER SIXTEEN

1. APAV, Diary, June 11, 1860, VFP-SCHS.

2. LGNA to CNP, June 19, [1860], PFP-SHC-UNC.

3. APAV, Diary, May 6, June 11, 1861, VFP-SCHS.

4. Ibid., June 19, 1861; JGPN to PJPoJr, June 16, 1861, PoFP-Car-USC; Fanny Alston to ATPA, September 7, 1861, RFWAP-SCHS.

5. APAV, Diary, February 12, 1862, and AV to APAV, April 27, 1862, VFP-SCHS.

6. AV to APAV, May 17, June 29, December 1, 1862, VFP-SCHS.

7. ATPA to BA, October 30, 1862, in Joel H. Easterby, ed., *The South Carolina Rice Plantation as Revealed in the Papers of Robert F. W. Allston* (Chicago: University of Chicago Press, 1945), 190.

8. JLAH to CPA, April 1863, AFP-Car-USC; RFWA to AV, May 6, 1863, and ATPA to RFWA, May 8, 1863, RFWAP-SCHS.

9. ATPA to RFWA, May 8, 1863, RFWAP-SCHS.

10. Elias Vanderhorst to APAV, June 15, 1863, VFP-SCHS.

11. AV to APAV, April 20, 1863, VFP-SCHS; APAV to ATPA, July 22, [1863], RFWAP-SCHS.

12. APAV to ATPA, August 4, 1863, RFWAP-SCHS; APAV, Diary, July 29, 1863, VFP-SCHS.

13. APAV, Diary, November 22, 1863, VFP-SCHS.

14. [JLAH] to APAV, August [1?], 1863, VFP-SCHS.

15. RFWA to ATPA, July 18, 1863, RFWAP-SCHS.

16. RFWA to BA, May 29, 1856, RFWAP-SCHS.

17. BA to ATPA, December 23, 1863, RFWAP-SCHS.

18. Ibid., January 24, 1864; EWAP to BA, April 11, 1864, RFWAP-SCHS.

19. ATPA, Diary, April 22, 1864, VFP-SCHS; EWAP to BA, April 11, 1864, RFWAP-SCHS.

20. LGNA to APAV, April 18, 1864, VFP-SCHS; CNP to ATPA, April 26, 1864; SDPK-B to ATPA, April 23, 1864; and JAPP to ATPA, April 13, 1864, all in RFWAP-SCHS.

21. Jesse Belflowers to ATPA, May 26, 1864, in Easterby, *South Carolina Rice Plantation*, 281; ATPA to CPA, July 11, 1864, AFP-Car-USC; ATPA to Jesse Belflowers, July 16, 1864, in Easterby, *South Carolina Rice Plantation*, 293.

22. F. W. Heriot to ATPA, November 14, 1864, RFWAP-SCHS.

23. CPA to BA, June 22, 1864, and CPA to ATPA, November 9, 1864, RFWAP-SCHS.

24. ATPA to BA, June 30, 1864, RFWAP-SCHS.

25. ESRA to ATPA, May 12, 1864, RFWAP-SCHS.

26. ESRA to BA, December 23, 1864, RFWAP-SCHS.

CHAPTER SEVENTEEN

1. CNP to CLP, December 25, 1863, PFP-SHC-UNC.

2. JGPN to JLP, November 13, October 27, 1862, PFP-SHC-UNC.

3. CNP to CLP, February 26, July 17, October 22, 1862, PFP-SHC-UNC.

4. Ibid., August 6, 1863.

5. Ibid., May 9, 1862; LPPo to CNP, July 22, 1864, PFP-SHC-UNC; MAPo to APAV, July 22, 1864, VFP-SCHS.

6. CNP to CLP, September 16, 1864, PFP-SHC-UNC; MCNA to APAV, July 28, 1864, VFP-SCHS.

7. LPPo to ATPA, June 16, 1864, RFWAP-SCHS; MAPo to APAV, December 16, 1864, VFP-SCHS.

8. CPC to EE, May 13, December 27, 1864, VFP-SCHS.

9. CNP to CLP, September 16, 1864, PFP-SHC-UNC; HPL to APAV, February 20, 1864, APHP-SCHS; LPPo to MCNA, May 23, 1864, PFP-SHC-UNC.

10. MAPo to APAV, May 15, 1864, VFP-SCHS; LPPo to CNP, July 22, 1860, PFP-SHC-UNC; ATPA to LPPo, April 17, 1864, PoFP-Car-USC.

11. JPC to WC, March 20, April 13, 1864, VFP-SCHS.

12. JPC to CPC, April 13, 1864; CPC to JPC, April 20, 1864; and CPC to EE, June 25, 1864, all in VFP-SCHS.

13. MAPo to APAV, December 16, 1864, VFP-SCHS; Mary Boykin Chesnut, Diary, December 12, 1864, in C. Vann Woodward, ed., *Mary Chesnut's Civil War* (New Haven: Yale University Press, 1981), 691–93.

14. Mary Boykin Chesnut, Diary, December 12, 1864, in Woodward, *Mary Chesnut's Civil War*, 692–93.

15. JGPN to ATPA, December 4, 1862, RFWAP-SCHS.

16. Elizabeth [Weston?] to ATPA, [March 16, 1865], RFWAP-SCHS; Jesse Belflowers to ATPA, March 18, 1865, in Joel H. Easterby, ed., *The South Carolina Rice Plantation as Revealed in the Papers of Robert F. W. Allston* (Chicago: University of Chicago Press, 1945), 328.

17. ATPA to Captain Morris, [March 1865], in Easterby, *South Carolina Rice Plantation*, 209.

18. Jane Lynch Pringle to ATPA, April 1, [1865], RFWAP-SCHS.

19. EWAP, *Chronicles of Chicora Wood* (New York: Charles Scribner's Sons, 1922), 273.

20. LPPo to MBPB[?], June 28, 1865, PFP-SHC-UNC.

21. MAPo to CNP, May [1865], PFP-SHC-UNC.

22. LPPo to MBPB[?], June 28, 1865, PFP-SHC-UNC.

23. LPPo to ATPA, August 22, 1865, VFP-SCHS.

CHAPTER EIGHTEEN

1. HPL to LPPo, May 14, 1865, PoFP-Car-USC; LPPo to MBPB [?], June 28, 1865, PFP-SHC-UNC.

2. HDL to ATPA, November 11, 1864, and HPL to ATPA, [January?] 15, 1866, RFWAP-SCHS.

3. LPPo to MBPB [?], June 28, 1865, PFP-SHC-UNC.

4. APAV, Diary, July 31, 1865, VFP-SCHS; BA to ESRA, September 28, 1865, RFWAP-SCHS.

5. ATPA to BA, September 10, 1865, in Joel H. Easterby, ed., *The South Carolina Rice Plantation as Revealed in the Papers of Robert F. W. Allston* (Chicago: University of Chicago Press, 1945), 212–13.

6. ATPA to BA, April 22, 1866, in ibid., 219.

7. Elias Vanderhorst to AV, May 22, 1864, VFP-SCHS; APAV to ATPA, September 20, 1865, RFWAP-SCHS.

8. APAV to BA, April 22, 1866, RFWAP-SCHS; WC to JAPP, April 20, 1865, VFP-SCHS; EWAP, *Chronicles of Chicora Wood* (New York: Charles Scribner's Sons, 1922), 299–300; Emma Huger Izard to Eliza Huger Smith, [1865], in Daniel E. Huger Smith et al., eds., *Mason Smith Family Letters, 1860–1868* (Columbia: University of South Carolina Press, 1950), 200; LGNA to CNP, January 12, 1868, PFP-SHC-UNC.

9. Emma Huger Izard to Eliza Huger Smith, [1865], in Smith et al., *Mason Smith Family Letters*, 200; LPPo to ATPA, April 22, 1865, VFP-SCHS.

10. William T. Sherman to CPC, March 24, 1865, copy, PC-LC.

11. MP to ATPA, March 9, [1866], and June 29, [1868] (misfiled as 1857), RFWAP-SCHS.

12. LPPo to CPo, September 14, 1867, PoFP-Car-USC.

13. LPPo to ATPA, October 7, 1867, and JGPN to ATPA, December 4, 1862, RFWAP-SCHS.

14. MCNA to CNP, January 15, [1867], PFP-SHC-UNC; EWAP, *Chronicles*, 321–22.

15. ATPA to CPA, April 5, 1868, AFP-Car-USC; EWAP, Journal, March 13, 1867, APHP-SCHS.

16. LGNA to CNP, November 7, 1866, September 27, 1868, [September 29, 1867?]; LGNA to CLP, December 8, 1867; and LGNA to CNP, January 26, 1868, all in PFP-SHC-UNC.

17. LGNA to CNP, March 22, 5, [1868], PFP-SHC-UNC.

18. Ibid., March 5, [1868].

19. Ibid., January 10, 1869.

20. CNP to MCNA, January 16, February 27, 1869, and MCNA to CNP, October 3, 1868, PFP-SHC-UNC.

21. J. W. Evans to ATPA, November 4, [1866], and W. W. Harlee to ATPA, July 3, 1867, RFWAP-SCHS.

22. Advertisement for Mrs. R. F. W. Allston's School, September 20, 1867, Miscellaneous Manuscripts, Car-USC.

23. Henry T. Williams to JLAH, August 30, 1868, APHP-SCHS.

CHAPTER NINETEEN

1. BA to EWAP, February 25, 1868, RFWAP-SCHS.

2. ATPA to APAV, July 21, 1865, RFWAP-SCHS.

3. ATPA to BA, January 14, 1867, RFWAP-SCHS.

4. ESRA to BA, January 16, 1865, RFWAP-SCHS.

5. Ibid., March 1, 15, 1865.

6. BA to ESRA, January 5, 1868, RFWAP-SCHS.

7. Ibid., April 7, February 2, 1868.

8. Ibid., February 15, March 14, April 16, 1868.

9. CNP to CLP, January 21, 1866, PFP-SHC-UNC.

10. [CNP] to CLP, March 14, 1866, PFP-SHC-UNC.

11. CNP to CLP, January 21, March 14, 1866, PFP-SHC-UNC.

12. CNP to MCNA, September 20, 1866, PFP-SHC-UNC.

13. Ibid., December 8, 1866.

14. Ibid., February 2, 1867.

15. Ibid., June 29, 1869.

16. CNP to LGNA, March 10, 1867, PFP-SHC-UNC.

17. CNP to MCNA, February 2, 1867, and CNP to WSP, November 25, 1872, PFP-SHC-UNC.

18. CNP to MCNA, July 16, 1868, and CNP to CLP, April 1, 1866, PFP-SHC-UNC.

19. CNP to MCNA, May 26, 1866, February 2, 1867, PFP-SHC-UNC.

20. CNP to WSP, July 29, 1867, August 8, 1868, PFP-SHC-UNC.

21. CNP to LGNA, July 16, 30, 1874, PFP-SHC-UNC.

22. CLP to [WSP], June 23, 1871, PFP-SHC-UNC.

23. CNP to WSP, March 31, 1873, PFP-SHC-UNC.

24. WSP to CNP, December 13, 1875, and CNP to WSP, [February 13, 1876], written on verso of CLouP to WSP, February 13, 1876, PFP-SHC-UNC.

25. CNP to WSP, July 13, 1874, [October 2, 1885], PFP-SHC-UNC.

26. CNP to LGNA, March 6, [1877], PFP-SHC-UNC.

27. HDL to CNP, November 12, 1872, and CNP to MCNA, July 9, [1870?], PFP-SHC-UNC.

28. CNP to LGNA, May 21, [188–?], and CNP to WSP, September 6, 1881, PFP-SHC-UNC; Genesis 16:13.

CHAPTER TWENTY

1. [MAPo] to CNP, May [1865], PFP-SHC-UNC.

2. LPPo to ATPA, August 22, 1865, and MJPoF to EWAP, August 20, 1865, VFP-SCHS; LPPo to ATPA, October 7, 1867, RFWAP-SCHS.

3. LGNA to CNP, January 26, 1868, and MCNA to CNP, January 15, [1867], PFP-SHC-UNC.

4. LPPo to ATPA, July 23, 1868, RFWAP-SCHS; LGNA to CNP, December 27, 1871, PFP-SHC-UNC.

5. CPA to APAV, May 26, 1869, VFP-SCHS.

6. LGNA to CNP, November 3, [1867], PFP-SHC-UNC; James Wood Davidson, ed., *The Living Writers of the South* (New York: Carleton Publishers, 1869), 314.

7. SDPK-B to JPC, August 5, 1870, VFP-SCHS; MCNA to CNP, September 4, 1870, PFP-SHC-UNC.

8. Undated newspaper clippings, probably all from *Charleston Courier*, Bowen File, Hinson Collection, CLS.

9. *Washington Patriot*, June 14, 1871, excerpt printed in *Charleston Daily Courier*, June 16, 1871.

10. *New York Times*, July 9, 1871.

11. William G. DeSaussure to WPoM, September 21, 1870, WPoMP-SHC-UNC; undated newspaper clipping from *Washington Chronicle*, Bowen File, Hinson Collection, CLS.

12. ATPA to APAV, February 23, 1871, VFP-SCHS.

13. *Charleston News and Courier*, June 18, 1875, reprinted in W. D. Porter, comp., *The Libel Cases of the News and Courier* (Charleston: News and Courier, 1875), 16.

14. James Lowndes to CPC, November 27, 1872, and SDPK-B to CPC, February 2, 1874, VFP-SCHS.

15. CPC to JPC, January 8, 1876, VFP-SCHS.

16. Claire Jervey, arr., *Inscriptions on the Tablets and Gravestones in St. Michael's Church and Churchyard, Charleston, S.C.* (Columbia: State Company, 1906), 48.

17. Christopher Columbus Bowen to CPC, December 23, 1875, VFP-SCHS.

18. CPC to JPC, May 19, June 16, 1889, VFP-SCHS.

CHAPTER TWENTY-ONE

1. CNP to [WSP], November 4, 1872, PFP-SHC-UNC.

2. HDL to CNP, November 12, 1872, PFP-SHC-UNC.

3. LGNA to CNP, May 27, [1858?], April 11, [1859], November 16, 1869, PFP-SHC-UNC.

4. LGNA to CNP, March 29, [1868], PFP-SHC-UNC.

5. ATPA to APAV, July 6, 1881, January 2, 1882; APAV to Elias Vanderhorst, March 29, 1882; and CPC to JPC, April 27, 1882, all in VFP-SCHS; CNP to WSP, March 21, [1882], PFP-SHC-UNC; BA to APAV, March 20, 1882, VFP-SCHS.

6. [MCNA to CNP], November 19, 1866, PFP-SHC-UNC.

7. MCNA to CNP, September 29, [1867], August 31, [1868], PFP-SHC-UNC.

8. LGNA to CNP, November 16, 1869, PFP-SHC-UNC.

9. BA to CPA, July 6, 1871, AFP-Car-USC.

10. CPA to APAV, February 23, 1872, RFWAP-SCHS; CNP to LGNA, August 24, 1876, PFP-SHC-UNC.

11. EWAP, Diary, May 24, 1885, APHP-SCHS; MCNA to CNP, April 4, [1886], PFP-SHC-UNC.

12. APAV to BA, April 22, 1866, RFWAP-SCHS; APAV, Diary, October 29, 1866, VFP-SCHS; LGNA to CNP, [September 29, 1867?], PFP-SHC-UNC.

13. Ann Morris Vanderhorst to APAV, October 9, 1876, VFP-SCHS.

14. AV to APAV, March 31, 1881, VFP-SCHS.

15. EWAP to Elias Vanderhorst, December 4, 1881, VFP-SCHS.

16. CPA to APAV, June 24, 1888, VFP-SCHS.

17. EWAP, "Dorothy" (ca. 1869), APHP-SCHS; ATPA to APAV, August 29, 1869, RFWAP-SCHS; MCNA to CNP, June 29, [1869], PFP-SHC-UNC.

18. APAV, Diary, April 20, 1870, VFP-SCHS; ATPA to CNP, May 23, 1870, PFP-SHC-UNC.

19. ATPA to APAV, August 11, 1870, and CPA to APAV, September 23, 1873, RFWAP-SCHS. .

20. EWAP, Diary, [ca. October] 1876, and Journal, November 13, 7, 1875, APHP-SCHS.

21. HPL to ATPA, September 5, 1876, APHP-SCHS.

22. EWAP to ATPA, September 19, 1876; JLAH to ATPA, September 10, [1876]; and EWAP, Diary, November 1, 1876, all in APHP-SCHS.

23. Patience Pennington [EWAP], *A Woman Rice Planter* (1913; reprint, Columbia: University of South Carolina Press, 1992), 1.

24. EWAP to JPC, March 12, 1893, and CPC to JPC, August 11, 1887, VFP-SCHS.

25. EWAP, Journal, November 18, 1875, APHP-SCHS; LGNA to CPC, April 26, 1885, VFP-SCHS.

26. JLAH to Henry Williams, December 12, 1869, APHP-SCHS; ATPA to CPA, February 29, 1872, AFP-Car-USC; APAV to AV, n.d. [188–?], VFP-SCHS; JLAH to ATPA, April 6, [1874], RFWAP-SCHS.

27. EWAP, Diary, June 2, 1884, APHP-SCHS; CPC to JPC, March 31, 1888, and ATPA to JLAH, May 6, 1888, VFP-SCHS.

28. ATPA, note to children, n.d. [1870s?], RFWAP-SCHS.

29. ATPA to APAV, November 10, 1878; ATPA to AV, May 17, 1875; and ATPA to APAV, August 8, 1888, August 29, 1883, all in VFP-SCHS.

30. ATPA to APAV, December 17, 1879, and ATPA to JLAH, January 8, 1882, VFP-SCHS.

31. ATPA to JNPW , February 7, 1871, PFP-SHC-UNC; ATPA to EWAP, September 20, 1876, APHP-SCHS; ATPA to AV, March 1, 1876, and LGNA to CPC, April 26, 1885, VFP-SCHS.

32. ATPA to APAV, September 10, 1881, March 21, 1889, VFP-SCHS.

33. EWAP, Diary, November 16, 1896, APHP-SCHS.

CHAPTER TWENTY-TWO

1. CPC to JPC, July 2, January 12, 1873, VFP-SCHS.

2. Ibid., December 20, 1873.

3. Ibid., March 10, June 2, 1874.

4. Ibid., April 22, 1873.

5. [Anna Brewster], clipping from *Philadelphia Evening Bulletin*, June 27, 1873, copy, VFP-SCHS.

6. CPC to JPC, April 8, December 10, 1875, March 10, 1876, VFP-SCHS.

7. Ibid., November 20, 1881, June 1, 1884.

8. Ibid., September 14, 1873.

9. Ibid., November 14, 1874.

10. CPC, Diary, October 12, 1877, VFP-SCHS.

11. CPC to JPC, January 15, 1889, VFP-SCHS.

12. Ibid., April 17, [1881].

13. Ibid., August 14, 1881.

14. CPC, Commonplace Books, 1:4, 2:21, Car-USC; CPC to WPoM, April 13, 1875, WPoMP-SHC-UNC; CPC to JPC, May 16, 1875, VFP-SCHS.

15. CPC to JPC, July 15, 1889, VFP-SCHS.

16. Ibid., December 14, September 18 [13?], 1888, and CPC to WC and JPC, December 10 [16?], 1889, VFP-SCHS.

17. CPC to JPC, April 12, 1892, VFP-SCHS.

18. WC to JPC, August 15, 1892, and CPC to Mr. Hooker, March 10, 1888, VFP-SCHS.

EPILOGUE

1. ATPA to APAV, November 10, 1878, VFP-SCHS.
2. LGNA to CNP, September 14, 1867, PFP-SHC-UNC.

As we did the research for a biography of James Louis Petigru, we stumbled onto a remarkable trove of correspondence among most of the Petigru women and the diaries and other writings of a few of them. We found these materials in the Robert Francis Withers Allston Papers, the Allston-Pringle-Hill Papers, and the Vanderhorst Family Papers at the South Carolina Historical Society in Charleston; in the Allston Family Papers and the Porcher-Ford Papers at the South Caroliniana Library at the University of South Carolina in Columbia, which also houses Caroline Carson's "Albums" (Commonplace Books); in the Pettigrew Family Papers and the Mitchell King Papers at the Southern Historical Collection, Wilson Library, University of North Carolina at Chapel Hill; in the collection of Pettigrew Family Papers at the Division of Archives and History, North Carolina Department of Cultural Resources, in Raleigh; and in the Petigru Correspondence at the Manuscripts Division of the Library of Congress in Washington, D.C. In addition to these major collections, several minor and minimally related ones contain random individual Petigru items, which are cited in the notes.

Several printed works were also valuable sources of primary material. James Petigru Carson, *Life, Letters, and Speeches of James Louis Petigru: The Union Man of South Carolina* (Washington, D.C.: W. H. Lowdermilk, 1920), and Joseph Blyth Allston, "Life and Times of James L. Petigru," a series of articles published in the *Charleston Sunday News* (1899–1900) that the Charleston Library Society bound as a scrapbook, both contain letters whose originals no longer exist. Joel H. Easterby, ed., *The South Carolina Rice Plantation as Revealed in the Papers of Robert F. W. Allston* (Chicago: University of Chicago Press, 1945), includes correspondence that is sometimes hard to locate in Allston's papers at the South Carolina Historical Society. Unfortunately, Sarah McCulloh Lemmon, ed., *The Pettigrew Papers*, vol. 2 (Raleigh: Division of Archives and History, North Carolina Department of Cultural Resources, 1988), only goes up to 1843. Michael O'Brien, ed., *An Evening When Alone: Four Journals of Single Women in the South, 1827–1867* (Charlottesville: University Press of Virginia for the Southern Texts Society, 1993), transcribes Caroline North's travel diaries, whose originals are in the Southern Historical Collection's Pettigrew Family Papers. Elizabeth Waties Allston Pringle's *Chronicles of Chicora Wood* (New York: Charles Scribner's Sons, 1922) is a memoir of her youth based on her diaries, some of which are in the Allston-Pringle-Hill Papers at the South Carolina Historical Society. Two of Sue King's works have been reprinted as *Gerald Gray's Wife* and *Lily: A Novel*, ed. Jane H. Pease and William H. Pease (Durham: Duke University Press, 1993). In addition, King published *Busy Moments of an Idle Woman* (New York: Appleton, 1854); *Sylvia's World: Crimes Which the Law Does Not Reach* (New York: Derby & Jackson, 1859); and stories in *Harpers Magazine* and *Russell's Magazine*. The

Charleston Courier and *Charleston Mercury* report on events and incidents involving the Petigrus. Especially useful is the *Charleston News and Courier's* pamphlet, *The Great Libel Case: Report of the Criminal Prosecution of the News and Courier, for Libelling Sheriff and Ex-Congressman C. C. Bowen, The State vs. F. W. Dawson* (Charleston: News and Courier, 1875). Caroline Carson's legal battle to regain Dean Hall can be traced in Edward McCrady, Jr., comp., *The Dean Hall Case: Carson v. Robertson, Hyatt v. McBurney*, a collection of documents in the South Carolina Historical Society.

The many books about Southern women that have expanded, refined, or refuted Anne Firor Scott's pioneering *The Southern Lady: From Pedestal to Politics, 1830–1930* (Chicago: University of Chicago Press, 1970) provide a useful context from which to view the Petigru women. Among those that treat the antebellum South are Catherine Clinton, *The Plantation Mistress: Woman's World in the Old South* (New York: Pantheon Books, 1982); Suzanne Lebsock, *The Free Women of Petersburg: Status and Culture in a Southern Town, 1784–1860* (New York: W. W. Norton, 1984); Jean E. Friedman, *The Enclosed Garden: Women and Community in the Evangelical South, 1830–1906* (Chapel Hill: University of North Carolina Press, 1985); Elizabeth Fox-Genovese, *Within the Plantation Household: Black and White Women of the Old South* (Chapel Hill: University of North Carolina Press, 1988); Jane H. Pease and William H. Pease, *Ladies, Women, and Wenches: Choice and Constraint in Antebellum Charleston and Boston* (Chapel Hill: University of North Carolina Press, 1990); and Marli F. Weiner, *Mistresses and Slaves: Plantation Women in South Carolina, 1830–80* (Urbana: University of Illinois Press, 1998). Victoria E. Bynum, *Unruly Women: The Politics of Social and Sexual Control in the Old South* (Chapel Hill: University of North Carolina Press, 1992), and Stephanie McCurry, *Masters of Small Worlds: Yeoman Households, Gender Relations, and the Political Culture of the Antebellum South Carolina Low Country* (New York: Oxford University Press, 1995), fill in the picture of nonelite white women. For African American women considered outside the white context, Charles Joyner, *Down by the Riverside: A South Carolina Slave Community* (Urbana: University of Illinois Press, 1984), and Margaret Washington Creel, *A Peculiar People: Slave Religion and Community Culture among the Gullahs* (New York: New York University Press, 1988), provide the best description.

Since 1989, a similar flourishing of work on women and the Civil War has revised Mary Elizabeth Massey's *Bonnet Brigades: American Women and the Civil War* (New York: Knopf, 1966). George C. Rable, *Civil Wars: Women and the Crisis of Southern Nationalism* (Urbana: University of Illinois Press, 1989); Catherine Clinton and Nina Silber, eds., *Divided Houses: Gender and the Civil War* (New York: Oxford University Press, 1992); Drew Gilpin Faust, *Mothers of Invention: Women of the Slaveholding South in the American Civil War* (Chapel Hill: University of North Carolina Press, 1995); and Lee Ann Whites, *The Civil War as a Crisis in Gender: Augusta, Georgia, 1860–1890* (Athens: University of Georgia Press, 1995), display a variety of approaches and interpretations. Whites's orientation on the war and postwar years as a single unit is particularly helpful. Julie Saville, *The Work of Reconstruction: From Slave to Wage Laborer in South Carolina, 1860–1870* (New York: Cambridge University Press, 1994), takes a somewhat similar tack and complements Willie Lee Rose, *Rehearsal for Reconstruction: The Port Royal Experiment* (Indianapolis: Bobbs-Merrill, 1964).

Among the many books elaborating the economic, social, and political structure of the places in which the Petigrus lived, the following proved particularly useful: George C. Rogers, Jr., *The History of Georgetown County, South Carolina* (Columbia: University of South Carolina Press, 1970); William H. Pease and Jane H. Pease, *The Web of Progress:*

Private Values and Public Styles in Boston and Charleston, 1828–1843 (New York: Oxford University Press, 1985; reprint, Athens: University of Georgia Press, 1991); Peter A. Coclanis, *The Shadow of a Dream: Economic Life and Death in the South Carolina Low Country, 1670–1920* (New York: Oxford University Press, 1989); Walter J. Fraser, Jr., *Charleston! Charleston!: The History of a Southern City* (Columbia: University of South Carolina Press, 1989); and Rachel N. Klein, *Unification of a Slave State: The Rise of the Planter Class in the South Carolina Backcountry, 1760–1808* (Chapel Hill: University of North Carolina Press, 1990).

The immediate impact of the Civil War on those places is elaborated in E. Milby Burton, *The Siege of Charleston, 1861–1865* (Columbia: University of South Carolina Press, 1970); Wayne K. Durrill, *War of Another Kind: A Southern Community in the Great Rebellion* (New York: Oxford University Press, 1990); Robert M. Browning, Jr., *From Cape Charles to Cape Fear: The North Atlantic Blocking Squadron during the Civil War* (Tuscaloosa: University of Alabama Press, 1993); Richard A. Sauers, "The Confederate Congress and the Loss of Roanoke Island," *Civil War History* 40 (June 1994): 134–50; Stephen R. Wise, *Gate of Hell: Campaign for Charleston Harbor, 1863* (Columbia: University of South Carolina Press, 1994); and Mark Grimsley, *The Hard Hand of War: Union Military Policy toward Southern Civilians, 1861–1865* (New York: Cambridge University Press, 1995).

South Carolina's postwar political climate is sketched out in Peggy Lamson, *The Glorious Failure: Black Congressman Robert Brown Elliott and the Reconstruction in South Carolina* (New York: W. W. Norton, 1973), and Thomas Holt, *Black over White: Negro Political Leadership in South Carolina during Reconstruction* (Urbana: University of Illinois Press, 1979). Charleston's Reconstruction politics is analyzed in great detail in William C. Hine, "Frustration, Factionalism, and Failure: Black Political Leadership and the Republican Party in Reconstruction Charleston, 1865–1877" (Ph.D. dissertation, Kent State University, 1979). Dan Carter, *When the War Was Over: The Failure of Self-Reconstruction in the South* (Baton Rouge: Louisiana State University Press, 1985), assesses how the idea of manly honor blocked white Southerners' ability to shape their section's recovery from war.

Several men of the Petigru connection have attracted historians' attention. Jeffrey D. Richardson, " 'Nothing More Fruitful': Debt and Cash Flow on the Antebellum Rice Plantation" (master's thesis, University of North Carolina, Chapel Hill, 1996), and William Dusinberre, *Them Dark Days: Slavery in the American Rice Swamps* (New York: Oxford University Press, 1996), examine Robert Allston more critically than did Joel Easterby in his introduction to Allston's collected correspondence, *The South Carolina Rice Plantation*. Robert D. Mellard lays bare a sordid past in "Christopher Columbus Bowen: A Scalawag Discovers Opportunity in the New World of Reconstruction Politics" (master's thesis, University of Charleston, 1994). Clyde N. Wilson's romantic study, *Carolina Cavalier: The Life and Mind of James Johnston Pettigrew* (Athens: University of Georgia Press, 1990), and William H. Pease and Jane H. Pease, *James Louis Petigru: Southern Conservative, Southern Dissenter* (Athens: University of Georgia Press, 1995), are full-length biographies.

Family history as a genre is hard to pin down, as Steven Ruggles points out in "The Transformation of American Family Structure," *American Historical Review* 99 (February 1994): 103–28. Most works on individual Southern families are genealogies rather than social histories, but some studies are particularly useful. Jane Turner Censer makes a broad systematic assessment in *North Carolina Planters and Their Children, 1800–1860* (Baton Rouge: Louisiana State University Press, 1984). Steven M. Stowe examines several individual families in *Intimacy and Power in the Old South: Ritual in the Lives of Planters*

(Baltimore: Johns Hopkins University Press, 1987). Both Malcolm Bell, Jr., *Major Butler's Legacy* (Athens: University of Georgia Press, 1987), and Bertram Wyatt-Brown, *The House of Percy: Honor, Melancholy, and Imagination in a Southern Family* (New York: Oxford University Press, 1994), are longitudinal family studies, although they largely omit consideration of less-gifted members. Robert Manson Myers, ed., *The Children of Pride: A True Story of Georgia and the Civil War* (New Haven: Yale University Press, 1972), a collection of letters exchanged within the family of Charles Colcock Jones, is more inclusive of family members but is limited to a ten-year period. The family history most comparable in structure to the present study is Stella Tillyard, *Aristocrats: Caroline, Emily, Louisa, and Sarah Lenox, 1740–1832* (London: Chatto & Windus, 1994), a narrative of the lives of and interchange among sisters.

Finally, the following works have relevance to the topics of individual chapters in this book: Judith Walzer Leavitt, *Brought to Bed: Childbearing in America, 1750–1850* (New York: Oxford University Press, 1986); Catherine Clinton, "Equally Their Due: The Education of the Planter Daughter in the Early Republic," *Journal of the Early Republic* 2 (Spring 1982): 39–60; Christie Anne Farnham, *The Education of the Southern Belle: Higher Education and Student Socialization in the Antebellum South* (New York: New York University Press, 1994); Patricia Cline Cohen, "Travel and Gender in Antebellum America" (paper delivered at the annual meeting of the Organization of American Historians, April 16, 1993); Charlene Boyer Lewis, "Southerners and Southern Society: Planter Society at the Virginia Springs, 1790–1860" (paper delivered at the annual meeting of the Society for Historians of the Early American Republic, July 21, 1995); Richard Rankin, *Ambivalent Churchmen and Evangelical Churchwomen: The Religion of the Episcopal Elite in North Carolina, 1800–1860* (Columbia: University of South Carolina Press, 1993); and Jane Turner Censer, "A Changing World of Work: North Carolina Elite Women, 1865–1885," *North Carolina Historical Review* 73 (January 1996): 28–55.

Middleton, John, 238–39
Miscarriage, 25, 26, 28, 233
Morven, 182
Mutual aid, 25–28, 37, 84–86, 148, 280

Naming practices, 28–29, 85, 99, 103–5, 121, 122, 156, 210–11, 252
Nashville Convention, 126–27
North, Albert Porcher, 16
North, Edward, 13
North, Jane Caroline (Carey). *See* Pettigrew, Caroline North
North, Jane Caroline Porcher, 13
North, Jane Gibert Petigru: courtship, marriage, and widowhood, 15–16; on education, 40–45, 58, 281–82; as family mediator, 36, 85, 145; household management, 34–35, 37; motherhood and relations with children, 39–40, 63–64, 97, 121–22; old age and death, 177; plantation management, 31–35, 92–94; politics and public affairs, 65–67, 125–26, 128, 129, 130–31, 140–41, 144, 151–52, 166; religion, 176–77
North, John Gough, 16
North, Louise (Lou) Gibert. *See* Allston, Louise Gibert North
North, Mary (Minnie) Charlotte. *See* Allston, Mary Charlotte North
Nullification crisis, 124–25
Nursing infants, 26, 28, 99, 100

O'Shea, Mary, 39, 91, 131
Overseers, 33–34

Patriarchy, 3–5, 278–79
Pawleys Island, 27, 261
Peninsular campaign in southern Virginia, 159
Petigru, Albert Porcher, 15
Petigru, Charles, 12, 21
Petigru, Daniel Elliott Huger, 15, 146, 170–71
Petigru, Harriette. *See* Lesesne, Harriette Petigru
Petigru, James Louis (Brother, Uncle): on education, 43–44; fatherhood and

relations with children, 51–52, 55–56, 73–75, 76, 81; finances, 48–49; fratriarch, 15–16, 18, 20, 22, 35, 84–85; old age and death, 171–72; politics and public affairs, 124–25, 128, 131, 141–42, 144; youth, courtship, and marriage, 11–15, 49, 56, 72–73
Petigru, James Louis, II, 18, 83–84
Petigru, Jane Amelia Postell (Sister), 25–26, 36; courtship and marriage, 12–15, 49, 56, 72–73; household management, 89, 90–91, 146; illnesses, 19, 71; motherhood and relations with children, 27–28, 48–51, 54–55, 71–72, 146, 172–74; politics and public affairs, 142; widowhood and old age, 172–74, 187, 211
Petigru, Jane Caroline. *See* Carson, Caroline Petigru
Petigru, Jane Gibert. *See* North, Jane Gibert Petigru
Petigru, John (Jack), 11, 21, 85–86, 213
Petigru, Louis, 18, 83–84
Petigru, Louise. *See* Porcher, Louise Petigru
Petigru, Martha (Mattie) Pawley, 18, 45, 67–68
Petigru, Mary, 12, 15, 17, 92, 130–33, 141, 143, 152, 177, 213–14
Petigru, Mary Ann (Ann) LaBruce, 17–18, 27, 36, 67–68, 83–85, 90, 144, 152–53, 215–16
Petigru, Susan (Sue) Dupont. *See* King, Susan Dupont Petigru
Petigru, Tempe, 21, 85–86, 213
Petigru, Thomas (Tom), 11, 17–18, 67–68, 83–84
Pettigrew, Adeline Theresa. *See* Allston, Adèle Theresa Petigru
Pettigrew, Alice Lockhart, 156
Pettigrew, Ann (Annie) Blount Shepard. *See* McKay, Ann Blount Shepard Pettigrew
Pettigrew, Ann Shepard, 105
Pettigrew, Caroline, 105
Pettigrew, Caroline (Carey) North: household management, 99–102, 155–

56; marriage, 96–99, 102–9, 154–58, 224–25, 229–30; motherhood and education of and relations with children, 98–100, 103–6, 194, 226, 230–34; plantation management at Belgrade, 229–31; plantation management at Bonarva, 98–109, 133, 224–27; plantation management at Cherry Hill, 157, 193–94, 224–25; politics and public affairs, 65–67, 126, 128–29, 131–33, 139, 140, 147, 227–28; as refugee in Hillsborough, 155–56; on slavery and rebellion, 131, 133–34, 151–52; travel in Europe, 97–98; travel in United States and Canada, 65–69; widowhood and death, 230–33; youth, education, and courtships, 16, 39–41, 45, 63–70, 95–96

Pettigrew, Charles Lockhart, 68–69, 95–109, 133–34, 154–58, 194, 226, 230

Pettigrew, Charles Louis, 99, 103, 230–31

Pettigrew, Ebenezer, 70

Pettigrew, James Johnston, 31, 68–70, 98, 106, 130–31, 143, 159, 175–76

Pettigrew, Jane Caroline (Carey) North. *See* Pettigrew, Caroline North

Pettigrew, Jane North, 103–4, 231–32

Pettigrew, Louise Guy Gibert, 9, 11–12, 15

Pettigrew, Louise Valerie, 194

Pettigrew, Mary Blount. *See* Browne, Mary Blount Pettigrew

Pettigrew, Mary Johnston, 226

Pettigrew, Thomas Petigru, 105

Pettigrew, William, 9–12, 31

Pettigrew, William Shepard, 106, 154, 194, 230–31

Pizzuti, Giacomo Carlo Angelo, 273

Porcher, Charles (Charley), 160, 196, 208

Porcher, Jane (Janey) Louise, 45, 60, 83

Porcher, Louise (Louly), 152–53

Porcher, Louise Petigru: household management, 89; on marriage, 55, 76; politics and public affairs, 125, 127, 131, 140, 141, 146–47, 195, 196–97, 201–3; postwar years, 235–37; religion, 178; youth, courtship, and marriage, 9, 12, 17, 27, 83

Porcher, Marion (Little Min) Johnston, 152–53, 237

Porcher, Mary Anna, 45, 129, 151, 152–53, 202, 235–36, 237

Porcher, Philip Johnston, 17, 83, 124–25, 236–37

Porcher, Philip (Phil) Johnston, Jr., 160, 196–97

Port Royal: federal seizure of, 150–51

Posi, Julio, 265

Postell, James, 13

Postell, Jane Amelia. *See* Petigru, Jane Amelia Postell

Pringle, Elizabeth (Bessie) Waties Allston, 27, 46–47, 59, 143, 185, 200–201, 214–15, 255–59, 263

Pringle, Jane Lynch, 199–200, 255–56

Pringle, John Julius, 255–57

Pyatt, Joseph Benjamin, 63–65

Race: as issue, 19, 90, 131–32, 227, 235–36, 276, 278

Reading, 75, 124, 129–30

Refugeeing, 152–56, 162, 192

Religion, 29–30, 83, 176–79

Roanoke Island: federal seizure of, 155

Robinson, Ellen Stanley. *See* Allston, Ellen Stanley Robinson

Schools for girls, 12, 42–47, 118, 218–19

Scott, Anne Firor, 5

Seaton, Gales, 66–67

Secession, 128, 140–42, 144

Sermoneta, Michaelangelo Caetani, Duke of, 268, 273

Servants: domestic, 87–94; Ayme, cook, 225, 226; Diana, maid, 241; Jacob, driver, 201; Laura, chambermaid, 225–27; Mack, 200–201; Primus, Daddy, head carpenter, 201; Sue, Maum, domestic, 227; Tony, dining room servant, 225, 227; white, 89, 91

Sherman, William Tecumseh, 211, 239

Simoni, Gustavo, 268

Slave marriages, 92–94, 101–2

Slave rebellion: rumors of, 132–35, 151–52

Slave trade, 130–31

Slavery: as political issue, 126–28, 130–33

Slaves: communication network, 91, 101–2, 134; as domestic servants, 87–94; emancipation of, 192–93

Slaves (by name): Aleck, Daddy, coachman, 88, 199–200; Andrew, waiter, 88; Beck, maid, 88–89; Caroline, cook, 100; Caroline, maid, 88; Caroline, seamstress, 37; Charlotte, dressmaker, 37, 92; Cindy, seamstress, 88; Clarinda, 92; Edmond, field hand, 101; Ellen, lady's maid, 101–2; George, scullion, 88; Grace, cook, waitress, 100, 134; James, domestic, 189; Jim, carpenter, 91, 93, 101; Joe, domestic, 90; Lavinia, lady's maid, 88, 91, 92; Linda, domestic, 84; Mary, Maum, cook, housekeeper, 88, 189; Milly, laundress, 88; Molly, 92; Moses, gardener, 88; Mullins, butler, 100; Nannie, lady's maid, 91; Ned, field hand, 93; Nelson, butler, 199; Peter, butler, 88; Peter, domestic, 90; Peter, driver, 133; Phoebe, Little, maid, 91; Phoebe, Old, seamstress, 91–92; Rosaline, errand girl, 90; Rose, lady's maid, 92, 101–2; Sally, poultry keeper, 92; Sukey, 91, 93; Susan, 93; Virgil, domestic, 90; William, butler, 90

Slaves (by plantation or city residence): at Badwell, 11, 32–33, 35, 92–94, 149, 151–52; at Bonarva, 102, 149, 155, 157–58, 193; at Cherry Hill, 157, 193–94, 199; at Chicora Wood, 18, 19, 85, 91, 92, 110, 130, 161, 180, 187–88, 189, 199–200, 201; at Dean Hall, 52, 165; at Dryslope, 195; at Goslington, 202; at Guendalos, 189, 201; of J. L. Petigru, 13, 48, 90–91; at Keithfield, 17, 89; the Kings', 89–90; the Lesesnes', 91; at Morven, 180, 187–88; at Nightingale Hall, 200–201; at Pipedown, 161; the Porchers', 36, 89, 151; of T. Petigru, 18, 90; the Vanderhorsts', 184; at Waverly, 122

Smith, Harriette Leila Lesesne, 237

Somerset Place plantation, 99–100, 225

Story, William Wetmore, 266

Sullivans Island, 15

Sylvia's World: Crimes Which the Law Does Not Reach, 81

Teaching, 32, 217–19, 280–81

Terry, Luther, 267

Thackeray, William Makepeace, 80, 83

Tilton, John Rollin, 267

Togno, Acelie, 45–47, 118

Uncle Tom's Cabin, 131

Vanderhorst, Adele (Della) Petigru Allston: childbearing and education of and relations with children, 210, 252–54; childhood, education, and youth, 27, 41–42, 45–47, 59, 118–19; courtship and marriage, 119, 180–85, 210, 252–54; household management, 184; personality, 181; widowhood, 254–55

Vanderhorst, Adele Petigru, 262

Vanderhorst, Ann Morris, 180, 252–53

Vanderhorst, Anna Morris, 252, 262

Vanderhorst, Arnoldus, 180–85, 208, 254

Vanderhorst, Arnoldus, II, 252

Vanderhorst, Elias, 180, 183

Vanderhorst, Elias, II, 252, 262

Vanderhorst, Elizabeth, 252, 262

Vanderhorst, Frances, 252

Vanderhorst, Robert Withers, 252

Virginia springs: cures and vacations at, 53, 65–66, 73, 107, 263

Wartime inflation and shortages, 148–49, 158, 170, 194

Waverly plantation, 122

Weddings, 19, 96–97, 183–84, 256

White House plantation, 256–57, 259

Widowhood, 16, 31–34, 84–85, 162–63, 172, 187–89, 200, 230–33, 254–55, 257–59, 280

Williams, Henry, 259–60

Williams, Jane North Pettigrew, 103–4, 231–32

Williams, Stephen Miller, 232

Windsor plantation, 259